International Criminal Justice Series

Volume 19

Series editors

Gerhard Werle, Berlin, Germany
Moritz Vormbaum, Berlin, Germany

Series Information

The *International Criminal Justice Series* aims to create a platform for publications in the whole field of international criminal justice. It, therefore, deals with issues relating, among others, to:

- the work of international criminal courts and tribunals;
- transitional justice approaches in different countries;
- international anti-corruption and anti-money laundering initiatives;
- the history of international criminal law.

The series concentrates on themes pertinent to developing countries. It is peer-reviewed and seeks to publish high-quality works emanating from excellent scholars, in particular from African countries.

Editorial Office

Prof. Dr. Gerhard Werle
Humboldt-Universität zu Berlin
Faculty of Law
Unter den Linden 6,
10099 Berlin, Germany
gerhard.werle@rewi.hu-berlin.de
moritz.vormbaum@rewi.hu-berlin.de

More information about this series at http://www.springer.com/series/13470

Emanuela Fronza

Memory and Punishment

Historical Denialism, Free Speech and the Limits of Criminal Law

ASSER PRESS

Springer

Emanuela Fronza
Department of Legal Sciences
Alma Mater Studiorum
Università di Bologna
Bologna
Italy

ISSN 2352-6718 ISSN 2352-6726 (electronic)
International Criminal Justice Series
ISBN 978-94-6265-233-0 ISBN 978-94-6265-234-7 (eBook)
https://doi.org/10.1007/978-94-6265-234-7

Library of Congress Control Number: 2017959910

Published by T.M.C. ASSER PRESS, The Hague, The Netherlands www.asserpress.nl
Produced and distributed for T.M.C. ASSER PRESS by Springer-Verlag Berlin Heidelberg

Printed on acid-free paper

This T.M.C. ASSER PRESS imprint is published by Springer Nature
The registered company is Springer Science+Business Media B.V.
The registered company address is: Van Godewijckstraat 30, 3311 GX Dordrecht, The Netherlands

For my father who taught me the culture of freedom and the culture of limits

For my mother who reminds me to forget

For Mattia, Cosimo and Simone,
my companions in time and memory

Foreword[1]

In the Outer London district of Walthamstow stands an eighteenth-century house originally used as a workhouse for the local poor, one of many that once dotted Britain. Today, the building is known (to the few who know it) as the Vestry House Museum. It is one of those museums whose two or three employees lavish an ardent welcome on visitors simply for walking through the door, delighted that someone is dropping in.

The collection comprises no more than half a dozen small rooms documenting local history through to the twentieth century, no different from countless small-town museums around Europe. What they lack in regal splendour they reclaim in humble charm.

Such places certainly tell us about the past. But do they teach us anything about how states use *law* to promote historical memory?

The Vestry House is not a private collection. Like many museums, it is government-run. The site was legally chartered by government as a museum as far back in 1931. Visitors who pay close attention will certainly carry away an impression different from the picture-book nostalgia which might at first have lured them in. They will leave with a remarkably bleak, un-celebratory history. The Vestry House stands not to sound trumpets of Britain's imperial past, but to invite critical reflection.

That, at its best, is what happens when governments use law, such as the Vestry House charter, to promote public understandings of history, not to woo the public with national self-flattery but to urge contemplation and dialogue. Even if that aim was not altogether clearly envisaged in the original charter, it is certainly how officials interpret it today.

Such use of law to shape historical consciousness does not always reflect any such socio-critical motive. Throughout the world today, states use legal means,

[1] Some passages from this Foreword are adapted from E. Heinze, 'Bans on Holocaust denial don't help Jews', 8 November 2016 (https://www.opendemocracy.net/can-europe-make-it/eric-heinze/bans-on-holocaust-denial-don-t-help-jews), originally published at *OpenDemocracy.net* under a Creative Commons Licence.

such as censorship and penalties for open dissent, to impose uncritically minded nationalism. In addition to such punitive means, states also use non-punitive means such as museums, but with no such dialectical aspiration in mind—spaces dedicated to one-sided national glorification, often at the expense of silencing more sinister pasts.[2]

Studies of state writings and rewritings of history are long established and well known. But detailed and comparative scholarly attention to the specific role played by law is remarkably new. One anthology undertaking that comparative study, edited by Uladzislau Belavusau and Aleksandra Gliszczyńska-Grabias, is entitled *Law and Memory: Towards Legal Governance of History*. It includes chapters on Canada, the Czech Republic, Greece, Hungary, Israel-Palestine, Peru, Poland, Romania, Russia, Ukraine and Spain.[3] Another collection, edited by Kalliopi Chainoglou, Barry Collins, Michael Phillips and John Strawson, is entitled *Injustice, Memory and Faith in Human Rights*. It includes chapters on Australia, Bangladesh, ISIS, New Zealand, Northern Ireland and Spain.[4] With such anthologies, and many other published works, we are witnessing the birth of a new discipline, or rather an 'inter-discipline'. We observe the study of law intersecting not only that of history but also with studies of politics, culture and society.

Emanuela Fronza leads in this field. The present monograph offers a probing, rigorous analysis not only of the complex laws, but of the fraught ethics and emotions animating the legislation and adjudication of memory laws, along with the risks they pose to democratic public discourse. In the spirit of London's Vestry House, Fronza wholeheartedly commits herself to states adopting a socio-critical stance towards their national histories. This book shows how difficult that ideal can be to achieve.

One of the salient problems to arise under the more controversial memory laws involves the necessary extent and limits of free speech within a robust democracy. That states must commemorate the victims of atrocities is certain; that they must punish those who, however benignly or maliciously, may challenge such histories, is, as Fronza explains, far less certain. The present study emerges from Fronza's years of painstaking and comprehensive examination of the criminal penalisation of 'negationism' (historical denialism), particularly of twentieth-century genocides. Fronza examines denialism as a criminal offence, its evolution and questions of constitutional legitimacy through a comparative European survey, exploring them as part of the internationalisation of legal norms and criminal justice—a study

[2] On distinctions between punitive and non-punitive approaches to disseminating state-approved histories, see, e.g. Heinze, E., 'Beyond "memory laws": Towards a general theory of law and historical discourse', *in* U. Belavusau and A. Gliszczyńska-Grabias (eds.), *Law and Memory: Towards Legal Governance of History*. Cambridge: Cambridge University Press (2017), pp. 413–33, at 415 21.

[3] U. Belavusau and A. Gliszczyńska-Grabias (eds.), *Law and Memory: Towards Legal Governance of History*. Cambridge: Cambridge University Press (2017), pp. 413–33, at 415–21.

[4] K. Chainoglou et al. eds., *Injustice, Memory and Faith in Human Rights*. Abingdon, UK: Routledge (2017).

particularly relevant in our era of 'post-truth' and fake news proliferated through new electronic technologies.

Consider the example of modern-day Germany. 'I'd rather not think about how horrible Germany would be', exclaimed Stephan J. Kramer, General Secretary of Germany's Central Council of Jews, 'if Holocaust denial were lawful'.[5] What else could he say? The Holocaust had almost extinguished Germany's Jewish community. Numbers have revived since the fall of the Berlin Wall, but remain tiny.[6] For many who have studied the rise of fascism in the early twentieth century, Kramer's response seems obvious. Of course, German law today provides iron-clad guarantees for free speech. For decades, the range and quality of the country's print and broadcast media have been second to none, noticeably superior in breadth and depth to those of English-speaking nations. Notwithstanding the bogus scientific façade, however, Holocaust denial is unequivocally hate speech, as research has repeatedly shown.[7]

For most of the German population, the scale and brutality of the Shoah have created a moral absolute. Nothing that would appear to minimise its gravity can be ethical. Many Germans believe that their law must reflect that ethics. For them, no moral value, not even the one most distinctive of a democratic sphere—free speech—can trump the nation's duty to honour both the dead and the survivors.

In 2008, Dr. Wolfgang Hoffmann-Riem, retiring from the Constitutional Court, nevertheless voiced his reservations about anti-negationist bans. Kramer then fired back. 'It is irresponsible for a legal authority to speak so thoughtlessly'. Yet Hoffmann-Riem is hardly famous as a political extremist. Any political affiliations traceable to him appear to be of a moderate centre-left. His reputation as guardian of civil liberties, on one of the most respected courts in the Western world, remains untainted. Whatever personal faults he may harbour as an individual or as a judge, careless speech scarcely counts among them.

What Hoffmann-Riem doubted was whether the bans serve their purpose, the same purpose Kramer pursues, namely, to safeguard the memory of millions of innocent dead. I share his doubt. Emerging and transitional democracies—as the Federal Republic had been in the war's aftermath—may benefit from bans on hateful expression. (And even that concession can be made only with weighty qualifications. In many such societies, hate speech bans are manipulated by

[5] See, e.g. Frank Jansen, 'Holocaust-Leugner nicht bestrafen', *Der Tagesspiegel*, 10 July 2008, at http://www.tagesspiegel.de/politik/ex-verfassungsrichter-holocaust-leugner-nicht-bestrafen/1275952.html (retrieved 25 September 2017).

[6] S. Urban, 'The Jewish Community in Germany: Living with Recognition, Anti-Semitism and Symbolic Roles', *Jerusalem Center for Public Affairs—Israeli Security, Regional Diplomacy, and International Law*, 29 October 2009, at http://jcpa.org/article/the-jewish-community-in-germany-living-with-recognition-anti-semitism-and-symbolic-roles/.

[7] Benz, W. (2005) *Was ist Antisemitismus?* (2nd edn.) Munich: Beck, R. Cohen-Almagor, 'Holocaust Denial is a Form of Hate Speech', 2 Amsterdam Law Forum 1 (2009); Taguieff, P.-A. (2002) *La Nouvelle judéophobie*. Paris: Mille et Une Nuits; Taguieff, P.-A. (2004). *Prêcheurs de haine : Traversée de la judéophobie planétaire*. Paris: Mille et Une Nuits.

governments not to protect vulnerable groups but to quell dissenters.) But Germany ceased long ago to be an emerging democracy. For many years now, *The Economist's* annual *Democracy Index* has placed Europe's dominant power among the world leaders, joined by societies like Norway and Canada—far in front of the USA, and also ahead of France and Britain.[8]

But don't those countries also ban certain forms of hate speech? Yes (aside from the USA). Even within the top-ranked democracies, however, we hear doubts about whether banning speech is right in principle. Some have also asked, as a practical matter, whether bans end up doing more harm than good.[9] Those concerns are not voiced by fanatics or by people indifferent to the plight of the historically repressed.

A common argument in defence of bans is that democracies are not immune from the excesses of hate speech.[10] The Weimar republic, on that view, shows how hate speech in today's democracy can snowball into tomorrow's genocide. The problem with that claim is its 'one size fits all' assumption. Not all democracies are alike. Risks associated with a highly flawed state cannot so casually be attributed to all democracies across the board. Weimar was scarcely more than an on-paper democracy, boasting none of the historical, institutional or cultural supports so conspicuous among the *Economist's* top ten or fifteen contenders.

In a word, the familiar cry of 'Never Again' meant something very different in 1946 than it means in 2016. The law must start to reflect that change. The Nazi regime represented absolute evil. It is by no means obvious, however, what the 'opposite' of that regime should look like. One evil of the Third Reich was indeed hate speech,[11] from which we might deduce the need for its opposite—the need for bans.

An equal evil, however, was suppression of *free* speech,[12] of the type that might have countered Nazi excesses. From that evil we can just as plausibly deduce a need for the abolition of censorship. Neither view is self-evident. Therefore neither is horrible, silly, nor worthy simply to be derided. Yet that is what Kramer did by chastising Hoffmann-Riem in such dismissive terms. Kramer did not simply condemn either the Holocaust or its denial—horrors which we must indeed decry. He instead took a very worrying step further. He ended up condemning a proposal made by an experienced, conscientious jurist concerning the best response of law and of government.

[8]The Economist—Intelligence Unit, 'Democracy Index 2015: Democracy in an Age of Anxiety'.

[9]Alexandre Lévy, 'Les groupes violents, plus faciles à fustiger qu'à interdire', *L'Opinion*, 09 June 2013, at http://www.lopinion.fr/edition/politique/groupes-violents-plus-faciles-a-fustiger-qu-a-interdire-868.

[10]Eric Heinze, 'Nineteen Arguments for Hate Speech Bans—And Against Them', *Free Speech Debate*, 3 March 2014, at http://freespeechdebate.com/en/discuss/nineteen-arguments-for-hate-speech-bans-and-against-them/.

[11]'Der Stürmer—*"Die Juden sind unser Unglück!"*', Holocaust Education & Archive Research Team, at http://www.holocaustresearchproject.org/holoprelude/dersturmer.html.

[12]'Nazi Propaganda and Censorship', *The Holocaust: A Learning Site for Students*, at https://www.ushmm.org/outreach/en/article.php?ModuleId=10007677.

When that abrupt 'Shut your mouth!' follows from the spirit of Holocaust commemoration, then something has gone wrong. I certainly share Kramer's raw emotion. And I admire the Council's longstanding and constructive contributions to European cultural life. But nothing could make the Jewish community look worse. And nothing renders such questionable homage to the Holocaust's victims. If we are to honour both the dead and the survivors, we are inevitably forced to talk about their experience in collective terms. There is something worrying, however, about the assumption that any one policy could ever speak for all the victims.

Yes, some of those who perished, if we could revive them today, would surely and understandably endorse anti-negationist bans. But it would be ludicrous, even insulting, to suggest that all of them would do so—or indeed that all Jews should take the same view on *any* complex moral question. The great German Jewish tradition from Moses Mendelssohn to Hannah Arendt wholly collapses if does not represent open, frank and intelligent discussion even of the most painful ethical dilemmas. The German Council of Jews is right to keep historical memory alive and informed. Hoffmann-Riem, however, is also right to ask whether speech bans do indeed further that effort. Europeans have not yet learned to have that debate.

Controversy about the role of the state in promoting historical memory will continue well into the future, in Europe and internationally. With *Memory and Punishment: Historical Denialism, Free Speech and the Limits of Criminal Law*, and at a time of ever greater divisions about Europe's past, Fronza offers a valuable tool indeed for evaluating and perhaps even revising current approaches.

Eric Heinze
Professor of Law and Humanities
School of Law Queen Mary
University of London

Preface

The term 'denialism' (*'négationnisme'*) was first used by the French historian Henry Rousso in his book *Vichy Syndrome*.[13] The term was specifically used by this author in reference to statements which denied the existence of gas chambers in the Nazi extermination camps.

Today, historical denialism must be distinguished from revisionism, which is a trend characterised by the tendency to revise confirmed historical facts based on new data, testimonies, documents and interpretations. In principle, of course, revisionism *per se* merely refers to the historiographical process of reviewing established historical opinions in the light of new information and knowledge, thereby making it possible to reinterpret and rewrite history. Every historian can be a revisionist by trade since his or her work consists in reviewing previous reconstructions according to changing theoretical paradigms and models. As long as it does not mix fact with fabrication, revisionism is a standard practice of historical scholarship. Historical denialism, by contrast, refuses to initiate a dialogue with well established historical data and methodological paradigm.

While it originally referred to denial of the Holocaust, today the phenomenon of denial of historical facts is much broader and much less controllable. It includes, more generally, genocide, crimes against humanity and war crimes, and it thrives on the same propagation mechanisms—filter bubbles, echo chambers and such—that contribute to the spreading of more trivial (yet just as worrisome) disinformation and misinformation on the World Wide Web. In this digital scenario, 'denialism' has also come to characterise phenomena and practices that have little in common with the original negation of the Holocaust which eventually resulted in criminalisation. From climate change denial to the moon landing, from the origins of the HIV-AIDS virus to the efficacy of vaccination, from Darwinist theories to the 9/11 attacks and other issues which might seem more insignificant, such as Barack Obama's birthplace, the creation and consumption of self-produced information on the Web has provided fertile ground for the multiplication of perspectives on issues

[13] Rousso 1987.

that in principle should not and must not be questioned, lest we wish to open the door to denying historically proven facts.

The concept of historical denialism has been revived to label those who dispute a dominant view ordinarily considered an agreed point of reference. In this new phase, the primary accusation is denying the 'truth', implying that what is being denied is an established fact. Conspiracy theories abound in the so-called post-truth era, triggering debates on whether a normative approach should be adopted to counter historical denialism, in what form, and on which players and stakeholders should be allowed to intervene without infringing the right to free speech and expression.

This consequently gives rise to other problematic aspects. An analysis of the experience of historical denialism itself, also as a crime, can therefore offer insights regarding these new phenomena as well, since they share similarities. Why are the foundations of core values increasingly attacked? Why are there consistently more statements based on simplistic beliefs, in political discourse, news and social media? Truth, post-truth, alternative facts, fake news and fact-checking—all these definitions have become a common currency in the global debate on information and the new media, and they all to some extent embody these dynamics and highlight the cacophony of opinions and the dangers at hand.

Despite their alarming significance, none of these manifestations of denialism will be analysed in this book. Instead this study focuses on criminal law as a response to the denial of the Holocaust and other mass atrocities. In particular, it examines historical denialism as a speech crime in Europe and discusses the implications of protecting historical institutional memory through criminal law. Nevertheless, this analysis also represents a jurist's contribution to the broader debate about the need for policies and regulations in the digital world, and more specifically in relationship to freedom of expression and the fake news phenomenon.

Holocaust denial both as conduct and as crime was originally concerned only with statements aimed at negating or belittling the Holocaust. For the purposes of this study, however, the phrase 'historical denialism' will have a wider scope, both as a form of conduct and as a criminal offence. As conduct, it consists in the denial, justification or trivialisation of historical events that constitute offences against humanity, as determined by the statute or case law of a domestic or international court. The related criminal offence, which varies among countries, generally punishes whoever purposely engages in public in one or more of those acts and thereby jeopardises an officially recognised narrative of those events.

Two basic assumptions underpin my research.

First, contemporary societies are strongly characterised by a 'cult for memory' (Todorov) and the 'will to remember' (Rousso), namely the tendency to remember the past to establish a sort of shared identity. Criminalisation of historical denialism is also a reflection of this trend, as it attributes a role to public memory and provides through law—increasingly criminal law—the means for establishing and protecting collective memory. The importance of a rigorous, open and critical scrutiny of memory in all aspects of public life is more frequently evident in Western societies.

The general tendency is that 'We must remember' in order to avoid the progressive weakening of a pillar of democratic society, namely the collective memory of historically significant crimes. Law, and especially criminal law, is considered to be the most powerful instrument available to promote collective historical memory within society. By imposing respect for the memory of a violent past that should never be forgotten, criminal law is used to pursue the objectives of narrating and reasserting historical memories. The importance of collective memory regarding past breaches of human rights is bolstered by the increasingly significant role of victims and results in the recognition of new categories of human rights (for instance, right to truth, memory and justice). Furthermore, international crimes are not subject to statutes of limitations or amnesty, and the principle of non-retroactivity of criminal law does not apply to them. The fight against impunity and the will to remember, therefore, redefines the relationship between memory and oblivion and between punishment and forgiveness. This polarisation between remembering and forgetting is the first area of conflict that makes criminalising historical denialism complex. It is in this context that the choice of giving a primary role to criminal law, which acts outside strictly national and global boundaries, is made. The *memory makers*, namely the actors through which memory is reaffirmed and consolidated,[14] also change and multiply. In fact, beyond national courts, one has to consider regional courts—such as the European Court of Human Rights and Inter-American Court of Human Rights—as well as the International Criminal Court and constitutional courts. Such institutions, albeit heterogeneous, are constantly in dialogue with each other.

Second, the crime of historical denialism reflects another European trend, whereby freedom of expression is limited to safeguard other values or to fight phenomena such as international terrorism. Indeed, Europe is displaying an increasing trend of limiting freedom of speech. The offence of historical denialism could catalyse this currently unfolding phase, resulting in 'new' speech crimes.

While it was first introduced in Israel, the crime of historical denialism has evolved primarily in Europe. In 1990, France was the first European country to include it as a crime in its national legislation and afterwards many other legal systems also opted to respond to this phenomenon with criminal law. Today, 21 European Union countries provide laws on historical denialism, distinguishing them from laws against condoning or instigating racial discrimination.

Initially, at the national level, an earlier, narrower formulation was introduced, which protected the founding identity of the Shoah by punishing justification, trivialisation and negation of that event (historical denialism in the 'original' sense). Other countries have since implemented an expanded formulation, which punishes statements regarding both the Nazi regime and other international crimes (historical denialism in the 'broader' sense).

---

[14]This concept refers to legislators and judges (national or international) and quasi-judicial bodies as actors influencing historical collective memory and contributing to its construction and evolution.

This latter paradigm of criminalisation is now the most common within European law,[15] signalling an important change. In addition to the core message rejecting attacks on the universal values that emerged after World War II and contributed to the creation of new European constitutions, further emphasis is placed on the construction of the identity of European societies founded upon respect for human rights and the memory of all their most serious violations. Not only the Holocaust, but also other international crimes now occupy and play a role, shifting memory that cannot be challenged from a European level (the Holocaust) to a universal one (human rights).

In addition to the conflict between memory and oblivion, the expansion of historical denialism to other international crimes demonstrates another polarisation that makes it difficult to use criminal law for this phenomenon: the polarisation of what is relative and what is universal. The stakes at play are not creating a divided community but establishing a fragile European and international community with a value system based on human rights. The expansion of the criminal offence is incorporated within the 'Framework Decision on combating certain forms and expressions of racism and xenophobia by means of criminal law' adopted in 2008. Also the European Union has chosen criminal law to combat denialist statements, endorsing a further step in the evolution of the offence: from the exclusive national level to which it was relegated, criminalisation has now become supranational.

Since the adoption of the EU Framework Decision, twelve countries have implemented it, prompting the beginning of a new phase. Instead of a single European memory to be protected, several historical narratives have emerged from the varying forms of historical denialism implemented in each country. The paradoxical dynamic is quite clear: the universality of the human rights contained in the Framework Decision encountered relativity in application, demonstrating that there is no single national memory in Europe but many national historical memories. Therefore, the 'broader' model of the offence entails new critical issues which did not exist in the 'original' model. First, due to the extended application to all international crimes, it requires identification of the significant historical facts worthy of criminal protection. But who is to select the memories to be protected? Depending on the legal system, this function is assigned to the judge or to the legislator. When qualifying a historical fact as an international crime, the agent of memory will also recognise it as a fact, the memory of which cannot be challenged. The criminal offence, in its broader version, is therefore structured to oblige the judge to intervene in matters of history considerably more invasively than ever before, when the object of the punishable conduct was only limited to the Holocaust. Criminal trials are conducted in order to establish the historical narration of facts through the judgement, which establishes what is to become the official historical truth. In this 'broader' form, the role of the judge or legislator is complex. They must operate within a mosaic of historical memories and must investigate international crimes which at times have not yet become the object of historical

[15] Eighteen countries introduced a 'broader' form of historical denialism.

study. We certainly risk a dangerous overlap between judicial activity and historical research. Such a risk was already present in the 'original' form of historical denialism, but here becomes major.

But a new risk also emerges through the difficulty of identifying criteria for selecting which memories to protect. As already demonstrated by the national and European legislation and case law, a further danger is the potential establishment of a *hierarchy* of historical memories.

This analysis reveals the image of Europe not only protecting but also constructing historical collective memory and defending its values through law. It is necessary to distinguish laws that criminalise historical denialism from other types of laws, which, without resorting to criminal law, intervene in order to recognise or define certain relevant historical facts. These include, for example, the so-called remembrance laws, which introduce 'days of memory' in national or international calendars, inviting citizens to remember. Although lacking a strictly criminal nature and following the introduction of the offence of historical denialism from a chronological point of view, these typologies of laws play an important role in the criminalisation of denialism: they attribute to a fact the value of an historical event. They thereby delimit the scope of application of criminal law which protects the memory of that event. After all, remembrance laws and denialism criminal statutes mutually nourish each other.

This study analyses the costs and benefits of this juridical culture, in the framework of the denial of the Holocaust and other mass atrocities. The complexity of the matter at hand is apparent. It reacts to an insidious and widespread phenomenon which involves free speech, historical research and open debate, ultimately contradicting the principles of a liberal criminal law. It also paves the way to a broader discussion about freedom of expression in a digital world, about fake news and post-truth scenario, and ultimately about the need (and the tools) to protect established facts from the pollution of misinformation. In the so-called post-truth era, it becomes of paramount importance to define the principles of what can and cannot be publicly affirmed, to draw a line between the two areas. Historic denialism and the related jurisdiction represent a key step in exploring this complex field.

Some of the most problematic issues arising from the criminalisation of historical denialism are general in nature and concern the identification of the protected interests, the risk of punishing a lifestyle rather than of an offensive conduct and resorting to criminal law as a first response. Furthermore, the risk of penalising 'words' alone does not seem to be averted, not even by those measures which at the legislative level attempt to classify the crime in terms of its level of potential endangerment (for example, requiring that the statement must possess an element of incitement), or limit punishment to those crimes for which a judgement or conviction has already been issued.

Other problems are exclusive to the crime of historical denialism due to the profound interaction between law and memory. For example, the judge becomes judge of history although there cannot be only one historical truth. Further complexities arise as the list of protected memories expands (e.g., including *all* international crimes, not just the Shoah). But which criteria are to determine the historical memories worthy of protection?

In the 'original' form of the offence, the role of the judge (or legislator) was more limited, as they were mainly called upon to reiterate that the memory of historical events already historically and judicially qualified as such (like the Holocaust) could not be questioned. At present, with the 'broader' form of the crime of historical denialism, the judge can be in the position of determining which historical memories should be protected. In addition to the risk of selective—and hierarchical—criminalisation, the danger of historical memory merely coinciding with judicial memory also increases. This configuration of public policies entails various implications for the structure and functions of the criminal trial. Its main aim should not be narrating history, but rather ascertaining individual responsibility in relation to identified facts. From a historical point of view there are a number of risks, such as elevating historical truth to the status of a legal truth and transforming historical truth into an official truth. In this manner, one gives credit to the idea that only one school of historical thought exists.

Congruent with the dual dynamic of the expansion of criminal law and the juridification of memory, the main purpose of the criminalisation of historical denialism is to build consensus around a sense of order and to send a message to the public regarding the reconstruction of collective identity and the establishment of a collective memory. The main purpose of the criminalisation of historical denialism is therefore not the protection of an important interest. The distorting effect that may ensue is caused by the prevalence of a purely pedagogical and expressive focus, with the consequence of punishing words and not criminal acts. However, certain fundamental principles comprise and limit liberal criminal law, namely a liberal state should never punish ideas. Thus, there is a paradox within the criminalisation of historical denialism since it results in the restriction of those same fundamental rights that form the foundation of what they seek to protect. This conundrum is more powerful today than ever since the World Wide Web made it possible to spread 'free' information without limits or boundaries.

Making historical denialism an offence differs from exploring in detail the debate, the validity and the content of denialist practices. This book intends only to analyse the former, namely the criminalisation of denialist conduct and not the larger issue of denial as a phenomenon. As for the latter, I wholly disapprove of the ideas advocated by denialists. Efforts should be made to stop similar practices from repeating themselves and prevent the ideologies that supported or fuelled mass atrocities (such as genocides and crimes against humanity) from gaining power and legitimacy. The urgency of a serious and comprehensive challenge to historical denialism requires that we address how to respond to it and the effectiveness of the instruments that have been chosen. Considering the importance of historical collective memory within a political and social system, the question arises as to what are the most appropriate and effective means to protect that memory.

Based on the assumption that it is necessary to respond to the denialist phenomenon and to protect collective historical memory, the underlying question that guides this study is the following: how can we respond adequately and effectively to such problems? Is there merit in the position, privileged both at the national and supranational level, that considers criminal law an effective and appropriate tool to counter historical denialism?

The criminalisation of historical denialism has spread far beyond Europe. In recent years, initiatives in several Latin American countries have proposed the introduction of the offence of historical denialism similar to that found in European legislation, although culturally tailored to protect the historical memory of formative events of their different national identities. The expansive capacity of historical denialism does not stop there. It also circulates as a concept, with a strong symbolic and emotional impact. Whenever the perceived aim is to eradicate interpretations considered to differ from an 'authoritative truth' intended to protect a collective point of reference, the accusation of 'historical denialism' is voiced. It presents the possibility to consider those who criticise that truth to be falsifiers of history worthy of being punished. Therefore, historical denialism becomes a means of validating a memory and/or a truth that seeks to be stabilised.

A further objective of this study is therefore to demonstrate the global dynamics at play. According to media scholars we live in a 'post-truth era' where opinions and prejudices can trump factual truths thanks to the uncontrolled and massive proliferation of fake news and biased information. Opinions continue to multiply, and there is an alarming increase in misinformation, and the role it plays in polluting the ocean of digital information and knowledge.

This book analyses the matrix of these phenomena: the denial of the Holocaust and the most serious crimes, to which Europe responded 'never again' when adopting national constitutions and a series of documents affirming the centrality of human rights. While saying 'never again' to mass atrocities, with the criminalisation of denialism legislators have decided to intervene in the difficult area of opinions, establishing a distinction between true and false via the (problematic) use of criminal law. Historical denialism not only consists of the discriminatory and shameful statements attacking the core of post-World War II principles which have shaped our constitutional models. It also creates a space within which states and international institutions have said 'No' by drawing a red line between true and false, frequently using criminal law to draw that line. Historical denialism demonstrates the clash between two practices: a misleading approach and an accurate method, in which the empiricist works with various experimental models based on hypotheses. This conflict, the centrality of memory, the over-expansion of criminal law and the proliferation of speech crimes are all elements that link the subject of this study to a fundamentally global dynamic currently underway. The relevance of the debate on post-truth and on how to define and protect a core idea of 'truth' in the flow of digital information share common terrain with this study: the delicate operation of resorting to legal means to establish the distinction between true and false and, therefore, between what can and what cannot be publicly affirmed. The issues at stake are not merely academic in terms of their effects on norms and jurisdiction, but are indeed the key to one of the most urgent questions facing our societies: what strategies can (and should) be implemented to prevent the misuse of the Internet as the most powerful information tool humanity has ever developed?

Consequently, the specific study of the offence of historical denialism focuses on a very contemporary and fundamental question about how to respond to refutations, radical dogmas and immutable ideologies that attack civic order. This analysis will explore the costs and benefits of choosing to respond with criminal law. There is no doubt that historical denialism and other racist phenomena require a response. But the point is *how* to respond to these serious, widespread and persistent statements? How can we avoid triggering a war of memories? How shall we prevent an excess of speech crimes? How not to question those same fundamental rights on which an open society is founded? How can we maintain those principles of legality and harm which must be the basis and limitation for every liberal criminal law? Why introduce another criminal offence when incitement is already punishable? These are questions that should be familiar to all those concerned with defining and protecting freedom of expression in the digital era and demonstrate the urgency of a shared analysis and approach.

Despite the fear of a logic based on myopic and unverifiable claims, particularly prominent in Holocaust denial, the premise is that criminal law may not be an appropriate response to historical denialism.

Given the political value of denialist statements and the limits of criminal law, it is necessary to attribute at least a minimum role to the restriction of freedom of expression, both on the dogmatic and criminal policy level. If it is required that the criminal trial intervenes to ascertain facts, to determine individual responsibility with regard to serious crimes, to consolidate memory and forgetting, and ultimately to stabilise civil order, then political intervention is required. The responsibility to react to denialist statements, as well as to all dogmas that seek to undermine fundamental values and civil order, should also pertain to the political sphere and not to criminal law alone. The response to historical denialism should therefore be a political commitment to the difficult long road of culture and education, and not the futile and merely symbolic shortcut of criminal law.

This book is the result of many years of research and reflection on the criminalisation of historical denialism. It continues an investigation of other previous publications and intends to contextualise the complex issues surrounding the criminal offence of historical denialism in the current dynamics of the criminal law system and its limits.

This publication is also part of my research as a Principal Investigator at the University of Bologna of the HERA-funded consortium 'Memory Laws in European and Comparative Perspective' which I would like to thank here for its support (http://www.melaproject.org/).

Bologna, Italy
January 2018

Emanuela Fronza

Reference

Rousso H (1987) Le syndrome de Vichy. Seuil, Paris (translated as: The Vichy Syndrome. History and Memory in France Since 1944. Harvard University Press, Massachusetts)

Contents

Part II Denialism in Practice

Table of International and National Instruments

Table of International Instruments

Agreement for the prosecution and punishment of the major war criminals of the European Axis, 8 August 1945

UN Doc A/RES/260(III) A, *Convention on the Prevention and Punishment of the Crime of Genocide*, UN General Assembly, 9 December 1948

UN Doc. A/RES/3/217 A, *Universal Declaration of Human Rights*, UN General Assembly, 10 December 1948

UN Doc. A/RES/2106(XX), *International Convention on the Elimination of All Forms of Racial Discrimination*, UN General Assembly, 21 December 1965

UN Doc. A/RES/2200(XXI), *International Covenant on Civil and Political Rights*, UN General Assembly, 16 September 1966

UN Doc. A/RES/3068(XXVIII), *International Convention on the Suppression and Punishment of the Crime of Apartheid*, UN General Assembly, 30 November 1973

UN Doc. CCPR/C/58/D/550/1993(1996), *Robert Faurisson v. France, Communication No. 550/1993*, Human Rights Committee, 2 January 1993

Council of Europe Joint Action 96/443/JHA *concerning action to combat racism and xenophobia*, 15 July 1996

International Criminal Court, *Statute of Rome*, 17 July 1998

Council of Europe, COM(2001)/664, *Proposal for a Council Framework Decision on combating racism and xenophobia*, 29 November 2001

Council Framework Decision 2002/475/JHA of 13 June 2002

Council of Europe ETS no. 189, *Additional Protocol to the Convention on Cybercrime concerning the criminalisation of acts of a racist and xenophobic nature committed through computer systems*, 28 January 2003

UN Doc. A/RES/60/7, *Resolution adopted by the General Assembly on the Holocaust Remembrance*, UN General Assembly, 1 November 2005

UN Doc. A/RES/61/255, *Resolution on Holocaust Denial*, UN General Assembly, 26 January 2007

European Parliament P6_TA(2008)0439, *Declaration of the European Parliament on the proclamation of 23 August as European Day of Remembrance for Victims of Stalinism and Nazism*, 23 September 2008
Council Framework Decision 2008/913/JHA *on combating certain forms and expressions of racism and xenophobia by means of criminal law*, 28 November 2008
European Parliament P6_TA(2009)0213, *European Parliament resolution on European conscience and totalitarianism*, 2 April 2009
UN Doc. CCPR/C/G34, *General Comment n. 34 concerning Article 19 of the Covenant on Civil and Political Rights*, Human Rights Committee, 12 September 2011
UN Doc. CERD/C/GC/35, *General Recommendation n. 35 on Combating Racist Hate Speech*, UN Committee on the Elimination of Racial Discrimination, 26 September 2013
Council of Europe COM(2014) 27, *Report from the Commission to the European Parliament and the Council on the implementation of Council Framework Decision 2008/913/JHA on combating certain forms and expressions of racism and xenophobia by means of criminal law*, 27 January 2014
Report of the Fifth International Caravana of Jurists to Colombia, *The search for peace with justice and human rights in Colombia*, November 2016

Table of National Instruments

Argentina

Ley para la prevencion y condena de la negacion del genocidio y crimenes contra la humanidad, October 2012

Austria

National Socialism Prohibition Act of 1947
Law no. 148, 19 March 1992

Belgium

Law tending to repress negation, minimisation, justification or approbation of the genocide committed by the German National-Socialist regime during the Second World War, 23 March 1995

Bulgaria

Law of 13 April 2011

Croatia

Law of 26 October 2011

Cyprus

Law no. 134 (I) on combating certain forms and expressions of racism and xenophobia by means of criminal law, 21 October 2011

Czech Republic

Law of 9 February 2009

France

Freedom of the Press Act, 29 July 1881

Law no. 90-615, 13 July 1990

Law no. 2000-644 of 10 July 2000, *Journée nationale à la mémoire des victimes des crimes racistes et antisémites de l'Etat français et d'hommage aux 'Justes' de France*

Law no. 2001-70 on the recognition of the Armenian genocide, 29 January 2001

Law no. 434 on the recognition of the slave trade and slavery as a crime against humanity, (*reconnaissance de la traite et de l'esclavage en tant que crime contre l'humanité*), 21 May 2001

Law no. 2005-1 regarding the positive aspects of French colonisation, *Loi portant reconnaissance de la Nation et contribution nationale en faveur des Français repatriés (loi Mekhachera)*, 23 February 2005

President of the National Assembly, Report: Gathering the Nation around a shared memory (*Rapport d'information de l'Assemblée nationale - Rassembler la Nation autour d'une mémoire partagée*), n. 1262, 18 November 2008

Law no. 647 aiming at repressing the contestation of the existence of the genocides recognised by law ('*Loi visant à réprimer la contestation de l'existence des génocides reconnus par la loi*'), approved by the National Assembly on 22 December 2011 and the Senate on 23 January 2012

State Council's Public Report, INT-387525, 12 April 2013

Law No. 2014-1353 of 13 November 2014, Strengthening Provisions on the Fight Against Terrorism (Loi *renforçant les dispositions relatives à la lutte contre le terrorisme*

Decree no. 7,18 February 2015

Law no. 43, 17 April 2015

Law no. 2017-86 of 27 January 2017

Germany

Act amending the Criminal Code, the Code of Criminal Procedure and Other Acts ('*Gesetz zur Änderung des Strafgesetzbuches, der Strafprozessordnung und anderer Gesetze*'), 28 October 1994

Act amending the Assemblies Act and the Criminal Code ('*Gesetz zur Änderung des Versammlungsgesetzes und des Strafgesetzbuches*'), 24 March 2005

Greece

Law no. 4285, 4 September 2014

Hungary

Law no. XLVIII of 2013

Italy

Law no. 167, 20 November 2017
Law no. 654 on the Ratification and Execution of the International Convention on the Elimination of Forms of Racial Discrimination, opened for signature in New York on 7 March 1966, 13 October 1975
Law no. 211 of 20 July 2000 establishing the Day of remembrance in memory of the extermination and persecution of the Jewish people, Italian military and political deportees to Nazi camps'
Law no. 115, 16 June 2016

Israel

Denial of Holocaust (Prohibition) Law, 5746-1986, 8 July 1986

Latvia

Law of 21 May 2009

Lithuania

Law no. 75-3792 of 2010

Luxembourg

Law of 13 February 2011

Malta

Law of 3 November 2009

Peru

Draft on *Negacionismo de los delitos de terrorismo*, 28 August 2012

Poland

Act on the Institute of National Remembrance - Commission for the Prosecution of Crimes against the Polish Nation, 18 December 1998

Portugal

Law no. 65, 2 September 1998

Romania

Emergency Ordinance of 13 March 2002
Decree no. 669, 22 July 2015

Slovakia

Law of 20 May 2005

Spain

Decree no. 3096 of 1973
Organic Law, no. 4, 11 May 1995
Organic Law, no. 10, 23 November 1995
Organic Law, no. 1, 30 March 2015
Law 52/2007 (Historical Memory Law), 31 October 2007

Slovenia

Law of 2 November 2011

United Kingdom

British Counter-Terrorism and Security Act, 12 February 2015

Table of Cases

European Court of Human Rights

ECtHR, *De Wilde, Ooms e Versyp ("Vagrancy") v. Belgium*, Judgement, 18 June 1971, Application nn. 2832/66, 2835/66, 2899/66

ECtHR, *Ireland v. United Kingdom*, Judgement, 18 January 1978, Application n. 5310/71

ECtHR, *Kuhnen v. Federal Republic of Germany*, Judgement, 12 May 1988, Application n. 12194/86,

ECtHR, *Lowes v. United Kingdom*, Judgement, 9 December 1988, Application n. 13214/87

ECtHR, *Remer v. Germany*, Judgement, 6 September 1995, Application n. 25096/94

ECtHR, *Pierre Marais v. France*, Judgement, 24 June 1996, Application n. 31159/96

ECtHR, Grand Chamber, *Lehideux and Isorni v. France*, Judgement, 23 September 1998, Application n. 24662/94

ECtHR, *Erdogdu v. Turkey*, Judgement, 8 July 1999, Applications n. 25067/94 and 25068/94.

ECtHR, *Garaudy v. France*, Judgement, 24 June 2003, Application n. 65831/01,

ECtHR, *Witzsch v. Germany*, Judgement, 13 December 2005, Application n. 7485/03

ECtHR, *Perınçek v. Switzerland*, Judgement, 17 December 2013, Application n. 27510/08

ECtHR, *M'Bala M'Bala v. France*, Judgement, 20 October 2015, Application n. 25239/13

France

Court of Cassation, Criminal Division, 17 November 1983

Court of Appeal of Paris, Judgement, 31 October 1990

Court of Appeal of Paris, Judgement, 1 April 1992, n. 5571/91

Court of Cassation, Criminal Division, *Faurisson*, 23 February 1993
High Court of Paris, 24 March 1994
Court of Cassation, Criminal Division, Judgement, 9 October 1995, n. 92-83.665
Constitutional Council, Decision n° 96-377 DC, 16 July 1996
Court of Appeal of Metz, Judgement, 27 September 2000, n. 971/2000
Court of Appeal of Paris, Judgement, 11 September 2002, n. 01/01445
High Court of Lyon, 6th Correctional Chamber, *George Theil*, Judgement, 3 January 2006, 0564977
Court of Appeal of Paris, Judgement, 18 June 2008, n. 07/08276
Court of Appeal of Paris, Judgement, 21 January 2009, n. 08/02208
Court of Appeal of Paris, Judgement, 2 April 2009, n. 08/0001
Court of Cassation, *Question Préliminaire Constitutionnalité*, 7 May 2010, n. 09-80.774
Constitutional Council, Decision, 28 February 2012, n. 2012-647 DC
Constitutional Council, Decision, 26 January 2017, n. 2016-745 DC

Germany

BVerfG, Decision, 25 February 1975, 39, 1 (67).
BGH, 18 September 1979, no. 140/78.
BGH, 15 March 1994, no. 40/97.
BverfG13 April 1994, no. 23/94 BVerfG, 4 November 2009, no. 2150/08.
BverfG, 4 February 2010, no. 369/04.
BverfG, 4 February 2010, no. 370/04.
BverfG, 4 February 2010, no. 371/04.
Regional Court of Regensburg, 23 September 2013, 4 Ns 102 Js, no. 1410/2009.
Higher Regional Court of Brandenburg, 16 December 2015, 1 Ws, no. 174/15.
BGH, 3 May 2016, 3 StR no. 449/15
BGH, 27 July 2016, 3 StR no. 149/16

Italy

Cass. Pen., Sec. I, no. 38220, 12 July 2011 (dep. 24 October 2011)
Cass. Pen., Sec. V, no. 48001, 14 July 2016 (dep. 14 November 2016)

Spain

Court of First Instance number 6 of Madrid, Judgement 16 June 1986, no. 1284/85.
Sentencia Tribunal Constitucional, 16 December 1987, no. 199/1987.
Regional Court of Madrid, First Chamber, Judgement, 9 February 1988, no. 572/86.
Supreme Court of Spain, First Chamber, Judgement, 5 December 1989, no. 771/88.
Constitutional Court of Spain, Judgement, 11 November 1991, no. 214/1991
Supremo Tribunal Constitutional, 11 December 1995, no. 176/1995.
Constitutional Court of Spain, Judgement, 7 November 2007, no. 235/2007.
Provincial Court of Barcelona (Section 3), 5 March 2008.

Provincial Court of Barcelona (Section 2), FD 6, 26 April 2010.
Supreme Court of Spain, Judgement, 12 April 2011, no. 259.
Supreme Court of Spain, Criminal Chamber, *Luciano Varela Castro*, 25 May 2017, no. 378/2017.

Switzerland

Federal Court, ATF 6B_398/2007, 12 December 2007

List of Judicial Bodies

Conseil Constitutionnel = French Constitutional Council
Tribunal de Grande Instance = High Court
Tribunal correctionel = Criminal Court
Cour de Cassation criminelle = Court of Cassation, Criminal Division
Cour d'Appel = Court of Appeal
Tribunal Constitucional = Spanish Constitutional Court
Bundesverfassungsgericht = Federal Constitutional Court (BVerfG)
Landesgericht = Regional Court
Oberlandesgericht = Higher Regional Court
Bundestag = German Bundestag
Tribunal Supremo = Spanish Supreme Court
Juzgado de Primera Instancia núm. 6 de Madrid = Madrid Court of First Instance n. 6
Audiencia Territorial de Madrid = Regional Court of Madrid
Sala Primera = First Chamber
Juzgado de lo Penal numéro 3 de Barcelona = Criminal Court, number 3 of Barcelona
Audiencia Provincial de Barcelona (séccion 3) = Provincial Court of Barcelona (section 3)
Sala de lo Penal = Criminal Chamber

Abbreviations

BGH	Federal Court of Justice (*Bundesgerichtshof*)
BverfG	German Federal Constitutional Court (*Bundesverfassungsgericht*)
ECHR	European Convention of Human Rights
ECtHR	European Court of Human Rights
EU	European Union
COE	Council of Europe
ICC	International Criminal Court
ICCPR	International Covenant on Civil and Political Rights
IMT	International Military Tribunal of Nuremberg
NPD	National Partei Deutschland
StGB	German Criminal Code (*Strafgesetzbuch*)
UN	United Nations
VStGB	German Code of Crimes against International Law (*Völkerstrafgesetzbuch*)

Part I
Historical Denialism as a Criminal Offence: Origins and Development

Chapter 1
The Birth of the Crime of Historical Denialism

Contents

Abstract This first chapter defines historical denialism by characterising it as a degeneration of the related notion of revisionism. Having introduced its evolution as a criminal offence, historical denialism is distinguished from remembrance laws. Its progressive criminalisation is further analysed from a European comparative angle. On the one hand, this process is characterised by the expansion of the object of the criminal prohibition, which was originally limited only to the negation of the Holocaust but now includes other international crimes. On the other hand, the criminalisation of historical denialism is illustrative of the blossoming of speech crimes. From this viewpoint, the protection of historical memory, guaranteed by the offence of historical denialism, aligns with a general trend that expands limitations of free speech in the name of the protection of other fundamental values of democratic societies.

Keywords Historical Denialism · Criminal Offence · Remembrance Laws · Speech Crimes · Freedom of Expression

E. Fronza, *Memory and Punishment*, International Criminal Justice Series 19,
https://doi.org/10.1007/978-94-6265-234-7_1

1.1 Origins of the Phenomenon

A definition of historical denialism cannot be separated from that of revisionism, with which it is often associated. 'Denialism' and 'revisionism' are both terms widely used in scholarly debate as well as in common discourse due to their increased appearance in the media since the late 1990s. Often considered as synonyms in printed and television news, they are generally used in a more evocative rather than descriptive sense. The commonly accepted interchangeability of the two terms in everyday language has diminished their conceptual specificity and blurred their distinguishing features, resulting in a miscomprehension of their roots and characteristics.

1.1.1 Historical Denialism and Revisionism

Historical denialism derives from revisionism, of which it is, strictly speaking, a degeneration. According to its broadest interpretation, the term revisionism[1] indicates a tendency to review historical reconstructions in the light of new information and knowledge acquired through research in order to reinterpret events and rewrite their narratives. Indeed, the continuous reinterpretation of the past in light of new research and the amendment of widely accepted positions are intrinsic to historical studies. The 19th-century idea that the historian's task is only to tell 'what actually happened'[2] has long been superseded. History is always constituted by a set of questions that the present asks of the past in an attempt to uncover the roots of its own problems and to better understand itself. The significant events of the past and their meaning within the historical narrative we construct must be clarified since they gradually change as society and the researchers investigating those events transform. Historians focus on events that are meaningful because they are relevant to current societal dynamics. As those dynamics and the problems created by these events dissipate, historians redirect their research on different aspects of history and its events.

In this sense, every historian and, more generally, every researcher is inevitably revisionist because the very nature of their work is underpinned by the succession of new theoretical models and changing paradigms. However, unanimity is rare when those models and paradigms are proposed—especially when they are substantial. As a result, if, generally speaking, 'revisionism' is an essential element of historical research, its application may have either a negative or positive meaning.

---

[1] See Vidal-Naquet 1981, p. 108.

[2] The well-known phrase is by Leopold Von Ranke (1795–1886), principal proponent of historiographical positivism. '*Man hat der Historie das Amt, die Vergangenheit zu richten, die Mitwelt zum Nutzen zukünftiger Jahre zu belehren, beigemessen: so hoher Ämter unterwindet sich gegenwärtiger Versuch nicht: er will bloß zeigen, wie es eigentlich gewesen*', Ranke, Leopold Von, Sämtliche Werke Bd. 33/34, Leipzig 1885, p. 7.

This depends on the dominant opinion it criticises, which, with reference to the context, may be perceived as either an orthodoxy to overcome or a common heritage to defend.

Denialism, on the contrary, is an eminently controversial term with an unequivocally negative connotation. It was coined in historical and journalistic circles in the mid-1980s to define a particular kind of historical revisionism deemed unacceptable by its critics for both its methodology and results. The origin of this historiographical trend dates back to immediately after World War II, even though its political significance and importance in public opinion are seen as relatively recent phenomena. At the end of the war, a few texts were published in Western Europe attempting to apologise for, or at least defend, defeated Nazism and to deny or minimise the Holocaust, considered to be mostly victors' propaganda. The authors of these publications called themselves 'revisionists'.

As with any historiographical revision, it is possible to distinguish two intertwined areas of criticism of the dominant historical reconstruction: a factual one, aiming to deny either that certain events ever took place or that they occurred in the way they are usually narrated; and an interpretative one, which does not contest the facts in themselves but seeks to deny that such facts have causal links with other events.

Two distinct approaches of these studies are immediately apparent. On the one hand, starting from the irrefutable fact that the Nazis eliminated much of the Jewish population of the occupied territories, the revisionist view aims mainly to redistribute blame, attribute limited responsibility to Adolf Hitler and the Nazi regime and downplay the issue of extermination within the overall framework of the war. On the other hand, the denialist view in the strict sense negates the very existence of the Holocaust and considers the facts underlying its historical reconstruction to be groundless.

The radical nature of denialist claims inevitably conflicts with any pre-established historiographical rule, given the wealth of evidence that proves the Holocaust, and bypasses the relationship of the nazi-genocide with the historical reality.[3] For these reasons, critics of extreme revisionist tendencies deemed denialists consider these theories to be unacceptable in terms of historical research and methodological accuracy and, therefore, also entirely ideological and largely counter-factual.

Over time, the terms revisionism and denialism have been expanded as regards their scope from being limited to the Holocaust to encompassing the criticism or denial of other mass killings and serious violations of human rights, such as genocides, the very mention of which is often highly contentious. Literature classified in journalistic terms as 'revisionist' pursues a radical questioning of the reconstruction of historical events that were taken as established facts. Today it

[3] Pisanty 2000, p. 44. On the phenomenon of denialism, see also Behrens et al. 2017, pp. 7-54; Vercelli 2013; Di Cesare 2012; Atkins 2009; Flores 2007; Pisanty 2005, p. 425 et seq.; Bastian 1997; Lipstadt 1994; Benz 1992. On negation, trivialization and sacralization as abuses of memory, see Pisanty 2012.

involves a broader thematic scope that is less strictly defined than, for example, the denial of a mass killing, which is a much more easily identifiable event.

The term 'denialism', meaning the systematic and ideological negation of reality and truth, was first used to identify the theories that negated the existence of gas chambers in Nazi concentration camps[4] and was associated for a long time mainly with Holocaust denial. Today, however, the concept of denialism has a much broader connotation. It now includes the questioning of other crimes such as genocide, crimes against humanity, and war crimes (for instance, the Armenian genocide by the Turkish Government during World War I; the *Porrajmos*, that is to say the Nazi extermination of European Gypsies; the *Holodomor,* also known as the Ukrainian Holocaust; or, more recently, the crimes perpetrated in the former Yugoslavia, in Rwanda and Cambodia).[5]

More recently, the term has circulated in contexts other than that of criminal law. For example, we speak of climate change denialism, the negation of the moon landing or the belief that AIDS is a hoax.[6] Therefore, it is important to differentiate historical denialism from historical approaches that aim to relativise and historicise mass exterminations or criticise given interpretations. In this book, the expression 'historical denialism' refers to those radical doctrines that argue that neither the genocide of Jews, gypsies and other groups considered 'subhuman' in Nazi Germany ever occurred nor other mass atrocities ever happened. Subsequently, it will be shown how historical denialists reject being classified as such. In particular, they refuse the epistemological status of historians, describing themselves as 'revisionist' historians marginalised by an ideologically-motivated academic and political consensus that conceals the 'facts' that they are ready to reveal.

A preliminary distinction must be made between these two approaches of criticising commonly established and accepted reconstructions of the Holocaust, as well as genocides and crimes against humanity in general, of which recent history is dramatically rich.

On the one hand, we understand revisionism as characterised by theories based on historical research, verification of events, and proper methodology with conclusions that appear to be the result of the research undertaken, however divergent they may be from the dominant reconstruction of a particular historical episode.

On the other, we characterise historical denialism by the proposition of theories with a thesis (the denial, the trivialisation or the justification of the facts in question) which prevails over the methodology of historical research. This directly influences the selection of circumstances or supporting facts. It also results in neglecting or

---

[4] See Rousso 1987.

[5] On the denial of the Rwandan genocide, see Behrens et al. 2017, pp. 94–144; Moerland 2016; Gasanabo et al. 2015; Longman 2011; Bizimana 2001. On Rwandan laws on genocide denial and on a recent case in which these provisions were used, see Jansen 2014. For more examples of historical denialism outside Europe, see Lechtholz Zey 2012; Kahn 1997, p. 17 et seq.; Hill 1989, p. 165 et seq.

[6] This new dimension of denialism will not be analysed in this study; see Fourie and Meyer 2013, p. 35 et seq.; Higwedere and Essex 2010.

downplaying other arguments that may contradict the main thesis, if not, as has occurred, directly fabricating or modifying facts and evidence.

1.1.2 A Brief History of Historical Denialism

As previously mentioned, the origins of historical denialism can be traced back to the years immediately following World War II. However, since the late 1970s there have been significant developments, facilitated, for example, by the *Institute for Historical Review* in the United States,[7] an organisation that promotes denialist work. In addition, it is worth to mention Paul Rassinier and Robert Faurisson's work and the writings of a new generation of 'historians' and publicists, among whom the best known is undoubtedly David Irving.[8] At least two factors were crucial to the spread of the phenomenon: first, the increasing temporal distance between World War II and the generations that directly experienced the war's events; second, the collapse of the Eastern bloc between 1989 and 1993.

With the dissolution of the Soviet Union, the bridging power of remembering the Holocaust disappeared. Previously, it served as a common ground between ideologies fighting a common enemy in the name of an enlightened 'humanism' based on human equality and respect for shared values, which had been indelibly marked by the Holocaust.

In addition, new right-wing movements providing reception for these theories emerged in Europe. Historical denialists also began to distance themselves from anti-Semitic claims in order to make their theories more neutral from an ideological point of view and less overtly racist so as not to be immediately rejected.

It is during this time that the radicalism of these theories, their dissemination and the ease of finding evidence for supporting their claims prompted the scientific community to challenge the classification of these authors as 'revisionist historians'. In reality, they were attempting to hide behind legitimate academic terms while espousing an ideology of minimisation and denial of established facts. Simultaneously, the expression 'denial'—variously translated in other languages—re-emerged, rejecting the legitimate historical concept of 'revisionism'. Emphasis was put on the word 'denial' in order to point out that the only purpose of these ideas was to deny the historical veracity of the Holocaust. In French-speaking countries the word '*négationnisme*' was used, in English-speaking countries 'Holocaust denial', in Germany '*Auschwitzlüge*' (from the verb '*leugen*', which means 'to deny' but also 'to lie'), in Italian '*negazionismo*', in Spanish-speaking countries '*negacionismo del Holocausto*' and in Portuguese-speaking countries '*negação do Holocausto*'.

Holocaust denial main claims are: the denial of gas chambers; the radical questioning of the number of victims; the rejection of the idea that the 'final solution of the Jewish problem', to which Nazi documents refer, was not a mass

[7] See the website of the *Institute for Historical Review* at http://www.ihr.org.

[8] For further references on the history of historical denial, see Terry 2017, especially pp. 35–40.

extermination, but only encompassed a forced emigration; and allegations against the Military Tribunal of Nuremberg, which prompted the first major collection of evidence, testimony and reconstruction of events, as a case of 'victor's justice' motivated by its unreliable and biased findings.[9]

Historians and intellectuals have harshly criticised these features of denialism and combine methodological indignation with moral revulsion. In effect, these assertions jeopardise the very existence of history. History can be understood and narrated and becomes part of collective memory only if proven, since irrefutable facts are considered an integral part of our historical experience. In the writings of deniers, however, this basic rule is completely disregarded: facts are hidden or altered, the chain of events is broken and isolated facts are 'edited' from time to time in order to support or deny, depending on what the theory in question requires for validation.

Values are inverted, since the truth is swapped with falsehood and reality with fiction. This is the consequence of historical denialism according to its harshest critics. History dissolves into social science, and simple current views—destined by historical absolutisation to turn into ideologies—explain everything and nothing at all: an artificial world is created that can compete with the real one. Such a world may not be logical, but it is coherent and organised to have an appearance of plausibility, similar to the Orwellian laws of totalitarian regimes which build a fictional world undisturbed by factuality.[10] Therefore, in historical denialism history is not reinterpreted as happens when history is simply revised (revisionism), but it is *tout court* denied (historical denialism).

A denialist historiographical uniform paradigm definitely does not exist as such. The only methodological fact common to the 'assassins of memory'[11] is historical denial. The proposed paradigm has no scientific dignity:[12] after opening with the shortcomings of official history and distorting documentary evidence, there is no attempt to provide arguments or evidence supporting the claims made. Therefore, anyone who wishes to adhere to these guidelines is required to do so as an act of faith, based on unproved theories such as the Jewish conspiracy, rather than on documented facts. The denialist mystification culminates in pure mythology or, in the words of Roland Barthes, in 'deprivation of history'.[13]

As a result, historical deniers are not considered historians nor do they pertain to the majority of intellectuals who work in the field of in-depth historiography. In other words, only those who adhere to the claims put forth by historical deniers view their work as a form of legitimate historical revisionism. In this sense, there is

---

[9] See Zimmerman 2000.

[10] Arendt 1966.

[11] The locution has been coined by the historian Yosef Hayim Yerushalmi, as cited and utilised by Pierre Vidal-Naquet 1981.

[12] *'Le révisionnisme de l'histoire étant une démarche classique chez les scientifiques, on préférera ici le barbarisme, moins élégant mais plus approprié, de «négationnisme», car il s'agit bien d'un système de pensée, d'une idéologie et non d'une démarche scientifique ou même simplement critique'*, Rousso 1987.

[13] See Finkielkraut 1982, p. 100.

a clear and insurmountable separation between the professional field and the 'historical' writings by the authors in question.

The denialist offensive has appeared mostly in Europe, in particular in Germany, Austria, France, Spain and Italy.[14] Its exponents come always from the margins of the political spectrum, often from the extreme right and the extreme left. They share an underlying anti-Semitic ideological platform or an opposition to 'Zionism', both of which constitute their main sources and driving force for finding other arguments and claims. Furthermore, historical denialism is not just advanced by individuals and groups, but also by states. The most significant examples of state historical denialism include the Turkish denial of the Armenian genocide and, more recently, former Iranian President Mahmoud Ahmadinejad's denialist view of the Holocaust. Especially in the Arab world, the latter claims have promoted a reductive and minimising vision of the Holocaust as the founding myth of Israel rather than a crucial 20th century event.[15]

In recent years, the ideologies of historical denialism have carved their own space in the market and in public opinion utilising media, such as leaflets, 'scholarly' books, simple propaganda, photocopied pamphlets, themed magazines, videotapes, DVDs and websites. Propaganda that denies, minimises or justifies genocide, crimes against humanity or war crimes has become a constant, albeit limited, phenomenon and, in most cases, has resulted in racism. Its presence is even more insidious today than before with the ease of disseminating texts and images via the Internet.[16]

1.2 Origins of the Offence

Historical denialism stems from a form of racism. It is mainly present in Europe and is flanked by various forms of anti-Semitism or the deliberate denigration of victims of serious violations of human rights. This phenomenon erodes the values transmitted by the public collective memory of the victimised community, understood as the communal and shared understanding of significant historical events.

Nowadays historical denialism is a diversified, multi-faceted phenomenon. Its arguments and discursive techniques appear in varied and subtle forms, and its representatives differ significantly in beliefs, interests and means, ranging from individuals to publishers, political or interest groups or states. Also, the scenario from which historical denialism usually emerges is very complex because it groups a great diversity of public opinions, as well as a communication system in which local radio, magazines, and especially the Internet and social networks facilitate

[14] See Terry 2017, p. 35 et seq.

[15] Details about the declarations of the former President of Iran: see http://www.bbc.com/news/world-middle-east-24442723. On state historical denialism, see Flores, La mappa dei negazionismi di Stato. Dallo sterminio degli armeni alla Shoah: dal colonialismo alla questione irlandese. Chi vuole falsificare il passato oggi può contare su nuove, potenti strategie comunicative, in *Corriere della Sera*, 26 February 2012.

[16] See Terry 2017, p. 50 et seq. Doward 2017; Gillespie 2015, pp. 488-507; Mensching 2014.

rapid and unlimited dissemination of unmediated messages. With the increasing frequency of historical denialist phenomena, many countries have responded with criminal law by making historical denialism a criminal offence.[17]

Over time, the criminal offence of denialism has evolved. From the outset, it was created to counter the denial, justification or minimisation of the Holocaust. This could be defined as a crime of 'original' denialism. Today, the offence of denialism has different features and, in the European context, a wide application: not only are expressions regarding the crimes of the Nazi regime punishable, but also those concerning other recognised international crimes. This second form can thus be defined as a crime of 'broader' denialism.

Criminal law protection has therefore become wider; it includes the Holocaust and other significant historical events, which are not always so historically undisputed. In most cases, the criminal provision identifies the historical facts to be protected by referring to the definition of international crimes contained in the Statute of the Military Tribunal of Nuremberg[18] and in the International Criminal Court Statute.[19] Sometimes, however, the provision does not refer to a specific text, leaving it to the judges or the prime legislator to identify and qualify historical

---

[17] By now there are numerous legal works on the criminalisation of historical denialism. Among the monographic works and the books: Behrens et al. 2017; Belavusau and Gliszczynska-Grabias 2017; Heinze 2017; Leotta 2015; Teruel Lozano 2015; Caruso 2013; Bifulco 2012; Garibian 2012, pp. 53-62; Hochmann 2012; Matuschek 2012; Resta and Zeno-Zencovich 2012; Hare and Weinstein 2011; Hennebel and Hochmann 2011; Pech 2011; Visconti 2008; Kahn 2004; Imbleau 2003; Laitenberger 2003; Wandres 2000. Among the studies in the field of criminal law, see Cavaliere 2016; Brunelli 2016; Fronza 2016a; Lobba 2014, 2015; Pulitanò 2015; Caputo 2014; Droin 2014; Insolera 2014; Gamberini 2013; Salomon 2012; Zabel 2010; Borgwardt 2009; Visconti 2009; Bilbao Ubillos 2008; Merli 2008; Dubuisson 2007; Gavagnin 2006; Peter 2006; Roxin 2006; Hörnle 2005; Laitenberger 2003; Wandres 2000; Beisel 1995; Dietz 1995; Werle 1992. Among the studies in the field of constitutional law, see Cortese 2012, 2016; Caruso 2013; Garibian 2014; Gliszczyńska-Grabias 2013; Parisi 2013; Bifulco 2012; Pollicino 2011; Pugiotto 2009; Bargiacchi 2008; Luther 2008; Merli 2008; Spigno 2008; Bloch 2006; Di Giovine 2006; Brugger 2005; Manetti 2005a, b. Among the studies from an international law perspective, see Della Morte 2011, 2016a, b; Shahnazarova 2015; Hervieu 2014; Matuschek 2013.

[18] On the definition of war crimes and crimes against humanity within the Statute of the Military Tribunal of Nuremberg, especially on the so-called war-nexus link, see Acquaviva 2011, pp. 881-903; Heller 2011; Merkel 2008, pp. 555–576; Schwarzenberger 2008, pp. 167–189; Mettraux 2008; Lippmann 1997; Clark 1990; Appleman 1954; Robinson 1946; Schwelb 1946, pp. 178–226. On the prosecution of crimes committed during the National Socialist Period, see Vormbaum and Bohlander 2014, p. 213 et seq.

[19] On the definition of international crimes in general, see Triffterer and Ambos 2016; Amati et al. 2016; Gil Gil and Maculan 2016, p. 345 et seq.; O'Keefe 2015; Ambos 2014, especially pp. 1–245; Cryer et al. 2014; Fouchard 2014; Werle and Jessberger 2014, p. 289 et seq.; Kolb and Scalia 2012. On the definition of war crimes in relation to international humanitarian law, see Sivakumaran 2012; Boed 2002, pp. 293–322; Kress 2001, pp. 103–177; Meron 1995, pp. 554–577; with a specific reference to the ICC Statute, see Prosperi and Terrosi 2017, pp. 509–525; Cullen 2008, pp. 419–445. On a more deep analysis of crimes against humanity within the ICC Statute, see Cupido 2011, pp. 275–309; Geras 2011; Sluiter 2011, pp. 102–141; Cryer 2009, pp. 283–296; Kress 2009, pp. 1–10; Ambos and Wirth 2002, pp. 1–90; Greppi 2001. On crimes against humanity and on humanity as victim, see Delmas-Marty 2005, pp. 75 seq. In relation to the

events whose memory cannot be violated (like in Greece or in the unapproved *Boyer* Bill in France).[20] As a consequence, identifying a specific historical fact as an international crime means that its memory must be protected by criminal law.

1.2.1 Evolution of the Criminal Offence

First nationally and then internationally, the response to the phenomenon of historical denialism has been to resort to the law, especially *criminal law*. This study focuses specifically on Europe as the geographical area where the criminalisation of historical denialism began and developed.

Denialism is punished as a criminal offence in special provisions in many national European laws, albeit with differences in the definition of the punishable conducts and the corresponding penalty. It is recognised either as a separate crime or as an aggravating circumstance in 21 of the 28 States that comprise the European Union (EU).[21] The 'original' model of criminalisation, which has since significantly expanded, punished statements regarding the Holocaust, resulting in a founding

---

crime of genocide, especially its special intent and the question of motives, see Behrens 2012, pp. 501–523; Jones 2003, p. 467; Nersessian 2002, pp. 231–276; Triffterer 2001, pp. 399–408.

[20] See Part. II, Chap. 3, Sect. 3.2.3

[21] Israel was the first country to introduce the offence of denialism with the Denial of Holocaust (Prohibition) Law, 5746-1986, 8 July 1986. In Europe, historical denialism is considered a criminal offence by: France (Article 24 bis of the Freedom of the Press Act); Austria (Article 3, para h of the National Socialism Prohibition Act of 1947, amended by law no. 148 of 19 March 1992); Germany (Article 130(3) Criminal Code amended by law of 28 October 1994); Belgium (Article 1 of the Law tending to repress negation, minimisation, justification or approbation of the genocide committed by the German National-Socialist regime during the Second World War of 23 March 1995); Spain (Article 510, para I, lett. c) Criminal Code, introduced by the Organic Law no. 1 of 30 March 2015 amending the measure originally provided by Article 607 Criminal Code by the Organic Law no. 10 of 23 November 1995); Portugal (Article 240, para II, lett. B) Criminal Code introduced by Law no. 65 of 2 September 1998); Poland (Article 55 of the Act on the Institute of National Remembrance - Commission for the Prosecution of Crimes against the Polish Nation of 18 December 1998); Romania (Article 6 of Law no. 217 of 27 July 2015 amending the Emergency Ordinance of 13 March 2002); Slovakia (Article 422d Criminal Code introduced by the law of 20 May 2005); the Czech Republic (Article 405 Criminal Code introduced by the law of 9 February 2009); Malta (Article 82B Criminal Code introduced by the law of 3 November 2009); Latvia (Article 74-1 Criminal Code introduced by the law of 21 May 21 2009 with the punishment provision amended in 2012); Lithuania (Article 170, para II Criminal Code introduced by law no. 75-3792 2010); Luxembourg (Article 457-3 of the Criminal Code introduced by the law of 13 February 2011); Bulgaria (Article 419a Criminal Code introduced by the law of 13 April 2011); Cyprus (Article 3 of law no. 134 (1) of 21 October 2011); Croatia (Article 325 Criminal Code introduced by the law of 26 October 2011); Slovenia (Article 297 Criminal Code introduced by the law of 2 November 2011); Hungary (Article 333 Criminal Code introduced by law no. XLVIII of 2013); Greece (Article 2 of law no. 4285 of 104 September 2014); and finally, more recently, Italy (Article 3 para 3 *bis* of law no. 654 of 13 October 1975, introduced by law no. 115 of 16 June 2016 and amended by Article 5 of law no. 167 of 20 November 2017. See the annexed Table.

event for the construction of the European identity. The use of criminal law as a solution is primarily intended to reassure the public opinion shaken by the questioning of tragic events and, as a result, it is characterised by a highly symbolic component. Far from remaining dormant, such criminal provisions have been the subject of several judgments in both national courts (ordinary and constitutional) and regional courts, in particular the European Court of Human Rights.

As mentioned, the criminalisation of these untrue statements raises several problematic issues because it implies the use of criminal justice as a preventive measure. Its preemptive logic is a key element in increasing limits on freedom of expression through criminal law.

This chapter briefly summarises the evolution of historical denialism as a crime, by focusing specifically on the dynamics of criminalisation of denialist statements, landmark moments in its development—in particular with the adoption of the EU Framework Decision—and the main actors in this process of juridification of historical memory.

1.2.1.1 From an 'Original' to a 'Broader' Form: the Offence

As previously mentioned, the criminal offence of historical denialism first appeared within the European cultural and geographical context, where it continues to undergo significant legislative and judicial evolution.[22]

From a chronological point of view, the first phase of the criminalisation of historical denialism is marked by the adoption of measures at the national level and subsequent remembrance laws, mostly in connection with the European experience of Nazi crimes. In the subsequent phase, the criminal offence or an obligation to criminalise is incorporated in EU and international law ('upward' movement).[23] Finally, based on this supranational input, criminalisation is once again subject to an implementation process at the national level. In some cases, the criminal offence is inserted *ex novo*. On the contrary, where it already existed, it is simply amended ('top-down' movement).[24]

The first European provision of this kind was introduced in France in 1990.[25] Since then, many other European countries have introduced such a crime, distinguishing it from both the offences of condoning and inciting racial discrimination, which were previously used to counter this behaviour.

[22] Other than Israel, outside the European continent New Zealand, Australia, Rwanda and Cambodia provide for this offence. For a comparative analysis, see Marcheri 2015; Helz 2012; Matuschek 2012, p. 46 et seq.; Hare and Weinstein 2011; Hennebel and Hochmann 2011; Wandres 2008. On the distinction between denialism and hate speech, among others see Belavusau 2017; Belavusau 2013, pp. 166–200. For a complete comparative overview—including Russia—from an historical perspective, see Koposov 2017.

[23] As so defined by Delmas-Marty 2006.

[24] *Ibid.*

[25] Article 24 *bis* of the French Freedom of the Press Act, amended by Article 173 of Law no. 2017-86 of 27 January 2017.

With regard to the introduction of the offence under consideration, two phases can generally be distinguished: the first in the early 1990s which, in addition to France, interested nine other countries (among them Austria, Germany, Belgium and Spain); a second phase, which started after 2008, the year of the adoption of the EU Framework Decision, and which concerns ten more countries, including some belonging to Eastern Europe, as well as Greece, Luxembourg, Slovenia, Malta and Cyprus.

During the first phase of criminalisation of denialism, the offence aimed at prohibiting the denial, justification and gross trivialisation of the Holocaust (the 'original' offence of historical denialism). Among the 21 European countries that introduced the offence, the following provide punishment only for statements regarding the Holocaust: Austria (Article 3. para H of the National Socialism Prohibition Law Act introduced by the law of 19 March 1992); Germany (§130 (3) Criminal Code); France with the *Gayssot* Act of 13 July 1990; Belgium (Article 1 of the Law tending to repress negation, minimisation, justification or approbation of the genocide committed by the German National-Socialist regime during the Second World War of 23 March 1995). Also, Romania, until the amendment of 2015, limited the offence only to original denialism (Emergency Ordinance of 13 March 2002). In this first phase, only four countries adopted the 'broader' offence of historical denialism: Poland (Article 55 of the Act on the Institute of National Remembrance - Commission for the Prosecution of Crimes against the Polish Nation), Portugal (Article 240, para II, lett. B) Criminal Code), Slovakia (Article 424a Criminal Code) and Spain (Article 510, para. I, lett. c) Criminal Code).

Currently, more than three decades after the introduction of the offence in France, the process of criminalisation of historical denialism is experiencing a new phase in an entirely different scenario. First of all, the context has changed: demand for penalisation of historical denialism is contained not only in national legislation but also in EU and international law. These, in turn, stipulate obligations for states to criminalise historical denialism, triggering an expansion of the criminal offence since it no longer solely encompasses the Holocaust.

In addition to these 'bottom-up' (from the national to the international level) and 'top-down' (from the international to the national level) dynamics of vertical interaction mainly concerning legislation, judicial interaction also occurs horizontally.[26] Citations, cross references and cross fertilisation of court decisions from different jurisdictions must be considered because they help in identifying the true nature of the current criminal offence of historical denialism and the problematic aspects of the juridification of collective memory. Indeed, domestic judges quote and utilise as references the rulings of the European Court of Human Rights or other foreign courts and vice versa.[27]

[26] For more on the criminal system as a system of interactions, see Delmas-Marty 2006, 2016.

[27] For examples, refer to the following judgments: Constitutional Tribunal of Spain, Judgment, 7 November 2007, no. 235/2007, in Official State Gazette (*Boletín Oficial del Estado*), 10 December 2007, no. 295, p. 50, where several cases of the European Court of Human Rights are cited, for example, ECtHR, *Lehideux and Isorni v. France* (Grand Chamber), no. 24662/94, 23 September 1998, Application no. 24662/94 and *Chauvy* et al. *v. France*, Judgment, 29 September 2004, Application no. 64915/01.

The moment the European Union became an actor in penalising historical denialism marked a new phase and reshaped the current form of the criminal offence. Consider that since 2008, the year the EU Framework Decision was adopted, 11 states have introduced a separate offence of denialism (Bulgaria, Croatia, Cyprus, Greece, Latvia, Lithuania, Luxembourg, Malta, Czech Republic, Slovenia, Hungary), one country has introduced an aggravating circumstance (Italy) and three other countries have amended the circumstances already existing within their legal systems prior to the adoption of the EU Framework Decision (France, Spain and Romania).

European Union law confirms the preference for criminal law as a means to respond to this pernicious phenomenon of historical denialism and embraces the definition of the crime that broadens the subject matter of the punishable statements: not only are expressions regarding denial of the Holocaust punishable but so are those concerning all categories of international crimes ('broader' offence of historical denialism).[28]

According to this paradigm of criminalisation, criminal protection is afforded to the Holocaust and other significant historical events that can be qualified as international crimes. To identify the historical facts directly connected to international crimes, the provision refers in most cases to the definition of international crimes contained in the Statute of the Nuremberg Military Tribunal or in the International Criminal Court Statute. Such protection is provided in France (Article 24 bis of the Freedom of the Press Act of 29 July 1881, as modified by Law no. 2017-86 of 27 January 2017) and Luxembourg (Article 457-3 Criminal Code). It can also be found in Cypriot Law no. 134 (I) on the combat against certain forms of racism and xenophobia of 21 October 2011, Slovakian Criminal Code (Article 422-d Criminal Code) and the aggravating circumstance provided in Italy by Article 3a of Law no. 654 of 13 October 1975 and introduced by Law no. 115 of 16 June 2016. Conversely, the Belgian legal system expressly refers to the Convention on the Prevention and Punishment of the Crime of Genocide of 9 December 1948.[29] In other cases, this function depends on court decisions: in Cyprus, the fact that cannot be denied must be defined by a judgment issued by an international tribunal, while in Luxembourg genocide, crimes against humanity and war crimes, as defined by Article 136a et seq. of the Criminal Code, can also be determined by national courts.

In some countries, it is up to the legislator (through legal qualification) to determine which historical events must be protected from denialism. Greece is exemplary in this regard because it requires that the object of the crime of denialism is to be established by a decision of an international court or by the national parliament.[30] In both of these models (the judge or the legislator as 'memory makers'), qualifying a historical fact as an international crime means establishing that the historical memory of that fact cannot be violated; if it is, the conduct will be punished.

---

[28] See Fronza 2015, p. 633 et seq.

[29] Article 1 of the Law punishing negation, minimisation, justification or approbation of the genocide committed by the German National-Socialist regime during the Second World War of 23 March 1995.

[30] Article 2 of Law no. 4285 of 10 September 2014.

As a result, expanding the punishment of historical denialism amplifies the 'original' message the penal measure conveys to public opinion. What was at first an expression of protecting the values that emerged after World War II has become something vaster. In fact, the message becomes that respect for human rights is the cornerstone of European democracies and identity, and, as a consequence, so is the collective memory of all their most serious violations, which must be preserved and protected, including through criminal law.

Before analysing the second phase of the criminalisation of historical denialism after the adoption of the EU Framework Decision, a brief comparative overview of criminal provisions on the issue at hand will be given. Despite the existence of an EU Framework Decision and of a trend of resorting to criminal law, there are numerous differences among the various paradigms of criminalisation at a national level.

1.2.1.2 A Crime with Varying Forms

Today legislation providing for the criminalisation of historical denialism is present in the majority of European States, albeit with significant exceptions.[31] Therefore, the emerging picture is a Europe that protects its historical collective memory through law and criminal trials. Even with this common punitive approach and a shared core of constitutional principles, a crime with varying forms in different legal systems surfaces, highlighting the unique nature of individual historical, political and legal national traditions.

The main differences in the approach to the criminalisation of historical denialism include: the source, within the legal system considered, that provides for the criminal offence; the configuration of the punishable conduct; and the domestic choice and extent to which Member States decide to prevent an excessive limitation of freedom of speech.

The provision of the crime in question may be included both in criminal codes[32] and special legislation.[33] Often, it has been added through subsequent revisions of already existing laws.[34]

---

[31] Among the European Union Member States, the United Kingdom, Ireland, the Netherlands, Denmark, Estonia, Sweden and Finland do not provide a specific criminal offence.

[32] Croatia (Article 325 Criminal Code), Hungary (Article 333 Criminal Code), Malta (Article 82b Criminal Code) and Slovenia (Article 297 Criminal Code) also place the offence of denialism within the section on crimes against public order. A different solution is foreseen in the Czech Republic (Article 405 Criminal Code), Latvia (Article 74-1 Criminal Code), Portugal (Article 240 Criminal Code) and Slovakia (Article 422d Criminal Code), which include the offence in the section dedicated to international crimes. Luxembourg, on the other hand, places the offence within the chapter devoted to racism, revisionism and other forms of discrimination (Article 457-3 Criminal Code).

[33] Other examples include Cyprus (Law No. 134 (I) on combating certain forms of racism and xenophobia) and Romania (Law no. 217 of 27 July 2015).

[34] For example, measures relating to the punishment of neo-Nazi and anti-Semitic activities in Austria (Article 3h National Socialism Prohibition Act) and the elimination of all forms of racial discrimination in Italy (Article 3 para 3 *bis* of law no. 654 of 13 October 1975).

The body of law the criminal offence belongs to is not insignificant because it can contribute to the identification of the interest protected by the crime of historical denialism. The identification of a protected interest is essential in order to balance freedom of expression with other fundamental rights. Protected interests may be public order, public peace, the human dignity of victims and the prohibition of discrimination. An interesting case is Lithuania, which punishes the denial of the serious crimes committed during the struggle for independence between 1990 and 1991. This offence, in addition to having a highly symbolic value, seems to identify the legal protected interest within the historical and collective memory of the country.[35]

With regard to the punishable conducts, in most cases the focus is on denial,[36] justification[37] and gross trivialisation.[38] In particular, trivialisation entails relativising the events, in either a quantitative or qualitative form. For example, reducing the number of victims is an example of quantitative trivialisation, whereas describing atrocious crimes as not so serious is a qualitative one.[39] Some legislations require the trivialisation to be 'crude' (Belgium, Lithuania, Croatia, Bulgaria and Malta)[40] or 'grave' (Austria and Cyprus).[41] Various legal systems, however, may also include approval (Austria, Belgium and the Czech Republic),[42] disputing (France, Luxembourg and Romania),[43] glorification (Latvia),[44] questioning (the Czech Republic)[45] or derision (Slovenia).[46]

[35] Article 170(2) Criminal Code of Lithuania.

[36] To express a doubt is not sufficient: an event must be questioned and the claim must be made that it has not taken place. Consider those who define the Holocaust as an invention or a lie.

[37] To justify means trying to prove the legitimacy of an event or at least the impossibility of avoiding it. Example: 'The Shoah was an unfortunate fact, but inevitable.'

[38] Austria (Article 3h National Socialism Prohibition Act), Germany (Article 130(3) Criminal Code), Portugal (Article 240 Criminal Code), Poland (Article 55 Act on the Institute of National Remembrance - Commission for the Prosecution of Crimes against the Polish Nation), Romania (Article 6 Law no. 217 of 27 July 2015), Hungary (Article 333 Criminal Code), Luxembourg (Article 457-3 Criminal Code) and Greece (Article 2 Law no. 4285 of 10 September 2014).

[39] Such conduct also includes expressing doubt: see Kindhäuser et al. 2013, p. 685; Fischer 2017.

[40] Belgium (Law tending to repress negation, minimisation, justification or approbation of the genocide committed by the German National-Socialist regime during the Second World War of 23 March 1995), Lithuania (Article 170(2) Criminal Code), Croatia (Article 325 Criminal Code), Bulgaria (Article 419 Criminal Code), Malta (Article 82b Criminal Code).

[41] Austria (Article 3h National Socialism Prohibition Act) and Cyprus (Law of 134(I) of 21 October 2011).

[42] Austria (Article 3h National Socialism Prohibition Act), Belgium (Law tending to repress negation, minimisation, justification or approbation of the genocide committed by the German National-Socialist regime during the Second World War of 23 March 1995) and Czech Republic (Article 405 Criminal Code).

[43] France (Article 24 bis Freedom of the Press Act), Luxembourg (Article 457-3 Criminal Code) and Romania (Article 6 of Law no. 217 of 27 July 2015).

[44] Article 74 Criminal Code.

[45] Article 405 Criminal Code.

[46] Article 297 Criminal Code.

Such diverse definitions, however, do not seem to correspond to a distinction among historical denialist statements actually subject to criminal punishment. This is not only due to the lack of precision in the terms utilised, but also because the various forms of historical denialism often tend to overlap. For example, the assertions can be denial of certain historical events and, at the same time, approval or justification of the atrocities committed.

Another indicator of the diversity of national approaches to historical denialism as a crime and of the complexity of criminalising such behaviours is the type and content of the thoughts punished by law.[47] This element eloquently expresses the differences among individual domestic legal systems and the critical issues of historical denialism as a crime. It also clearly demonstrates the expansion sparked by the EU Framework Decision, which adopted the 'broader' form of the offence by providing for the criminalisation of statements not only about the Holocaust but also regarding all international crimes. Some legal systems still require the subject of punishable statements to be exclusively about the genocide committed by the Nazi regime (Germany, Belgium and Austria). In this case, claims regarding other genocides or other crimes against humanity cannot be punished. Following the indications of European law, however, other countries extended protection to statements about genocide, crimes against humanity and war crimes (Greece, Liechtenstein, Portugal and Slovenia).[48] Furthermore, some countries expressly refer to Articles 6–8 of the International Criminal Court Statute and Article 6 of the Charter of the Nuremberg Military Tribunal, as required by the EU Framework Decision (Cyprus and Slovakia).[49] Finally, eight countries also punish the denial of crimes against peace.[50]

In addition, within the EU, some legislatures, in implementing the EU Framework Decision, have introduced a new separate criminal offence that punishes statements about Nazi crimes as well as those about crimes committed by the communist regime. This is the case of Czech Republic, Hungary, Lithuania and Poland.[51]

The comparative analysis also demonstrates the different ways national legal systems include optional elements in order to avoid an excessive restriction of freedom of expression.

---

[47] On this aspect, see Koposov 2017, especially p. 120 et seq.

[48] Greece (Article 2 Law no. 4285 of 10 September 2014), Liechtenstein (Article 283 Criminal Code), Portugal (Article 240 Criminal Code) and Slovenia (Article 297 Criminal Code).

[49] Cyprus (Law no. 134(I) on combating certain forms of racism and xenophobia of 21 October 2011) and Slovakia (Article 422d Criminal Code).

[50] Bulgaria (Article 419a Criminal Code); Croatia (Article 325 Criminal Code); Latvia (Article 74-1 Criminal Code); Portugal (Article 240 Criminal Code); Slovakia (Article 422d Criminal Code); Slovenia (Article 297 Criminal Code). Lithuania limits denialism only to violence perpetrated by the Nazis and the Soviet regime (Article 170(2) Criminal Code). Poland punishes denialism of crimes against peace committed from 1 September 1939 to 31 December 1989 (Article 55 Act on the Institute of National Remembrance - Commission for the Prosecution of Crimes against the Polish Nation).

[51] Czech Republic (Article 405 Criminal Code), Hungary (Article 333 Criminal Code), Lithuania (Article 170(2) Criminal Code) and Poland (Article 55 Act on the Institute of National Remembrance - Commission for the Prosecution of Crimes against the Polish Nation).

In this regard, an element shared by domestic laws is the public nature of the statements. Thus, it is not the statement itself that determines the harmfulness of the conduct, which is not punishable if it remains within the private sphere, but only the fact that it is made in public. The public nature of the statement is based on whether it was made in a public place as well as on the ability of the message to spread to a potentially larger and indeterminate group of persons.[52]

According to a liberal approach to criminal law,[53] some legislators further limit the scope of application with the introduction of specific elements related to the criminal offence. These can vary in content and may be provided individually or cumulatively. For example, the conduct must be capable of disturbing public peace[54] or inciting violence or hatred;[55] be carried out in a threatening, violent or offensive manner or disturb public order;[56] or be directed towards an individual or group of persons because of their race, ethnicity, religion or nationality.[57] The limiting element can also relate to the *mens rea*, for example the claims must be accompanied by discriminatory motives[58] or committed with the intention of inciting or encouraging racial or religious discrimination.[59]

---

[52] The majority of countries which criminalise denialism requires that the punishable conduct be carried out in a public place: Austria, Belgium, Croatia, Cyprus, Czech Republic, France, Germany, Greece, Hungary, Latvia, Lithuania, Luxembourg, Malta, Poland, Portugal, Romania, Slovakia, Slovenia and Spain. Bulgary is an exception, but its legislation requires the risk that the conduct causes violence or discriminatory hatred. (Article 419a Criminal Code). In this regard, it is interesting to mention the Italian law which restricts limitations on freedom of expression by providing clauses related to the final judgment and the requirement that the offence be carried out through advertising. However, such clauses were not included in the approved final version. Italian legislation requires that the conduct of the basic offence (propaganda, instigation and incitement) be carried out 'so that there is a real danger of diffusion.' The adverb 'publicly' is rather outdated because it is incapable of expressing the distortion of public-private boundaries due to social networks and the Internet (see Stenographic Report No. 617 of 28 April 2016, D'Ascola). The introduction of the requirement of a 'real danger of diffusion' would also eliminate the presumption of statements made in public and would permit extending the punishment to more cases than were previously punishable only through the use of 'advertising,' such as 'encouraging violence through electronic media (see the example of international terrorism) (see Resolutions of the House of Deputies on 23 May 2016, Sarro).

[53] The English expression 'liberal criminal law' is intended in this book as conceived, for example, in the works of Andrew Ashworth and Darryl Robinson. See Simester et al. 2014; Ashworth and Zedner 2008, pp. 21–51; Robinson 2008, pp. 925–963.

[54] Germany (Article 130(3) Criminal Code).

[55] Croatia (Article 325 Criminal Code); Greece (Article 2 Law no. 4285 of 10 September 2014); Lithuania (Article 170(2) Criminal Code); Malta (Article 82b Criminal Code); Spain (Article 510 Criminal Code).

[56] Malta (Article 82b Criminal Code).

[57] Slovakia (Article 422d Criminal Code).

[58] Portugal (Article 240 Criminal Code) and Slovakia (Article 422d Criminal Code). Outside the EU countries, see Switzerland (Article 262a Criminal Code).

[59] Italy (Article 3 para 3 *bis* of law no. 654 of 13 October 1975, introduced by Law no. 115 of 16 June 2016), Portugal (Article 240 Criminal Code) and Spain (Article 510 Criminal Code).

1.2.1.3 The Spread of the 'Broader' Form

The comparative analysis of national legislation provides important elements for observations of a more general nature.

The first phase characterised by the criminalisation of historical denialist statements is followed by a second phase, in which both the scope of punishment and the protected mnemonic framework are expanded.

Furthermore, the offence, as well as its definition of 'historical denialism', circulate in different geographical contexts outside the original European area, further confirming expansive dynamics. Examples include Peru, where a proposal to introduce the offence of denial of terrorist crimes was presented in October 2012,[60] and in Argentina, where Article 1 of the *Ley para la prevención y condena de la negación del genocidio y crímenes contra la humanidad* (Law for the prevention and condemnation of the denial of genocide and crimes against humanity) envisages the punishment of anyone who publicly denies, trivialises, condones or justifies genocide or a crime against humanity. Moreover, the second paragraph provides for an aggravating circumstance if the offence is committed by a public official.[61]

Therefore, the development of the offence after the EU Framework Decision points to another difficulty of the criminal law intervention: the plural nature of national historical memories. Indeed, the supposedly common memory is neither shared nor collective and can therefore become a source of conflict.[62] Diverse legal solutions emerge, and the resulting diversity demonstrates the lack of a common European 'language' of common values which, in a way, contradicts the EU Framework Decision.

Following the EU Framework Decision, we can observe a bidirectional development which entails the adoption of a gradually broader model of the offence as well as a paradoxical dynamic of the Decision itself. On the one hand, it is important to underline that most EU Member States introduced the offence of historical denialism. On the other hand, however, the crimes gradually implemented in countries with different legal traditions and political histories do not seem to reflect the universal values the EU Framework Decision intended to promote. The conflict between universal and relative appears clearly. The dissemination of this

---

[60] On 28 August 2012, a legislative proposal was presented by Ollanta Humala to the Peruvian Parliament under the title '*Negacionismo de los delitos de terrorismo*'. It introduced a new criminal offence, Article 316 a of the Criminal Code. on the one side, it shows how this criminal offence can travel long distances and be introduced in legal systems that have radically different historical backgrounds in comparison to the European countries; on the other, it shifts the focus of protection, as it moves away from international crimes in a strict sense, up to include terrorist acts. The text of the legislative proposal is available at http://www2.congreso.gob.pe/Sicr/TraDocEstProc/CLProLey2011.nsf.

[61] *Ley para la prevencion y condena de la negacion del genocidio y crimenes contra la humanidad*, see http://www.parlamentario.com/noticia-98654.html.

[62] On 'memory wars', see Koposov 2017; Stone 2013; Cajani 2008–2009, pp. 39–55. This dynamic is also defined as *querelle des mémoires* or *mémoires abusives*; see Veyrat-Masson and Blanchard 2008; Stora 2007; Rousso, Mémoires abusives, *Le Monde*, 24 December 2005; Todorov 1995.

criminal offence would be more aptly identified not as a general acceptance of the 'broader' paradigm, but as a proliferation of many different and specific 'original' paradigms, each tailored to the diverse and unique historical characteristics of the countries in question. From this perspective, when extending the offence of historical denialism beyond Western Europe—for example, Eastern Europe, Turkey or South American countries—the difficulties associated with propagating the 'broader' form of the crime are greater than if various 'original' configurations were adopted.

1.2.2 Criminal Law and Remembrance Laws

It is important to distinguish between legislation that criminalises historical denialism from other provisions that recognise and/or establish certain historical facts *without* resorting to punishment. These are the so-called remembrance laws, which mainly take the form of laws that add 'remembrance days' to the national or international calendar, thereby sending a clear message to citizens: 'you must remember'. In these cases, remembering is necessary and pertains to civic ethics to which each citizen is called upon to adhere.[63]

Even in the absence of strictly criminal content, this legislation plays a part in the criminalisation of historical denialism. Remembrance laws define a fact as a historical event, thereby defining also the scope of application of criminal laws that protect the memory of that event.[64] As a result, remembrance laws can constitute the basis for punitive measures, although not automatically. The similarities and differences between the two types of laws are immediately apparent. The crime of denialism imposes an imperative of memory.[65] The offence conveys a different and more specific message than the official recognition of an event: 'we must remember' becomes 'remembering differently will be punished'. Therefore, not only is *one* interpretation of history made official, but also those who attempt to narrate and remember it in a different way are punished. This choice is justified based on the assumption that denialist claims are subversive. It is argued that these practices of questioning moments from the past that constitute the founding historical

[63] On remembrance laws which do not include criminal law, see Hochmann 2012, p. 133 et seq.; Wartanian 2008; Stofleth 2012. On the concept of memory laws, see Heinze 2017; Belavusau and Gliszczynska-Grabias 2017; on the concept and on the history of memory laws, see Koposov 2017.

[64] For instance, consider the adoption of the laws which recognises the Armenian genocide as the French Law no. 2001-70 on the recognition of the Armenian genocide, 29 January 2001. On the international level, see European Parliament P8_TA(2015)0094, *Resolution on the centenary of the Armenian Genocide*, 15 April 2015; European Parliament A5-0297/2000, *Resolution on the 1999 Regular Report from the Commission on Turkey's progress toward accession*, 15 November 2000, para 10; European Parliament A2-33/87, *Resolution on a political solution to the Armenian question*, 18 June 1987.

[65] Regarding the history of memory imperatives, see Lollini 2003, pp. 449–470.

experience of communities cannot be tolerated: a past that is capable of guiding, depending on how it is remembered, the understanding of current events and the very decisions that citizens make.

The complexity of choosing punishment is clearly evident. It is a reaction to a dangerous phenomenon in the name of fundamental values such as the historical roots of the ethical pact among citizens which forms the basis of their respective national constitutions. It also, however, interferes with other fundamental values: freedom of speech, historical research, open discussion and, ultimately, with the foundations of positive law and democracies.

Certain implications of these issues are related to those of the more general category of speech crimes. Others, however, are exclusive to the crime of historical denialism due to the intersection between law and memory arising from this offence.

Finally, as previously mentioned, new and critical issues are triggered by the larger number of crimes that must not be questioned according to the 'broader' form of historical denialism.

1.3 The Relationship Between Law and Memory

In recent years, interactions between and overlapping of law and memory have multiplied and at times have been problematic. Law has been increasingly identified by states and international organisations as the means for responding to the fear that the memory of historical significant facts may gradually weaken, become muddled and eventually lose meaning.[66] To prevent this from happening, law is employed as a bridge between past, present and future.

This trend has been further reinforced by the centrality of international politics over at least the last two decades and the newly-found role of victims in contemporary system of criminal law both at national and international level.[67] Giving a voice to victims and recognising their history of sufferings are necessary for doing justice.[68] In this way, history and law become even more intertwined.

These dynamics are part of what has been defined as '*malaise de la mémoire*' (malady of memory)[69] or 'commemorative obsession'.[70] Memory is considered a vital, necessary and collective stronghold of common values of equality and justice,

---

[66] For more on 'judicial derivations of history' and the proliferation of memorial laws in France, particularly since 1990, see Nora 2016, p. 60 et seq.

[67] Within the literature on the rights of the victims of mass atrocities see, also for further references, Gil Gil and Maculan 2017a; see also Ochoa 2013. On the risks of this dynamic for liberal criminal law, see Fornasari 2013.

[68] 'One of the key figure of the mondialisation of memory is the victim', Rousso 2016, 287.

[69] Rousso 1987. The same author uses also the expression 'memory industry' (cited in Rieff 2016, 108).

[70] Traverso 2006. The author refers to the 'obsession for commemoration' to indicate the general trend, whereby national and international jurisdictions increasingly resort to the law—not only to the criminal law—to address the fear that the historical memory of particularly atrocious criminal acts be progressively questioned.

which must be protected from fading: a memory that requires care. However, this need can at times lead to a 'memory obsession',[71] which fixates on a memory being as unambiguous as possible. This public memory is employed in order to solidify a world that eludes us; in this way, it becomes a space of conflict and a place where divergent and opposing power strategies are applied. The inalienability of memory and the inevitably of threats to it, in a world that has lost its points of reference and feels increasingly 'liquid', to use Zygmunt Bauman's term,[72] converge in an appeal for stability and authority to ensure that our past—an important and fragile heritage—retains at least those aspects which establish a common identity.

Collective memory of mass atrocities is viewed as containing an important cautionary message for the present. The interpretation of past tragic events such as crimes of genocide, crimes against humanity and war crimes (of which Auschwitz is emblematic) seems to naturally opt for law as a remedy. Law itself has been an important element in codifying memory: consider the role of the Nuremberg International Military Tribunal in defining the Holocaust. 'We remember' because the magnitude of those atrocities affects the deepest common values. We know with certainty that they are crimes because they have been judged as such and convictions were made in the name of the law and of those funding values that represent us all, and thus 'we remember' in an 'established' way.

To summarise, law increasingly tends to be the primary vehicle for the protection of historical collective memory, and memory is identified as an 'interest' that must be defended and a 'space' where crimes can be committed.[73]

1.4 The Leading Role of Criminal Law

There are numerous and complex intersections between law and memory.[74] Within the dynamics of the juridification of the past, or rather, the identification of law as a more effective medium between past, present and future, we can observe a specific

[71] On the four phases of memory and law overlapping in French history see Rousso 1987, p. 19 et seq. In the French historian's opinion the issue of memory becomes an 'obsession' in the fourth phase. Also, Todorov uses the expression 'Obsession for the cult of memory' (cited in Rieff 2016, p. 119), while Rieff chooses the concept of 'hyperthymesia', which is the condition of possessing an extremely detailed autobiographical memory (Rieff 2016, 120); for the opinion of this author and the idea of memory as *kitsch*, *ibid.*, 800. For a list and analysis of similar expressions, see Caroli 2017, p. 290. This is the starting point of a broader debate about uses and abuses of memory and on the trade-off between memory and oblivion on a collective level (see *ibid.*, pp. 272 and ff.). For the concept of 'abuses of memory' see Todorov 1995, 2001.

[72] Bauman 2000.

[73] Criticism on criminalising historical denialism and the line between legal and illegal thoughts is even more crucial in today's environment of post-truth politics.

[74] In this book, I will prefer the conceptual binomial of law and memory to that of law and history because the concept of memory, generalised in recent years, but now widely recognised as a reference term, embraces the social process of reworking the past in its entirety. The concept of

tendency: trials and the penalties imposed by way of them are expedient tools for defending a past that must not be forgotten.[75] The criminal trial makes a distinction between guilt and innocence and therefore defines what is right ('just') and what is wrong ('unjust') with respect to certain events. Furthermore, it ultimately defines the importance and the sense—we could say the moral significance—that should be attributed to the content of the judgment.

In this scenario, symbolic and performative aspects intertwine and reinforce each other. The trial is a 'theatre of the word' like no other, and the resulting punishment seals the efficacy and performativity of the words pronounced therein, changing and indelibly marking the lives of the people on trial. In *res judicata*, those same words have a definitive quality and an ability to establish facts that no other narrative method possesses, which is what makes its final result so highly symbolic. The narrative becomes effective via the criminal judgment that ensues, and the punishment becomes symbolic via the narrative made factual by it.

Due to the highly symbolic potential of judicial proceedings and punishments, law and criminal trial are seen as key instruments for establishing memory. The criminal trial is not only a place for gathering evidence, ascertaining liability and imposing penalties to protect an interest guaranteed by law, but also—together, and by virtue of the same mechanisms—a theatre in which history may be pedagogically re-enacted[76] in order to revitalise a precise and morally significant memory of the past, thus laying the foundations for the future pact between citizens.

The demands made on the courtroom increasingly tend toward punishing offenders and, simultaneously, imposing a historical truth. This historical truth must be unequivocal, supported by evidence, reinforced by the penalty issued by the court, and made definitive by force of *res judicata*.[77]

---

memory, although there are various declinations in doctrine, is generally considered broader, more inclusive and more dynamic than historical and historiographic investigations. The phenomena of mnemonic crystallization, as a set of dynamics distinct and distinguishable from history, have progressively involved an increasing number of scholars. Here reference is made mainly to the pioneering work of Halbwachs 1925, 1950 and to the detailed studies of Todorov 1995; Ricoeur 2000; Yerushalmi 1988; Assmann 2012. For a more critical perspective, see Traverso 2006. On the uses and abuses of historical memory and on the question about whether collective remembrance has truly—or indeed ever could—inoculate the present against repeating the crimes of the past, see the book of Rieff 2016.

[75] We will see how many issues and contradictions arise when historical memory is considered a protected interest and how difficult it is, if not impossible, to establish an adequate definition within criminal law which seeks to protect it.

[76] See Osiel 1999.

[77] Here emerges a central aspect of the different epistemological status of 'judicial truth' and 'historical truth', both of which are specific and distinct from the well-known concept of the truth as perceived by the common sense, see Ferrajoli 2009. Behind the major debate around the kind of truth that results from the criminal trial (a debate that cannot be resumed here), there is also a methodological issue. On the one hand, both the criminal judge and the historian are asked to investigate the past and to find out the truth, on the other, the method and the tasks of the criminal judge appears to be very different from the method and the tasks of the historian. See on this issue Chapter 3.

1.4.1 Memory as Collective Redefinition of a Common Past

The relatively recent concept of memory has largely replaced or absorbed the concept of history from which it is important to differentiate. Unlike history, memory embraces and assembles the past utilising a broad network and contributing a much larger dose of subjectivity and personal experience. It is a continuous process, and—unlike its common meaning referring to the individual—it is a collective, social and eminently public activity. In this new role, memory has lost its original quality of referring to a private and intimate sphere as much as history, by definition, originally referred to the public sphere. In this sense, memory is now at the centre of Western societies. It invades the public space with the help of media and settles into the collective imagination defining the way in which the past co-exists with and orientates the present.[78]

These characteristics elucidate its relationship with the law that intervenes to protect it. Collective representations of the past are constructions that take place in the present. They are produced in every society and structure social identity and shared values by placing them in historical continuity and attributing meaning, content and direction to them. Previously, this function was mainly attributed to history, a field that is relatively rigid, sophisticated, based on distance and a linear understanding of the causal sequences on which it tends to focus. Memory in a collective, familial or community sense has always been present and has played a distinctly subordinate role.

Today, on the contrary, the prevailing significance of this structuring and reprocessing of the collective experience in our societies has transitioned to the closest, most recently lived memory, which is less formalised and more open to a variety of inputs. This process is accelerated by the changes introduced into the public sphere by the media and the internet.

Memory is a fluid activity affecting everyone's heritage and is characterised by internal dynamics similar to those of public opinion. It has recently inherited a role that only a few decades ago in Western societies belonged to an academic discipline that was mainly accessible to people with specific preparation.

'Each history is always contemporary, that is political'[79] noted the Italian theorist and politician Antonio Gramsci, who criticised the historicist conception of history that tells the past 'exactly as it was'. He was referring to the studies of the Italian historian and philosopher Benedetto Croce, who insisted that our need for history is born from the needs of the present. Gramsci's observation fully applies to the subject under investigation. Memory always operates from the present, which determines the manner and the selection of events whose remembrance, interpretation and lesson must be preserved. This is a particularly important lesson in the case of historical events which have certain large-scale political, social and institutional tendencies, such as the emerging democracies in the Axis countries after World War II, the overcoming of Apartheid in South Africa, the end of the Franco

[78] Traverso 2006.

[79] Gramsci 1994.

dictatorship in Spain or the fall of 'real socialism' in Eastern Europe. In similar cases, the institutions, societies and constitutions of the countries that have experienced similar events encourage the memory of such past tragic events as a cautionary reminder of the policies and ideologies that made them possible, as well as an historical foundation of a shared 'new beginning' and a renewed 'ethical pact' among citizens enshrined in their constitutions.

The relationship between past and present filtered through a fluid medium does, however, mean that the relationship becomes two-way. As a consequence of a more meaningful, open and flexible relationship with the past than with history, memory results in having a closer relationship with the present, but, paradoxically, it is also subject to repercussions. On the one hand, using an analogy with fundamental charters and based on the ability of the memory to provide meaningful collective experience at the highest level, we could define its relationship with the present as constituent. On the other hand, the same characteristics make it a reciprocal relationship: memory defines the present just as the present redefines memory.

As an essential point of reference for the values society considers most significant, memory must be consolidated within the set of experiences and events that represent and establish those values. For memory to fully perform its function of stabilising the *ethical pact* among citizens, it is important not to allow the present to transform it or choose other events, other witnesses and other constellations of meanings from its infinite space which could alter its original significance.

1.4.2 Collective Historical Memory as an Ethical Pact

Historical denialism threatens the collective European memory. This memory is the result of the dramatic experiences of the early 1900s and World War II. It constitutes a political and moral divide, particularly for the interpretation of historical events according to the value choices European countries assign to them. The nations that experienced these tragic developments subsequently created democratic forms of government and currently place the protection of human rights and collective liberties among their most urgent priorities. Therefore, it is a memory with a lesson that is an integral part of the universe of values underlying the European constitutions adopted after the conflict, as well as the European Union and the United Nations itself.

As will be made evident by examining legislation and case law, the relationship between law and protection of collective memory is not linear and comprises very different cases as expressions of the same tendency toward the juridification of history.[80]

At first glance, we can detect the presence of a wide array of experiences that view law as a medium between past and present. These range from cases in which

[80] See Delage and Goodrich 2012; Resta and Zeno-Zencovich 2012, p. 11 et seq.; Lalieu 2001, p. 83 et seq.; Melloni 2008, p. 3; Cartier 2006, pp. 527–533; Garapon 2002. On some of the problems arising from the 'juridification' of history, see the analysis of a concrete case taken from the Italian postwar experience by Resta and Zeno-Zencovich 2013, p. 849 et seq.

law is limited to establishing the correct way of remembering certain events and their importance, such as days of remembrance, to cases where the court that ends up defining the correct interpretation of historical events through a prosecution and a trial. Such declarations assist in defining the necessary context of the judgments issued, as occurred, for example, with the *ad hoc* International Criminal Tribunals for former Yugoslavia and Rwanda.[81]

We can also find laws that, within the framework of a criminal trial, create mechanisms that do not threaten punishment but instead declare a historical truth, such as the *juicios por la verdad* (truth-finding trials) in Argentina. In this case, crimes committed under the military dictatorship (1976–1983) were brought to trial before the ordinary federal court with the sole objective of establishing the truth, without any punishment being issued.[82] Of the same trend, but beyond the scope of this study, are mechanisms for determining historical and factual truth and ascertaining accountability like the South African Truth and Reconciliation Commission.[83] This mechanism, which resulted from the political impossibility to agree on a strictly criminal approach for coming to terms with the past,[84] operates on two levels. First, it has a political effect on the public sphere and the constituent construction of shared values; second, it establishes a punishment with a conditioned amnesty for those who confess guilt. In the South African Truth and Reconciliation Commission system, once the punishment has been eliminated, self-accusation takes on a different shape. In South Africa, the intent was that the protagonists of the 'apartheid war' formally state the 'truth' that everyone was already aware of as opposed to a judge certifying with a judgment the reconstruction of events that everyone witnessed.[85]

---

[81] On the role and the ability of international prosecutions and trials to define the historical records of the crimes and to write an historical narrative, see Delage and Goodrich 2012; Findlay and Henham 2012; Wilson 2011, pp. 1–23; Osiel 1999, 2008; Damaska 2006; Damaska 2007; Drumbl 2007; Fronza and Tricot 2003, p. 292 et seq.; Minow 1998; Koskeniemmi 1989. On the importance of civil trials, see Garapon 2008.

[82] See Maculan 2012, pp. 53–82; Méndez 2009; Pastor 2009, pp. 102–109; Méndez and Bariffi 2007; Guembe 2005; Abregú 1996, pp. 11–41.

[83] See Swart and van Marle 2017; Lollini 2011; Du Bois-Pedain 2007; Werle 2006, pp. 39–99; Sarkin 2004; Villa-Vicencio and Doxtader 2003. For a general overview on the Truth Commissions as a mechanism to deal with grave violations of human rights, see within a vast literature Fornasari 2015, pp. 547–570; Ibáñez Majar 2014; Bisset 2012; Freeman 2006; Hayner 1994, pp. 597–665. A criminal trial is a mechanism that embodies conflict and declares a victor; in this way it perpetuates the conflict in the courtroom and in the public sphere, see Lollini 2011, 12 et seq.; Garapon 1995; Damaska 1991.

[84] See Lollini 2011, 132.

[85] Lollini 2011, 168. In the author's view, 'even if historians or meticulous analysts of the TRC's activity have often stressed that the 'truth' of the amnesty process is partial and that confessors often manipulated facts in their self-accusation in order to have their punishment eliminated, the primary effect of the confession was nevertheless produced. More than the truth about the past, what really was at play here was the capitulation of all those who practiced political violence—the true enemy of democracy—before the new constitutional order. By formally rejecting political violence, the individual implicitly asked for citizenship in the new democratic constitutional order', Lollini 2011, 168.

Finally, some criminal laws punish those responsible for crimes committed 'against' memory, which leads to defining which historical memory is admissible and which is the correct interpretation of it. This is perhaps the most interesting case considering its richness of implications and contradictions. It is enough here to recall the potential conflict of such a configuration with fundamental values such as freedom of opinion or freedom of research. Within this paradigm, we can include criminal provisions adopted in many countries in order to punish historical denialism, which is the main focus of this investigation.

1.4.3 Memory, Law and Punishment

The relationship between criminal law and memory is full of shadows. One of the reasons has to do with the nature of criminal law and in particular with the fact that punishment is intrinsic to it. In this perspective, we are dealing with a trinomial: *law, memory and punishment.* Analysis of experiences in different historical and geographical realities demonstrates that this trio has evolved in radically different ways.

If in Argentina a request for truth about the violent past results also in criminal law without punishment (*juicios por la verdad*), in most cases, on the contrary, the importance of punishment and retributive justice is emphasised as a vehicle for satisfying the needs of narration and combating attempts to manipulate the violent past or blur the memory of dramatic events to which meaning and value are attributed.[86]

[86] There are many examples in this regard: from the establishment and proliferation of *ad hoc* international criminal tribunals to all the trials conducted many years, if not decades, after the events. Think, for example, of what happened in Italy with the reopening of war crimes trials after the discovery of the so-called *Armoir of Shame* in 1994, the elaboration of the so-called *Aylwin Doctrine* in Chile or the prosecution of forced disappearances in Argentina and, in particular, the annulment by the Supreme Court of the *Obediencia Debida* and the *Punto Final*. Ruti Teitel uses the expression 'transitional justice postponed' (Teitel 2014, p. 188).

Within this dynamic toward a retributive response to international crimes has played a pivotal role in the Inter-American Human Rights Court. On the most relevant case law and for some critical remarks about the risks that arise from such a configuration, see the volume by Gil Gil and Maculan 2017b, especially pp. 23–46; pp. 187–242; for an overview in relation to South America, Palermo 2014; Lessa and Payne 2012; Ambos et al. 2009; Malarino 2009; Parenti 2009; Fronza and Fornasari 2009. On the phenomenon of the annulment of amnesty laws, see Della Morte 2011, p. 261. Concerning certain parallel approaches ('*approdi paralleli*') of the European Court of Human Rights and the Inter-American Court of Human rights related to the duty to criminalise in order to protect human rights, see Viganò 2011, pp. 2645–2704; critical to this case law Malarino 2009. Criticism are expressed also in Pastor 2006; Fletcher 1998. See also the work by Silva Sánchez 2007, p. 339. On the influence of the 'struggle against impunity' related to clemency measures, see Della Morte et al. 2007.

Historical experiences like the Nuremberg International Military Tribunal indicate that 'show trials'[87] and their resultant punishments embed in our memory the dramatic nature of the facts being judged and the meaning of those events. Where trials lead to no punishment or, instead, where punishment is subsequently and rapidly issued, like in Italy with the transition from Fascism to democracy (1945–48),[88] the establishment of a common historical memory of the events in question has been much more problematic.[89] In trials that deal with crimes of historical significance it seems that punishment has an additional characteristic whereby it removes historical factuality from the natural processes of mnemonic absorption (and transformation) and makes it part of an eternal and immutable present in a definitive manner.

Therefore, this trinomial carries an additional layer of complexity: the rules that punish denial, justification or trivialisation of the Holocaust or other genocides and crimes against humanity[90] view law and punishment as instruments for building collective memory and protecting it from dangerous phenomena such as historical denialism. Here, the law and the trial become a space for reconstructing the collective memory of facts from the past and the values that this narrative conveys via the refutation of conducts that seek to deny memory. In this case, the trinomial remains intact: punishment, imposed by the law, is retribution for a violated memory.

In a different scenario a group of three elements (law, memory and punishment) becomes a binary combination of law and memory without the provision of punishment. This is the case of the aforementioned remembrance laws (*lois mémorielles*

[87] See Koskeniemmi 1989. Koskeniemmi's view has been developed with specific relation the international criminal justice by Makau Mutua, see Mutua 2001. According to Osiel, lawyers and judges should thus heed the "poetics" of "legal storytelling." The judge should use 'the law to recast the courtroom drama in terms of a "theater of ideas", which engages large questions of collective memory and even national identity.' 'To maximize their pedagogic impact, such trials should be unabashedly designed as monumental spectacles.' See for this concept of trial as 'pedagogic theatre', Osiel 1999, p. 3.

[88] For the introduction of sanctions against Fascism in Italy, see Domenico 1991, p. 74 et seq. For a brief overview of the transitional process, see Caroli 2015. On the Italian political transition from a legal point of view, see Caroli 2017; Fronza 2016b; Seminara 2014; Fornasari 2013, p. 15 et seq.; Donini 2009; Vassalli and Sabatini 1947; Woller 1996. From a historical point of view, see Domenico 1991. See also the relationship between the majority and minority within the Parliamentary Investigative Commission at: http://www.camera.it/leg17/522?tema=negazionismo Accessed 30 September 2017.

[89] Baldissara 2016, pp. 6–20; Focardi and Klinkhammer 2004, p. 330; Resta and Zeno-Zencovich 2012; Focardi 2014; Caroli 2017, pp. 245 and ff.; Rovatti 2009. It has to be noted that the political and social debate which led to the recent introduction of the criminal offence of denialism in Italy began just in recent years, after the death of Erich Priebke in 2013. Priebke is one of the few Nazi officers who was tried and sentenced in Italy; in the '1990s, his trial was an important turning point in the Italian transition. See Resta and Zeno-Zencovich 2013; Portelli 2003.

[90] On denialism, from an historical perspective, see Vercelli 2013; Ginzburg 2002, pp. 50–60; Vidal-Naquet 1981; Vidal-Naquet 1995; Tiedemann 1996; Bastian 1997; Igounet 2000; Ternon 1999; Lipstadt 1994.

according to the broader French expression)[91] through which the legislature makes a clear request that citizens remember very specific events.

There are numerous instances that can be cited. For example, Italy's Law no. 211 of 20 July 2000 establishes a day for commemorating a 'Day of remembrance in memory of the extermination and persecution of the Jewish people, Italian military and political deportees to Nazi camps': January 27 (the anniversary of the liberation of the Auschwitz concentration camp).[92] Another case is France, which is undoubtedly one of the most interesting examples. In 2000, it passed a law establishing a 'National day in memory of victims of racist and anti-Semitic crimes of the French State and homage to the 'righteous' people of France' (*Journée nationale à la mémoire des victimes des crimes racistes et antisémites de l'Etat français et d'hommage aux 'Justes' de France*).[93] Between 2001 and 2005, other memory laws were passed recognising the Armenian genocide, the trafficking of humans and slavery as crimes against humanity. In October 2007, Spain adopted the Law of Historical Memory, which recognises and expands the rights of victims of the civil war and dictatorship.[94] Finally, on a global level, the United Nations have introduced the 'International Day of Remembrance'. With resolution 60/7, entitled 'Holocaust Remembrance' and adopted on 1 November 2005, the General Assembly proclaimed January 27 as the international day dedicated to Holocaust victims.[95]

In remembrance laws, the definition of mnemonic frameworks lies in the legislative domain, rather than in the judicial one. However, in the case of laws providing for the punishment of historical denialism, the protection and construction of a collective memory is accomplished through a powerful and highly symbolic tool: criminal law. A measure which falls in the general field of legally sanctioned 'imperatives of memory', where it is the task of criminal law—the most unequivocal and powerful gesture of public authority—to institute a binding obligation on both a legal and a symbolic level. As a result, actions involving only laws or the judicial sphere demonstrate a distinction between two models of legal protection of memory: a *soft* model (remembrance laws) and a *hard* model (criminal statutes).

---

[91] Here the French expression '*lois mémorielles*' is used without including the provisions which introduce the offence of denialism. On this concept (and on the broad and narrow meanings), which includes different legal measures, see Koposov 2017; Assemblée Nationale: Rapport d'information no. 1262, Rassembler la Nation autour d'une mémoire partagée, 2008, p. 11 et seq.

[92] See Pugiotto 2009, p. 25 et seq.; for a critical approach to this Law, see also Lowenthal 2014; Gordon 2013. Also in Italy Law no. 56 of 4 May 2007 established 9 May, the day Aldo Moro was assassinated by the Red Brigades, as the official day of memory honouring victims of terrorism. Outside of Europe, for instance in Argentina, 24 May is a national day of remembrance for truth and justice in memory of the 1976 *coup détat* (*Día Nacional de la Memoria por la Verdad y la Justicia*).

[93] See Law no. 644 of 10 July 2000, accessible at http://www.senat.fr/leg/ppl99-244.html, which invites French people to remember the victims of racist and anti-Semitic crimes on 16 July.

[94] See Tamarit Sumalla 2014, pp. 43–65; Gil Gil 2009.

[95] UN General Assembly, A/RES/60/7, Resolution adopted by the General Assembly on the Holocaust Remembrance, 1 November 2005.

The phenomenon of imperatives of memory is not historically new. Indeed, remembering and forgetting have been imposed through legal norms on a number of occasions.[96] Suffice it to mention the well-known ban on publicly remembering the serious crimes committed in Athens during the dictatorship of the Thirty Tyrants, which was later rescinded in 403 BC after democracy was restored.[97]

A fundamental question emerges: can collective memory and the narrative of past events be protected through criminal law? Historians and philosophers have always emphasised the importance of memory. However, the fact that the legal field also focuses its attention on memory demonstrates a profound element of post-World War II society. The possibility of immediately forgetting evokes its antidote, which is indeed memory.[98] Simplifying the issue in such opposing terms, however, hinders a full grasp of the unique nature of the relationship between memory and criminal law.

The relationship between law and memory can be discussed much in the same terms as the relationship between criminal law and ethics. Indeed, criminal law reinforces the legal protection of certain values and interests: by criminalising certain conduct, legal provisions delineate the core values of different societies—those same values that are an essential part of their constitutions—and therefore represent one of the most noticeable manners for defending what is socially considered worthy of protection.

As mentioned, several elements demonstrate that law, and in particular criminal law, plays a crucial role in establishing and imposing a collective memory. The criminal trial becomes a place for affirming historical truths considered significant to counteract revisionism and historical denialism, which threaten to distort and erase those truths, thereby impeding their message from being conveyed.

From a juridical point of view, considering the activity of remembering—or, rather, of remembering the past in an established way—as a valuable form of legal protection means making it a significant component of social life and community policy, as well as recognising its role as a constitutive element of public space and for the construction of the meaning of collective action therein. This is demonstrated by the introduction of the crime of historical denialism and by other dynamics through which memory becomes a legal and ethical imperative, such as the tendencies of case law regarding the recognition of the right to truth and the right or duty of memory.[99]

[96] See Ost 1999.

[97] Loraux 1997; Loraux 1988, pp. 23–47. On the history of Athen's amnesty see Elster 2004; Lollini 2003, pp. 358–359; Quaritsch 1992, pp. 389–418.

[98] On the necessity of forgetting, see Ricoeur 2000; recently on forgetting as 'safe response', see Rieff 2016, p. 39 et seq.

[99] These new rights against states are recognised in UN law and international human rights law and constitute a pillar of the 'struggle against impunity', because they affirm an obligation to investigate and punish international crimes. See Garibian 2014, pp. 515–538; Maculan and Pastor 2013; Campisi 2014; Ledoux 2012, pp. 175–185; Maculan 2012; Rioux 2008, pp. 186–192; Naqvi 2006, p. 245 et seq.; Pastor 2009; Seibert-Fohr 2009, especially p. 51 et seq.; Méndez 2009, p. 255 et seq.; UN Doc. A/HRC/5/7, Office of the United Nations High Commissioner for Human Rights 'Right to the Truth', 7 June 2007, para 16.

This book exclusively considers the rules that punish historical denialism. These dramatically express the complexity of the dialogue between law and memory and are of great interest for comprehending the dynamics with legal, historical and social implications that have a political impact on collective ethics and morals.

1.5 Historical Denialism, Anti-Terrorist Legislation and the Protection of Collective Historical Memory

Historical denialism is punished as a criminal offence in several national legal systems, though its scope and sanctions vary considerably.[100]

The crime of historical denialism has found its way into case law: it has been the subject of several judgments issued by constitutional courts (for example, in Germany, Belgium, Spain and France), by courts of first instance, as well as by the European Court of Human Rights.[101]

The reason why this crime has been introduced within domestic legislations lies essentially with international legal instruments, at a regional (in particular the EU Framework Decision)[102] and international level (for example, Article 6 of the Protocol to the Cybercrime Convention).[103] Such legislation has also been fostered by the increasing recognition granted to rights of victims as well as by case law concerning international crimes, which regards criminal penalties as a reassertion of the severity of certain human rights violations.[104] In this vein, the courts—in particular the Inter-American Court of Human Rights—have stressed the existence of a right to historical memory, a right to truth, an obligation to punish and a prohibition of pardoning the most severe wrongdoings, thereby outlining the aforementioned trinomial: law, memory and punishment.

---

[100] The same conduct can be qualified as a crime in one state and be imposed by law in another. For instance, Article 301 of the Turkish Criminal Code punishes public denigration of the Turkish nation, state, government and judiciary institutions. This law has been used to punish confirmation of the Armenian genocide. This approach, on the one hand, is equivalent to norms establishing the crime of historical denialism because it creates a separate offence for expressing opinions about a historical event other than the official memory. On the other, it is contrary to historical denialism since it punishes the affirmation and not the denial of a genocide. Despite this formal difference, this kind of prohibition is essentially the same: doubting a historical truth asserted by the state is forbidden by criminal law.

[101] See Chaps. 3 and 4.

[102] Council Framework Decision 2008/913/JHA of 28 November 2008 on combating certain forms and expressions of racism and xenophobia by means of criminal law, in *Official Journal of the European Union*, L 328/55, 6 December 2008.

[103] Additional Protocol to the Convention on Cybercrime, concerning the criminalisation of acts of a racist and xenophobic nature committed through computer systems (the so-called 'Budapest Convention') of 28 January 2003, in *European Treaty Series*, 189.

[104] See Traverso 2006. On the fundamental role played by the victims in the process of globalisation of memory, see Rousso 2016, p. 287.

Upon a closer look, the crime of historical denialism seems to dovetail with the proliferation of constraints affecting the right to freedom of expression, including the ones that entail criminal sanctions: historical denialism can indeed be considered the paradigm of the germination of speech crimes—in the sense of their proliferation, transformation and expansion. Proof of this is the renewed success of such criminal offences in the legal framework against sexual discrimination and racism, just as much as in the legislation against international terrorism.[105]

In this respect, it is worth mentioning some national criminal provisions in a European comparative perspective: though not specifically focused on historical denialism, these norms are the touchstone of the recent renaissance of speech crimes. As the following examples will show, the distinctive trait of this combination between anti-terrorism legislation and speech crimes appears to be the increasing pervasiveness of an approach that favours the expansion of criminal law and the limitation of free speech.

A first example is provided by the recent amendment to the section on terrorist offences of the Spanish Criminal Code. The reform provides new far-reaching repressive instruments for countering terrorism, and goes as far as to criminalise mere forms of expression. The Organic Law no. 2/2015 substantially reshapes the definition of terrorism by eliminating the connection between the conduct and the existence of some forms of organisation. The criminal conduct is poorly defined as opposed to under the previous legislation (Article 573, first paragraph of the Spanish Criminal Code); in line with other provisions prioritising the intervention of criminal law (such as the provisions concerning child pornography), the scope of the criminalised '*conductas periféricas*' has been widened considerably and now includes the acts of merely owning books or visiting websites related to terrorism.

In the preamble, the Spanish law claims that the amendments are 'modelled' on the EU Framework Decision 2002/475/JHA of 13 June 2002 (later amended by the EU Framework Decision 2008/919/JHA), though its provisions are diverted for completely different purposes. Indeed, the reform also introduces a series of speech crimes.

First of all, the second paragraph of Article 575 punishes all persons 'visiting webpages' or simply '[…] owning books, whose contents might be directed or able to encourage somebody to enter or actively take part in a terrorist groups' with a view to '*capacitarse*' (rendering oneself able) to commit terrorist crimes. Then there is the second paragraph of Article 577, which punishes any act of '*adoctrinamento*' (indoctrination) aimed at coercing others to enter a terrorist organisation or commit terrorist crimes. Furthermore, the first paragraph of Article 578 punishes any act of '*enaltecimiento*' (praise) or '*justificación*' (justification) of terrorist offences or their authors. Lastly, the first Paragraph of Article 579 establishes as punishable the preparatory act of the '*difusión de mensajes*' (dissemination of messages) that are intended or able, due to their content, to incite others to commit

[105] On the proliferation of 'modern speech crimes', see also Pulitanò 2006, p. 84.

terrorist acts, and it also punishes any person merely posting text on a website which positively portrays the activity of terrorist groups.[106]

Another testament to the tendency described above is the Cazeneuve Act against terrorism, which entered into force on 14 November 2014.[107] This piece of legislation transposed into the French Criminal Code several forms of instigation or condoning of criminal acts, such as terrorism, which was already punishable by the 1881 Freedom of the Press Act. Apart from relocating this offence—as well as the crime of instigation—from the Freedom of the Press Act to the Criminal Code (specifically, in the second and fifth paragraphs of Article 421), the new law also toughens the sanctioning levels and the applicable procedural rules: it provides for the immediate appearance of the accused before a court, extends the limitation period from one to three years and expands the available investigative tools.[108]

As a consequence, these offences are no longer dealt with by specialised judges belonging to a specific branch of the judicial system (like judges for press offences), but fall within the general criminal jurisdiction. Nevertheless, they are subject to the severe procedural rules of anti-terrorism legislation: the criminal trial is faster, penalties are harsher and an additional aggravating circumstance is applicable if the offence is committed via web.[109]

The relocation of the crimes of instigation and condoning within the French Criminal Code proves that these offences are no longer viewed through the lens of freedom of expression. There is a change in perspective whereby 'freedom of the press' is no longer a protected value: the location of these crimes among common criminal offences overshadows the controversial questions involved in their application and frustrates any attempt to balance the conflicting rights and liberties.

The implications are clearly tangible. After the terrorist attacks in Paris, on 7 and 9 January 2015, several Internet users—approximately 70—were charged with these crimes for having expressed their approval of what had happened; they were later punished with striking severity. This approach is reflected in a statement issued by the Ministry of Justice on 12 January 2015, which defines condoning terrorism as the act of 'presenting or commenting in a positive light any terrorist act, by expressing positive moral consideration of the latter'.

---

[106] The aforementioned Organic Law 1/2015 also reintroduces life imprisonment (defined as '*prison permanente revisable*').

[107] Law no. 2014-1353 of 13 November 2014 to Reinforce Provisions Regarding the Fight Against Terrorism (*renforçant les dispositions relatives à la lutte contre le terrorisme*) is available at *Journal Officiel de la République Française* (JORF), no. 0263, 14 November 2014, 19162 et seq.

[108] Poncela 2016, p. 9; Alix 2015, p. 11 et seq.; Alix 2014, p. 849 et seq.; Alix 2010.

[109] Here it is worth noting the second Paragraph of Article 421-2-5 of the French Criminal Code (*Consultation à titre habituel de sites internet terroristes*), introduced by Law no. *2016-731* of 3 June 2016 (*renforçant la lutte contre le crime organisé, le terrorisme et leur financement, et améliorant l'efficacité*). This criminal offence has been declared unconstitutional, see Constitutional Council, Décision, no. 2016-611 QPC, 10 February 2017. Concerning this Law as as a law strongly 'intrusive' and 'preemptive', see Décima 2016; Ribeyre 2016.

The very description of the criminal conduct is so ill-defined that it paves the way for judicial policies based on double standards[110] such a differentiated statutory regime might be conceivable—to say the most—only if the relevant provisions were extremely accurate and the offences carefully targeted.

French legislation is extremely interesting for this study. In recent years, France has played a leading role in the EU by being the first Member State ever to introduce the crime of Holocaust denial; it later restricted the right to freedom of expression through a security-oriented criminal policy as a response to the threat of international terrorism.[111]

Italy began to address the issue of terrorism within criminal law during the 1970s in an effort to fight against national subversive crimes of the so-called 'Years of Lead'. Legislation has frequently revisited the matter since the 9/11 attacks and introduced a series of offences, many of which pre-emptively redraw the line between punishable and non-punishable behaviour and are based on subjective criteria (the intent of 'terrorism, including international terrorism', which embodies the very essence of the punishable nature of many speech crimes).

One of the most interesting measures is the 'anti-terrorism package' of the recent decree no. 7 of 18 February 2015 (issued as a symbolic and emotional response to the Charlie Hebdo attack in Paris on 7 January 2015 and converted into law no. 43 of 17 April 2015). It expanded the wide range of terrorist crimes contained in the Italian Criminal Code by adding, for instance, in Article 270 *quater*-1, the crime of organising relocation for the purpose of terrorism, which punishes even propaganda for trips abroad for performing terrorist acts.

The aforementioned law also changed the offence of 'training for purposes of terrorism, even international terrorism' as per Article 270d by extending punishment to persons who, although not trained, 'after acquiring instructions, including autonomously, for performing acts as described in the first sentence, enact behaviour for the unequivocal purpose of committing conduct as per Article 270es.'

In this context, the Italian Supreme Court of Cassation case law plays an important role in limiting this dangerous trend of drawing the line of punishable acts so as to include merely adhering to abstract—albeit aberrant—ideologies. The

[110] This expression (along with the so-called freedom '*à deux vitesses*', the double standard in the freedom of speech) has been largely referred to in the debate, which sparked after the vast wave of solidarity and calls for freedom of expression that followed the attacks to the French magazine *Charlie Hebdo*, while the French comedian *Dieudonnée* had been charged with condoning terrorism for having posted on January 11th '*Je me sens Charlie Coulibaly*' on his Facebook page (thereby associating the solidarity slogan '*Je suis Charlie*' to the name of Amédy Coulibaly, who had killed four Jewish people and a police man in a Casher supermarket).

[111] From a comparative perspective, one last example—which is not possible to analyse here extensively—is the British Counter-Terrorism and Security Act of 12 February 2015, which entered into force on July 2015 and is available at http://www.legislation.gov.uk/ukpga/2015/6/contents/enacted.

case law in question has always employed an interpretive approach that characterises terrorist crimes in more concrete terms.[112]

The legal landscape is changing dramatically and a new status of the right to freedom of expression is emerging. Indeed, while at the end of the 20th century it had gained great importance and was being reinforced by national legislators and constitutional courts, such right has lately been subjected to considerable constraints throughout Europe as a consequence of the action taken to fight international terrorism.[113] This brief comparative overview shows how the introduction of a new generation of speech crimes—based on unbending partisanship and addressing the demands for safety of (real or imaginary) crime victims—fundamentally undermines the right to freedom of expression.

When analysing these forms of criminalisation, one aspect worth pointing out is that the germination of speech crimes—a broad category under which historical denialism falls—is one of the components of the fight against international terrorism. In other words, speech crimes are experiencing a parallel growth in the legislation against international terrorism.[114]

In this respect, the crime of historical denialism can be conceived as a 'bridge-provision' between the protection of historical collective memory through criminal law and post-9/11 legislation, which reflects an evermore pervasive, far-reaching and security-oriented criminal policy.

Considering the above, the crime of historical denialism can in many ways become a pivotal vehicle for the construction of identity, thereby leading to the uncontrolled rise of other speech crimes. In other words, such form of criminalisation risks becoming the Trojan horse for political consensus, which legitimises the punishment of other forms

---

[112] The Supreme Court of Cassation wrote in Judgment no. 1072/2007 (Court of Cassation, Section no. 1, Judgment, 17 January 2007, no. 1072) on subversive terrorist association *ex* art. 270 *bis* Criminal Code: 'While it is true that the incriminating provision punishes the very fact of the formation of the association, regardless of the commitment of criminal acts falling within the program and instrumental to the particular purpose pursued, it is equally true that the organizational structure must have a certain degree of effectiveness so as to at least make possible the enactment of criminal activity and therefore justify the legal assessment of the danger. Otherwise […] preemptive repression would end up striking, through the framework of the associative offence, only the fact of adhering to an abstract ideology.' On the subject of terrorist association, see the recent Court of Cassation, Section no. 5, Judgment, 14 July 2016, no. 48001, at www.dirittopenalecontemporaneo.it. See also, on the subject of Training for Activities with International Terrorism Purposes as per Article 270 *quinquies* Criminal Code, Court of Cassation, Section no. 1, Judgment, 12 July, no. 38220, also published on www.dirittopenalecontemporaneo.it.

[113] On the comparison between the European and the US approaches, see Grande 2015, pp. 47–61; Barak-Erez and Scharia 2011, pp. 1–30. For an analysis of hate speech and hate speech laws in the US, see Khan 2006, pp. 165–181; Bakircioglu 2008, pp. 13–27; Tourkochoriti 2014, pp. 574–580. For a comparison between the ECtHR and the US Supreme Court jurisprudence on hate speech, see Kiska 2012. On the implications for free speech after 9/11, see the study of Gelber 2016.

[114] This dynamic is strictly related to what has been defined as the 'criminal law of enemy': for example, think about the growing pervasiveness of criminal offences, the author-based criminal legislations or the tendency to disregard the difference between the author of a crime and his/her accomplices. See Jakobs 2014, p. 415. See Chap. 5.

of expressions.[115] Within this context, it has been justifiably emphasised that freedom of expression must be safeguarded: it is necessary not to go so far as to introduce so many speech crimes that we can no longer distinguish hate crimes from other despicable—but nonetheless legitimate—forms of expression.

The following pages will address the fundamental question that has now been brought into light: the relationship between historical denialism and speech crimes.

1.6 Criminalising Dissent Versus Protecting Consensus

In reflecting on the criminalisation of dissent and the protection of consensus, the 'original' form of historical denialism will be taken into account. Such a form of denialism criminalises the denial of the Shoah only (rather than the denial of all international crimes), regardless of whether a risk arises from the criminal conduct or not.

Historical denialism constitutes a speech crime like any other, though it displays some very peculiar—if not unique—characteristics as compared to other speech crimes.

But what exactly distinguishes historical denialism from other speech crimes? The most notable peculiarity—though arguably not the only one–is that historical denialism, in its 'original' form, represented a paradigm of criminalisation based on *consensus*: it reaffirmed and actively protected a shared and well-established understanding of past events.

As has been observed, 'such a form of criminalisation attracted a real, universal and deep-rooted consensus, which constituted a component of the cultural and ethical foundations of the society'.[116] The criminal norm was there to affirm that 'you shall remember in an established way' and punish whoever wishes to 'remember differently'. Criminalisation, at least in Europe, had thus acquired a proactive role.

The traditional types of speech crimes (for example, the various forms of vilification, propaganda or instigation that are still part of the Italian Criminal Code)[117] targeted instead forms of expression that were considered dangerous because they built upon social conflict. Due to their historical background, such offences can be regarded as a way of criminalising social discord. These are crimes of political opinion and were intended to preserve the power of the ruling class; speech crimes were thus an instrument of political warfare, or—more correctly—'they were the formal re-elaboration of a real conflict, the hegemonic re-elaboration of such conflict, that reflected the structure and the dynamics of underlying forces, as well

[115] In line with the principle of communicating vessels, whereby the ever-growing restrictions in certain fields of the law lead to greater restriction in others. On limits as a central element within the notion of human rights, see Delmas-Marty 2017.

[116] See Paliero 1992, p. 895.

[117] On speech crimes, see Pelissero 2015, pp. 37–46; Gamberini 1973; Fiore 1972. Concerning the criminalization of dissent, see the articles published in the special issue on *Rivista italiana di diritto e procedura penale* 2/2016. Concerning the reform of 2006 of speech crimes, see Pelissero 2015, p. 37 et seq.; Spena 2007, p. 689; Gamberini and Insolera 2006, pp. 135–143.

as the balance of power between the actors involved'.[118] Therefore, such speech crimes represented the paradigm of criminalisation based on *conflict* and served a repressive purpose.

From this perspective, the crime of historical denialism stands out as a sort of great exception within the realm of speech crimes. Such an offence is not intended to punish social unrest in the context of a pluralistic democracy, but rather to strengthen a consensus: not simply the commonly understood democratic consensus, but a common understanding of the truth of certain past events that are of great significance and thus, greatly needed by contemporary democratic societies.

The foundations of this offence do not lie within the kind of social unrest that characterised the criminological and practical backbone of the traditional forms of speech crimes. Historical denialism is instead a way to protect the established notion of a recent past. For this reason, it cannot be categorised among those criminal offences that were used—although improperly—for political warfare: this offence does punish whomever resists an established political consensus, but its meaning is actually found in the protection (and reassertion) of a collective historical understanding.

In light of the above, historical denialism does not seem to fall within the category of speech crimes, at least not in a traditional sense. It might be considered a peculiar type of speech crime, as it shares most of their controversial aspects: by ascribing historical denialism to this category, it may be easier to stress the relevance of certain legal safeguards, as for instance the correct application *in abstracto* and *in concreto* of the harm principle.[119] Nevertheless, its sheer distinctiveness will always be present.

Historical denialism, in its 'original' definition, punished an attack on a historical memory and the ethical pact that places the Holocaust at the centre of modern social conscience.[120] In brief, it consecrates the memory of the Holocaust and—later on— of other grave violations of human rights, by punishing—either as a specific crime or as an aggravating circumstance of another offence[121]—all attempts to deny that

---

[118] See Paliero 1992, p. 894 et seq.

[119] On this principle as a constitutional limit of substantive criminal law, and limiting the scope to general English language literature, see Hörnle 2015, 169 ss.; Dubber and Hörnle 2014, p. 113 et seq.; Dubber 2004, p. 1 et seq.; Finkelstein 2000, p. 335 et seq.; Harcourt 1999, p. 109 et seq.; Baker 2008, p. 3 et seq.

[120] Donini 2008, p. 1588 affirms that 'the collective memory cannot be protected through the criminal law: it could arguably be protected by the law, but not by the criminal law (nor could the threat to such historical heritage be sanctioned in itself), as the criminal regulation would transform a scientifically established truth into a real 'taboo', a form of truth divorced from scientific research, the content of which could not—by definition—be protected by the State'. On this issue, see also Cavaliere 2016; cf. Caputo 2014; Bifulco 2012; Romano 2007; Manes 2007, p. 782 et seq.; Roxin 2006, p. 730 et seq.; Hörnle 2005, p. 315 et seq.

[121] Only Italy opted for this peculiar solution. The reform entered into force on 13 July 2016. The aggravating circumstance was then amended by Article 5 of law no. 167 of 20 November 2017. See no. 149 Gazzetta Ufficiale 28 June 2016. See Fronza 2017; Puglisi 2016, p. 24 et seq.; Della Morte 2016b; Galazzo 2016. Among commentaries published before the reform, see Pelissero 2015, p. 37 et seq.; Pulitanò 2015, p. 1 et seq.; Montanari 2013, p. 1 et seq.; Fronza and Gamberini 2013, p. 1 et seq.; Di Martino, Negazionismo, reato di opinione, in *Il Manifesto*, 20 November 2013; Cassano 2013, p. 276 et seq.

these facts have occurred. For this reason, historical denialism is founded upon a general consensus and protects a common cultural identity.[122] Against this historical and moral background, the need for the unlawful conduct to be clearly and strictly defined appears less stringent.

An interesting issue to analyse is whether the offences introduced by anti-terrorism legislation resemble the traditional forms of speech crimes (criminalisation of conflict) or rather the crime of historical denialism (protection of consensus), or whether they pertain to a third different category. In our understanding, they represent a modern variation of the more traditional forms of speech crimes. Indeed, they all serve a clear and concrete repressive purpose, whereas the crime of historical denialism is mainly symbolic.[123] Nevertheless, unlike traditional speech offences, terrorism is not challenged through the means—improper as they may be—of political warfare, but rather by introducing *délits obstacle*, namely offences that are designed to prevent potential future crimes or other particularly dangerous acts.[124] Thus, these offences represent the rediscovery, from a security-oriented perspective, of traditional speech crimes. However, this point of view is taken to its extremes, as the potential crimes that the new offences seek to prevent are defined by *danger* to society rather than by social discord.

In light of this background and the fundamental traits and peculiarities of the 'original' form of historical denialism as a form of protecting consensus, this study will proceed to focus on the offence's reception and evolution internationally and in particular within the EU.

References

Abregú M (1996) La tutela judicial del derecho a la verdad en la Argentina. Revista Instituto Interamericano de derechos humanos 24:11–41

Acquaviva G (2011) At the Origins of Crimes Against Humanity: Clues to a Proper Understanding of the Nullum Crimen Principle in the Nuremberg Judgment. Journal of International Criminal Justice 9: 881–903

Alix J (2010) Terrorisme et droit penal. Etude critique des incriminations terroristes. Dalloz, Paris

Alix J (2014) Réprimer la participation au terrorisme. Revue des Sciences Criminelles et de Droit Comparé 4:849–866

Alix J (2015) La répression de l'incitation au terrorisme. Gazette du Palais 55:11–23

Amati E, Costi M, Fronza E, Lobba P, Maculan E, Vallini A (2016) Introduzione al diritto penale internazionale. Giappichelli, Turin

Ambos K (2014) Treatise on International Criminal Law. Volume II: The Crimes and Sentencing. Oxford University Press, Oxford

Ambos K, Malarino E, Elsner G (eds) (2009) Justicia de Transición. Informes de América Latina, Alemania, Italia y España. Konrad-Adenauer-Stiftung, Berlin

---

[122] See Sotis 2007.

[123] See Chap. 5.

[124] Think about the possibility of punishing the mere possession of material—not necessarily propaganda—in order to prevent a potential terrorist attack.

Ambos K, Wirth S (2002) The Current Law of Crimes Against Humanity. An Analysis of UNTAET Regulation 15/2000. Criminal Law Forum 13:1–90
Appleman JA (1954) Military Tribunals and International Crimes. Bobbs-Merrill, Indianapolis
Arendt H (1966) The Origins of Totalitarianism. Harcourt, New York
Ashworth A, Zedner L (2008) Defending the Criminal Law: Reflections on the Changing Character of Crime, Procedure, and Sanctions. Criminal Law and Philosophy 2:21–51
Assmann A (2012) Cultural Memory and Western Civilization: Functions, Media. Cambridge University Press, Cambridge
Atkins SE (2009) Holocaust Denial as an International Movement. Praeger, Westport, Connecticut
Baker DJ (2008) Constitutionalizing the Harm Principle. Criminal Justice Ethics 3–18
Bakircioglu O (2008) Freedom of Expression and Hate Speech. Tulsa Journal of Comparative and International Law 16:1–49
Baldissara L (2016) Politiche della memoria e spazio del ricordo in Europa. Il Mulino, Bologna 1:6–20
Barak-Erez D, Scharia D (2011) Freedom of Speech, Support for Terrorism, and the Challenge of Global Constitutional Law. National Security Journal 2:1–30
Bargiacchi P (2008) Cenni sulle tendenze della prassi internazionale ed europea in tema di negazionismo. Rivista della cooperazione giuridica internazionale 10:70–86
Bastian T (1997) Auschwitz und Auschwitzlüge. Beck, Munich
Bauman Z (2000) Liquid Modernity. Polity Press, London
Behrens P (2012) Genocide and the Question of Motives. Journal of International Criminal Justice 10:501–523
Behrens P, Jensen O, Terry N (eds) (2017) Holocaust and Genocide Denial: A Contextual Perspective. Routledge, Abingdon-on-Thames
Beisel D (1995) Die Strafbarkeit der Auschwitzlüge. Neue Juristische Wochenschrift 997–1000
Belavusau U (2013) Freedom of Speech. Routledge, London
Belavusau U (2017) Hate Speech. In: Grote R, Wolfrum R, Lachenmann F (eds) The Max Plank Encyclopedia of Comparative Constitutional Law. Oxford University Press, Oxford
Belavusau U, Gliszczyńska-Grabias A (eds) (2017) Law and Memory: Towards Legal Governance of History. Cambridge University Press, Cambridge
Belavusau U, Gliszczynska-Grabias A (2017) Memory Laws: Mapping a New Subject in Comparative Law and Transitional Justice. In: Belavusau U, Gliszczyńska-Grabias A (eds) Law and Memory: Towards Legal Governance of History. Cambridge University Press, Cambridge
Benz W (1992) Legenden Lügen Vorurteile. Ein Wörterbuch für Zeitgeschichte. Deutscher Taschenbuch, Monaco
Bifulco D (2012) Negare l'evidenza, Diritto e storia di fronte alla 'menzogna' di Auschwitz. Franco Angeli, Milan
Bilbao Ubillos JM (2008) La negación del holocausto en la jurisprudencia del Tribunal Europeo de Derechos humanos: la endeble justificación de tipos penales contrarios a la libertad de expression. Revista de Derecho Político (UNED) 71–72:19–56
Bisset A (2012) Truth Commissions and Criminal Courts. Cambridge University Press, Cambridge
Bizimana JD (2001) L'Eglise et le génocide au Ruanda: les Péres blancs et le négationnisme. L'Harmattan, Paris
Bloch P (2006) Response to Professor Fronza's The Punishment of Negationism. Vermont Law Review 30:627–643
Boed R (2002) Individual Criminal Responsibility for Violations of Article 3 Common to the Geneva Convention of 1949 and of Additional Protocol II Thereto in the Case Law of the International Criminal Tribunal for Rwanda. Criminal Law Forum 13:293–322
Borgwardt H (2009) Die Strafbarkeit der "Auschwitzlüge". In: Ostendorf H (ed) Rechtsextremismus. Eine Herausforderung für Strafrecht und Strafjustiz. Nomos, Baden-Baden, pp 233–266
Brugger W (2005) Ban on or Protection of Hate Speech? Some Observations Based on German and American Law. Tulane European and Civil Law Forum 17:1–21

Brunelli D (2016) Attorno alla punizione di negazionismo. Rivista italiana di diritto e procedura penale 2:978–998
Cajani L (2008–2009) Historians between Memory Wars and Criminal Law: the Case of European Union. Annales International Society for Historic Didactis XXIX–XXX:39–55
Campisi MC (2014) From a Duty to Remember to an Obligation to Memory? Memory as Reparation in the Jurisprudence of the Inter-American Court of Human Rights. International Journal of Conflict and Violence 8:62–74
Caputo M (2014) La "menzogna di Auschwitz", le "verità" del diritto penale. La criminalizzazione del c.d. negazionismo tra ordine pubblico, dignità e senso di umanità. Diritto penale contemporaneo. Online: https://www.penalecontemporaneo.it/upload/1389084288CAPUTO%202014a.pdf. Accessed 1 October 2017
Caroli P (2015) The role of the judiciary within the construction of collective memory. The Italian Transition. Wroclaw Review of Law, Administration and Economics 5 1:162–179
Caroli P (2017) La giustizia di transizione in Italia. L'esperienza dopo la seconda guerra mondiale. http://eprints-phd.biblio.unitn.it/1981/1/Paolo_Caroli_-_Tesi_dottorato_.pdf. Accessed 13 August 2017
Cartier E (2006) Histoire et droit: rivalité ou complémentarité? Revue francaise de droit constitutionnel 67:509–534
Caruso C (2013) La libertà di espressione in azione. Contributo a una teoria costituzionale del discorso pubblico. Bononia University Press, Bologna
Cassano M (2013) Negazionismo e opportunità di una risposta penale. Criminalia 276–287
Cavaliere A (2016) La discussione intorno alla punibilità del negazionismo, i principi di offensività e libera manifestazione del pensiero e la funzione della pena. Rivista italiana di diritto e procedura penale 2:999–1015
Clark RS (1990) Crimes Against Humanity at Nuremberg. In: Ginsburgs G, Kudriavtsev VN (eds) The Nuremberg Trial and International Law. Nijhoff, Boston, pp 177–212
Cortese F (2012) Memoria e diritto. Contributo per un approccio non necessariamente centripeto (tra storia, giustizia e letteratura). Rassegna Di Diritto Pubblico Europeo, 2:19–45
Cortese F (2016) What can the Perincek case teach? DPCE online http://www.dpceonline.it/index.php/dpceonline/article/view/93. Accessed 16 July 2017
Cryer R (2009) The Definitions of International Crimes in the Al Bashir Arrest Warrant Decision. Journal of International Criminal Justice 7:283–296
Cryer R, Friman H, Robinson D, Wilmshurst E (2014) An Introduction to International Criminal Law and Procedure. Cambridge University Press, Cambridge
Cullen A (2008) Definition of Non-International Armed Conflict in the Rome Statute of the International Criminal Court: An Analysis of the Threshold of Application Contained in Article 8(2)(f). Journal of Conflict and Security Law 12:419–445
Cupido M (2011) The Policy Underlying Crimes Against Humanity: Practical Reflections on a Theoretical Debate. Criminal Law Forum 22:275–309
Damaska M (1991) The face of Justice and State Authority. A Comparative Approach to the Legal Process. Yale University Press, New Haven
Damaska M (2006) The Uncertain Self-Identity of International Criminal Courts. Criminalia: 9–55
Damaska M (2007) What is the Point of International Criminal Justice? Chicago Kent Law Review, 83:329–364
Décima (2016) Terreur et métamorphose. À propos de la loi n° 2016- 731 du 3 juin 2016 sur la lutte contre le terrorisme. Dalloz, Paris
Delage C, Goodrich P (eds) (2012) The Scene of the Mass Crime: History, Film, and International Tribunals. Routledge, London
Della Morte G (2011) Le amnistie nel diritto internazionale. Cedam, Padua
Della Morte G (2016a) When is a criminal prohibition of genocide denial justified? The *Perinçek* Case and the risk of a double standard. Questions of International Law, online: http://www.qil-qdi.org/criminal-prohibition-genocide-denial-justified-perincek-case-risk-double-standard/. Accessed 15 September 2017

Della Morte G (2016b) Sulla legge che introduce la punizione delle condotte negazionistiche nell'ordinamento italiano: tre argomenti per una critica severa. SIDI Blog, online: http://www.sidiblog.org/2016/06/22/sulla-legge-che-introduce-la-punizione-delle-condotte-negazionistiche-nellordinamento-italiano-tre-argomenti-per-una-critica-severa/. Accessed 20 September 2017
Della Morte G, Abdelgawad EL, Martin-Chenut K (2007) La clémence saisie par le droit: Amnistie, prescription et grâce en droit international et comparé. Collection de l'UMR de droit comparé de Paris 14, Paris
Delmas-Marty M (2005) Le relative et l'universel. Les forces imaginantes du droit. I. Seuil, Paris
Delmas-Marty M (2006) Les forces imaginantes du droit. II. Le pluralisme ordonné. Seuil, Paris
Delmas-Marty M (2016) Aux quatre vents du monde. Petit guide de navigation sur l'océan de la mondialisation. Seuil, Paris
Delmas-Marty M (2017) The Limits of Human Rights in a Moving World. Elements of a dynamic approach. In: Fassbender B, Traisbach K (eds) The Limits of Human Rights. CUP, Cambridge
Di Cesare SD (2012) Se Auschwitz è nulla: contro il negazionismo. Nuovo Melangolo, Genoa
Di Giovine A (2006) Il passato che non passa. «Eichmann di carta» e repressione penale. Diritto pubblico comparato e europeo 1:XIII–XXVIII
Dietz S (1995) Die Lüge von der "Auschwitzlüge" - Wie weit reicht das Recht auf Meinungsäußerung? Kritische Justiz 28:210–222
Domenico RP (1991) Italian fascists on trial 1943–1948. University of North Carolina Press, Chapel Hill
Donini M (2008) «Danno» e «offesa» nella cd. tutela penale dei sentimenti. Note su morale e sicurezza come beni giuridici, a margine della categoría dell' «offense» di Joel Feinberg. Rivista italiana di diritto e procedura penale 4:1546–1558
Donini M (2009) La gestione penale del passaggio dal fascismo alla Repubblica in Italia. Materiali per una storia della cultura giuridica XXXIX 1:183–216
Doward J (2017) New online generation takes up Holocaust denial https://www.theguardian.com/world/2017/jan/22/online-conspiracy-theories-feed-holocaust-denial. Accessed 13 August 2017
Droin N (2014) État des lieux de la répression du négationnisme en France et en droit comparé. Revue Trimestrielle des Droits de l'Homme 98:363–394
Drumbl MA (2007) Atrocity, Punishment, and International Law. Cambridge University Press, Cambridge
Du Bois-Pedain A (2007) Transitional Amnesty in South Africa. Cambridge University Press, New York
Dubber MD (2004) Toward a Constitutional Law of Crime and Punishment. Hastings Law Journal 55:1–33
Dubber M, Hörnle T (2014) Criminal Law: A Comparative Approach. Oxford University Press, Oxford
Dubuisson F (2007) L'incrimination générique du négationnisme est-elle conciliable avec le droit à la liberté d'expression. Revue de Droit Université Libre de Bruxelles 35:135–195
Elster J (2004) Closing the Books: Transitional Justice in Historical perspective. Cambridge University Press, Cambridge
Ferrajoli L (2009) Diritto e ragione. Teoria del garantismo penale. Laterza, Bari
Findlay M, Henham R (eds) (2012) Transforming International Criminal Justice. Retributive and restorative justice in the trial process. Routledge, London
Finkelstein C (2000) Positivism and the Notion of an Offense. California Law Review 335–348
Finkielkraut A (1982) L'avenir d'une négation. Réflexion sur la question du genocide. Seuil, Paris
Fiore C (1972) I reati di opinione. Cedam, Padua
Fischer T (2017) Strafgesetzbuch und Nebengesetze. Beck, Munich
Fletcher GP (1998) Basic Concepts of Criminal Law. Oxford University Press, Oxford
Flores M (2007) Revisionismo storiografico. In: Enciclopedia Italiana Treccani, VII Appendice
Focardi F (2014) Il cattivo tedesco e il buon italiano. Laterza, Bari

Focardi F, Klinkhammer L (2004) The question of Fascist Italy's war crimes: the construction of a self-acquitting myth (1943–1948). Journal of Modern Italian Studies 3:330–348
Fornasari G (2013) Giustizia di transizione e diritto penale. Giappichelli, Turin
Fornasari G (2015) Giustizia di transizione. Enciclopedia del Diritto. Annali VIII:547–570
Fouchard I (2014) Crimes internationaux. Entre internationalisation du droit pénal et pénalisation du droit international. Bruylant, Brussels
Fourie P, Meyer M (2013) The Politics of AIDS Denialism: South Africa's Failure to Respond. Routledge, London
Freeman M (2006) Truth Commission and Procedural fairness. Cambridge University Press, New York
Fronza E (2015) Negazionismo. Enciclopedia del Diritto Annali VIII:633–658
Fronza E (2016a) Criminalizzazione del dissenso o tutela del consenso. Profili critici del negazionismo come reato. Rivista italiana di diritto e procedura penale 2:1016–1033
Fronza E (2016b) La poursuite des crimes nazis et fascistes en Italie, in Vv. AA. Mélanges en l'honneur de Geneviéve Giudicelli-Delage. Dalloz, Paris, pp 344–364
Fronza E (2017) L'introduzione dell'aggravante di negazionismo. Diritto penale e processo 2:155–167
Fronza E, Fornasari G (eds) (2009) Il superamento del passato e il superamento del presente. La punizione delle violazioni sistematiche dei diritti umani nell'esperienza argentina e colombiana. Università degli Studi di Trento, Trento
Fronza E, Tricot J (2003) Fonction symbolique et droit pénal international. Une analyse du discours des Tribunaux pénaux internationaux. In: Fronza E, Manacorda S (eds) La justice pénale internationale dans les décisions des tribunaux ad hoc. Dalloz-Giuffré, Milan
Galazzo G (2016) Reato di negazionismo e libertà di manifestazione del pensiero: una riflessione. Giurisprudenza penale 9:1–10
Gamberini A (1973) I "pensieri leciti" della Corte Costituzionale. Rivista italiana di diritto e procedura penale
Gamberini A (2013) Tutela della memoria e diritto penale: una riflessione sistematica e comparativa a partire dal reato di negazionismo. Diritto penale contemporaneo. Online: https://www.penalecontemporaneo.it/d/2716-tutela-della-memoria-e-diritto-penale-una-riflessione-sistematica-e-comparativa-a-partire-dal-reato. Accessed 2 October 2017
Gamberini A, Insolera G (2006) Legislazione penale compulsiva, buone ragioni e altro. A proposito della riforma dei reati di opinione. In: Insolera G (ed) La legislazione penale compulsiva. Cedam, Padua, pp 135–143
Garapon A (1995) Bien juger: essai sur le rituel judiciaire. Odile Jacob, Paris
Garapon A (2002) Des crimes qu'on ne peut ni punir ni pardonner: pour une justice internationale. Odile Jacob, Paris
Garapon A (2008) Peut-on réparer l'histoire? Colonisation, esclavage, Shoah. Odile Jacob, Paris
Garibian S (2012) Droit, histoire, mémoire. Le négationnisme: exercice d'une liberté ou violation d'un droit? Revue arménienne des questions contemporaines 15: 53-62
Garibian S (2014) Ghosts Also Die: Resisting Disappearance through the 'Right to the Truth' and the Juicios por la Verdad in Argentina. Journal of International Criminal Justice 12:515–538
Gasanabo JD, Simon DJ, Ensign MM (eds) (2015) Confronting Genocide in Rwanda: Dehumanization, Denial, and Strategies for Prevention. Apidama, Bogota
Gavagnin G (2006) Il negazionismo nella legislazione penale francese, austriaca e tedesca. In: Riondato S (ed) Discriminazione razziale, xenophobia, odio religioso. Diritti fondamentali e tutela penale. Cedam, Padua, pp 199–215
Gelber K (2016) Free Speech After 9/11. Oxford University Press, Oxford
Geras N (2011) Crimes Against Humanity: Birth of a Concept. Manchester University Press, Manchester
Gil Gil A (2009) La Justicia de Transición en España: de la Amnistía a la Memoria Histórica. Atelier, Barcelona
Gil Gil A, Maculan E (eds) (2016) Derecho penal internacional. Librería Dykinson, Madrid

Gil Gil A, Maculan E (eds) (2017a) Colombia como nuevo modelo para la justicia de transición. Instituto Universitario General Gutiérrez Mellado, Madrid

Gil Gil A, Maculan E (2017b) La influencia de las victimas en el tratamiento juridico de la violencia colectiva. Librería Dykinson, Madrid

Gillespie A (2015) Hate and Harm: The Law on Hate Speech. In: Savin A, Trzaskowski J (eds) Research Handbook on EU Internet Law, pp 488–507

Ginzburg C (2002) Beweis, Gedächtnis, Vergessen. Memory 30:50–60

Gliszczyńska-Grabias A (2013) Penalizing Holocaust Denial: A View from Europe. In: Small CA (ed) Global Antisemitism: A Crisis of Modernity. Brill-Nijhoff, Leiden

Gordon RSC (2013) Scolpitelo nei cuori. L'Olocausto nella cultura italiana. Bollati Boringhieri, Turin

Gramsci A (1994) Letters from Prison. Columbia University Press, New York

Grande E (2015) I mobili confini della libertà di espressione negli Stati Uniti e il metro della paura. Questione Giustizia 4:47–61

Greppi E (2001) I crimini di guerra e contro l'umanità nel diritto internazionale. Utet, Turin

Guembe MJ (2005) Reopening of trials for crimes committed by the Argentine military dictatorship. http://www.scielo.br/scielo.php?pid=S1806-64452005000200008&script=sci_arttext&tlng=es. Accessed 13 August 2017

Halbwachs M (1925) Les cadres sociaux de la mémoire. Presses Universitaires de France, Paris

Halbwachs M (1950) La mémoire collective. Presses Universitaires de France, Paris

Harcourt BE (1999) The Collapse of the Harm Principle. Journal of Criminal Law and Criminology 109–124

Hare I, Weinstein J (eds) (2011) Extreme Speech and Democracy. Oxford University Press, Oxford

Hayner P (1994) Fifteen Truth Commissions - 1974 to 1994: A Comparative Study. Human Rights Quarterly 16:597–665

Heinze E (2017) Beyond 'Memory Laws': Towards a General Theory of Law and Historical Discourse. In: Belavusau U, Gliszczyńska-Grabias A (eds) Law and Memory: Addressing Historical Injustice by Law. Cambridge University Press, Cambridge

Heller KJ (2011) The Nuremberg Military Tribunals and the Origins of International Criminal Law. Oxford University Press, Oxford

Helz M (2012) The Content and Context of Hate Speech: Rethinking Regulation and Responses. Cambridge University Press, Cambridge

Hennebel L, Hochmann T (eds) (2011) Genocide Denials and the Law. Oxford University Press, Oxford

Hervieu N (2014) Le négationnisme, prisme révélateur du dilemme européen face à lutte contre l'extrémisme. Revue des droits de l'homme online https://revdh.revues.org/503. Accessed 16 July 2017

Higwedere P, Essex M (2010) AIDS Denialism and Public Health Practice. AIDS and Behavior 14:237–247

Hill LE (1989) The Trial of Ernst Zundel. Revisionism and the Law in Canada. http://motlc.wiesenthal.com/site/pp.asp?c=gvKVLcMVIuG&b=395157. Accessed 13 August 2017

Hochmann T (2012) Le négationnisme face aux limites de la liberté d'expression. Étude de droit comparé. Pedone, Paris

Hörnle T (2005) Grob anstössiges Verhalten: strafrechtlicher Schutz von Moral, Gefühlen und Tabus. Verlag, Frankfurt am Main

Hörnle T (2015) Theories of Criminalization. In: Dubber MD, Hörnle T (eds) The Oxford Handbook of Criminal Law. Oxford University Press, Oxford

Ibáñez Majar JE (2014) Justicia transicional y las Comisiones de la Verdad. Aufklarung, Bogota

Igounet V (2000) Histoire du négationnisme en France. Seuil, Paris

Imbleau M (2003) La négation du génocide nazi, liberté d'expression ou crime raciste? L'Harmattan, Paris

Insolera G (2014) Negazionismo e controllo penale. Criminal law studies and materials 1:1–25

Jakobs G (2014) On the Theory of Enemy Criminal Law. In: Dubber MD (ed) Foundational Texts in Modern Criminal Law. Oxford University Press, Oxford, pp 415–424
Jansen YO (2014) Denying Genocide or Denying Free Speech? A Case Study of the Application of Rwanda's Genocide Denial Laws. Northwestern Journal International Human Rights 12:191–213
Jean JP (2009) Le procès et l'écriture de l'histoire. Revue de sciences humaines 9:61–74
Jones JRWD (2003) Whose Intent is it Anyway? – Genocide and the Intent to Destroy a Group. In: Vohrah LC et al. (eds) Man's Inhumanity to Man. Brill-Nijhoff, Boston
Kahn RA (1997) Who Takes the Blame? Scapegoating, Legal Responsibility and the Prosecution of Holocaust Revisionists in the Federal Republic of Germany and Canada. Glendale Law Review 16:17–64
Kahn RA (2004) Holocaust Denial and the Law. A Comparative Study. Palgrave, New York
Kahn RA (2006) Cross-Burning, Holocaust Denial, and the Development of Hate Speech Law in the United States and Germany. University of Detroit Mercy Law Review 83:163–194
Kindhäuser U, Neumann U, Paeffgen HU (ed) (2013) Strafgesetzbuch: Band 2. Nomos, Munich
Kiska R (2012) Hate Speech: a Comparison between the European Court of Human Rights and the United States Supreme Court Jurisprudence. Regent University Law Review 25:107–151
Kolb R, Scalia D (2012) Droit international pénal. Précis. Helbing & Lichtenhahn, Basel
Koposov N (2017) Memory Laws, Memory Wars. Cambridge University Press, Cambridge
Koskeniemmi M (1989) From Apology to Utopia. The Structure of International Legal Argument. Cambridge University Press, Cambridge
Kress C (2001) War Crimes Committed in Non-International Armed Conflict and the Emerging System of International Criminal Justice. Israeli Yearbook on Human Rights 30:103–177
Kress C (2009) The Crime of Genocide and Contextual Elements. A Comment on the ICC Pre-Trial Chamber's Decision in the Al Bashir Case. Journal of International Criminal Justice 7:1–10
Laitenberger A (2003) Die Strafbarkeit der Verbreitung rassistischer, rechtsextremistischer und neonazistischer Inhalte: Unter besonderer Berücksichtigung der Verbreitung über Netzwerke. Ein Rechtsvergleich. Peter Lang, Frankfurt am Main
Lalieu O (2001) L'invention du 'devoir de mémoire'. Vingtième Siècle Revue histoire 69:83–94
Lechtholz Zey J (2012) The Laws Banning Holocaust Denial. Genocide Prevention Now 9: 1-18
Ledoux S (2012) Ecrire une histoire du "devoir de mémoire". Le Débat 170:175–185
Leotta CD (2015) Profili penali del negazionismo. Riflessioni alla luce della sentenza della Corte EDU sul genocidio armeno. Cedam, Padua
Lessa F, Payne LA (eds) (2012) Amnesty in the Age of Human Rights Accountability. Comparative and International Perspectives. Cambridge University Press, New York
Lippmann M (1997) Crimes Against Humanity. Boston College Third World Law Journal 17:171–278
Lipstadt DE (1994) Denying the Holocaust: The Growing Assault on Truth and Memory. Plume, New York
Lobba P (2014) Il negazionismo come abuso della libertà di espressione: la giurisprudenza della Corte di Strasburgo. Rivista italiana di diritto e procedura penale 57:1815–1853
Lobba P (2015) Holocaust Denial Before the European Court of Human Rights: Evolution of an Exceptional Regime. European Journal of International Law 26:237–253
Lollini A (2003) Le rôle (pre)costituant de la Commission Verité et Reconciliation. Le renouvellement du constitutionnalisme en Afrique du Sud. Thesis
Lollini A (2011) Constitutionalism and Transitional Justice in South Africa. Berghahn Books, Oxford
Longman T (2011) Christianity and Genocide in Rwanda. Cambridge University Press, Cambridge
Loraux N (1988) De l'amnistie et de son contraire. In: Yerushalmi YH, Loraux N, Mommsen H, Milner JR, Vattimo G (eds) Les usages de l'oubli. Seuil, Paris, pp 23–47
Loraux N (1997) La cité divisée. Payot, Paris

Lowenthal E (2014) Contro il giorno della memoria. Online: http://www.lastampa.it/2014/01/16/cultura/contro-il-giorno-della-memoria-GKkosn3Gh3Ddz5qNYBOQMJ/pagina.html. Accessed 28 September 2017
Luther J (2008) L'antinegazionismo nell'esperienza giuridica tedesca e comparata. Diritto pubblico comparato ed europeo 1192–1212
Maculan E (2012) Prosecuting international crimes at national level: lessons from the Argentine "truth-finding trials". Human Rights Review 1:53–82
Maculan E, Pastor D (2013) El derecho a la verdad y su esercicio por medio del proceso penal. Hammurabi, Buenos Aires
Malarino E (2009) Il volto repressivo della recente giurisprudenza argentina sulle gravi violazioni dei diritti umani. Un'analisi della sentenza della Corte Suprema di Giustizia della Nazione del 14 giugno 2005 nel caso Simón. In: Fronza E, Fornasari G (eds) Il superamento del passato e il superamento del presente. La punizione delle violazioni sistematiche dei diritti umani nell'esperienza argentina e colombiana. Università degli Studi di Trento, Trento, pp 31–98
Manes V (2007) Attualità e prospettive del giudizio di ragionevolezza in materia penale. Rivista italiana di diritto e procedura penale 2–3:739–789
Manetti M (2005a) Libertà di pensiero e negazionismo. In: Ainis M (ed) Informazione, potere, libertà. Giappichelli, Turin, pp. 41–51
Manetti M (2005b) L'incitamento all'odio razziale tra realizzazione dell'eguaglianza e difesa dello Stato. In: Di Giovine A (ed) Democrazie protette e protezione della democrazia. Giappichelli, Turin, pp. 1–34
Marcheri PL (2015) Legislação europeia de combate ao nazismo, doutrinas de ódio e discriminação racial. Cia Do Ebook, Timburi
Matuschek M (2012) Erinnerungsstrafrecht. Eine Neubegründung des Verbots der Holocaustleugnung auf rechtsvergleichender und sozialphilosophischer Grundlage. Verlag, Berlin
Matuschek M (2013) Thomas Hochmann, Le négationnisme face aux limites de la liberté d'expression, étude de droit comparé. Droit et cultures 66:231–234
Melloni A (2008) Per una storia della tribunalizzazione della storia. In: Marquard O, Melloni A (eds) La storia che giudica, la storia che assolve. Laterza, Rome/Bari
Méndez J (2009) An Emerging 'Right to Truth': Latin American Contributions. In: Karstedt S (ed) Legal Institutions and Collective Memories. Hart, Oxford
Méndez J, Bariffi F (2007) Right to Truth. In: Wolfrum R (ed) Max Plank Encyclopedia of Public International Law. Oxford University Press, Oxford
Mensching C (2014) Hassrede im Internet. Grundrechtsvergleich und regulatorische Konsequenzen. Duncker & Humblot, Berlin
Merkel R (2008) The Law of the Nuremberg Trial: Valid, Dubious, Outdated. In: Mettraux G (ed) Perspectives on the Nuremberg Trial. Oxford University Press, Oxford, pp 555–576
Merli A (2008) Democrazia e diritto penale. Note a margine del dibattito sul cosiddetto negazionismo. Edizioni Scientifiche Italiane, Naples
Meron T (1995) International Criminalization of Internal Atrocities. American Journal of International Law 89:554–577
Mettraux G (ed) (2008) Perspectives on the Nuremberg Trial. Oxford University Press, Oxford
Minow M (1998) Between Vengeance and Forgiveness: Facing History After Genocide and Mass Violence. Beacon, Boston
Moerland R (2016) The Killing of Death: Denying the Genocide Against the Tutsi. Intersentia, Cambridge
Montanari M (2013) Il disegno di legge in materia di negazionismo passa all'esame dell'aula del Senato. Diritto penale contemporaneo. Online: https://www.penalecontemporaneo.it/d/2597-il-disegno-di-legge-in-materia-di-negazionismo-passa-all-esame-dell-aula-del-senato. Accessed 28 September 2017
Mutua M (2001) Savages-Victims-Saviors: The Metaphor of Human Rights. Harvard International Law Journal 42

Naqvi Y (2006) The right to truth in international law: fact or fiction? International Review of the Red Cross 88:245–273
Nersessian DL (2002) The Contours of Genocide Intent. Troubling Jurisprudence from the International Criminal Tribunals. Texas International Law Journal 37:231–276
Nora P (2016) Come si manipola la memoria. Lo storico il potere, il passato. La Scuola, Brescia
O'Keefe R (2015) International Criminal Law. Oxford University Press, Oxford
Ochoa JC (2013) The Rights of Victims in Criminal Justice Proceedings for Serious Human Rights Violations. Brill-Nijhoff, The Hague
Osiel M (1999) Mass Atrocity, Collective Memory, and the Law. Transaction, London
Osiel M (2008) In Defence of Liberal Show Trials – Nuremberg and Beyond. In: Mettraux G (ed) Perspectives on the Nuremberg Trial. Oxford University Press, New York, pp 704–726
Ost F (1999) Le temps du droit. Odile Jacob, Paris
Palermo PG (2014) Mecanismos políticos y jurídicos aplicados durante la transición uruguaya para la superación del pasado. In: Sabadell AL, Simon JM, Dimoulis D (eds) Justiça de Transição. Das Anistias às Comissões de Verdade. Revista dos Tribunais, Sao Paulo, pp 101–150
Paliero CE (1992) Consenso sociale e diritto penale. Rivista italiana di diritto e procedura penale 3:849–922
Parenti P (2009) La persecuzione penale di gravi violazioni dei diritti umani in Argentina. A 25 anni dal ritorno della democrazia. In: Fronza E, Fornasari G (eds) Il superamento del passato e il superamento del presente. La punizione delle violazioni sistematiche dei diritti umani nell'esperienza argentina e colombiana. Università degli Studi di Trento, Trento, pp 13–30
Parisi S (2013) Il negazionismo dell'Olocausto e la sconfitta del Diritto penale. Quaderni costituzionali 4:879–904
Pastor D (2006) La deriva neopunitivista de organismos y activistas como causa del desprestigio actual de los derechos humanos. Jura Gentium online: http://www.juragentium.org/topics/latina/es/pastor.htm. Accessed 30 September 2017
Pastor D (2009) Processi penali solo per conoscere la verità? L'esperienza argentina. In: Fronza E, Fornasari G (eds) Il superamento del passato e il superamento del presente. La punizione delle violazioni sistematiche di diritti umani nell'esperienza argentina e colombiana. Università degli Studi di Trento, Trento
Pech L (2011) Ruling Denial Prohibition. In: Hennebel L, Hochmann T (eds) Genocide Denials and the Law. Oxford University Press, Oxford, pp 183–234
Pelissero M (2015) La parola pericolosa. Il confine incerto del controllo penale del dissenso. Quest. giust. 4:37–46
Peter R (2006) Making "Holocaust Denial" a Crime: Reflections on European AntiNegationist Laws from the perspective of US constitutional experience. Vermont Law Review 30, pp 155–181
Pisanty V (2000) Sul negazionismo. In: Collotti E (ed) Fascismo e antifascismo. Rimozioni, revisioni, negazioni. Laterza, Rome/Bari, pp 43–68
Pisanty V (2005) I negazionismi. In: Cattaruzza M, Flores M, Levi Sullam S, Traverso E (eds) Storia della Shoah. Volume I. Utet, Turin
Pisanty V (2012) Abusi di memoria. Negare, banalizzare, sacralizzare la Shoah. Mondadori, Milan
Pollicino O (2011) Il negazionismo nel diritto comparato: profili ricostruttivi. Diritti umani e diritto internazionale 1:85–105
Poncela P (2016) Les naufragés du droit pénal. Archives de politique criminelle 38:9–25
Portelli A (2003) The Order Has Been Carried Out: History, Memory, and Meaning of a Nazi Massacre in Rome. Palgrave, Basingstoke
Prosperi L, Terrosi J (2017) Embracing the 'Human Factor': Is There New Impetus at the ICC for Conceiving and Prioritizing Intentional Environmental Harms as Crimes Against Humanity? Journal of International Criminal Justice 15: 509–525
Pugiotto A (2009) Quando (e perché) la memoria si fa legge. Quaderni costituzionali 1:7–36
Puglisi G (2016) A margine della c.d. "aggravante di negazionismo": tra occasioni sprecate e legislazione penale simbolica. Diritto penale contemporaneo, online: https://www.penalecontemporaneo.it/upload/1468507001PUGLISI_2016b.pdf. Accessed 20 September 2017

Pulitanò D (2006) Laicità e diritto penale. Rivista italiana di diritto e procedura penale 1:55–94
Pulitanò D (2015) Di fronte al negazionismo e al discorso d'odio. Diritto penale contemporaneo. Online: https://www.penalecontemporaneo.it/upload/1426333841PULITANO_2015.pdf. Accessed 28 September 2017
Quaritsch H (1992) Über Bürgerkriegs- und Feind-Amnestien. Der Staat 4:389–418
Resta G, Zeno-Zencovich V (2013) "Judicial "Truth" and Historical "Truth": The Case of the Ardeatine Caves Massacre". Law and History Review 31 4:843–886
Resta G, Zeno-Zencovich V (eds) (2012) Riparare, risarcire, ricordare. Un dialogo tra storici e giuristi. Editoriale Scientifica, Naples
Ribeyre C (2016) Loi n° 2016-731 du 3 juin 2016 renforçant la lutte contre le crime organisé, le terrorisme et leur financement, et améliorant l'efficacité et les garanties de la procédure pénale - Et maintenant? Droit pénal
Ricoeur P (2000) La mémoire, l'histoire, l'oubli. Seuil, Paris
Rieff D (2016) In praise of forgetting: Historical Memory and Its Ironies. Yale University Press, New Haven
Rioux JP (2008) Les avatars du 'devoir de mémoire'. Le Débat 170:186–192
Robinson D (2008) The Identity Crisis of International Criminal Law. Leiden Journal of International Law 21:925–963
Robinson J (1946) The Nuremberg Judgment. Congress Weekly: A Review of Jewish Interests 13
Romano M (2007) Principio di laicità dello Stato, religioni, norme penali. Rivista trimestrale di diritto e procedura penale 495–512
Rousso H (1987) Le syndrome de Vichy. Seuil. Paris (tr. The Vichy Syndrome. History and Memory in France since 1944. Harvard University Press, Massachusetts)
Rousso H (2016) Face au passé. Essais sur la mémoire contemporaine. Belin, Paris
Rovatti T (2009) Fra politiche di violenza e aspirazioni di giustizia. La popolazione civile vittima delle stragi di Monchio e Tavolicci (1943–45). Carocci, Rome
Roxin C (2006) Was darf der Staat unter Strafe stellen? Zur Legitimation von Strafdrohungen. In: Dolcini E, Paliero CE (eds) Studi in onore di Giorgio Marinucci, I. Giuffrè, Milan
Salomon TR (2012) Meinungsfreiheit und die Strafbarkeit des Negationismus. Zeitschrift für Rechtspolitik 48–50
Sarkin J (2004) Carrots and Sticks: The TRC and the South African Amnesty Process. Intersentia, Antwerp
Schwarzenberger G (2008) The Judgment of Nuremberg. In: Mettraux G (ed) Perspectives on the Nuremberg Trial. Oxford University Press, Oxford, pp 167–189
Schwelb E (1946) Crimes Against Humanity. In: British Yearbook of International Law 23: 178–226
Seibert-Fohr A (2009) Prosecuting Serious Human Rights Violations. Oxford University Press, Oxford
Seminara S (2014) Die Aufarbeitung der faschistischen Vergangenheit in Italien. Strafrechtliche Probleme. Jahrbuch der Juristischen Zeitgeschichte 15:3–65
Shahnazarova I (2015) Criminalisation of genocide denial and freedom of expression. Inderscience online 1:322–340
Silva Sánchez JM (2007) Nullum crimen sine poena? Sobre las doctrinas penales de la "lucha contra la impunidad" y del "derecho de la víctima al castigo del autor". Derecho Penal del siglo XXI 339–357
Simester AP, Du Bois-Pedain A, Neuman U (eds) (2014) Liberal Criminal Theory. Essays for Andreas Von Hirsch. Hart, Portland
Sivakumaran S (2012) The Law of Non-International Armed Conflict. Oxford University Press, Oxford
Sluiter G (2011) "Chapeau Elements" of Crimes Against Humanity in the Jurisprudence of the UN ad hoc Tribunals. In: Sadat LN (ed) Forging a Convention for Crimes Against Humanity. Cambridge University Press, Cambridge, pp 102–141
Sotis C (2007) Il diritto senza codice. Uno studio sul diritto penale europeo vigente. Giuffrè, Milan

Spena A (2007) Libertà di espressione e reati di opinione. Rivista italiana di diritto e procedura penale 689–703
Spigno I (2008) Un dibattito ancora attuale: l'Olocausto e la sua negazione. Diritto pubblico comparato ed europeo 1921–1931
Stofleth DE (2012) Memory Laws as Mechanisms of "remembering to forget": The Spanish Law of Historical Memory as an Archetype. https://www.academia.edu/11087676/Memory_Laws_as_Mechanisms_of_Remembering_to_Forget_The_Spanish_Law_of_Historical_Memory_as_an_Archetype. Accessed 13 August 2017
Stone D (2013) The Holocaust, Fascism and Memory: Essays in the History of Ideas. Palgrave, London
Stora B (2007) La guerre des mémoires: la France face à son passé colonial (entretiens avec Thierry Leclere). Éditions de l'Aube, La Tour d'Aigues
Swart M, van Marle K (eds) (2017) The Limits of Transition: The South African Truth and Reconciliation 20 years on. Brill Nijhoff, The Hague
Tamarit Sumalla JM (2014) Memoria histórica y justicia transicional en España: el tiempo como actor de la justicia penal. Anuario Iberoamericano de Derecho Internacional Penal, Bogota
Teitel RG (2014) Globalizing Transitional Justice. Oxford University Press, Oxford
Ternon Y (1999) Du négationnisme: mémoire et tabou. Desclée de Brouwer, Paris
Terry N (2017) Holocaust denial in the age of web 2.0. In: Behrens P, Jensen O, Terry N (eds) Holocaust and Genocide Denial: A Contextual Perspective. Routledge, London
Teruel Lozano GM (2015) La libertad de expresión a los delitos de negacionismo y de provocación al odio y a la violencia: sombras sin luces en la reforma del código penal. Revista para el análisis del derecho 4:1–51
Tiedemann M (1996) In Auschwitz wurde niemand vergast. Verlag, Berlin
Todorov T (1995) Les abus de la mémoire. Arléa, Paris
Todorov T (2001) The uses and abuses of memory. In: Marchitello H (ed) What Happens to History: The Renewal of Ethics in Contemporary Thought. Routledge, London, pp 11–39
Tourkochoriti I (2014) Should Hate Speech Be Protected? Group Defamation, Party Bans, Holocaust Denaial and the Divide Between (France) Europe and the United States. Columbia Human Rights Law Review 45:552–622
Traverso E (2006) Il Passato. Istruzioni per l'uso. Storia, memoria, politica. Ombre Corte, Verona
Triffterer O (2001) Genocide, its Particular Intent to Destroy in Whole or in Part the Group as Such. Leiden Journal of International Law 14:399–408
Triffterer O, Ambos K (eds) (2016) Commentary on the Rome Statute of the International Criminal Court. Observer's Notes, Article by Article. C.H. Beck/Hart/Nomos, Munich/Oxford
Vassalli G, Sabatini G (1947) Il collaborazionismo e l'amnistia politica nella giurisprudenza della Corte di Cassazione. La Giustizia penale, Rome
Vercelli C (2013) Il Negazionismo: Storia di una menzogna. Laterza, Rome/Bari
Veyrat-Masson I, Blanchard P (eds) (2008) Les guerres de mémoires. La France et son histoire. La Decouverte, Paris
Vidal-Naquet P (1981) Assassins of Memory: Essays on the Denial of the Holocaust. Columbia University Press, New York
Vidal-Naquet P (1995) Les Assassins de la Mémoire. «Un Eichmann de Papier» et autres essais sur le révisionnisme. Seuil, Paris
Viganò F (2011) L'arbitrio del non punire. Sugli obblighi di tutela penale dei diritti fondamentali. In: Studi in onore di Mario Romano. Vol. IV. Jovene, Naples, pp 2645–2704
Visconti C (2008) Aspetti penalistici del discorso pubblico. Giappichelli, Turin
Visconti C (2009) Il reato di propaganda razzista tra dignità umana e libertà di espressione. Ius17@unibo.it 1:191–213
Villa-Vicencio C, Doxtader E (eds) (2003) The Provocations of Amnesty. Africa World Press, Trenton-Asmara
Vormbaum T, Bohlander M (eds) (2014) A Modern History of German Criminal Law. Springer, Berlin
Wandres T (2000) Die Strafbarkeit des Auschwitz-Leugnens. Duncker & Humblot, Berlin

Wandres T (2008) Expanding Holocaust Denial and Legislation Against It. Online: http://jcpa.org/article/expanding-holocaust-denial-and-legislation-against-it/. Accessed 27 September 2017

Wartanian R (2008) Memory Laws in France and their Implications: Institutionalizing Social Harmony. http://www.humanityinaction.org/knowledgebase/117-memory-laws-in-france-and-their-implications-institutionalizing-social-harmony. Accessed 13 August 2017

Werle G (1992) Der Holocaust als Gegenstand der bundesdeutschen Strafjustiz. Neue Juristische Wochenschrift 2530–2548

Werle G (2006) (ed) Justice in Transition - Prosecution and Amnesty in Germany and South Africa. Berliner Wissenschafts, Berlin

Werle G, Jessberger F (2014) Principles of International Criminal Law. Oxford University Press, Oxford

Wilson RA (2011) Writing History in International Criminal Trials. Cambridge University Press, Cambridge

Woller H (1996) Die Abrechnung mit dem Faschismus in Italien, 1943–1948. Oldenbourg, Munich

Yerushalmi YH (1988) Réflexions sur l'oubli. In: Yerushalmi YH, Loraux N, Mommsen H, Milner JR, Vattimo G (eds) Les usages de l'oubli. Seuil, Paris, pp 7–28

Zabel B (2010) Soll das Strafrecht Erinnerungen schützen? Zeitschrift für die Gesamte Strafrechtswissenschaft 122:834–853

Zimmerman JC (2000) Holocaust Denial: Demographics, Testimonies, and Ideologies. University Press of America, Maryland

Chapter 2
The Crime of Historical Denialism and International Law

Contents

Abstract This chapter focuses on the evolution of historical denialism as a criminal offence and, more specifically, on the migration of the offence from the domestic to the international level. This bottom-up movement culminated with the adoption of the EU Framework Decision, which established a duty to criminalise denialist statements upon member states. The Framework Decision contributes to shaping the criminal offence by, on the one hand, prescribing that it applies not only to Holocaust denial but also to the negation of other international crimes and, on the other hand, by introducing limitations in order to safeguard free speech. This panorama is further enriched by the provisions of the ECHR system and the case law of its Court.

Keywords EU Framework decision · international crimes · obligation to criminalise · clauses limiting punishment · European Court of Human Rights

2.1 The International Obligation to Criminalise Historical Denialism

International sources are particularly important for understanding the dynamics of criminalisation and the expansion of historical denialism as a crime.

Indeed, the crime of historical denialism is now provided for not only in national law but also in EU and international law. In addition, we are assisting to a shift from the criminalisation of Holocaust denial only to the penalisation of the denial or

E. Fronza, *Memory and Punishment*, International Criminal Justice Series 19,
https://doi.org/10.1007/978-94-6265-234-7_2

trivialisation of genocides and other mass atrocities, consequently expanding the protected mnemonic framework. The offence is no longer confined to the European experience but is incorporated within the universal system of human rights. Thus, the list of crimes whose denial may be punished as historical denialism is in expansion, the geographical and chronological dimension is broadened and the criminal offence is no longer historically limited to European history, Nazism and World War II.

Extending protection to all international crimes has made criminalising historical denialist claims even more complex. All the conflicts that make it difficult to use criminal law for this phenomenon emerge more distinctly: the conflict between remembering and forgetting, between punishing and pardoning, and between universal and relative.

This tension emerges from the evolution of the offence of historical denialism.

The paradigm of 'original' historical denialism stemmed from a bottom-up process that hinged on a specific, unique and historically defined event: the Holocaust. In contrast, 'broadened' historical denialism emerged from a top-down process whereby the universal category of human rights—which also constitutes a fundamental tenet of the European Union—serves as the selection criteria for the protection of the memory of serious crimes. Thus, human rights give substance to a universal ethical pact that the offence of 'broadened' denialism safeguards. Consequently, historical denialism is no longer confined to the dramatic, yet delimited, experience of WWII, but ascends to a global level by protecting the memory of events with no specific geographical or temporal ties. Historical denialism no longer protects a specific community who, with reference to a specific past event, has declared 'never again'. Rather, it protects a collective public memory founded on universal values which, in turn, are globally legitimised through their incorporation in the European and international legal system. In other words, historical denialism protects a foundational set of values characterised by abstraction, universality and specificity.

This process also influences the progressive development of the criminal offence which, on the one hand, transitions from protecting the memory of the Holocaust to safeguarding the memory of all international crimes and, on the other hand, is now provided for not only in domestic but also in international legal sources. However, as we shall see later on, expanding the scope of protection has an unforeseen effect when implemented at the domestic level. It adapts to the particularities of each national experience, memory, and historical heritage, thus highlighting the plurality of these phenomena. Hence, global efforts to preserve a collective memory founded on human rights (universal level) clash with the specificities of each domestic historical memory (relative level).

The tension between universal and relative becomes even more apparent at the international level as demonstrated by the group of general and specific provisions adopted internationally and regionally for combating racism and historical denialism.

National responses to historical denialism have been incorporated within a comprehensive body of international law and soft law intended to counter the spread of racist phenomena.

Before examining the EU Framework Decision on 'combating certain forms and expressions of racism and xenophobia by means of criminal law', it is therefore appropriate to briefly analyse the international law framework regarding historical denialism. Here it is not possible to analyse or even mention all the legal provisions under international law that have been established to counteract the various forms of racial discrimination and possible abuses of freedom of expression related to this offence. However, it should be noted that, despite their diversity, international law provisions are a point of reference both for legislation and for case law on the punishment of historical denialism at the domestic and regional level. Furthermore, this analysis also confirms how international law—and not only European Union law—establishes an obligation for member states to criminalise historical denialism.

2.1.1 International Level

Under international law, there are many provisions that, on the one hand, affirm the fundamental right to freedom of expression and, on the other hand, prohibit any form of discrimination, above all racist propaganda, thus permitting restrictions of the former right in some cases and under certain circumstances.[1]

An overview of the existing international instruments related to historical denialism should begin with the Universal Declaration of Human Rights. Proclaimed by the United Nations General Assembly in Paris on 10 December 1948,[2] it envisages freedom of opinion and expressions for every individual at Article 19.[3] The Declaration, however, also establishes restrictions to guarantee acknowledgement of and respect for the rights and freedoms of others, in addition to defining the requirements for morality, public order and general welfare in a democratic society based on the principles of equality and non-discrimination (Article 29).

Likewise, the International Covenant on Civil and Political Rights (ICCPR) of the United Nations of 1966[4] protects freedom of expression[5] in Article 19, paras 1

---

[1] See UN General Assembly, 21 December 1965, *International Convention on the Elimination of All Forms of Racial Discrimination*, UN Doc. A/RES/2106(XX); Articles 19 and 20 of UN General Assembly, 16 September 1966, *International Covenant on Civil and Political Rights*, UN Doc. A/RES/2200(XXI). For an overview on responses at an international level, see Behrens et al. 2017, p. 227 et seq.; Della Morte 2014; Hare and Weinstein 2011, p. 380 et seq.; Cooper Williams 1999, pp. 593–613; on approaches to these statements by international adjudicators, see Oster 2015, p. 230 et seq.

[2] UN General Assembly, 10 December 1948, *Universal Declaration of Human Rights*, UN. Doc. A/RES/3/217 A.

[3] Article 19: 'Everyone has the right to freedom of opinion and expression; this right includes freedom to hold opinions without interference and to seek, receive and impart information and ideas through any media and regardless of frontiers'.

[4] UN General Assembly, 16 September 1966, UN. Doc. A/RES/2200(XXI) (above n 1).

[5] Article 19: '1. Everyone shall have the right to hold opinions without interference. 2. Everyone shall have the right to freedom of expression; this right shall include freedom to seek, receive and impart information and ideas of all kinds, regardless of frontiers, either orally, in writing or in print, in the form of art, or through any other media of his choice'.

and 2, but also provides restrictions expressly established and deemed necessary to ensure the respect of the rights or reputation of others[6] as well as the protection of national security, public order, public health and public morality (Article 19, para 3). The subsequent provision prohibits propaganda promoting war (Article 20, para 1) and incitement to national, racial or religious hatred that constitutes incitement to discrimination, hostility or violence (Article 20, para 2).

The International Convention on the Elimination of All Forms of Racial Discrimination of the United Nations of 21 December 1965[7] promotes non-discrimination by providing special and concrete measures against incitement to, or acts of, such discrimination and dissemination of ideas based on racial superiority or hatred.[8]

Also highly relevant is the guidance provided by the UN Human Rights Committee, which is a quasi-judicial body of independent experts that monitors the implementation of the International Covenant on Civil and Political Rights by its State parties. In addition to ruling on historical denialism in the *Faurisson v. France* case,[9] this Committee has stated that public denial of facts that amount to

---

[6] See Human Rights Committee, 2 January 1993, *Robert Faurisson v. France, Communication No. 550/1993*, UN. Doc. CCPR/C/58/D/550/1993(1996), which states that not only are legitimate restrictions on freedom of expression provided in order to protect the reputation of others, but that denialist phenomena constitute one of the main vectors of anti-Semitism.

[7] UN General Assembly, 21 December 1965, *International Convention on the Elimination of All Forms of Racial Discrimination*, UN Doc. A/RES/2106(XX).

[8] Article 4: 'States Parties [...] (a) Shall declare an offence punishable by law all dissemination of ideas based on racial superiority or hatred, incitement to racial discrimination, as well as all acts of violence or incitement to such acts against any race or group of persons of another color or ethnic origin, and also the provision of any assistance to racist activities, including the financing thereof'. This provision is an example of the penalisation impulses originating in international law. In the case of Italy, it is interesting to note that the law implementing the Convention also contains the aggravating circumstance of historical denialism in accordance with the obligations imposed by European law, see Law no. 654 on the Ratification and Execution of the International Convention on the Elimination of Forms of Racial Discrimination, opened for signature in New York on 7 March 1966, 13 October 1975, as last amended by Law no. 115 of 16 June 2016; see Pavich and Bonomi 2014.

[9] Robert Faurisson is a Franco-British former academic and one of the most famous Holocaust deniers. In December 1978 and January 1979, Faurisson, at that time professor of Literature at the University of Lyon, published two letters in *Le Monde* claiming that the gas chambers never existed. Those led first of all to an academic controversy (the so-called '*Faurisson* case'). The controversy involved also Noam Chomsky (in defence of Faurisson's freedom of speech) and Pierre Vidal-Naquet (as one of the main opponents). The social pressure against his statements led to the introduction of the crime of denialism in France in 1990. Shortly after that, he was interviewed by the French monthly magazine '*Le Choc du Mois*'. In the interview, he reiterated his personal conviction that there were no homicidal gas chambers for the extermination of Jews in Nazi concentration camps. Following the publication of this interview, eleven associations of French resistance fighters and of deportees to German concentration camps filed a private criminal action against Faurisson, who was found guilty in 1991, in application of the new criminal offence. In 1992, the Court of Appeal of Paris (Eleventh Chamber) upheld the conviction. In his communication to the Human Rights Committee, Faurisson contended that the '*Gayssot Act*' curtailed his right to freedom of expression and academic freedom in general, and considered that the law

international crimes must be subject to criminal prosecution only if they constitute incitement to violence and racial hatred.[10] Therefore, it can be stated with confidence that, in the absence of these ulterior elements, historical discourse, all the more so if revisionist or controversial, cannot be subject to restriction or punishment.[11]

The list of international instruments is still very long. Among these, it is worth mentioning the United Nations Charter signed in San Francisco in 1945; the Convention on the Prevention and Punishment of the Crime of Genocide of 1948, which punishes direct and public incitement to commit genocide (Article III, letter c); the International Covenant on Civil and Political Rights (Article 20, para 2); the Convention on the Suppression and Punishment of the Crime of Apartheid of 1973;[12] the Convention on the Elimination of All Forms of Discrimination against Women of 1979 and in other several statements and various documents issued by specialised UN agencies, such as UNESCO and UNICEF, or by the ILO.

This legislation is symptomatic of an international tendency that permits limitations of freedom of speech as a response to denialist claims. An undisputable fact emerges from this brief analysis, namely the incompatibility of the right to freedom of expression with the criminal repression of public discourse about historical events and historical research, even when they appear false, incorrect or misleading. Due to this ever-present conflict, there is no endorsement of criminal repression within international sources or the obligation to provide criminal protection against denialist discourse in general, unless it is likely to cause incitement. Quoting the words of the UN Human Rights Committee regarding the *Faurisson* case, 'general prohibition of expressions of an erroneous opinion or an incorrect interpretation of past events'[13] is not permitted.

2.1.2 EU Level

The European regional context and its dual system comprised of the European Union and the Council of Europe, with the Strasbourg Court in the foreground, are

targeted him personally. *Robert Faurisson v. France, Communication No. 550/1993*, U.N. Doc. CCPR/C/58/D/550/1993(1996); see Gliszczyńska-Grabias, p. 254 et seq.; Tracol 1997. For a comprehensive study, see Igounet 2012.

[10] On the relationship between the position of the UN Human Rights Committee and the UN Committee on the Elimination of Racial Discrimination, see Temperman 2014, pp. 158–161. On the position of the UN Human Rights Committee, see Kučs 2014, pp. 303–308. On the position of the UN CERD as regards Holocaust denial, see Thornberry 2016, pp. 292 and 928.

[11] UN Committee on the Elimination of Racial Discrimination, 26 September 2013, *General Recommendation n. 35 on Combating Racist Hate Speech*, UN Doc. CERD/C/GC/35, para 14.

[12] See Eden 2014, pp. 171–191; Burz 2013, pp. 205–233; Booysen 1976, p. 56.

[13] Human Rights Committee, 12 September 2011, *General Comment no. 34 concerning Article 19 of the Covenant on Civil and Political Rights*, UN Doc. CCPR/C/G34, para 49.

a fundamental component of the evolution of historical denialism as a criminal offence. In fact, both prove the existence of a trend of employing punishment to counteract this phenomenon.[14]

As part of a more general effort to counter racism and xenophobia, the first specific initiative of the European Union regarding the denialist phenomenon and criminal prosecution dates back to 1996. On 15 July 1996, the Council of the European Union adopted a *Joint action* to combat racism and xenophobia.[15] This instrument recommends that member states punish as a criminal offence the public denial of the crimes contained in Article 6 of the Nuremberg Statute (Title 1(A)(a)).

As early as 2001, the Commission began negotiations for the formulation of a Framework Decision to respond to racism and xenophobia with criminal law.[16] In the proposal put forth on 29 November 2001,[17] the Commission introduced a crime of original historical denialism, punishing only the denial of acts included in the Nuremberg Statute when such conduct is likely to disturb public peace (Article 4, letter D). As will be shortly discussed, instead, the EU Framework Decision of 2008 enshrines a 'broader' crime of historical denialism. The expansion of the punishable conducts is balanced by optional clauses that member states may introduce to limit the application of criminal law, and that are inspired by the protection of freedom of speech and scientific research. This also explains the seven years of intense negotiations before the Framework Decision 2008/913/JHA was unanimously adopted.

2.1.3 The 2008 Framework Decision

The EU Framework Decision[18] marks both the transition from a purely national to a pan-European criminalisation of historical denialism and a paradigm shift to a

[14] See UN General Assembly, 1 November 2005, *Resolution on the Holocaust Remembrance,* UN Doc. A/RES/60/7 and UN General Assembly, 26 January 2007, *Resolution on Holocaust Denial*, UN Doc. A/RES/61/255. For a more in-depth account, see Della Morte 2014, p. 1181 et seq.

[15] Council of the European Union, 15 July 1996, *Joint Action of 15 July 1996 adopted by the Council on the basis of Article K.3 of the Treaty on European Union, concerning action to combat racism and xenophobia*, 96/443/JHA, in *Official Journal of the European Union*, L 185/5. Dominic McGoldrick and Therese O'Donnell, 'Hate-speech laws: consistency with national and international human rights law' (2006) 18(4) *Legal Studies* 453–485, 464–465.

[16] See Pech 2011, p. 226.

[17] Council of the European Union, 26 March 2002, *Proposal for a Council Framework Decision on combating racism and xenophobia*, in *Official Journal of the European Communities*, COM (2001)/664, C 75 E/269.

[18] Council of the European Union, 28 November 2008, *Council Framework Decision on combating certain forms and expressions of racism and xenophobia by means of criminal law*, 2008/913/JHA, in *Official Journal of the European Union* L 328/55, 6 December 2008.

'broader' form of historical denialism already adopted by some national legal systems.[19]

The importance of the EU Framework Decision is highlighted by the many legal and political aspects intertwined therein. It unequivocally establishes a turning point and distinguishes a 'before' and an 'after' by proposing a potentially more unifying paradigm, here defined as the 'broader' form of historical denialism.

There was a long debate leading up to the EU Framework Decision guided by an ambition to represent the core values of the European Union, its roots in human rights and its determination to defend them.

Of equal importance are the difficulties encountered prior to the Decision, that is the plethora of differences concerning historical narratives among the diverse national legislations and the autonomy given to domestic legal systems by the measure, an indicator of significant variations in the perspectives of Member States regarding these issues.[20] These variations were already evident in the expansion of the broadened paradigm, and continue to evolve through the multiplication of offences of historical denialism on a national scale.

The Framework Decision represents the common European core for the criminalisation of historical denialism, which the States are required to implement. In other words, the European Union calls on its Member States to employ criminal law to combat historical denialism.[21]

The EU Framework Decision played a key role in the process of criminalisation of denialism. The way in which it characterises the offence led to a second phase of the criminalisation of denialism and influenced the adoption and characterisation of the criminal offence at the national level after 2008. During the first phase, before the adoption of the Framework Decision, the 'original' form of denialism was predominant: only five states adopted this paradigm, characterised by the punishment of

---

[19] Before the adoption of the EU Framework Decision, the following countries punished denialism in its broader sense: Poland (Article 55 Act on the Institute of National Remembrance - Commission for the Prosecution of Crimes against the Polish Nation), Portugal (Article 240 Criminal Code), Romania (Emergency Ordinance of 13 March 2002), Slovakia (Article 422-d Criminal Code), Spain (Article 607 Criminal Code; now Article 510 Criminal Code).

[20] Harmonization of criminal law is achieved by providing room, or margin, to the member States, which in turns allows them to adopt national laws which are not identical but achieve the purposes set by the European normative acts. On the concept of national margin of appreciation, introduced by the ECtHR as a pillar of the European legal system, see Delmas-Marty 2005, pp. 64–74; Delmas-Marty 2006, pp. 96–97 and 273–274; Delmas-Marty 2004. On the margin of appreciation as "outil indispensable" for a global legal order and in order to avoid a relativisme, see Delmas-Marty 2011.

[21] See Lobba 2017, pp. 189–210; Cajani 2017; Behrens et al. 2017, p. 227 et seq.; for further references, see Ambos 2017, p. 380, footnote 133; Gorton 2015, pp. 421–445; Lobba 2014, p. 58 et seq.; Turner 2012, pp. 555–583; Yakis 2011, pp. 63–92; Renauld 2010, pp. 119–140; Weiler 2009, p. 77; Knechtle 2008, pp. 41–65; Turner 2012, pp. 555–583; Weiler 2009. See also Ash 2007, and the critical remarks on the FD of the American Historical Association, *Statement on the Framework Decision of the Council of the European Union on the Fight against Racism and Xenophobia*, in 'Perspectives', 45 (8) (2007).

Holocaust denial (Austria, Belgium, France, Germany and Romania),[22] and four other nations opted for a 'broader' model (Poland, Portugal, Slovakia and Spain).[23] However, after 2008 we can see a clear predominance of the broader approach in all the 12 states that introduced an offence of denialism that does not limit punishable acts to the denial of the Holocaust but extends it to other international crimes (Bulgaria, Croatia, Cyprus, the Czech Republic, Greece, Hungary, Latvia, Lithuania, Luxembourg, Malta, Slovenia and Italy).[24]

In this phase, the heterogeneity of national laws is more evident in terms of the scope of protection and the composition of collective memory within each country. The effect is almost paradoxical. A provision that is part of a general strategy of building a common European identity by creating a collective memory with a shared meaning[25] ends up prompting vastly different approaches in each country, thus demonstrating that a shared collective memory does not exist.

The preamble to the EU Framework Decision describes the reasons for its adoption. Paragraph 1 states that racism and xenophobia are direct violations of the principles of liberty, democracy, respect for human rights and fundamental freedoms, and the rule of law, principles upon which the European Union is founded and which are common to the Member States. Although the Council is aware that a full harmonisation of criminal laws is currently not possible given the different cultural and legal traditions among Member States, particularly in this field, Article 1 provides for various offences concerning racism and xenophobia.

[22] Austria (Article 3h National Socialism Prohibition Act of 1947), Belgium (Law tending to repress negation, minimisation, justification or approbation of the genocide committed by the German National-Socialist regime during the Second World War, 23 March 1995), France (Article 24a of the Freedom of the Press Act, 19 July 1881), Germany (Article 130(3) Criminal Code) and Romania (Emergency Ordinance of 13 March 2002).

[23] Poland (Article 55 Act on the Institute of National Remembrance - Commission for the Prosecution of Crimes against the Polish Nation, 18 December 1998), Portugal (Article 240 Criminal Code), Slovakia (Article 422-d Criminal Code) and Spain (Article 607(2) Criminal Code).

[24] See European Commission, 27 January 2014, *Report from the Commission to the European Parliament and the Council on the implementation of Council Framework Decision 2008/913/JHA on combating certain forms and expressions of racism and xenophobia by means of criminal law*, COM(2014) 27.

[25] European enlargement should include the expansion of public knowledge of the past. Western Europeans should accept the legacy of both Nazism and Communism in Europe. For this reason a common European narrative should include both the Holocaust and the communist traumas. With reference to the attention given at the European level to the construction of a European 'common memory', see European Parliament, 23 September 2008, *Declaration of the European Parliament on the proclamation of 23 August as European Day of Remembrance for Victims of Stalinism and Nazism*, P6_TA (2008)0439 and European Parliament, 2 April 2009, *European Parliament resolution on European conscience and totalitarianism,* P6_TA (2009)0213. See also the website of the 'Platform of European Memory and Conscience'; this is a project established in 2011, which represents a part of a bigger project of the European Union related to the reconciliation of European violent pasts. See Baldissarra 2016; Cajani 2008. Concerning the EU initiatives establishing a duty to criminalise in the name of the protection of his ethical identity, see the remarks of Paliero 2016.

Under this provision, each Member State shall take the measures necessary to ensure that the following intentional conduct is punishable:

> publicly condoning, denying or grossly trivialising crimes of genocide, crimes against humanity and war crimes as defined in Articles 6, 7 and 8 of the Statute of the International Criminal Court, directed against a group of persons or a member of such group defined by reference to race, colour, religion, descent or national or ethnic origin when the conduct is carried out in a manner likely to incite to violence or hatred against such a group or a member of such group (Article 1 let. c);
>
> publicly condoning, denying or grossly trivialising the crimes defined in Article 6 of the Charter of the International Military Tribunal appended to the London Agreement of 8 August 1945, directed against a group of persons or a member of such group defined by reference to race, colour, religion, descent or national or ethnic origin when the conduct is carried out in a manner likely to incite to violence or hatred against such a group or a member of such group (Article 1 let. d).

2.1.3.1 The Mandatory Clause Limiting Punishment

A common provision, as per *letter* (c) and (d) of Article 1 of the Decision, establishes that condoning, denying or grossly trivialising crimes of genocide, crimes against humanity war crimes as defined in Articles 6, 7 and 8 of the Statute of the International Criminal Court is punishable if carried out in a manner likely to incite violence or hatred against such a group or a member of such a group.

This element tends to restrict the scope of applicability of the crime: denialist statements are not punished *per se* but only insofar as they harm a protected interest.

As in other cases of criminalisation of speech, the punishability of certain acts based on their propensity to incite violence or hatred may result in the lack of a material act against which to measure the actual effect of incitement, resulting from the expressed statement (in particular with reference to 'hatred'). However, as noted, propensity to incite must be given substance when dealing with denialist assertions, and it is often very difficult to provide evidence of concrete harm. Present in various legal systems, this element proves to be particularly important because it is a key factor in distinguishing between licit and illicit statements. To date, four States explicitly provide that propensity to instigate is an essential constitutive element of the offence: Spain (Article 510 Criminal Code), Croatia (Article 325 of the Criminal Code), Greece (Article 2 of the Law no. 4285, 4 September 2014) and Malta (Article 82b of the Criminal Code). However, Bulgaria makes reference to a 'risk that the conduct generates violence or discriminatory hatred' (Article 419a Criminal Code). Finally, Portugal provides a requirement related to the *mens rea* of the agent, requiring the willingness on the part of the perpetrator to incite or encourage hatred and discrimination (Article 240 Criminal Code).

2.1.3.2 Optional Clauses Limiting Punishment

In addition to the propensity to incite violence, Article 1(2) and (4) of the EU Framework Decision introduce two additional optional elements that Member States may adopt.

In order to remedy the restriction of freedom inherent in every speech crime, and similar to what has already been experimented in Germany with the 'Auschwitz lie' (*Auschwitzlüge*) offence, the first of these elements stipulates that Member States may choose to punish only acts which are either carried out in a manner likely to disturb public order or which are threatening, abusive or insulting (Article 1, (2)).

Therefore, in the interaction between the European Union and Member States regarding the identification of punishable acts, the concept of *public order* becomes a crucial element, and each state enjoys a considerable degree of discretion in its definition. To date, five states incorporate provisions related to historical denialism within penal legislation protecting public order. These states are Croatia (Article 325 Criminal Code), Germany (Article 130 Criminal Code), Hungary (Article 333 Criminal Code), Malta (Article 82B Criminal Code) and Slovenia (Article 297 Criminal Code). Given the numerous optional elements, the introduction of this concept confirms that the European Union creates an offence that is implemented in different ways at the national level. As a further consequence, opinions about certain historical events may indeed be criminally punishable in one country but not in another.

Other concerns also re-emerge related to the concept of public order not defined by the EU Framework Decision, which leads to a broader question: which interest —among historical memory, public order and human dignity of the victims—does the offence of historical denialism protect?

2.1.3.3 Res judicata

The second optional element intended to limit an expansion of the offence pertains to *res judicata*.

According to Article 1, para 4 of the Framework Decision

> Any Member State may, on adoption of this Framework Decision or later, make a statement that it will make punishable the act of denying or grossly trivializing the crimes referred to in paragraph 1(c) and/or (d) only if the crimes referred to in these paragraphs have been established by a final decision of a national court of this Member State and/or an international court, or by a final decision of an international court only.

If adopted at the national level, this variable would restrict punishment to crimes ruled as such by national courts of the Member State and/or an international court in a final way. However, it is important to note that this applies to denial and gross trivialisation but not condoning.

All these optional elements, along with the adoption of a broadened approach to the crime, are the litmus test of the transformative dynamics established by the Framework Decision. The judge continues to dominate the narrative, both when defining the historical fact and when legally qualifying it. Starting from the assessment of the crimes mentioned above, the judge also becomes the one who selects the collective memories to be protected by punishment.

Ascertaining the existence of a court decision regarding the historical fact becomes—or rather could become—an element of the criminal offence if the denialist statement is made by a member state. To date, the states that provide such a requirement are Cyprus,[26] Greece,[27] Luxembourg[28] and France.[29] However, the French legal system requires that the crimes being denied have resulted in a conviction by a French or international court.

Penalising only those crimes established in a *res judicata* by national and/or international courts (with no further distinctions between the various bodies) and opting for a formal establishment of collective memory implies that historical collective memory coincides with judicial memory, with all the problems this entails. In this way, as already observed, a fact may well be considered a crime in one country but not in another.[30] We may consider, for example, the facts related to genocide, not defined and not legally qualified as such by a criminal trial: this would be enough to render the speech criminally irrelevant. Such an element thus creates the risk of establishing a hierarchy of collective historical memories and denialisms.

These observations become very relevant with respect to the context in which the provision is to be enforced, characterised by a plurality of historical and mnemonic legacies and in which the phenomenon of competing memories is powerfully present. They show again how the tension between universal and relative increases when international laws criminalise historical denialism, and this tension demonstrates the existence of multiple memories and truths.

---

[26] Law no. 134(I) on combating against certain forms of racism and xenophobia by means of criminal law, 21 October 2011, which requires the prior final ruling of an international tribunal.

[27] Law no. 4285, 4 September 2014, which requires the prior investigation of crimes by an international court.

[28] Article 457-3 Criminal Code, which requires that the crimes be ascertained by a Luxembourg or international court.

[29] Article 24a Freedom of the Press Act, 29 July 1881.

[30] Cajani 2011, pp. 28–29.

2.1.4 European Convention of Human Rights

The phenomenon of historical denialism is included in various acts of the Council of Europe.[31] Among these is the Additional Protocol to the Convention on Cybercrime, which provides in Article 6 that:

> each Party shall adopt such legislative measures as may be necessary to establish the following conduct as criminal offences under its domestic law, when committed intentionally and without right: distributing or otherwise making available, through a computer system to the public, material which denies, grossly minimises, approves or justifies acts constituting genocide or crimes against humanity, as defined by international law and recognised as such by final and binding decisions of the International Military Tribunal, established by the London Agreement of 8 August 1945, or of any other international court established by relevant international instruments and whose jurisdiction is recognised by that Party.[32]

At the European level, another important landmark for the criminalisation of historical denialism is the European Convention on Human Rights and Fundamental Freedoms (ECHR) and the attached European Court of Human Rights (ECtHR), which ensures compliance with the rights and freedoms protected by the Convention.

ECHR-related litigation concerning domestic restrictions on Holocaust denial has produced 30 years of decisions by the ECtHR and European Commission of Human Rights.[33] The Court has highlighted the importance of combating historical denialist statements by making use of criminal law. These judgments shed light on the complexity of the offence of historical denialism *tout court* and also contain argumentative structures and balancing patterns that play a significant role in the solutions of other cases in other jurisdictions.

Often requested to rule on the compatibility of the offence of historical denialism with the right to freedom of expression, the Court frames the phenomenon in question within the broader category of 'hate speech'.[34] This reaffirms the

---

[31] Council of Europe Parliamentary Assembly, 20 April 2016, '*Renewed commitment in the fight against antisemitism in Europe*', Resolution 2106 (2016); European Commission against Racism and Intolerance, 25 June 2004, '*The fight against antisemitism*', General Policy Recommendation No. 9 (2004); Council of Europe Committee of Ministers, 31 October 2001, '*Recommendation Rec (2001)15 of the Committee of Ministers to member states on history teaching in twenty-first-century Europe*'.

[32] COE, 28 January 2003, *Additional Protocol to the Convention on Cybercrime, concerning the criminalization of acts of a racist and xenophobic nature committed through computer systems*, in *European Treaty Series no. 189.*

[33] See Lobba 2015, pp. 237–253.

[34] Several ECtHR judgments frame Holocaust denial as an hate speech crime, see ECtHR, *Witzsch v. Germany*, Judgment, 13 December 2005, Application n. 7485/03; ECtHR, *Garaudy v. France*, Judgment, 24 June 2003, Application n. 65831/01; ECtHR, *Lehideux and Isorni v. France* (Grand Chamber), Judgment, 23 September 1998, Application n. 24662/94; ECtHR, *Kuhnen v. Federal Republic of Germany*, Judgment, 12 May 1988, Application n. 12194/86; ECtHR, *Lowes v. United Kingdom*, Judgment, 9 December 1988, Application n. 13214/87. ECtHR, *Perinçek v. Switzerland*

seriousness of historical denialist statements and permits recourse to criminal law as a means of countering them.

The provisions used by the ECtHR in historical denialism cases are also extremely relevant for this study. They provide insight into exceptions to fundamental rights and their limits. Moreover, they help to identify the legal instruments capable of restraining, containing, limiting or controlling the choices—including those regarding criminal law—made by national legal systems, if they violate ECHR provisions.

In adjudicating alleged violations of free speech by national states, the Strasbourg Court has applied two provisions of the Convention. The first is Article 10, para 2, entitled *Freedom of Expression.*[35]

According to this Article

> 'the exercise of freedoms enshrined in the treaty may be subject to such formalities, conditions, restrictions or penalties as prescribed by law and must be necessary in a democratic society, in the interests of national security, territorial integrity or public safety, for the prevention of disorder or crime, for the protection of health or morals, for the protection of the reputation or rights of others, for preventing the disclosure of information received in confidence, or for maintaining the authority and impartiality of the judiciary'.

It sets forth a balancing test. In this way, the Strasbourg system allows member states a measure of discretion. The national margin of appreciation[36] granted to states is an example of this discretion. On the one hand, the conflict between the ECtHR's margin of appreciation doctrine and the European judicial review is an expression of the tension between the demands for pluralism and variety and, on the other hand, a response to calls for a common European legal order and for the nation state to grant power to regional institutions.

Historical denialist conducts also trigger the application of Article 17 of the ECHR, entitled *Prohibition of Abuse of Rights*, according to which no provision contained in the Convention may be interpreted as requiring any state, group or individual to engage in any activity or perform any act aimed at the destruction of

(Grand Chamber), Judgment, 15 October 2015, Application n. 27510/08, (see also Chap. 3). See Caruso 2011; Caruso 2017; Gliszczyńska-Grabias 2013; Lobba 2015; Lobba 2016; Buratti 2012, p. 3; Kiska 2012; Bilbao Ubillos 2008, p. 19 et seq.

[35] On this provision, see Schabas 2015, pp. 444–482; Grabenwarter 2014, pp. 251–296; Bartole et al. 2012.

[36] See ECtHR, *Affaire "relative à certains aspects du régime linguistique de l'enseignement en Belgique"*, 23 July 1968, para 10 and ECtHR, *De Wilde, Ooms e Versyp ('Vagrancy') v. Belgium*, Judgment, 18 June 1971, Application nn. 2832/66, 2835/66 and 2899/66, para 93; ECtHR, *Ireland v. UK*, Judgment, 18 January 1978, Application n. 5310/71, para 207. See, for a more in-depth analysis, see Saul 2015, pp. 745–774; Barbosa Delgado 2012; Letsas 2007; Tulkens and Donnay 2006, pp. 3–24; Mathieu-Izorche 2006, p. 25; Greer 2006; Sweeney 2005, pp. 459–474; Delmas-Marty and Mathieu-Izorche 2000, pp. 753–780. Consider also Mireille Delmas-Marty's key work on this technique within the internationalization of law as a tool which contributes to a pluralistic order (and to a diversity of legal systems) and to a common legal order, Delmas-Marty 2006.

the recognised rights and freedoms, or to impose on such rights and freedoms broader restrictions than those established by the Convention.[37]

Within the ECtHR case law on the offence of historical denialism, it is possible to identify distinct phases in which Article 10 or Article 17 would apply.[38]

The first phase coincides with the recourse to the general principles of freedom of expression as governed by Article 10. Once it is accepted that free speech is not an absolute right, the Court applies the so-called balancing test in order to verify whether the restrictions are really necessary in a democratic society. This means that the analysis of the factual circumstances is both formal, because it is intended to verify the legality of the restriction, and above all substantial, because it is carried out to verify the correspondence of the restriction with the objectives of protection pursued by a democratic state (necessity and proportionality).

In addition, the application of Article 10 places the burden of proof on the state deemed to have violated the Convention, which means that the state is responsible for demonstrating that the measures taken comply with the requirements provided by law.

Article 17 clause on the abuse of rights does not play a significant role in this first phase. In fact, the Commission stated in *Lowes v. United Kingdom* that only racist conduct—and not even that which is anti-Semitic, as in this case—may justify recourse to Article 17, ECHR.[39]

The second phase is characterised by a greater importance attributed to Article 17 ECHR, which acts as an interpretive aid in addition to Article 10 ECHR.[40] If the balancing test between rights and restrictions provided for in Article 10 ECHR still complies with the criteria (and method) for adjudicating such violations, Article 17 ECHR becomes much more significant. It now means that not only an act aimed at the destruction of the recognised rights and freedoms can be characterised as abusive, but also one that is in contrast with the fundamental values expressed in the Convention.

This change of perspective is significant. There is no longer a referral to the concept of 'destruction' of recognised rights and freedoms. Instead the scope is expanded to include behaviour that 'is contrary' to the Convention. Appealing to the 'spirit' of the Convention risks classifying different activities as abusive and all unified by a single idea (for example, Nazi ideology and anti-Semitism) without verifying—as required by Article 10 ECHR—if, on a case by case basis, their restriction is in conflict with free speech.

[37] On this provision, see Schabas 2015, pp. 611–622; Bartole et al. 2012.

[38] Lobba 2015, pp. 240–243.

[39] ECtHR, *Lowes v. United Kingdom* (above n 36). For criticism of the non-application of the clause provided by Article 17, see van Drooghenbroeck 2001, pp. 552–553.

[40] ECtHR, *Kuhnen v. Federal Republic of Germany* (above n 36). See Lobba 2015, p. 240.

Within the third and final phase, there is a veritable monopoly of Article 17 ECHR over Article 10 ECHR. As a consequence, a series of expressions of opinion (such as historical denialism) are excluded in principle from the protection guaranteed under Article 10 ECHR.

This new approach leads to various consequences. First, there is a risk that the Court will not evaluate in detail the reasonableness, necessity and proportionality of the restriction imposed by the state, while instead automatically applying expressions within the abuse clause (Article 17). Second, resolving the case through Article 17, at the expense of Article 10, means that the state no longer bears the burden of proof regarding the restriction of freedom of expression as a necessary measure in a democratic society. The potential of this approach has been demonstrated in several subsequent cases in which the Court applied the abuse clause to deal with appeals concerning convictions for historical denialism, such as the *Garaudy*[41] and *Witzsch*[42] cases.

However, as noted, establishing punishment for historical denialism under the ECHR is not a linear path. A key role here is played by the likelihood of denialist statements to incite and concretely constitute 'hate speech'.[43] This connection is essential in the model of broadened historical denialism and is consolidated around the Holocaust with cases of original historical denialism addressed by the Court; however, after a few recent decisions this no longer appears necessary.

Similar to the German distinction between 'qualified' historical denialism (where incitement to hatred is a necessary element for punishment) and simple historical denialism (where incitement is not a necessary element), the Strasbourg Court recently recognised the possibility of denial not constituting incitement to hatred with reference to the Armenian genocide (thus outside the original scope of the Holocaust) in the *Perincek v. Switzerland* case.[44] In this case, denial is not punishable as such because it lacks the characteristics of discriminatory intent that determines the prevalence of Article 17 over Article 10.

Within a well-defined general trend, this reveals a much livelier and more confrontational dynamic than only a cursory reading of the laws would suggest, and which is well represented in the judgments of the Strasbourg Court.

---

[41] Which also references clearly established historical facts and the threat to public order. ECtHR, *Garaudy v. France* (above n 36).

[42] In which reference is made not only to denial of the Holocaust but also to other similar and significant circumstances. ECtHR, *Witzsch v. Germany*, Judgment, 13 December 2005, Application no. 7485/03.

[43] Waldron 2012; Cohen-Almagor 2009, pp. 33–42; Knechtle 2006, pp. 539–578.

[44] See Chap. 3, Sect. 3.3.

2.2 The Relationship Between Criminal Law and Memory

Providing a separate crime of historical denialism, which requires 'remembering in an established way' and punishes those who seek to remember in a different way, results in various problematic implications regardless of the various national solutions.

Some of these can be traced to the more general category of speech crimes. Others, however, are unique to the offence of historical denialism due to the extended area of intersection between law and memory. It is indeed primarily the process of forming and sharing memory as a common heritage and collective reference for the community which these laws address, in addition to holding trials and punishing 'deniers of history'. Further problems are triggered by expanding the list of crimes the memory of which cannot be questioned. This is determined in two distinct ways depending on whether the reference is to the general system of human rights or if it is to particular events of national history.

Despite their diversity in structure, these problems are shared by many legal systems which adopt the model of 'broadened' historical denialism, aimed at protecting the memory of recognised macro-violations of human rights considered as such by the Framework Decision. Similarly for the multiplication of laws protecting individual heritages of national memory, which can be viewed as new original denialisms sanctioned by law (the Ukrainian Holodomor, crimes of various communist regimes, terrorism) and are particularly evident in the countries of central and eastern Europe and South America.

First, there is an undeniable conflict between criminal law and freedom of expression, evidenced by the difficulty to identify a legal protected interest for the purpose of balancing. As a result, we dangerously move away from a criminal law approach based on the punishability of *acts* to one based on the punishability of *authors* and ways of being, and this trend is not thwarted by harm principle elements that qualify the offence as criminal (propensity to incite, threat to public order).

Second, the criminalisation of historical denialism reveals another key area of conflict between criminal law and history. Today, this tension is intensified by the provisions of the EU Framework Decision and global dynamics that favour criminal law as a foundation of the broader public policy on collective memory.

On the one hand, there is the well-known risk of transforming the judge into an arbiter of history[45] without taking into account the specific logic of the two spheres. This transformation under the wide approach can fuel conflicts of identity.

On the other hand, there is a public 'will of memory'[46] that identifies criminal law and criminal trial as the *medium* connecting past, present and future. It can imply risks even within the criminal trial, influencing the development of the trial in the name of a purpose—the establishment of foundational events. This is indeed

[45] Ginzburg 1991, p. 108 et seq.

[46] In the sense of securing the memory that is needed, see Rousso 1987, p. 265 et seq.

quite different from a court's objective of determining individual criminal responsibility based on a precisely identified fact.

Therefore, the outcome may result in the minimisation of the judicial decision to an exemplary punitive conviction influenced by emotional factors and which precedes any verification. In this way, the criminal trial loses its mediated, neutral and rational design and takes on external functions. As a consequence, conflict may also be created within the dynamics of the public sphere, which is a sphere linked to vital and active politics and is structurally different from criminal law.[47] A conflict between criminal law and the public space, between the criminal trial and politics can only take place in both directions, bringing elements of one dynamic into the other and vice versa with the constant risk of mutual entanglement.

In the second part of this study, these conflicts will be further explored through an analysis of the emblematic case law, which will demonstrate that law, in particular criminal law, is not the most adequate instrument for the protection of historical collective memory.

References

Ambos K (2017) Derecho penal europeo. Thomson Reuters, Civitas

Arendt H (1998) The Human Condition. University of Chicago Press, Chicago

Ash TG (2007) A blanket ban on Holocaust denial would be a serious mistake. The Guardian

Baldissara L (2016) Politiche della memoria e spazio del ricordo in Europa. Il Mulino, Bologna 1:6–20

Barbosa Delgado FR (2012) El margen nacional de apreciación y sus límites en la libertad de expresión: análisis comparado de los sistemas europeo e interamericano de derechos humanos. Universidad Externado de Colombia, Bogota

Bartole S, De Sena P, Zagrebelsky V (2012) Commentario breve alla Convenzione europea dei diritti dell'uomo. Giuffrè, Milan

Behrens P, Jensen O, Terry N (eds) (2017) Holocaust and Genocide Denial: A Contextual Perspective. Routledge, Abingdon-on-Thames

Bilbao Ubillos JM (2008) La negación del holocausto en la jurisprudencia del Tribunal Europeo de Derechos humanos: la endeble justificación de tipos penales contrarios a la libertad de expression. Revista de Derecho Político (UNED) 71–72:19–56

Booysen H (1976) Convention on the Crime of Apartheid. South African Yearbook of International Law 2:56–96

Buratti A (2012) L'uso della storia nella giurisprudenza della Corte europea dei diritti dell'uomo. Rivista telematica giuridica dell'Associazione italiana dei Costituzionalisti 2:1–18

Burz A (2013) Redefining Apartheid in International Criminal Law. Criminal Law Forum 24: 205–233

Cajani L (2008) Historians between Memory Wars and Criminal Laws: The Case of the European Union. In: Erdmann E et al. (eds) Jahrbuch der Internationalen Gesellschaft für Geschichtsdidaktik, 27–42

Cajani L (2011) Criminal Laws on History. The Case of the European Union. Historein. How to deal with tormented pasts 3:19–29

[47] Arendt 1998.

Cajani L (2017) La storia nel mirino del diritto penale. The relationship between memory and criminal law. DPCE Online 25, http://www.dpceonline.it/index.php/dpceonline/article/view/91. Accessed 14 September 2017
Caruso C (2011) Ai confini dell'abuso del diritto: l'hate speech nella giurisprudenza della Corte Europea dei Diritto dell'Uomo. In: Mezzetti L, Morrone A (eds) Lo strumento costituzionale dell'ordine pubblico europeo. Giappichelli, Turin, pp 339–352
Caruso C (2017) L'hate speech a Strasburgo. Il pluralismo militante del sistema convenzionale. Quaderni costituzionali 4
Cohen-Almagor R (2009) Holocaust Denial is a Form of Hate Speech. Amsterdam Law Forum 2:33–42
Cooper J, Williams AM (1999) Hate Speech, Holocaust Denial and International Human Rights Law. European Human Rights Law Review 6:593–613
Della Morte G (2014) L'introduzione del reato di negazionismo in Italia. Una prospettiva critica alla luce dell'ordinamento internazionale. Diritto pubblico comparato ed europeo 3:1181–1203
Delmas-Marty M (2004) Le flou du droit. Du code pénal aux droits de l'homme. Puf, Paris
Delmas-Marty M (2005) Le relative et l'universel. Les forces imaginantes du droit. I. Seuil, Paris
Delmas-Marty M (2006) Le pluralisme ordonné. Les forces imaginantes du droit. II. Seuil, Paris
Delmas-Marty M (2011) Vers une Communauté de Valeurs. Les Forces Imaginantes du Droit 4. Seuil, Paris
Delmas-Marty M, Mathieu-Izorche ML (2000) Marge nationale d'appréciation et internationalisation du droit: réflexions sur la validité formelle d'un droit commun pluraliste. Revue internationale de droit comparé 52:753–780
Eden P (2014) The Role of the Rome Statute in the Criminalization of Apartheid. Journal of International Criminal Justice 12:171–191
Ginzburg C (1991) Il giudice e lo storico. Considerazioni a margine del processo Sofri. Einaudi, Turin
Gliszczyńska-Grabias A (2013) Penalizing Holocaust Denial: A View from Europe. In: Small CA (ed) Global Antisemitism: A Crisis of Modernity. Brill-Nijhoff, Leiden
Gorton S (2015) The Uncertain Future of Genocide Denial Laws in the European Union. George Washington International Law 47:421–445
Grabenwarter C (2014) European Convention on Human Rights: Commentary. CH Beck/Hart/ Nomos, Helbing Lichtenhahn
Greer S (2006) The European Convention on Human Rights. Achievements, Problems and Prospects. Cambridge University Press, Cambridge
Hare I, Weinstein J (eds) (2011) Extreme Speech and Democracy. Oxford University Press. Oxford
Igounet V (2012) Robert Faurisson: Portrait d'un négationniste. Denoël, Paris
Kiska R (2012) Hate Speech: A Comparison between the European Court of Human Rights and the United States Supreme Court Jurisprudence. Regent University Law Review 25:107
Knechtle JC (2006) When to Regulate Hate Speech. Pennsylvania State Law Review 110:539–578
Knechtle JC (2008) Holocaust Denial and the Concept of Human Dignity in the European Union. Florida State University Law Review 36:41–65
Kučs A (2014) Denial of Genocide and Crimes against Humanity in the Jurisprudence of Human Rights Monitoring Bodies. Journal of Ethnic and Migration Studies 40:301–319
Letsas G (2007) A Theory of Interpretation of the European Convention on Human Rights. Oxford University Press, Oxford
Lobba P (2014) Punishing Denialism Beyond Holocaust Denial: EU Framework Decision 2008/ 913/JHA and Other Expansive Trends. New Journal of European Criminal Law 5:58–77
Lobba P (2015) Holocaust Denial Before the European Court of Human Rights: Evolution of an Exceptional Regime. European Journal of International Law 26:237–253
Lobba P (2016) Testing the "Uniqueness": Denial of the Holocaust vs. Denial of Other Crimes Before the European Court of Human Rights. Diritto penale contemporaneo, http://www.penalecontemporaneo.it/upload/LOBBA_2016a.pdf. Accessed 13 August 2017

Lobba P (2017) From introduction to implementation: First steps of the EU Framework Decision 2008/913/JHA against racism and xenophobia. In: Behrens P, Terry N, Jensen O (eds) Holocaust and Genocide Denial: A Contextual Perspective. Routledge, London, pp 189–210

Mathieu-Izorche ML (2006) La marge nationale d'appréciation, enjeu de savoir et de pouvoir, ou jeu de construction? Revue de Sciences Criminelles 1:25–34

Oster J (2015) Media Freedom as Fundamental Rights. Cambridge University Press, Cambridge

Pavich G, Bonomi A (2014) Reati in tema di discriminazione: il punto sull'evoluzione normativa recente, sui principi e valori in gioco, sulle prospettive legislative e sulla possibilità di interpretare in senso conforme a Costituzione la normativa vigente. Diritto penale contemporaneo. Online: https://www.penalecontemporaneo.it/upload/1412690237PAVICH-BONOMI_2014.pdf. Accessed 28 September 2017

Pech L (2011) Ruling Denial Prohibition. In: Hennebel L, Hochmann T (eds) Genocide Denials and the Law. Oxford University Press, Oxford, pp 183–234

Renauld B (2010) La décision-cadre 2008/913/JAI du Conseil de l'Union européenne: du nouveau en matière de lutte contre le racisme? Revue trimestrielle des droits de l'homme 21/81:119–140

Rousso H (1987) Le syndrome de Vichy. Seuil, Paris (tr. The Vichy Syndrome. History and Memory in France since 1944. Harvard University Press, Massachusetts)

Saul M (2015) The European Court of Human Rights' Margin of Appreciation and the Process of National Parliaments. Human Rights Law Review 15:745–774

Schabas WA (2015) The European Convention on Human Rights: A Commentary. Oxford University Press, Oxford

Sweeney JA (2005) Margins of Appreciation: Cultural relativity and the European Court of Human Rights in the post-Cold War era. International and Comparative Law Quarterly 2: 459–474

Temperman J (2014) Laws against the Denial of Historical Atrocities: A Human Rights Analysis. Religion and Human Rights 9:151–180

Thornberry P (2016) The International Convention on the Elimination of All Forms of Racial Discrimination: A Commentary. Oxford University Press, Oxford

Tracol X (1997) L'affaire Faurisson devant le Comité des droits de l'homme des Nations-Unies. Légipresse 141 II:57

Tulkens F, Donnay L (2006) L'usage de la marge d'appréciation par la Cour européenne des droits de l'homme. Paravent juridique superflu ou mécanisme indispensable par nature? Revue de Sciences Criminelles et de Droit Comparé XXII:3–24

Turner JI (2012) The Expressive Dimension of EU Criminal Law. American Journal of Comparative Law 60:555–583

van Drooghenbroeck S (2001) L'article 17 de la Convention européenne des droits de l'homme est-il indispensable? Revue trimestrielle des droits de l'homme 46:541–553

Waldron J (2012) The Harm in Hate Speech. Harvard University Press, Cambridge

Weiler JHH (2009) Fundamental Rights and Fundamental Boundaries: Common Standards and Conflicting Values in the Protection of Human Rights in the European Legal Space. In: Kastoryano R (ed) An Identity for Europe: the Relevance of Multiculturalism in EU Construction. Palgrave, London, pp 73–77

Yakis YA (2011) European Union Framework Decision On the Offence of Denying a Crime. Review of Armenian Studies 23:63–92

Part II
Denialism in Practice

Chapter 3
Criminal Law and Memory

Contents

Abstract This chapter focuses on the conflicts between the criminal offence of historical denialism and history. It dissects the three main problematic consequences of criminalisation: the risk of tampering with historical reconstructions; the risk of establishing one historical truth only and the risk of introducing a hierarchy among historical memories. First, the analysis focuses on a few landmark cases adjudicated by French courts. The French legal experience is paradigmatic of the problematics emerging from the criminalisation of historical denialism. Second, two judgments of the ECtHR are examined. The Garaudy case epitomises the consequences of the 'original' form of historical denialism. The Perinçek case demonstrates the risks involved in adopting a 'broader' paradigm of historical denialism.

Keywords Memory makers · *Gayssot* Act · European Court of Human Rights · *Garaudy* · *Perinçek*

E. Fronza, *Memory and Punishment*, International Criminal Justice Series 19,
https://doi.org/10.1007/978-94-6265-234-7_3

3.1 Criminal Law and Historical Memory

Criminalising historical denialism involves two major areas of conflict: the first stems from the relationship between criminal law and memory; and the second between criminal law and free speech. The third and fourth chapters will examine each respectively.

Among the key characteristics of the conflicting relationship between criminal law and memory is the significance of the judgment issued by a court as an *act of memory*. A court decision is capable of ratifying a violent past that deserves criminal law protection, including all that this implies with respect to history.

Once the jurisdiction of the court to rule on past events has been determined, the only way for the court to evaluate them is through a trial and then a final court decision. The judgment sets in stone those events qualified as international crimes and produces a sort of *certification of the truth* which cannot be challenged. This amounts to what is known as judicial truth, which differs from the notion of truth accepted in historical research.[1]

This is the delicate terrain on which judges (but also legislators and law in general) tread when dealing with historical occurrences, which must be sanctified as founding events of democratic societies. In other words, memory that transmits and breathes life into the experience and sense of our past.

The conflict between the two plays out on various levels. First, one has to consider history and law as separate disciplines with significantly diverse ways of reconstructing past events. The dynamic of mutual attraction and reciprocal mingling of judicial truth and historical truth is another source of conflict. On the one hand, judicial truth enjoys a 'stronger' status which tends to dominate over historical reconstruction. On the other hand, there are the fluid and constantly changing demands that society places on each individual reconstruction of the past, which also plays a part in judicial reconstruction.

This causes a vicious circle on both historical and judicial levels. History and memory (with their changing landscapes, multiple components, layered and mutable nature) are at first invaded and stripped of some of their constituent functions by criminal law and the criminal trial. These are both instruments which are necessarily simplistic and have as their end goal a final judgment issued in court. In other words, a *fixed* reconstruction that can no longer be modified, except by the extraordinary means provided in legal systems for guaranteeing the rights of those who have been unjustly convicted.

Before formulating any critical remarks regarding the complex interaction between criminal law and historical memory, we will mention some cases in which the French courts and the ECtHR have had to rule on historical denialism. These

[1] On this distinction, see Ferrajoli 1989: 18–69. Concerning the relationship between the concept of 'historic truth' and 'forensic truth', see Hartog et al. 1998, pp. 4–44; Le Crom and Jean-Clément 1998, pp. 1–59.

examples have been selected as they exemplify dilemmas and 'short-circuits' that may result from criminalisation.

The first of these cases are the French Constitutional Council's (*Conseil Constitutionnel*) decisions regarding the Boyer Bill and Law no. 2017-86 of 27 January 2017. These laws are attempts to gradually extend the 'original' offence of historical denialism to cover genocides other than the Holocaust and blatant crimes against humanity. This case law exemplifies the issues related to the role of the legislator or the judges as agents of memory.

The second is the *Theil* case, which permits judges to rule on the validity of the historical method used, thereby broadening their power to the extent that they may establish the scientific status of a discipline that is entirely different and separate from the legal one.[2]

The third example is the ECtHR *Garaudy* case. It is the source of two key points of the argument made here: the judge being granted the power to reconstruct historical facts and, conversely, historical facts being qualified as elements which may be scrutinised, clarified and established within the criminal trial, similar to the circumstances of *res judicata*. The main question raised by this case is whether the historical fact can be *established* and whether such a legal qualification can imply a limitation of freedom of expression.

Shortly afterwards, and in large part related to issues arising from the 'broader' form of the offence, is another case of the ECtHR. The *Perinçek* case deals with the Armenian genocide. These ECtHR judgments are particularly relevant because they introduce the distinction between *fact* and *legal qualification of the fact*. This distinction confirms, once again, the difficulties and potentially inherent paradoxes of criminalising historical denialism.

3.2 The French Experience: The Legislator and Judge as Memory Makers

We draw from the French experience where the politics of memory were first developed, tested and implemented (even before remembrance laws).

As previously mentioned, the *Gayssot* Act of 1990 is the first European law punishing a 'crime of memory'—Holocaust denial.[3] Since the beginning of the 1990s, France, more than any other European country, has been the scene of a veritable public politics of memory through the use of the law. This is manifested in both the form of remembrance laws, with the solemn legislative recognition of

[2] See Traverso 2006, p. 9 et seq. and p. 17 et seq.

[3] The Law no. 90-615 of 13 July 1990 (the so-called 'Gayssot Act') modified Article 24 *bis* of the Freedom of the Press Act of 29 July 1881.

genocide and tragic events in several Acts, as well as in imperatives of memory with the introduction of the criminal offence of historical denialism.[4]

France has taken the lead on this matter especially when it comes to two specific issues. The first is the expansive tendency of memory protection through law within the complex interweaving of remembrance laws and criminal law. The second is the debate on opposing values, most notably freedom of expression and historical research against the protection of the dignity of victims and historical memory as a cornerstone of the democratic system.

Therefore, in many ways the French case law offers a rich experience of the multiple dynamics at play between history and law within laws protecting collective memory.

This section incorporates an analysis of the decision of the Constitutional Council that declared the *Boyer* Bill unconstitutional. This law aimed to expand the scope of application of the criminal offence to other genocides determined by the legislature. The judgment exemplifies many of the problems that are caused by the relationship between criminal law and memory, especially regarding the conflict with freedom of expression. Others issues also emerge, such as complications inherent to criminal law protection of historical memory and the particular role of lawmakers with respect to judges as memory makers.

A short digression on the *Gayssot* Act and the production of remembrance laws is relevant to our discussion. It demonstrates the activism of the French legislature and the trend of judicially sanctioning the past. Additionally, some of the issues involved are closely related to the criminalisation of denialist statements. The provisions relating to the recognition of the Armenian genocide are exemplary in this respect. The provision that enshrines this official recognition was in fact followed by a law that criminalises the negation of this event, which in the future could possibly extend the mechanisms of criminal law protection created for the Holocaust to all international crimes. This law is then followed by the contrary decision of the Constitutional Council which will be subsequently discussed.

3.2.1 *Lois Mémorielles*

The expression 'remembrance laws' (*lois mémorielles*) was first used to describe a set of heterogeneous laws and measures characterised by the decision to memorialise significant events of the past and it has quickly attained generalised use in this sense.[5]

---

[4] It is worth mentioning that France is to be considered a unique historical case, due to the fact that the 1789 Declaration (the Declaration on the Rights of Man and the Citizen) already limited freedom of expression.

[5] This relatively recent notion is defined as 'Laws [that], beyond the differences in their content, seem to proceed from the same intention: to tell history, even to qualify it, by using contemporary legal concepts such as genocide or crime against humanity, in one way or another, to do justice

This expression is found in the *Gayssot* Act (see below) and in the Law no. 2000-644 of 10 July 2000, which establishes the national day of remembrance of the victims of racist and anti-Semitic persecutions by the French State and of tribute to the 'righteous' of France;[6] the Law no. 70 of 29 January 2001 on the recognition of the Armenian genocide, the *Taubira* Law no. 434 of 21 May 2001 on the 'recognition of the slave trade and slavery as a crime against humanity' ('*reconnaissance de la traite et de l'esclavage en tant que crime contre l'humanité*') and the *Mekachera* Law no. 158 of 23 February 2005 regarding the French presence overseas, where the 'positive aspects' ('*aspects positifs*') of French colonisation were recognised.[7] Although they share the aim of establishing a duty to remember, and the expression memory laws in its generic sense is often used for both interventions,[8] these laws should be considered as very distinct from the other form of legal intervention, which resorts to criminal law and introduces the offence of historical denialism.[9]

From a historical point of view, even in the absence of strictly criminal content, remembrance laws contextualise and express recognition of events which are by nature classifiable as crimes (for example the law recognising the Armenian genocide). Aside from referencing the criminal offence—only possible through criminal law—memory laws are important because it attributes to a fact the value of a historical event, thereby defining the scope of application of criminal laws protecting the historical memory of that event.

Therefore, in such cases it is the legislator who performs the function of defining and qualifying the facts of the past. The legislator nominates, declares and frames a

through the recognition of past suffering' ('*lois, [qui] au-delà des différences de leur contenu, semblent procéder d'une même volonté: 'dire' l'histoire, voire la qualifier, en recourant à des concepts juridiques contemporains comme le génocide ou le crime contre l'humanité, pour, d'une manière ou d'une autre, faire œuvre de justice au travers de la reconnaissance de souffrances passées*', see *Rapport d'information de l'Assemblée nationale* (the so-called Accoyer Report, named after the President of the National Assembly), titled 'Gathering the Nation around a shared memory' (*Rassembler la Nation autour d'une mémoire partagée*), no. 1262, 18 November 2008. There are many studies on such provisions. See Hochmann 2013, pp. 57–69; contributions from the journal *Droit et cultures* titled *Espaces de politique mémorielles. Enjeux de mémoire*, no. 66, 2013; Hochmann 2012, p. 133 et seq.; Mallet-Poujol 2012, p. 219 et seq.; Michel 2010; Morange 2009, p. 154 et seq. On public politics of memory in France: Baruch 2013; Fraisseix 2006, p. 483 et seq; Garibian 2006, p. 158 et seq.; Frangi 2005, p. 241 et seq. Concerning criticism of the French historians, see Nora and Chandernagor 2008; Rémond 2006; *Appel des juristes contre les lois mémorielles*, contained in Assemblée Nationale, *Rapport d'information fait en application de l'article 145 du règlement au nom de la mission d'information sur les questions mémorielles*, Président-Rapporteur M. Bertrand Accoyer (*enregistré à la Présidence de l'Assemblée nationale le 18 novembre 2008*), pp. 475 ss. There are numerous criticisms made by historians against the intervention within the field of public memory: see footnote no. 40 of Chap. 5. Note that remembrance laws are backward-looking, that is they focus on the past. Conversely, laws that protect 'future generations' are forward-looking, and thus focus on the future.

[6] See Law no. 2000-644, 10 July 2000, http://www.senat.fr/leg/ppl99-244.html

[7] See Law no. 2005-158, 23 February 2005 (*Loi portant reconnaissance de la Nation et contribution nationale en faveur des Français repatriés*).

[8] For instance, see the Spanish Law no. 52/2007 on Historical Memory of 31 October 2007.

[9] See Chap. 1, Sect. 1.2.

historical occurrence, describing it with precision and acting as agent of memory. This transition, as the subsequent investigation demonstrates, is not to be underestimated.

3.2.2 *The First-Ever Crime of Historical Denialism: The* Gayssot *Act*

Before the adoption of remembrance laws, France had already passed separate provisions for the criminal protection of memory, which criminalised statements denying the Holocaust and, in a subsequent moment, other crimes against humanity: the *Gayssot* Act. It was adopted in 1990 in the wake of the debate sparked by the *Faurisson* case, and it introduced a specific offence which punished historical denialism (despite France already having several provisions for the prevention and punishment of neo-racist phenomena). Denialism took root in France in the late 1970s through the writings of Robert Faurisson and Paul Rassinier, and by the second half of the 1980s it had become significantly more widespread.[10]

To impede the spread of phenomena of racism (among them historical denialism), the French legislature enacted the punishment for Holocaust denial according to Article 11 of the Declaration of Human Rights and of the Citizen of 1789,[11] on which the Preamble of the French Constitution confers the value of positive law. The offence was inserted in the French Freedom of the Press Act of 29 July 1881 which defines public forms of freedom of speech.[12]

The French legislature had already intervened several times over the years in matters of racial discrimination. In 1939, the aforementioned law on freedom of the press had been amended with provisions that soon proved to be insufficient to encompass and punish the various types of racism (the so-called *Marchandeau* Decree).[13] In 1972, based on the International Convention on the Elimination of All Forms of Racial Discrimination, France implemented a new law against racism to supplement previous legislation.[14] Between 1977 and 1990 (the year the *Gayssot*

[10] On French denialists, see, among others, Terry 2017, p. 34 et seq.; Hochmann 2011, p. 235 et seq.; Jouanneau 2008; Vidal-Naquet 1981.

[11] See Article 11.

[12] More specifically, the law forbids publicly inciting discrimination, hatred or violence (Article 24, para 6, amended by the law of 1 July 1972), defamation (Article 32, para 2) and insult (Article 33, para 3) for belonging or not belonging to an ethnicity, race or religion. Article 24, para 3, after the 1987 amendment, also includes the offence of defending crimes against humanity, to which case law adds publications or publicly made assessments that incite the audience to view favourably or justify a crime against humanity.

[13] This law adds a paragraph to Article 32 of the 1881 law prohibiting defamation and insult of people belonging to a specific race or religion if intended to incite hatred among citizens and inhabitants.

[14] This law includes punishing instigating discrimination, hatred or violence against a person or a group on the bases of belonging or not belonging to a specific ethnicity, nation or religion. It also introduced provisions to the Criminal Code punishing discrimination, making a distinction

Act was adopted), several amendments were made to the Criminal Code: new offences were introduced (including, for example, the act of impeding the exercise of any economic activity) as well as discriminatory motives (sex, origin, family situation, health status and disability).

The legal framework for counteracting racist phenomena was expanded in 1990 with the *Gayssot* Act,[15] which aimed to 'combat all racist, anti-Semitic and xenophobic acts.' France was thus the first European country to introduce a specific law punishing historical denialism with a separate provision (Article 24 *bis* Freedom of the Press Act).[16]

3.2.2.1 Features and Dilemmas

The *Gayssot* Act is a complex law that creates new offences and reorganises the matter of press crimes. This provision is a veritable turning point in French criminal law policy because it punishes racist or denialist ideology as such.[17] No pre-existing law explicitly provided for the prosecution of such conducts, which means that previously such statements were punishable only through the crime of racial defamation.

Article 24 *bis* of the Freedom of the Press Act of 1881, as introduced by Article 9 of the *Gayssot* Act, states that it will punish:

> [...] those who question the existence of one or more crimes against humanity as defined by Article 6 of the Statute of the International Military Tribunal annexed to the London Agreement of 8 August 1945, which have been committed either by a member of an organization declared criminal under Article 9 (d) of the Statute or by a person found guilty of such crimes by a French or international court.

---

between discrimination by a civil servant and by an individual. See Guyaz 1996, pp. 87–90; Korman 1989, p. 3404; Costa-Lascoux 1976, p. 181 et seq.

[15] *Gayssot* Act is named after the communist deputy (Jean-Claude Gayssot) who proposed it. On this Act, see Droin 2014, p. 363 et seq.; Francillon 2013a, p. 99 et seq; Francillon 2013b; Hochmann 2012; Droin 2010, p. 211 et seq.; Garibian 2008, p. 479 et seq.; Frangi 2005; Levinet 2004, p. 653; Troper 1999, p. 1239 et seq.; Tracol 1997, p. 57; Roumelian 1996, p. 10; Massias 1993, p. 183; Véron 1990.

[16] Note that the Freedom of the Press Act represents a specific and distinct subsystem of the Criminal Code, owing to its reference to specialised judges on the freedom of the press. Conversely, as pointed out in Chapter 1, the introduction of the offence of apology of terrorism in the Criminal Code through the Cazeneuve Law has the effect of excluding the applicability of the said regime to the new offence. With consequences on the significantly burdensome sentencing practice.

[17] Article 23: 'The ones who will be punished [...] are those who either through speeches, calls or threats uttered in public places or meetings, or through writings [...] will have directly caused the author or the authors to commit the aforementioned action, if the provocation has been followed by an effect' ('*Seront punis* [...] *ceux qui par le discours, cris ou menaces proférés dans des lieux ou réunion publics, soit par des écrits* [...] *auront directement provoqué l'auteur ou les auteurs à commettre la dite action, si la provocation a été suivie d'effet*').

This provision punishes with the same sanctions those, who by one of the means announced in Article 23 of the same law,[18] commit '*apologie*' of crimes provided for in the first paragraph, war crimes, crimes against humanity, as defined by Article 6 of the Statute of the International Military Tribunal annexed to the London Agreement of 8 August 1945, and which were committed by members of an organisation declared criminal pursuant to Article 9 of the same Statute, or committed by an individual who has been convicted of the above crimes by a French or international judicial body.[19]

An essential element of the crime is the public nature of the offence, which is considered as such if the statements are made in public or loud enough to be understood by anyone in the vicinity.[20] Furthermore, according to Article 48-2 of this act, associations defending the moral interests and honour of the Resistance to Nazism or deportees may be civil plaintiffs in denialist trials. The penalty is imprisonment (up to one year) and a fine (up to € 45,000), with the possibility that it would be included in public criminal records.

The particularities of the French legislation of interest here are mainly related to the scope of application of the law. It is interesting to consider the wording before the change took place, which includes the debate and subsequent pressure related to the expansion of criminal protection to international crimes other than the Holocaust, i.e. international crimes established by Articles 6–8 of the ICC St and genocide and crimes against humanity as defined by the national Criminal Code (from Article 211-1 to Article 212-3 Criminal Code). Limited protection was also motivated by the concern to not excessively restrict freedom of expression.

Until the 2017 amendment, the law limited the scope of the offence only to historical denialism of crimes against humanity as defined by Article 6 of the Statute of the Nuremberg Tribunal. Thus, the crime only consists of the denial of genocide and crimes against humanity committed by organisations or persons acting on behalf of the countries belonging to the Axis Powers, according to what is stipulated by the Nuremberg Tribunal or based on findings from a French or international court.

Therefore, the provision does not permit statements concerning the denial of other international crimes to be criminalised. Consequently, the existence of crimes against humanity committed in other places and at other times may be questioned. This decision is consistent with the scope of the criminal offence, which—as specified by the case law—seeks to prevent the public questioning of the Nuremberg Tribunal's final decisions, made in the interest of the victims of Nazism,

[18] Article 23 on defamation defined as a means of diffusion, discourse in public spaces or public meetings, writings, drawings, emblems, images and paintings that are sold or distributed, put up for sale or exhibited in public places or public meetings or through posters exposed to the public.

[19] See Feldman 1998. For critical remarks, see Droin 2014, p. 384 et seq. Concerning the case law, see Court of Appeal of Paris, Judgment, 31 October 1990, in *Gaz. Palais*, 311; the 1991 judgment on the *Faurisson* case and the judgment of the Court of Cassation, Judgment, 23 February 1993, *Bulletin criminel*, no. 86, 1993, 208.

[20] *Crim. 17 nov. 1983*, in *Bulletin Criminel*, no. 260.

and to ensure respect of their memory in accordance with the objectives of the European Convention of Human Rights and Fundamental Freedoms.[21]

However, in an apparent contradiction, the *Gayssot* Act refers to the general concept of crimes against humanity. At the time of the *Gayssot* Act, this was a notion which extended far beyond the Holocaust, and thus it was immediately capable of exerting pressure to expand the provision in order to encompass other crimes.

There are important consequences due to the limited scope of applicability of the law. First, with regard to *locus standi*, only associations defending the moral interests and honour of the Resistance to Nazism or of deportees may intervene in court, and not those associations active in countering the general phenomenon of racism.

There are also significant repercussions concerning the scope of criminalisation. A prime example of this, which anticipates problems emerging in subsequent cases, is the trial of historian Bernard Lewis regarding the Armenian genocide. Lewis was accused of having denied the existence of crimes against humanity (Article 24 *bis* of the Freedom of the Press Act) by denying the Armenian genocide. This is a particularly significant case, given the discussion that ensued in France about extending the criminal protection of the memory of this genocide. The Criminal Court of Paris declared the charges inadmissible because the offence of denialism only included 'crimes against humanity committed during the Second World War by organizations or persons acting on behalf of the countries that are part of the Axis' and thus the denial of the Armenian genocide was not within the scope of the *Gayssot* Act. The *Bernard Lewis* case, however, did not end with an acquittal but with a conviction in a civil trial issued by the High Court of Paris.[22] The Tribunal stated that 'it is not for the courts to assess whether the massacre committed from 1915 to 1917 constitutes genocide or not. [...]. The historian has in principle the freedom to present the facts according to his point of view [...].' The Court moves in the direction of protecting freedom of research, but, in the end, finds the accused responsible for not having provided proof, sources or documents contrary to his thesis, such as the United Nations Declaration of 1985 and the European Parliament Resolution of 1987, which classified the massacre of Armenians as genocide. Therefore, the ruling considers the method, which is in line with what has been observed previously. Likewise, by referring to legislative recognition of the Armenian genocide, the Court's decision demonstrates the expansive force inherent in referring to the greatest of crimes against humanity.

The French criminal provision on historical denialism and its application demonstrates the conflict with freedom of research and the emergence of a more general problem that inevitably accompanies all the measures of this kind: the conflict

---

[21] See Court of Cassation, Criminal Division, Judgment, 9 October 1995, no. 92-83.665.

[22] Regarding the *Lewis* case in particular, TGI Paris, 21 June 1995, *Forum des Association Arméniennes de France c. Lewis*, *Les petites affiches* 117 (1995): 17, holding Bernard Lewis responsible under Article 1382 of the French Civil Code for negationism of the Armenian genocide. The *Lewis* case, which began with the Le Monde interview, dated 13 November 1993 and ended with the court decision of 21 June 1995, see *Libération,* 17 October and 19 November 1994; *Le Monde,* 23 June 1995 and *Le Figaro,* 26 June 1995. See also Arslan et al. 2017; Gunter 2011, p. 77 et seq.; Ternon 1999, pp. 237–248.

with free speech. Indeed, it should become evident here how, instead of facing the danger of creating a mere speech crime, the French legislature (like other countries and later the European Union) felt the need to restrict the expansive potential of the law and chose to criminalise only those statements denying the crimes against humanity defined by the Statute of the Nuremberg Tribunal and identified by a national or international court: *res judicata* becomes, therefore, a constituent element of the offence. In this way, an excessive restriction of free speech is avoided.

Finally, citing the judgment of Nuremberg results in limiting punishment, but it also highlights a weakness of those trials in relation to the current definition of crimes against humanity[23] and the multiple forms of historical denialism. An additional example is the *Guionnet* case, which arose after the publication of an article in the magazine *Revision* stating that 'only' 125,000 people had died at Auschwitz. In this case, the High Court of Paris did not consider crimes against humanity applicable to Guionnet since the mortality rates of Auschwitz had not been published at the time of the Nuremberg judgment[24] and therefore were not protected by the law being examined by the Court.

3.2.2.2 The 'Assassins of Memory' and the Court of Cassation

The *Gayssot* Act has been frequently applied over the years. Memory deniers have often been subject to trials and convictions, and all attempts to challenge the constitutionality of this law for the alleged violation of the right to freedom of speech have been rejected.

In terms of punishable conducts, the act of questioning ('*contestation*') a crime against humanity consists in not admitting the crime occurred.[25] According to case law, such conduct can take different forms: belittling the events in an outrageous manner,[26] denying that human beings were burned in concentration camps,[27] quoting parts of a book on Holocaust denial that are prohibited in France,[28] bluntly denying that the Jewish genocide occurred and hinting at a different historical truth in front of a class at school,[29] promoting a revisionist theory and enclosing the terms Holocaust, genocide and extermination in quotation marks,[30] or qualifying Auschwitz as a paradise compared to the conditions suffered by African people.[31]

[23] See Werle and Jessberger 2014, p. 866 et seq.; Ambos 2014, pp. 46–116; Delmas Marty et al. 2013; Luban 2004, pp. 85–167.

[24] High Court of Paris, 24 March 1994.

[25] On the notion of questioning ('*contestation*'), see Ader 2012, p. 236. On the possibility of punishing the 'indulgent presentation' ('*présentation complaisante*'), see the *Gollnisch* case.

[26] Court of Appeal of Paris, Judgment, 21 January 2009, no. 08/02208.

[27] Court of Appeal of Paris, Judgment, 18 June 2008, no. 07/08276.

[28] Court of Appeal of Paris, Judgment, 11 September 2002, no. 01/01445.

[29] Court of Appeal of Metz, Judgment, 27 September 2000, no. 971/2000.

[30] Court of Appeal of Paris, Judgment, 1 April 1992, no. 5571/91.

[31] Court of Appeal of Paris, Judgment, 2 April 2009, no. 08/0001.

Although the Gayssot Act had not been subject to an *a priori* judicial review before entering into force, the Court of Cassation has on several occasions submitted inquiries to the Constitutional Council challenging its constitutionality. The Constitutional Council, however, has always rejected such demands 'thereby showing its intention to thwart all attempts to call such piece of legislation into question'.[32]

One clear example is the trial against the far-right journal *Rivarole*, which was convicted for 'questioning crimes against humanity' ('*contestations de crimes contre l'humanité*') after it published an interview with Jean-Marie Le Pen, according to whom 'the German occupation was not particularly inhuman'. The Court of Cassation dismissed the questions concerning the violation of the principle of legality and of the right to freedom of speech; it affirmed that 'the offence [...] is based on legal instruments that were lawfully introduced within the national legal system and that define in a clear and precise manner the crime of denying one or more crimes against humanity [...], a crime whose prosecution does not, by the way, infringe upon the constitutional rights to freedom of expression and freedom of speech'.[33] This line of reasoning was confirmed, in slightly different terms, in a judgment from 2013.[34]

The legal framework utilised did not change substantially after the new Criminal Code which introduced crimes against humanity and entered into force on 1 March 1994.[35] The new Criminal Code was completed by the introduction of a decree published on 29 March 1993 that makes any racially-based form of non-public insult and defamation (Article from R. 624-3 to R. 624-6) and incitement to racial hatred or discrimination (Article R. 625-7) a minor offence (*contravention*).[36]

3.2.3 *From the Holocaust to the Armenian Genocide: The* Boyer *Bill*

The need for the application of the *Gayssot* Act beyond the Holocaust translated into reality with a bill extending the offence of historical denialism to the Armenian genocide.[37] In this respect, it is worth noting that in 2001 the Parliament approved a legislative act 'recognising the Armenian genocide'[38] and in 2006 some Members

---

[32] Francillon 2010, p. 640 et seq.

[33] See Court of Cassation, *Question Préliminaire Constitutionnalité*, 7 May 2010, no. 09-80.774. Camby 2012.

[34] See Lapage 2013.

[35] The special part of the Criminal Code starts with the section on '*Les crimes contre l'humanité*', at Articles. 211-1 et seq. See Couvrat 1993, p. 469.

[36] The last amendment on the matter is from 27 January 2017 and is analysed in Sect. 3.2.5.

[37] See *Rapport Accoyer*, cit., 49 et seq.

[38] For this reason, the historian Pierre Nora argues that this act is a resolution rather than a law. This is significant remark, if we agree with the opinion that the proliferation of remembrance laws is the consequence of the limitations of the Parliament's prerogative, see *Rapport Accoyer*, cit., 23-25. See Derieux 2012, p. 6. See Maus and Bougrab 2005.

of Parliament proposed modifying Article 24b so as to include this genocide, which remained unapproved until late 2011.[39]

Indeed, it was not until 11 December 2011 and 23 January 2012 that the National Assembly and the Senate, respectively, adopted the *Boyer* Bill that modified two articles of the Law of 29 July 1881 on Freedom of the Press and introduced Article 24 *ter*, which punishes whoever 'questions or belittles in an outrageous manner the existence of one or more genocides, defined by Articles 211-1 of the Criminal Code and qualified as such under French law'.[40] Article 2 of the *Boyer* Bill also amended Article 48-2 of the 1881 law, thereby entitling 'all victims of crimes of genocide, of crimes of war, crimes against humanity or crimes of collaborating with the enemy' to monetary compensation during criminal proceedings.

3.2.3.1 A Complicated Reform

The *Boyer* Bill was deemed unconstitutional and never entered into force. Nevertheless, this proposed law and other attempts to provide criminal law protection for the memory of the Armenian genocide raise politically sensitive issues and invite further reflection.[41]

First of all, one notable aspect is the decision of the French legislator concerning the role played by agents of public remembrance: in France, it is the legislator who holds the power of extending the protection ensured by the offence of denialism to other genocides. Once again, a wide array of problematic issues seems to reappear because this choice impacts the dynamism of historical research.

It should be noted that the Armenian genocide was—and is—the only genocide ever to be recognised under French law autonomously—that is, without any reference to other external forms of recognition or judicial findings. Furthermore, Armenian genocide denial is unique because it is the result of a denialist public policy or 'official truth' set under Turkish law and falls under the category of 'state denials'. This element should be taken into due consideration when choosing to use criminal law, which by definition is meant to determine individual liability.[42]

[39] Something similar happened in Belgium. See Grandjean 2011, p. 137 et seq.

[40] Emphasis added. Article 24 *ter* states that: 'The criminal penalties provided for by Article 24 *bis* shall apply to those who have challenged or excessively minimised, by one of the means set forth in Article 23, the existence of one or more crimes of genocide as defined by Article 211-1 of the Criminal Code and recognised as such by the French law'.

[41] See legislative proposal no. 690, registered on February 6th 2013, on the implementation of the 2008 EU Framework Decisions into the domestic legal system, which has been presented by Valérie Boyer and others. See Droin 2014, pp. 390–391. See also legislative proposal no. 479, registered by the Presidency of the French Senate on 22 April 2014, presented by Guy Fischer and others.

[42] See Chap. 1, Sect. 1.1.

Finally, before addressing the Constitutional Council judgment, it is worth pointing out that its rejection of the *Boyer* Bill demonstrates the difference between a remembrance law and a criminal offence contained in a criminal law statute as an imperative of memory. Although a remembrance law might serve as the legal background for an imperative of memory, the former does not necessarily lead to the latter, since a number of issues must be dealt with in the transition from establishing a historical memory to punishing conducts denying it under criminal law.

3.2.3.2 The Constitutional Council Decision of 28 February 2012

The Senate's approval of the *Boyer* Bill in January 2012 is exemplary of the tendency to go beyond the Holocaust and the crimes of the Nazi regime—a tendency already noted with the 'crimes against humanity' referred to by the Freedom of the Press Act. The extension of criminal protection to the memory of the Armenian genocide, indeed, exemplifies such a development: a remembrance law initially 'recognises' a given historical fact as a crime against humanity. Once the historical fact is established, another law then declares an imperative of memory by punishing 'under criminal law' whoever tries to deny it. This mechanism set a paradigm that could be extended to other mass atrocities like the genocide in Rwanda or the crimes committed in former Yugoslavia, to cite two cases that have been established by international criminal tribunals.

Unlike the *Gayssot* Act on the Holocaust, the *Boyer* Bill on the Armenian genocide was deemed unconstitutional by the French Constitutional Council.

On 28 February 2012,[43] the French Constitutional Council ruled that Law no. 647 of 2012 'punishing as a criminal offence the denial of genocides recognised under French law' was unconstitutional.

The *Boyer* Bill sought to introduce a new provision to the *Gayssot* Act of 29 July 1881. Article 2c was supposed to punish with up to one year of imprisonment and with a fine of up to 45,000 € whoever 'denies or belittles in an outrageous manner a genocide recognised under French law'. When the proposal was being approved, the Armenian genocide was the only genocide that had been recognised autonomously under French law, that is, without referring to decisions of international tribunals, such as the Nuremberg Tribunals. The legislative act aimed at furthering the protection ensured by another piece of legislation approved on 29 January 2001, which had recognised the Armenian genocide.

According to the Council's tradition of laconic decisions, the judgment is extremely concise.[44] The Council ruled that the *Boyer* Bill encroached upon the

[43] Available at http://www.conseil-constitutionnel.fr/conseil-constitutionnel/francais/page-d-accueil.1.html.

[44] See Koposov 2017, p. 103 et seq.; Garibian 2013, pp. 25–56; Baruch 2013; Levade and Mathieu 2012, pp. 680–684; Hamon 2012, pp. 7–11; Roux 2012, pp. 987–993; Camby 2012, pp. 17–22; Puig 2012, pp. 78–84; Francillon 2012, pp. 179–182; Mouysset 2012, pp. 26–27; Brunet 2012, pp. 343–354; Danti-Juan 2012, pp. 399–402.

right to freedom of speech (enshrined in Article 11 of the 1789 Declaration of the Rights of Man and of the Citizen) and was therefore unconstitutional. Notably, the Council further added that Article 2c also violated Article 6 of the Declaration, according to which the law must be the expression of the general will.

This was the first time that the Constitutional Council was called upon to review the constitutionality of a remembrance law (‘*loi mémorielle*’)—in this case in the form of an imperative of memory under criminal law—and ruled against it. As noted, the Constitutional Council had never reviewed this law, and in 2010 the Court of Cassation had dismissed a claim concerning its unconstitutionality because it lacked ‘seriousness’.[45]

The Council responded to only one of the numerous questions raised by the delegates and senators: the encroachment on the right to freedom of expression and speech. However, several other substantial and far-reaching questions had been submitted to the Council,[46] drawing on the complexity of the debate that had been sparked by various remembrance laws.

In addition to encroaching upon the right to freedom of speech, the applicants claimed that the *Boyer* Bill failed to represent the general will. Indeed, it introduced an indirect (*par ricochet*) form of criminalisation, as only the memory of certain genocides—those recognised under French law—was considered worthy of protection through criminal law. Therefore, criminalisation depended on the Parliament's decision to recognise a genocide rather than on the findings of criminal proceedings. As a result, the choice of which historical memory to protect rested upon political bargaining, thereby violating the principle of separation of powers, as the legislative branch—instead of the judiciary—had the power to ascertain historical facts in the eyes of the law.

The applicants also argued that the *Boyer* Bill encroached upon the fundamental principles of a democratic legal system, and in particular upon the principles of substantive equality and of the legality of crimes and punishments: it only punished the denial of episodes defined as genocides by the law (that is, only the Armenian genocide), thus leaving out all the others that could fall under that category. In addition, Article 211-1 of the French Criminal Code, which defines the crime of genocide, punishes all and every genocide, thus making no further distinction.[47]

The Court did not address all the intricate issues raised by the applicants, but rather based its concise decision exclusively on the violation of the right to freedom of expression and speech.

---

[45] Several authors had said that the law was unconstitutional, see for example Verpeaux 2007, p. 242.

[46] The claim was filed according to the French *a priori* constitutional review before the Constitutional Council.

[47] This law encroaches upon the principle of equal treatment, as it does not consider the crimes against humanity, which are punished under Article of the Criminal Code. In this sense, see also Camby 2012.

3.2.3.3 From the *Boyer* Bill to Remembrance Laws

The conciseness of the ruling should not misguide the reader. In its apparently clear decision, the Council addresses two crucial issues connected to the punishment of denialism: the limitations on freedom of speech and memory makers.

The judgment starts by stressing the role of the right to freedom of speech in constructing democratic societies. The legislator may restrict it in order to protect other public or private interests, but this restriction is lawful only insofar as it is necessary, proportionate and capable of attaining the desired result.[48] Should instead the legislator punish all persons questioning the existence—or legal qualification—of crimes that the legislator 'has previously defined as crimes', then the right to freedom of expression and speech would be undermined.

This line of argument represents one of the key points of the entire decision and, on a larger scale, of the debate concerning French policies of public remembrance. Indeed, it touches upon a question of method, which is not apparent at first glance but is absolutely crucial: by defining a historical and judicial truth that cannot be called into question, the legislator becomes a judge. The Constitutional Council thus criticises the method employed, which entrusts the law-making body with the power of recognising history and deciding whether denying it should be punished or not. In addition, the purpose envisaged—to combat all revisionist opinions deemed to be scientifically unfounded and socially dangerous—failed to justify the decision to give such power to the legislature.

The Council appears to reaffirm such principle when stating that 'a legislative provision seeking to recognise a crime of genocide fails to display the normative scope that is attached to the law'. Laws should have a normative scope that the legal provision for 'recognising' a genocide does not appear to have. In this respect, the Council reasoning, while partially moving away from the issue of freedom of expression,[49] echoes the issue raised by delegates and senators that a legislative act, which only 'declares' or 'recognises', fails to represent the general will and to display the normative substance that characterises legislation.

The Constitutional Council thus discusses the violation of the right to freedom of speech by focusing on how the criminal law is structured with respect to Article 24b (which refers to another existing law recognising genocide). It does not, however, address the issue concerning the need for—and legitimacy of—the *Boyer* Bill in terms of proportionality between the criminal sanction and the intended purpose.

The decision clearly affirms that Article 24 *bis* (Law of 29 January 2001 on the recognition of the Armenian genocide) cannot be considered as having normative scope because it does not introduce an actual norm into the legal system, but merely

[48] In spite of this reference, the Council does not focus on such parameters.

[49] Francillon 2010 argues that the Constitutional Council should not have made reference exclusively to the right to freedom of speech, but also to the constitutional principle of the respect for human dignity.

recognises the historical existence of a genocide. Although the decision makes no direct reference to the constitutionality of the 2001 law, the Council seems to imply that this act fails to provide a normative scope and cannot be qualified as a proper 'law' and thereby violates the French Constitution.[50]

This leads to another crucial question, that is the significance of the Council's decision for the larger debate on the protection of collective historical memory through the use of criminal law. The importance of the judgment may indeed go beyond the matter discussed before the Council by indicating a general disfavour towards provisions punishing the denial of a significant historical event based on the right to freedom of speech.[51] More explicitly, this decision could serve as the basis for a new judgment on the constitutionality of the *Gayssot* Act, especially in light of the Council's position on the violation of the right to freedom of speech, which calls into question any memory law leading to the introduction of a speech crime.[52]

It is important to note that the *Boyer* Bill and the *Gayssot* Act are considerably different. Nevertheless, we are not concerned with the elements that distinguish one from the other, but rather with understanding if these elements can guarantee that the Gayssot Act, which punishes whoever denies a genocide and therefore restricts freedom of speech, will not be declared unconstitutional in the future.[53] In other words, it is fair to assume that the Council's decision concerns the limitation of a fundamental right through criminal law rather than the use of law-making as a way of recognising a genocide.[54]

Commentary on the judgment is careful to clarify that the Constitutional Council 'did not want to question the constitutionality of other penal provisions punishing Holocaust denial'.[55] This wording seems to imply—although indirectly—that the *Gayssot* Act is not unconstitutional because the Holocaust has been recognised as a genocide by international tribunals rather than by the French Parliament alone. As a consequence, the *Gayssot* Act does not exhibit the conflict of powers created by the *Boyer* Bill, which allowed the legislator alone to act as an agent of memory. From this perspective, the Council draws attention to the opposition between judge and legislator and reasserts the full powers of the judiciary and court decisions. Nevertheless, the Council never goes so far as to say that the *Gayssot* Act restricts the right to freedom of speech in a proportionate, necessary and adequate manner.

---

[50] Badinter, *Le Monde*, 14 January 2012; Cassia, 'La fin de la saga des lois mémorielles', in *Libération*, 29 February 2012; Hochmann, 'Un paradoxe de portée limitée: le Conseil Constitutionnel et le négationnisme', in *Le Monde*, 20 March 2012.

[51] Pech 2011, p. 8 et seq. underlines both the actual and the *potential* impact of such a decision.

[52] Camby 2012 raises the question as to whether this decision concerns this specific piece of legislation or rather every existing speech crime.

[53] In this sense, see Camby 2012, Chap. vi.

[54] *Ibid.*

[55] See *Commentaire*, p. 12, available at: www.conseil-constitutionnel.fr/decision/2012/2012647dc.htm, accessed 15 August 2017.

The constant comparison between the two laws, which underpins the Council's decision, actually seems to suggest otherwise. Both regulations, as do all memory laws, consist of two correlated components: the memorial element, which seeks to recognise and reaffirm the collective memory of past events, and the normative element, which provides criminal protection for that historical memory. The Council's position on the criminal provisions of the *Boyer* Bill, and its implications for the law recognising the Armenian genocide, impact the *Gayssot* Act in an opposite but equally problematic way.

In the case of the *Boyer* Bill, the use of criminal law was deemed unconstitutional because it violated the right to freedom of speech and provided the legislator with the uncontrolled power to ascertain and qualify facts. As a result, the law referred to by the *Boyer* Bill is likely to be unconstitutional: not only did the correlation with this law provide the legislator with the abovementioned excess of power (undermining the autonomy of the criminal provision), but the act itself cannot be qualified as a proper law because it lacks normative substance.

The *Gayssot* Act seems to be in a symmetrical and equally difficult position: its memorial element appears to have all the characteristics required by law because it is contained in a criminal law provision that reinforces such substance. Nevertheless, this criminal provision punishes a speech crime and therefore seems to reiterate—almost inevitably—the violation of the right to freedom of expression which the Council deemed unconstitutional.

3.2.4 The Role of the Legislator and Freedom of Speech Before the French Courts

Three issues need to be addressed: the role of the legislator, the necessary normative substance of laws and the relationship between criminal law and the right to freedom of speech.

Whenever a criminal law directly refers to a remembrance law, which thereby acts as its 'legal anchor', such criminal law results being based on an act that lacks normative substance and is therefore unconstitutional. Furthermore, this mechanism gives the legislator a double role that the Constitutional Council considers a breach of the French Constitution. In addition, limitations on the right to freedom of expression can themselves be grounds for a declaration of unconstitutionality.

When, instead, criminal law succeeds in providing normative substance to the commemorative law and the legislator does not play the aforementioned double role, the question remains as to whether freedom of speech is being restricted in a necessary, proportionate and adequate manner; a question that is all the more delicate because it pertains to a fundamental right.

Considering the above, the transition from establishing a collective historical memory to protecting it through criminal law is fraught with critical problems, and it is almost impossible to avoid conflicts and paradoxes. Indeed, the legislator and the judge as memory makers seem destined to face them continuously.

Another issue that may be directly affected by the decision of the Constitutional Council is the duty to criminalise, provided for by the EU Framework Decision. Indeed, the question arises as to whether France and the European Union might end up fighting one another since the very Member State that issued the proposal—and on various occasions reasserted its necessity under European law—has ruled that such form of criminalisation is unconstitutional.

Finally, the Council's decision seems to hint at the debate concerning the unique and incomparable nature of the Holocaust.[56] There are official historical truths that are protected by certain countries, and there are secret historical truths that are hidden and persecuted. There are strong and weak truths.[57] This is confirmed by the fact that the memory of the Armenian genocide is still prohibited and punished under Turkish law.[58]

Currently, the Constitutional Council appears to acknowledge the peculiarity of the Holocaust and to suggest that it deserves specific protection under the law. In this respect, the judgment directly touches upon the discussion concerning the relationship between law and history, and therefore concerning the 'normative' substance of a law that 'declares' history. This aspect (a rather crucial one in this analysis) was not a core part of the judgment issued by the Constitutional Council, which instead focused on the conflict between the *Boyer* Bill and the right to freedom of speech and expression. Indeed, the French judges did not assert the violation of the fundamental principles of criminal law or the violation of separation of powers, nor did they use the argument concerning the violation of the exclusive power of the judiciary to establish judicial findings.

Despite these observations about the reasoning of the Constitutional Council, its ruling of 28 February 2012 certainly aided in restraining the objectionable tendency of conferring an official character upon history: by stressing the conflict between remembrance laws and the right to freedom of speech, the Council criticised the constraints imposed by the law on history and ensured that history continued to be open to debate.[59]

3.2.5 Constitutional Developments

Some common elements can be found in the comparative study of historical denialism, and especially the choice for criminal punishment among all possible

[56] This aspect is always implicitly or explicitly present in criminal trials on historical denialism. See for instance the debate on the *Boyer* Bill, Sect. 3.2.3.3.

[57] On this distinction, see Traverso 2006, p. 51.

[58] See Chap. 1, Sect. 1.5, n 100.

[59] Camby 2012, p. 8.

answers. Many differences, however, also emerge, and some of them hinge upon the broader paradigm of criminalisation.[60]

In this regard, it is worth examining an important decision of the French Constitutional Council, which is demonstrative of the problem of memory makers and the judge's role in the legal protection of historical memory. As this offence evolves, the conflict between law and history does not subside but instead tends to be accentuated when implementing measures originating in European law.

The Council's ruling led to the amendment of the provision on original denialism, which is limited to the Holocaust and already existed in French criminal law. As mentioned above, France was the first country to introduce a specific offence tailored to this phenomenon[61] by inserting a separate provision within Article 24 *bis* of the Law on the Freedom of the Press. The amendment the Council ruled on is in line with previous attempts[62] to extend the application of the criminal provision beyond the Holocaust and in particular to the Armenian genocide of 1915.[63]

The proposed amendment was incorporated in the final text of the 'Equality and Citizenship' Law of 22 December 2016. Article 173, para 2 of this provision introduces an expansive modification of punishment for the current offence of denialism. By adding a paragraph to Article 24 *bis* of the law on Freedom of the Press, it declares as punishable those who in the same way:

> deny, minimise or outrageously trivialise, through one of the means specified in Article 23, the existence of a crime of genocide other than those mentioned in the first paragraph of this Article, another crime against humanity, a crime of enslavement, exploitation of a person reduced to slavery or a crime of war as defined in Articles 6, 7, and 8 of the Statute of the International Criminal Court signed in Rome on 18 June 1998 and Articles 211-1 to 212-3,

---

[60] On the problematic implication deriving from the expansion of the criminal offence, see the remarks, Dubuisson 2007, p. 164.

[61] As mentioned, the 1990 *Gayssot* Act introduces the offence of '*contestation des crimes contre l'humanité*'. From a temporal point of view, it should be emphasised that the offence of historical denialism is introduced before the remembrance laws.

[62] A first attempt to do so had already been carried out in 2006, but the bill was blocked in 2008. Another major initiative began in 2012 when Law no. 647 'Aiming at repressing the contestation of the existence of the genocides recognised by law' ('*Visant à réprimer la contestation de l'existence des génocides reconnus par la loi*') was approved by the National Assembly on 22 December 2011 and the Senate on 23 January 2012.

[63] The Armenian genocide was officially recognised by France on 29 January 2001 Law no. 2001-70. On the 'judicial derivations of history' and the proliferation of memorial laws in France, especially since 1990, see Nora 2016, p. 60 et seq. Important is the Law no. 647 'Aiming at repressing the contestation of the existence of the genocides recognised by law' ('*Visant à réprimer the contestation of the existence of the genocides reconnus par la loi*') approved by the National Assembly on 22 December 2011 and the Senate on 23 January 2012, which provided punishment for 'who disproves or grossly trivializes the existence of one or more crimes of genocide', 211-1 of the Criminal Code and recognised as such by French law. It was declared unconstitutional by the already mentioned decision of the Constitutional Council, Decision, 28 February 2012, n 2012-647 DC, available at the following link: http://www.conseil-constitutionnel.fr/decision/2012/2012-647-dc/decision-n-2012-647-dc-du-28-fevrier-2012.104949.html. See Hochmann 2016.

224-1 from A to C 224-1 and 461-1 to 461-31 of the Criminal Code, when: 1. Such a crime has led to a conviction handed down by a French or international court; 2. Or, that the denial, minimisation or trivialisation of such a crime constitutes an incitement to violence or hatred directed against a group of people or to a member of a group defined on the basis of race, colour, religion, provenance or national origin.

The Council examines the two distinct hypotheses created by the new paragraph, which correspond to two different crimes in terms of structure, violation and core of negative values. When the claim relates to a historical event that has already been the subject of a conviction ('*condamnation*') issued by a French or international court, it does not require compliance with other requirements.[64] Conversely, when it lacks this prior conviction punishment may be applied only if the denial, minimisation or trivialisation results in incitement to violence or hatred directed against a group (or members of a group) on the basis of race, colour, religion, provenance or national origin.[65]

Prompted by a group of senators and delegates who raised various objections to this law, the constitutional judges came to the conclusion that only the second scenario is unconstitutional with decision no. 745 of 26 January 2017[66]. The finding of unconstitutionality of this section is based on the offence being superfluous and a potential source of double jeopardy. Indeed, the Council argues that it overlaps with the crime of condoning denialism provided for by Article 24 of the same Freedom of the Press Act.[67]

After having affirmed that not every denial, trivialisation or minimisation constitutes incitement to hatred, the Council states that the offence of denialism established by the second paragraph[68] (which also requires proof of instigation) punishes acts which are not considered abusive of freedom of expression.[69] The Council also recognises another defect of the provision contained in the second paragraph:[70] in the absence of a prior '*condamnation*' related to the crime denied, minimised or trivialised, (in the trial for denialism) the judge is delegated with the

[64] The original text presents further complications, due to the fact that it does not specify whether the conviction should be final or not. Furthermore, it provides for the punishment of claims concerning slavery, whether this constitutes an international crime or not.

[65] The measure would not apply except in the case of denial of hatred or violence and does not provide for automatic punishment of mere historical denialism, as is established in the aforementioned Law, declared unconstitutional in 2012 by the Constitutional Council. On the distinction introduced in Germany between mere/simple historical 'denialism' and 'qualified' denialism, see Chap. 4, n 16.

[66] Available at the following link: http://www.conseil-constitutionnel.fr/conseil-constitutionnel/francais/les-decisions/acces-par-date/decisions-depuis-1959/2017/2016-745-dc/decision-n-2016-745-dc-du-26-janvier-2017.148543.html.

[67] Constitutional Council, Decision, 26 January 2017, no. 2016-745 DC, para 195.

[68] *Ibid.*, para 194 exposes the contradiction between these two statements.

[69] *Ibid.*, para 197. For criticism on this point, see Hochmann 2017, p. 2, available at: http://www.revuedlf.com/droit-constitutionnel/pas-de-lunettes-sous-les-oeilleres-le-conseil-constitutionnel-et-le-negationnisme/.

[70] Constitutional Council, Decision, 16 July 1996, no. 96-377 DC, para 196.

task of qualifying the criminal nature of the facts punished. Therefore, this would lead to uncertainty about the legality of comments made about facts which are likely to be the subject of historical debate, and thus a question of constitutionality in terms of the proportionality of the intervention of criminal law.

However, it has been observed[71] that the Council should have addressed the problem of foreseeability[72] rather than the problem of proportionality in relation to freedom of expression given the broad spectrum of crimes. Likewise, denialist acts do not require an assessment of the truth of the denied facts, which are not the subject of the judgment.[73] Indeed, the latter relates not to a question of fact (the reality of the denied facts) but to a question of law consisting of the qualified denial of the facts.[74]

It remains difficult to understand why the Council's judgment of unconstitutionality was not extended to the new hypotheses considered in the first paragraph.[75] The rationale of the Council is not explained with regard to delegating the judge with the task of determining the truth of the facts. Furthermore, there has been no extension to another provision of the 'Equality and Citizenship' Law (contained in Article 173), which amended the offence of condoning under Article 24 of the Freedom of the Press Act. The amendment establishes that those who condone the crimes referred to in the first paragraph, namely war crimes, crimes against humanity or crimes of collaboration with the enemy, shall be punished 'even if such crimes have not led to the conviction of those who committed them'.[76]

To date the amended Article 24 *bis* reads:

> the punishment shall be one year in prison and € 45,000 in penalties for those who question, through one of the means specified in Article 23, the existence of one or more crimes against humanity as defined in Article 6 of the Statute of the International Military Tribunal annexed to the London Agreement of 8 August 1945 and have been committed either by members of an organisation declared criminal under Article 9 of said Statute, or by an individual who has been convicted of the above crimes by a French or international court.
>
> Punished with the same penalties are those who deny, minimise or outrageously trivialise, through one of the means specified in Article 23, the existence of a crime of genocide other than those mentioned in the first paragraph of this Article, another crime against humanity, a crime of enslavement, exploitation of an enslaved person or a crime of war as defined in Articles 6, 7, and 8 of the Statute of the International Criminal Court signed in Rome on 18 June 1998 and Articles from 211-1 to 212-3, 224-1 from A to C 224-1 and 461-1 to 461-31 of the Criminal Code, when: 1. This crime has led to a conviction handed down by a French or international court.

---

[71] Hochmann 2017, p. 2.

[72] As discussed in the State Council's Public Report of 2014, INT-387525, 12 April 2013, 294, available at the following link: http://www.conseil-etat.fr/Decisions-Avis-Publications/Etudes-Publications/Rapports-Etudes/Rapport-public-2014.

[73] Hochmann 2017, p. 2.

[74] *Ibid.* See also Hochmann 2012, p. 187 et seq.; Thomas 1998, p. 24.

[75] However, the possibility of raising a question of constitutionality in the future remains.

[76] Hochmann 2017, p. 4.

What emerges from the Council's judgment, even if only implicitly, is that the existence of a prior conviction (by a French or international court) establishes the element of constitutional legitimacy for punishing historical denialism.

On a practical level, the consequence is that, although the new provision expands the capacity to punish, it is still not applicable to the denial of the Armenian genocide, because this genocide still has not been the subject of a conviction by a French or international court.[77] Additionally, the new configuration of the provision does not include a number of instances which would fall under the second paragraph, such as facts qualified as crimes of genocide or against humanity by a non-French national court and by a French or international non-judicial body (such as a military commission or a parliamentary commission of inquiry).

The result is that crimes that are not the subject of a '*condamnation*' by a French or international court, such as the Armenian genocide, will enjoy less protection. As a result, the new provision creates ambiguity by stating that events are 'established' historical facts and as such do not fall within freedom of expression if they have already been the subject of a court ruling. The historical and judicial spheres thus reinforce one another. The French example and the Council's most recent judgment reaffirm that only historical facts designated as such by a judge (French or international) can be protected. Protecting the memory of a fact through criminal law inevitably entails protecting the legal qualification of the fact. It risks creating a vicious circle within law determined by emphasising court rulings and neglecting the context in which the statements are made, which are the only means for assessing whether they are likely to incite or not. These very themes arise in the case of *Perinçek v. Switzerland*, which is emblematic of the broadened offence of denialism and led the European Court of Human Rights to issue two distinct judgments.

3.2.6 *Protecting Historical Research Methodology: The* Theil *Case*

The complex relationship between history and law is also at the centre of another important judgment, issued by the High Court (*Tribunal de Grande Instance*) of Lyon. On 3 January 2006, this Court condemned George Theil to six months imprisonment and a fine of 10,000 € for questioning crimes against humanity ('*contestation des crimes contre l'humanité*') pursuant to Article 24 *bis* of the Freedom of the Press Act, which punishes denialism.[78] He had denied the existence

[77] *Ibid.*, p. 5. Differently, the Rwandan genocide has been the object of convictions handed down by both the ICTR and French courts; see, for instance, the life sentence for crimes against humanity and genocide imposed on Tito Barahira and Octavien Ngenzi by the Cour d'Assise de Paris, 6 July 2016, or the conviction and 25-year imprisonment sentence of Pasval Simbikangwa by the Tribunal de Bobigny, 3 December 2016.

[78] High Court of Lyon, 6th Correctional Chamber, *George Theil*, Judgment, 3 January 2006, no. 0564977.

of gas chambers during a television interview. Though not very recent, this decision is of interest because the judges explain the rationale behind the law (*ratio legis*) and the scope of Article 24 *bis* as part of a broader discussion on conflicts of memory.[79]

The Tribunal cites the *Travaux préparatoires* of the law, which express the need for punishing behaviour related to anti-Semitism and sympathising with Nazism. According to their reading, the judges consider a protected interest to be the equal human dignity of all people regardless of ethnicity, nation, race or religion. This protection would require punishment for every offence regarding the memory of the victims of crimes against humanity, as defined by Article 6 letter c) of the Statute of the Nuremberg Military Tribunal. Therefore, Article 24 *bis* serves to counter all forms of denial of memory that mask anti-Semitism. The judges also stress that they should not overstep the boundaries of historical research by becoming guardians of an official historical truth as this would compromise the 'good faith' of this discipline.[80] The ruling thus expresses the need to ensure that the trial does not result in the removal of certain historical events from historical research and that their transformation into indisputable *truths* remains intact.

In order to resolve this case, the judges identified certain criteria, such as the use of the 'correct method' by the historian. In line with the case law of the ECtHR, which evaluates the context, purpose and method of the historical assessment more than the content, this Court decision argues that it is essential to analyse the merits of the argument put forward by *Theil* as well as his method.

To this end, they had to verify whether the historian had followed a procedure in good faith by taking into account the type and number of sources used. The Lyon court found the accused guilty, *ex* Article 24 *bis*,[81] on the basis of these arguments, citing previous French and European Court case law[82] as well as certain studies on denialism, some of which are by now considered outdated in light of copious contemporary literature.[83]

This decision leads to another questionable scenario in which the judge intervenes to clarify elements of the defendant's guilt (their 'good faith') and to determine what the correct historical method is. But under what terms can the method be judged? What does it mean to criminally protect a scientific method and, in this case, the historical method? If the value to be protected—as indicated in the preparatory work of the Freedom of the Press Act—is human dignity, why focus on method rather than the content of the statements?

[79] On memory wars, see Chap. 1, Sect. 1.2.1.3, n 62.

[80] High Court of Lyon, *George Theil*, above n 76, 36.

[81] It is worth noting that the Court based its Judgment on the previous version of Article 24 *bis* of the Freedom of the Press Act.

[82] In particular the cases ECtHR (Grand Chamber), *Lehideux and Isorni v. France*, Judgment, 23 September 1998, Application no. 24662/94 and ECtHR, *Garaudy v. France*, Judgment, 24 June 2003, Application no. 65831/01. See High Court of Lyon, *George Theil*, above n 76, p. 29.

[83] See High Court of Lyon, *George Theil*, above no. 76, p. 30.

The judgment seems to implicitly recognise that there are different and potentially conflicting values at stake. In order to protect the dignity of the victims, it is important to identify specific criteria within the processes of scientific research. Otherwise, by simply reacting to the final outcomes, freedom would be threatened —and freedom itself is a protected value. However, this reasoning creates other issues: it puts history on trial and questions the validity of the historical method. A judge is put in the position to assess the method of historical research, but is he not a judge rather than a historian? In trying to avoid a 'paradox of content', which entails establishing an event as truth by removing it from the scrutiny of historical research, do we not risk a 'paradox of method'? This in turn judges the scientific validity of a discipline other than law by actually establishing correct and 'definitive' standards. This consequence is that in many ways the methodological foundations of the discipline are put on trial. Is it sufficient to simply make reference to a scientific method, albeit one that is widespread, considered effective and with a long tradition, as a basis for adjudication?

3.3 The European Court of Human Rights

The following analysis of relevant jurisprudence continues to explore the complex interaction between criminal law and memory.

We now move from the national to the regional level with the examination of two cases dealt with by the ECtHR. We consider first the *Garaudy* case concerning original denialism and, second, the *Perinçek* case which highlights some problematic issues related to broadened denialism.

3.3.1 *'Clearly Established Historical Facts': The* **Garaudy** *Case*

The ruling of the European Court of Human Rights in the *Garaudy* case is crucial to examining the complex relationship between history, memory and criminal law generated by the crime of historical denialism and, more generally, the trend of filtering the past or significant historical events through court decisions.

The *Garaudy v. France* decision[84] expresses the complexity of criminalisation as well as the adverse effects of transforming tribunals into sanctuaries for constructing collective historical memory. Moreover, it has become an important legal precedent and is often referred to by other national and international court decisions.

[84] Safi 2017, p. 686; Roets 2004, p. 239; Cohen-Jonathan 1999, p. 366 et seq.

In this case, the European Court declared the defendant's request to be inadmissible, citing a restriction on the free expression of thought protected by Article 10 ECHR.

Roger Garaudy was convicted in France of 'committing crimes against humanity, public racial defamation' and 'provoking racial hatred' after publishing a book titled *The Founding Myths of Israeli Politics*. It is not possible here, nor is it our purpose, to summarise and analyse all of the aspects contained in the decision.

The Court recalls the distinction between the 'clearly established historical facts, such as the Holocaust'[85] and 'facts about which there is still an ongoing debate among historians'.[86]

Therefore, the ECtHR examines the possibility and legitimacy of limits on a historical debate about the events of World War II. While an open and peaceful debate about history is considered necessary for any country,[87] the ECtHR affirms the exclusion of the application of Article 10 ECHR to denialist or revisionist discourse concerning the existence of the Holocaust.[88]

According to this judgment, given the methods used and the content of the statements, it is up to the Court to decide whether 'historical facts'[89] can be challenged. Based on this assumption, the ECtHR declared the defendant's request inadmissible since the book published by *Garaudy* was intended to cast doubt on the Holocaust. Therefore, the purpose of the publication was not to find the truth, but the accusation of the victims of the Nazi regime of falsifying history; the publication achieved this end by altering events and redeeming Nationalist Socialist rule.[90] Consequently, considering the historical, human and political significance of that event, Holocaust denial on its own takes on a racist character with discriminatory intent and the ability to incite hatred.

As stated in the judgment, assertions regarding the Holocaust 'question the underlying values in the fight against racism and anti-Semitism, and as such are able to seriously disturb public order. Offending the rights of others, these

---

[85] See ECtHR (Grand Chamber), *Lehideux and Isorni v. France*, Judgment, 23 September 1998, Application no. 24662/94, paras 53, 47; ECtHR, *Garaudy v. France*, Judgment, 24 June 2003, Application no. 65831/01, para 28.

[86] This expression was used for the first time in the aforementioned judgment of the ECtHR (Grand Chamber), *Lehideux and Isorni v. France*, Judgment, 23 September 1998, Application no. 24662/94, para 47 and then referred to by the Court in the cited judgment.

[87] See para 55.

[88] The statements analysed in this landmark case do 'not belong to the category of clearly established historical facts—such as the Holocaust—whose negation or revision would be removed from the protection of Article 10 by Article 17' (Para. 47). According to this interpretation the protections in Article 17, the prohibition of abuse of rights, could restrict the right of free speech granted under Article 10. Hence, Article 17's new role was only announced in Lehideux but not applied.

[89] ECtHR, *Garaudy v. France*, Judgment, 24 June 2003, Application no. 65831/01, para 26, citing ECtHR (Grand Chamber), *Lehideux and Isorni v. France*, Judgment, 23 September 1998, Application no. 24662/94, para 53.

[90] ECtHR, *Garaudy v. France*, Judgment, 24 June 2003, Application no. 65831/01, para 29.

behaviours are incompatible with democracy and human rights and perpetrators of them pursue objectives which are prohibited by Article 17 ECHR'.[91]

For this reason, such conduct is not protected by Article 10 ECHR, and stands in opposition to the values of justice and peace, which are fundamental to the Convention and expressed in the Preamble.[92]

On the one hand, this judgment demonstrates the tendency of determining history through the context of legal categories. On the other hand, it reveals the tendency of responding to historical denialism with criminalisation.

The distinction between '*established historical facts*' and 'facts still subject to debate' is particularly significant. This distinction presents history as a process that, although gradual, ultimately aims to produce a definitive knowledge of the past or of the relevant events. The influence exerted by the dynamics of fact-finding in a criminal trial related to a discipline such as history could not be more apparent, as it strives to gain knowledge of the facts of the past using diverse means and for very different purposes.

With specific procedures, both history and the criminal trial seek to reconstruct the past. At first glance, the image of the past as a 'definitive acquisition [of the facts]' seems to share undisputable similarities with the judicial truth and with the contents of the final decision issued in court. However, this notion is profoundly misleading.

The idea that history narrates the facts 'as they actually took place' is a relic of 19th century positivism. It proved to be deceptive and today historians consider the concept to be in serious conflict with current research practices. Currently it has largely been replaced by historians' reflections on their own discipline.

In this way, the fundamental differences between the criminal trial and historical research remain hidden. First, the strict limitations on relevant facts in the criminal trial are instrumental for ascertaining the responsibility of the accused *versus* the fundamental limitlessness of historical investigations. Second, over time the present asks numerous questions of the past in order to understand its roots: every new present has new questions for the past, significant new facts to be discovered and new causal links between already distinguished facts which acquire a new meaning.

Furthermore, the legal definition of past events entails the use of existing legal categories to interpret the past (consider enslavement, which today is qualified as an international crime but for long periods of human history was a basic institution of society). Doing so marginalises the goal of historical research: the interaction among men and human communities at the political level.

The categories of guilt and innocence are defined by a determined legal framework and it is difficult for them to encompass the conflicting and transformational dimensions of the public realm, as well as the unexpected, fundamental

---

[91] *Ibid.*

[92] *Ibid.* See also ECtHR, *Pierre Marais v. France*, Judgment, 24 June 1996, Application no. 31159/96, p. 191; ECtHR *Remer v. Germany*, Judgment, 6 September 1995, Application no. 25096/94.

elements of human history. This can trigger another potential dilemma that concerns not only the relationship between history, memory and rights, but also between politics and law.

In this context, the criminal judgment can therefore imply depriving the political sphere of power, which is in line with a society that deepens its regulatory laws. The judgment on the past occurs in the present, thus constricting a field that is, by definition, one of conflict, of change, of continuous redefinition and brings with it the risk of damaging a cornerstone of our social existence.

From this point of view, the relationship between politics and law, that is between the constituent and the constituted, is inverted. However, through the use of seemingly 'neutral' categories, there is the danger of a latent, barely perceptible tendency towards the de-politicisation of the public sphere.

With reference to the relationship between law and history, a similar trend emerges with the progressive removal of significant events of the past from research because *they have already been judged*. This creates a paradox with a scientific, objective vision of history and the very nature of the relationship between human society and the past, which is always in a process of continuous renegotiation.

3.3.2 'Fact' and 'Legal Qualification of Fact': The **Perinçek** *Case*

The *Perinçek* case is symbolic of the broadened model of criminalisation of denialism and in particular regarding the conflict between law and history.

We will briefly review the two judgments of the European Court of Human Rights, the last from the Grand Chamber in 2015, which ruled that a violation of Article 10 ECHR did not occur.

As already noted, the European Court has frequently been asked to rule on cases of historical denialism, which, however, were always related to the Holocaust. The *Perinçek* case not only demonstrates that some of the critical issues related to the 'original' form of historical denialism are exacerbated in the 'broader' form provided for by the Swiss Criminal Code, but will also highlight the emergence of new and unusual dilemmas stemming from criminalisation.

In the *Perinçek* case, the European Court was asked for the first time to consider the denial of the Armenian genocide, widely recognised as such by the community of historians and the legislation of various countries, both European and non-European, but outside of the frequently analysed context of the Holocaust and of court cases concerning it. Another aspect worth mentioning is that the Armenian genocide is the subject of legislation in the country where it occurred, but in a contrasting manner with respect to all the cases examined so far. The 'official memory' of the nation, protected by Turkish law, indeed denies that it occurred and asserting its existence is a specific offence in an equal and opposite way that denialism of international crimes is in other countries.[93]

As mentioned, the ECtHR ruled on the *Perinçek* case twice. In 2013, the Second Section of the European Court of Human Rights ruled by five votes to two that Switzerland violated the right to freedom of expression (Article 10 ECHR) by convicting Doğu Perinçek for publicly denying the existence of the genocide against the Armenian people.[94] On 15 October 2015, (the centennial year of the Armenian genocide), after a referral, the Grand Chamber confirmed by ten votes to seven the finding of a violation of Article 10 ECHR. The judgment was again contrary to the Confederation and in favour of the defendant, albeit for reasons partly divergent but at the same time relevant to this analysis.

This ECtHR jurisprudence is the first intervention which limits the *expansive tendency* of criminalising denialism of other recognised genocides and, in perspective, crimes against humanity.

The subsequent analysis identifies and examines only the most relevant points for the purpose of this study, especially those regarding the conflict between criminal law and history.[95]

3.3.2.1 The Swiss Conviction

Dogu Perinçek, a law graduate and president of the Turkish workers' party, participated in three conferences in Switzerland between May and June 2005, during which he publicly stated that qualifying the atrocities committed by the Ottoman Empire against Armenians as crimes of genocide constitutes an 'international lie'. According to *Perinçek*, those crimes were actually committed due to the nature and demands of war and were not committed for the specific purpose to destroy, in

[93] See Algan 2008, pp. 2237–2252. It is worth mentioning Article 301 of the Turkish Criminal Code, which punishes those who publicly denigrate the nation, state, government or legal institutions of the Turkish state. This provision has been used to attempt to punish those who recognizes and affirm the existence of the Armenian genocide. It thus stands in equal and opposite terms to the offence of denialism: equal because foresight of an autonomous offence prohibits the expression of an opinion that does not conform to an official and majority view of the memory of a historical event; opposite because in the Turkish case the affirmation of a genocide is punished and not its denial. Although the offence provided by Turkish law is antithetical (penalising affirmation and not denial), it is absolutely identical in form and structure: it is prohibited by criminal law to question a 'historical truth' sanctioned as such by the State.

[94] The ECtHR considered the defendant's statements as legal and ruled that the case did not apply to ECHR Article 17 (abuse clause). Article 17 ECHR states: 'Nothing in this Convention may be interpreted as implying for any State, group or person any right to engage in any activity or perform any act aimed at the destruction of any of the rights and freedoms set forth herein or at their limitation to a greater extent than is provided for in the Convention'. ECtHR, *Perinçek v. Switzerland*, Judgment, 17 December 2013, Application no. 27510/08.

[95] Examination of those judgments in the light of the case law of the European Court of Human Rights is not within the scope of this study. For an analysis of the judgment from this perspective, see Hervieu 2014; Lobba 2014; Decoeur 2014.

whole or in part, the Armenian people, which is an essential requirement of the crime of genocide.[96] However, the purpose or the specific intention (*dolus specialis*) was absent, and therefore, *Perinçek* asserted that the crimes could not be defined as crimes of genocide. *Perinçek* recognised that the massacre had occurred but did not believe it could be legally qualified as genocide. The crux of the *Perinçek* case is immediately evident: by giving these crimes a different name *Perinçek* denies the significance attributed to them.

Denounced by the Swiss-Armenian Association in July 2005, *Perinçek* received a final sentence (a monetary penalty) from the Swiss authorities in accordance with Article 261a on racial discrimination of the Criminal Code and, in particular, pursuant to para 4 of this provision, which stipulates punishment for 'everyone [...] who publicly, [...] denies, grossly minimises or attempts to justify genocide or other crimes against humanity'.[97]

Initially, with the judgment of 9 March 2007, the Police Tribunal in the District of Lausanne found *Perinçek* guilty of the offence under Article 261a, para 4 of the Criminal Code, considering that the Armenian genocide was protected under this provision. The judgment was later upheld by the county Criminal Court of Cassation.

Finally, with the 12 December 2007 judgment[98] the Swiss Federal Court rejected *Perinçek*'s appeal, reiterating the applicability of the provision also to the Armenian genocide.[99]

These decisions are interesting to note because in many ways they are exemplary of the inner mechanisms and trends already observed in the transition from original denialism to its broadened version.

The expansion of the criminal offence is an issue that had emerged during the preparatory phase of the law, in which there had been a discrepancy between the German and French texts. The German text reads 'who [...] denies genocide or other crimes against humanity' ('*wer* [...] *Völkermord oder andere Verbrechen gegen die Menschlichkeit leugnet*'). In this text, the word genocide (*Völkermord*) is not preceded by any article. The German version thus suggests a general ambiguity about possible extension beyond the Holocaust that should be resolved by judicial interpretation. The structure of the French version (as well as the Italian one) does not allow for this uncertainty and therefore the provision must clearly indicate that the offence regards denialism of '*le génocide*' (the genocide) or '*un génocide*' (a genocide). Initially the Legal Affairs Committee of the National Council adopted the first proposed solution, which according to some of its members, created a situation of conflict between the French restrictive text and the potentially broad

[96] On the constituent elements of the crime of genocide, see Schabas 2016, pp. 143–157; Fronza 2016, pp. 323–350; O'Keefe 2015; Ambos 2014, pp. 1–45; Werle and Jessberger 2014, pp. 309–312; May 2010; Schabas 2009; Cassese 2002, pp. 335–351.

[97] See Niggli and Wiprächtiger 2013; Trechsel and Pieth 2012; Corboz 2002; Weber 1998. The *Perinçek* case was the first conviction under Article 261a.

[98] See Federal Court, 12 December 2007, ATF 6B_398/2007, in http://www.bger.ch.

[99] *Ibid.*, Sect. 3.2.

German text. After passing through the Council of States (the High Chamber of the Swiss Parliament), the provision was amended and the expression '*le génocide*' was replaced with '*un génocide*' and that version was then finally adopted. It is therefore the French version that today more explicitly enshrines the expanded paradigm of denialism beyond the Holocaust.

The Swiss judges, particularly those of first instance court, address this matter by inquiring whether a consensus like the one about the Holocaust also existed for the Armenian genocide. If the two historical events can be identified as genocide, and are officially and definitively established as such, it follows that they require a similar response and protection with regard to denialism.

It should also be reiterated that the judges were not expected to 'make history' but only to recognise whether a genocide is 'known and recognised' and 'proven'. However, the defendant in this case claimed that no international judgment or expert commission had expressly qualified the events of 1915 as a crime of genocide. The Federal Court, on the other hand, did not consider this point relevant because the existence of a general consensus within the historical debate on such a qualification was sufficient to exclude a predominately criminal law debate on the same matter. The Swiss Supreme Court also stressed that general consensus does not mean unanimity and therefore is not excluded based on the fact that some states have decided not to recognise the Armenian genocide, a decision which may have been dictated by political motives. General consensus is to be sought instead within the scientific community.[100] The Federal Tribunal affirmed that, on the one hand, the Swiss Federal Council never officially recognised the Armenian genocide and, on the other hand, it encouraged Turkey to develop its own historical memory by promoting the creation of an international commission of experts among Turkish authorities.[101] Thus, Switzerland did not implicitly recognise the genocide but opted for a different policy solution and approach to this issue. With respect to the scientific community, the Tribunal added that the defendant had not proven the existence of sufficient doubt about qualifying the events of 1915 as genocide.

Another particular aspect worth mentioning is the provision of a subjective element required by Article 261, para 4 of the Criminal Code.[102] Unlike other offences of denialism, Swiss law requires that punishable acts are carried out for intentionally discriminatory reasons.

In the proceedings before the Federal Court that intention was considered proven on the basis of external factors: Perinçek's degree in law, his activity as a politician, and the fact that he is a writer and historian. For all these reasons, he would have acted with knowledge of the facts, expressly stating among other things that he would never have changed his opinion. Therefore, according to the judges, qualifying a people who are victims of genocide as the aggressor constitutes an attack on the identity of the members of a community.

[100] See n 94 above, para 4.3.

[101] *Ibid.*, para 4.5.

[102] *Ibid.*, para 5.

The Federal Court also held that Perinçek's assertions were not part of the historical debate (thus they cannot benefit from the protection given to the freedom of research) and were expressed intentionally to promote racial and ethnic discrimination.

As mentioned above, the defendant's appeal was rejected and the conviction was confirmed. Although Perinçek denied that the events of 1915 constituted genocide, he did acknowledge the existence of massacres and deportations and provided justification for the same. According to the judges, even if such massacres and deportations were not qualified as a crime of genocide, they would in any case be legally considered as crimes against humanity, and therefore to justify them based on the law of war or alleged security reasons would still make them punishable under the offence in question.[103]

The procedure that led the Swiss judges to confirm Perinçek's conviction is emblematic of the dynamics of the criminal offence in its expanded version. Perinçek proposed a reconstruction of history which presented the events as merely tragic consequences of war without the specific intent to destroy a group, which itself is a minimisation and justification, and therefore a punishable act of denialism.

3.3.2.2 The Decisions of the European Court of Human Rights

After the final Swiss court judgment, Perinçek appealed to the European Court claiming that under Swiss Article 261a, para 4 of the Criminal Code his conviction was not justified by a legitimate aim and that the restriction of his right to free speech was not necessary in a democratic society and was a violation of Article 10 ECHR.

The appeal was received, and the Court issued its first judgment on 17 December 2013, thus finding the Swiss authorities in breach of Article 10 ECHR because they had unjustifiably limited freedom of expression.[104] As previously mentioned, the first judgment was followed by a second one handed down by the Grand Chamber in 2015, which the Swiss authorities appealed, and resulted in a similar outcome.

As a testament to the complexity of the decision to criminalise denialism, the judgments contain a number of relevant issues, as well as the symptomatic ambiguities of the dilemma on which the European Court has been asked to rule twice.[105]

---

[103] *Ibid.*, para 7.

[104] See Lobba 2014, pp. 59–77; Hervieu 2014.

[105] See Fronza and Cortese 2017; Belavusau 2016, pp. 627–629; Della Morte 2016; Garibian 2016; Longo and Ubiali 2016; Leotta 2015; Hervieu 2014; Montanari 2013.

'Fact' and 'Legal Qualification of Fact'

In the first judgment of 2013, the European Court was asked whether the clause contained in Article 17 ECHR[106] applied to this case, that is, if the statements under scrutiny constituted incitement to violence and hatred. As noted above, this is the very same reasoning which led to the dismissal of the appeal in the case of *Garaudy v. France*. If the answer was yes, the case should have been declared inadmissible because the statements made by Perinçek would no longer have been protected by Article 10.[107]

Following an established procedure, the European judges reiterate that in accordance with the tolerant and open character of a democratic society, freedom of speech 'applies not only to the statements or ideas that are favourably received or regarded as inoffensive or indifferent, but also for those that offend, shock or disturb the State or any part of the population'.[108]

According to the judges, Perinçek's statements pertained to a topic of general public interest—an element which requires caution when placing limits on the freedom of expression—and they did not have as their objective the questioning of the massacres or deportation, which can widely be considered established historical facts. Rather they were exclusively concerned with the legal qualification of those facts as 'genocide' and as 'international crimes'. 'Furthermore, it is considered important that the applicant has never disputed that massacres and deportations took place during the years in question. Instead, all he denies is the legal characterisation of those events as 'genocide''.[109]

Departing from the previous jurisprudence on denialism (however, as mentioned, the Court had never ruled on the Armenian genocide), the judges excluded the applicability of Article 17 ECHR: 'since Perinçek's statements challenging the legal classification of the events of 1915 cannot in themselves incite hatred against

[106] 'The Court will determine whether the applicant's statements should be excluded from the scope of Article 10 on the basis of Article 17 of the Convention': ECtHR, *Perinçek v. Switzerland*, above n 92, para 49.

[107] Article 10 ECHR therefore operates in unison with other provisions of the ECHR, including Article 17 ECHR. See Schabas 2015; Buyse 2014, pp. 491–503; Bartole et al. 2012; Keane 2007, pp. 641–663; van Drooghenbroeck 2001, pp. 552–553. For cases in which the European Court used Article 17 ECHR in relation to denialist statements, see Lobba 2015, pp. 62–64; ECtHR, *Lehideux and Isorni v. France*, Grand Chamber, above n 80, para 47. For a recent case of application of Article 17, though not strictly concerning a denialist episode, see ECtHR, *M'Bala M'Bala v. France*, Judgment, 20 October 2015, Application no. 25239/13, with a commentary by Caroli 2015.

[108] See ECtHR *Lehideux and Isorni v. France*, above n 80, paras 55, 51.

[109] ECtHR, *Perinçek v. Switzerland*, above n 92, para 51. On this point, refer to the partially dissenting opinions of the judges Vučinić and Pinto de Albuquerque, according to which: 'the distinction between mere denial and trivialising or justifying is artificial in linguistic terms and can be easily circumvented by a sophisticated speaker, through euphemistic and elaborate speech' (para 19). The differentiation between denial of a historical fact and denial of its legal qualification may not make sense to some, see Garibian 2016, p. 238.

the Armenian people, and do not express contempt for the suffering endured', which Perinçek did not dispute.[110] In this way the applicability of the clause is limited to cases involving an abuse that displays specific severity.

The statements made by Perinçek must therefore be evaluated in light of Article 10 ECHR, under which any limitations on the right to freedom of expression are legitimate if provided by law, if in the interest of any of the aims of the Convention, and if necessary in a democratic society (Article 10, para 2 ECHR). The reasoning of the Court focuses on the latter requirement, considering the first two met respectively by the existence of the provision specified in legal code (the aforementioned Article 261, para 4 of the Swiss Criminal Code)[111] and the need to protect the rights of the victims' families.[112]

The Court reiterates that it cannot intervene and resolve issues that fall into an on-going debate among historians, nor rule on the qualification of historical events as genocide or crimes against humanity.[113] These aspects are under the responsibility of national authorities and, in particular, courts which are delegated to interpret and apply national law.[114]

The Strasbourg court should instead rule on the compatibility and proportionality of the restrictions adopted by the national authority with Article 10 ECHR, and verify if these are justified by a 'pressing social need', considering, on one hand, the rights of the families of the victims, and, on the other, the defendant's freedom of expression.[115]

The defendant's assertions, which the Court recognises as indisputably public in nature, are part of a heated and controversial debate about those events. They must be considered anchored in a historical context when evaluating tragic and significant events of the past as these statements also have a political and legal nature.[116]

In view of these elements, the European Court considers the margin of appreciation of the Swiss authorities to be reduced: the free exercise of the right to openly discuss sensitive and controversial issues is one of the fundamental aspects of freedom of opinion and the recognition of this exercise forms the boundary line

---

[110] 'The case-law cited above (see paras 44–50) indicates that the threshold for determining whether statements may fall within the scope of Article 17 relates to whether their aim is to stir up hatred or violence. The Court considers that the rejection of the legal characterization of the events of 1915 was not in itself sufficient to amount to incitement of hatred towards the Armenian people. In any event, the applicant has never been prosecuted or punished for incitement to hatred, which is a separate offence under the first paragraph of Article 261 *bis* of the Criminal Code (see para 14 above). Nor does it appear that the applicant has expressed contempt towards the victims of the events in question': ECtHR, *Perinçek v. Switzerland*, above n 92. On the Court's use of the clause on abuse of rights (Article 17), see Lobba 2015, pp. 240–243.

[111] ECtHR, *Perinçek v. Switzerland*, above n 92, paras 58–72.

[112] *Ibid.*, paras 73–75.

[113] *Ibid.*, para 99.

[114] *Ibid.*, para 111.

[115] *Ibid.*, paras 99–100 of the Judgment.

[116] *Ibid.*, para 112.

between a tolerant and democratic society and a totalitarian and dictatorial regime. Therefore, restricting the scope of this free exercise requires true necessity, which the majority of the judges did not find to be present in this case.

The absence of a social need to punish Perinçek's statements also emerges from a comparative analysis of national legislation. According to the Court, only two States extend the punishment of denialism to all genocides. In comparison to other countries, there is not a stronger social need in Switzerland to punish speech that denies only the legal qualification of crimes committed by the Ottoman Empire as crimes of genocide.[117]

In line with this reasoning are the decisions of the Spanish Constitutional Court and of the French Constitutional Council, as well as the General Observation 34/2011 of the Human Rights Committee of the United Nations, according to which 'the provisions that punish the expression of opinions about historical facts are incompatible with the obligations that the pact requires of State parties concerning the respect of freedom of expression. The pact does not permit general prohibition of statements about an erroneous opinion or an incorrect interpretation of past events'.[118]

The Swiss court decision would therefore be disproportionate to the aim of protecting the honour of the victims' families as it risks constituting censure capable of dissuading other individuals from publicly discussing issues affecting society as a whole.

These arguments and the comparison with other foreign laws convinced five out of seven judges to rule that the restriction established by Swiss authorities was not necessary in a democratic society. Consequently, Perinçek's conviction was not justified as it would violate the rights guaranteed by Article 10 ECHR.

The Nature of Historical Research and the Exception of the Holocaust

The other highly relevant aspect of the 2013 judgment in the context of this analysis is the Court's determination of freedom as an integral part of historical research. According to the judges, history by definition does not lend itself to definitive conclusions. However, they also affirm that this principle has one exception: the Holocaust. It is an exception that has a legal and historical basis as evidenced by extensive case law.

The reasoning of the judges was decisive regarding the concept of 'general consensus' on the legal definition of the crimes committed against the Armenian people. Contrary to the Swiss ruling, the European Court finds that there is no general consensus on the 'legal qualification' of these crimes as crimes of genocide. Thus, two interrelated aspects become relevant here: (1) the lack of unanimity in the scientific community, which is related to fundamental aspects of research and not

[117] *Ibid.*, para 120.

[118] *Ibid.*, para 124.

only specific to the Ottoman Empire's crimes against the Armenians; and (2) the lack of legal recognition of the same, unlike for instance the impact of the Nuremberg Tribunal's final decision on the Holocaust.

The judges observed that only 20 of 190 States in the world have officially recognised the Armenian genocide and note that there are differing points of view even within Swiss political bodies.[119] Recognising an overexpansion of the crime of genocide, the Court reiterates that the criminal offence (therefore beyond the specific case of the Armenian people) only occurs when the perpetrator has the specific intent to destroy the targeted group.[120] In addition, the judges acknowledge the difficulty of providing evidence that proves this intention. According to the Court, due to these specific aspects it is difficult to discern the general consensus the Swiss authorities refer to. As stated by the Court, a general consensus that does not even exist in the scientific community with regard to these events, 'given that historical research is controversial and debatable by definition and does not lend itself to definitive conclusions or to objective and absolute truths'.

However, this statement is partially challenged two lines below when the Court states that Holocaust denial discourse is a different matter. First, it denies very concrete historical facts, such as the existence of gas chambers.[121] Second, the convictions for crimes committed by the Nazis have a clear legal basis, namely Article 6, letter c) of the Statute of the Nuremberg International Military Tribunal. Last, these historical events questioned by the accused were subject to a ruling by an international court.[122] According to the Court, in the case of Holocaust denial, a pressing social need justifies interference with the right of freedom of expression because such statements are vehicles of anti-Semitism and require a firm response.

As a result, the denial of Nazi crimes constitutes an exception and may be punished without having to prove incitement to hatred or violence. Conversely, the same repercussions cannot result from denying the legal qualification of the tragic 1915 events against the Armenian people as genocide.[123] In the judges' opinion, these statements establish a different response to Holocaust denial, including in how it is treated. This conclusion, however, is quite perplexing considering that the judgment regards such a universally recognised genocide as that of the Armenian people.

---

[119] *Ibid.*, para 115.

[120] *Ibid.*, para 116.

[121] *Ibid.*, para 117.

[122] *Ibid.*, para 118. For criticism of these statements, see Hervieu 2014, citing that the judgments of the International Military Tribunal in Nuremberg are not unanimously accepted as 'historical facts', just as the qualification of Armenian as genocide is not unanimously accepted. According to the article, such a difference in status between Nazi and Armenian genocides based on the existence of a judicial decision is entirely 'artificial'. The article highlights the minority opinion of judges Vučinić and Pinto de Albuquerque who consider that the Armenian genocide has been widely recognised both by courts and internationally (see paras 2–10 of the Opinion).

[123] *Ibid.*, para 119.

Finally, the decision affirms the importance of freedom of expression on matters of public importance, even when this may include opinions that offend, shock or disturb the State or any sector of the population. Likewise, it reiterates the open nature of historical debate, but it also establishes an exception for the Holocaust, as it encompasses historical events established by international law and by the rulings of international tribunals. Contradiction seems to play out on two levels. In terms of the specific case, the Armenian genocide enjoys less protection. In terms of the larger picture, independence of historical research is upheld, and yet the court argues that one event (the Holocaust) is a historical fact and is excluded from freedom of expression when it is the subject of a law or a court decision. At first the judicial and historical spheres are separated, but then more emphatically re-joined.

A Hierarchy of Memories?

According to the judges of the Chamber, Holocaust denial and denial of the Armenian Genocide are to be distinguished by using the criteria of a pressing social need, which is different from and not simply attributable to the need to punish hate speech and violence. This leads to duplicity when balancing rights: free speech, which prevails in the case of the Armenian genocide, and the prohibition of discrimination, which takes precedence in the case of the Holocaust based on the fight against anti-Semitism. Thus, a clear hierarchy of historical memories emerges, which translates into a differentiation of treatment.[124]

What differentiates the Holocaust and its underlying anti-Semitism from other crimes against humanity is its historical character as the 'founding memory' of the values enshrined in the UN Charter and in the post-war constitutions: but can those same values justify this kind of hierarchy among memories?

This perspective was outlined in the 2013 ruling and then confirmed in the Grand Chamber's 2015 judgment. This very rich and complex decision (including the dissenting opinions) echoes the Chamber's ruling but with a different line of argumentation. It should be noted that the problematic issue of 'general consensus' is absent, at least explicitly. However, the ruling insists strongly on the context of Perinçek's statements and on the greater lapse of time between them and the crimes in question, thus making the need to punish denialist statements about the Armenian Genocide in a democratic society circumstantially dependent.

> This is particularly relevant with regard to the Holocaust. For the Court, the justification for making its denial a criminal offence lies not so much in that it is a clearly established historical fact but in that, in view of the historical context in the States concerned [...] its denial, even if dressed up as impartial historical research, must invariably be seen as connoting an antidemocratic ideology and anti-Semitism. [...] By contrast, it has not been argued that there was a direct link between Switzerland and the events that took place in the Ottoman Empire in 1915 and the following years.[125]

---

[124] Garibian 2016, p. 249.

[125] *Perincek*, Grand Chamber, para 243.

However, these elements cannot serve as the basis for a difference in treatment with respect to the Shoah.

A long lapse of time is capable of subduing the emotions sparked by the memory of events. In the span of a few more years this argument could also be made for the Holocaust. Likewise, the principle of evaluating the context in which the statements were made in order to assess their potential danger to public order (in this case the democratic country of Switzerland, not involved historically with the facts and for which those same facts bear no founding relevance) risks legitimising denialist statements about the Holocaust itself, especially in countries geographically and culturally foreign to it.

Furthermore, in both cases certain basic features of genocide and crimes against humanity are questioned, just like their statutes of limitation or the universal human rights affected by them, which, as has been noted,[126] is the basis of the very existence of the ECHR. In this light, differentiating memories seems hardly sustainable. 'Legislation expressing solidarity with victims of genocide and crimes against humanity must be possible everywhere, even if there are no direct links to the events or the victims, even if a long period of time has elapsed, and even if the legislation is not directly aimed at preventing conflicts'.[127]

A similar position can be found in Judge Nussberger's dissenting opinion. After criticising the inconsistency of the majority's approach, she contests that the state must proceed with a clear formulation of the criminal provision so that permissible and punishable opinions are clearly foreseeable. Judge Nussberger's claim seems intimately connected with the principle of *nullum crimen sine lege*, as coined by Feuerbach, according to which a precise prior legal provision is essential for guiding the behaviour of individuals in a democratic society (general positive prevention). Swiss Criminal Code Article 261a appears unclear and vague as it does not identify which historical events must be legally qualified as genocide. Therefore, the vagueness of legislation caused by the legislator creates methodological uncertainty to be dealt with by the judge and which concerns the legal qualification of certain historical events. A national law which does not clearly define precise historical events is destined to remain indeterminate and constitutes an interference with freedom of expression since uncertainty about the boundaries of criminal responsibility—and the consequent threat of punishment—may limit historical research.[128]

This leads to another observation: the protection of freedom of expression, regardless of collective opinion, is ultimately the protection of the cornerstone of the 'public space' of democratic societies and is confirmed by public interest in the statements under scrutiny. Thus, the utmost caution is required on the part of the judges in the Armenian case as another dilemma arises: recognising an expansive

---

[126] Cortese 2016, p. 10.

[127] See ECtHR, *Perinçek v. Switzerland*, above n 92, *partly concurring and partly dissenting opinion of Judge Nussberger*, p. 86.

[128] *Ibid.*, p. 86.

tendency of criminal legal protection of memory which eventually threatens that very memory, while at the same time accepting that same criminal legal protection in the case of the Holocaust. In this sense, the uniqueness of the Holocaust translates into legal and judicial uniqueness: but are such different consequences sustainable for crimes of equal gravity?

The protection of public space in one case, and the protection of foundational memories in the other, are juxtaposed in the 2013 judgment with no real mediation other than the role of the Holocaust and its historical 'certification' (and historical truth) via the judgments of the Nuremberg Tribunal and international legal instruments recognising the genocide.

An observation can also be made more specifically about the relationship between historical memory and judicial authority, which here acquires the *auctoritas* to decide which memories are worthy of protection under criminal law. In this regard, it is interesting to cite judges Vucininc and Pinto de Albuquerque's partially dissenting opinion in the 2013 Chamber judgment. According to them, the Armenian people, like the Jewish people, and in line with the statement made by the European Court in the case of *Garaudy v. France*, constitute a vulnerable minority. Consequently, the suffering endured by the Armenians is not of less value than the suffering of the Jews under the genocidal Nazi policy.[129]

Finally, the capability to incite violence and hatred as a determining factor in punishable statements should be a guiding force of balancing prohibition of discrimination and free speech in all cases. Part of the provision uses the phrase 'aggravated denial' to identify statements that are discriminatory and offensive when directed against a group of persons or a member of the group.[130]

This leads to the same conclusion, although with a different argumentative method. The Court's balanced approach between freedom of expression (Article 10 ECHR) and the right of a group to maintain their identity and dignity (stipulated in Article 8 ECHR) masks a certain ambiguity when identifying the legal interest to be protected. Declaring that Perinçek's statements cannot be regarded as offensive to the dignity of Armenians because they are harmless by nature and due to their place in space and time, the Grand Chamber seems to confuse the legal interest of 'dignity' with that of 'public order', in this case meaning peaceful coexistence among individuals. In this specific case, it could not be denied that the scope of Perinçek's statements harmed the dignity of the victims and their descendants. However, what is lacking in the defendant's assertions is the ability to incite hatred and violence. In this sense, the protection of dignity through criminal law would be desirable only if denialist discourse creates a need to defend public order and to prevent crimes, which are identified as legitimate aims by Article 10, para 2 ECHR. Accordingly, free speech should be restricted only when such statements have the ability to instigate hatred and violence.

[129] See *ibid.*, paras 21 and 22.

[130] See Garibian 2016, p. 237.

3.3.2.3 Final Remarks

The *Perinçek* case demonstrates the dilemmas resulting from criminalising denialism and the problematic relationship between law and history concerning 'crimes of memory'.

As previously mentioned, both European Court judgments take a favorable position on freedom of expression as a fundamental element of a democratic society, stressing that when denialist statements do not incite hatred or violence they are protected by Article 10 ECHR and, therefore, follow the guidelines contained in the EU Framework decision.

This conclusion is reached through some of the aspects analysed here, in particular the distinction between denialism of historical fact and denialism of the legal qualification of historical fact, given that Perinçek had recognised the crimes against the Armenians but did not attribute them to the legal category of genocide. The judges raised many questions related to this reasoning, the most important of which is: who decides that a fact is a historical fact? An event constitutes a historical fact when it acquires significance within a causal sequence and a given historical context. The same event may constitute a relevant fact for the historical reconstruction of one circumstance while having absolutely no influence in another reconstruction or context. From time to time the question we ask our past to answer is: what facts among the infinite plurality of events are historical facts? How can the narrative of the facts be distinguished from the facts themselves? How can we distinguish meaning from a symbol? Within a narrative of historical memory, the facts and the meaning attributed to them are inevitably interrelated.

The *Perinçek* decision raises a fundamental question in this regard: is the purpose of the offence of denialism to protect the legal qualification of a historical fact or to protect a historical fact from denialism? If the latter, when is a fact historical? The key consideration here is that the only protectable historical fact is the one designated by legislators or by judges, who continue to govern semantics and narrative. Once entrusted to criminal law, the protection of the memory of a fact can only end in the protection of the legal qualification of that fact.

Another fundamental characteristic of these rulings is the precedence of Article 10 ECHR (the protection of Freedom of expression) over Article 17 ECHR (Prohibition of abuse of rights). Specifically, the statements in question do not deny the facts but their legal qualification and are devoid of expressions of denigration, ridicule or lack of respect for suffering and as a result they do not constitute hate speech. However, in this way it is possible that denialist statements regarding serious crimes are not in themselves an expression of hatred. Unlike for the Holocaust, in these cases denial does not have an inherent ability to instigate.

This is exactly where the legal and judicial uniqueness of the Holocaust becomes important. When referring to the Holocaust, denialism in all its forms seems to be always immediately dangerous and therefore worthy of protection. The denial of the Nazi extermination seems to inherently contain instigation to hatred, discriminatory intent and a threat to social peace and thus constitutes the offence.

The problem of the legal and judicial uniqueness of the Holocaust is that the capacity to instigate is presumed. On the contrary, the case of the Armenian genocide reconfirms the possibility of a denial that is not inherently dangerous and hence, we could argue, 'non-denialist', which is the logic behind the approval of the appeal.

However, this uniqueness implies a difference in treatment of memories of all mass atrocities that is hardly sustainable if not absolutely discriminatory. It also creates an unstable equilibrium and a conflicting dynamic between opposing scenarios, which run the risk of eventually becoming mutually exclusive.

By considering 'non-denialist denialism' legal, and potentially not an offence because it lacks the capability of inciting hate, and distinguishing it from a specific intrinsically denialist denialism (with judgments and laws recognising it), a hierarchy of memories is created with a powerful status given only to the Holocaust. It follows that expanding the offence to other genocides and crimes against humanity (even with all the remedies available under the EU Framework Decision and various national legislations), in the name of combating every type of discrimination, is destined to fail when confronted with the need to protect freedom of expression.

If, on the other hand, we exclude the possibility of non-denialist denialism and consider that denial of the Holocaust and all mass crimes can inherently instigate hate, then the scenario moves in the direction of broadening the established criminalisation paradigm for the Holocaust to all other seriously grave crimes. Each type of denialism will then tend to be punished, with a prevalence of prohibiting discrimination with respect to freedom of expression, resulting in the full (and potentially unlimited) unfolding of the expansive iteration of the offence proposed by the EU Framework Decision.

However, there is a risk of triggering a vicious circle with the self-referential nature of entrusting the qualification of historical fact to a judgment and with the conflicting relationship between historical research criteria and that of legal qualification. These two profoundly different sets of criteria are far from being clearly defined and end up overlapping with the prevalence of the latter over the former based on the misleading equivalence of historiography and judicial investigation in ascertaining the facts of the past.

3.4 Courts of Memory

The analysis of legislation and case law conducted thus far clearly shows the complex intersection between law, trial and memory that the decision to punish historical denialism implies. The complications of using criminal law increase with the 'broadened' paradigm and to an even further extent when moving from a strictly national level to an international one. Indeed, when observed at an international level, we can clearly see a plurality of memories and the conflict between relative and universal.

It is worth remembering the many cases in which the criminal trial intervenes to 'establish' events of the past and to impose an official 'truth', which is the aspect that is most relevant to this book.

It should be emphasised that these are not exceptional cases.[131] Consider, for example, the numerous criminal trials in which reconstruction of the historical context plays a decisive role or in which a historian intervenes as an expert witness. This occurred with many cases brought before military prosecutors against Nazi and Fascist war criminals following the discovery of documents related to war crimes which were hidden for political reasons for decades,[132] as is also the case in certain in proceedings related to international terrorism.

Indeed, trials on historical denialism share this characteristic with trials concerning serious violations of human rights, in particular those which are internationally recognised. In both kinds of trial, historical reconstruction becomes one of the primary functions. This can be easily observed from the judgments, which always contain a significant portion on historical events.[133]

In this way, the ascertainment of past facts loses the much more limited characteristic of a mere preliminary moment and becomes crucial to determining individual criminal responsibility in a role independent from to that of the criminal trial.

However, historical reconstruction and judicial reconstruction have different methods, logics and objectives. Establishing historical reconstruction as a prevalent 'parallel objective' of the criminal trial has consequences for law and for the criminal trial, but it has perhaps an even greater impact on history. The truth that

---

[131] The trial is memory and orders time. *'Toute la cérémonie judiciaire converge vers ce moment final, libérateur. Car si le temps de la poursuite est imprescriptible, celui du jugement est bel et bien définitif'*, see Salas 2002, p. 24.

[132] The armoire of shame was a wooden cabinet discovered in 1994 inside a large storage room in *Palazzo Cesi-Gaddi* in Rome, which, at the time, housed the chancellery of the military attorney's office. The cabinet contained an archive of 695 files documenting war crimes perpetrated on Italian soil during the Nazi occupation. The discovery led to the opening of two Commissions of Inquiry. The Commision of Inquiry of the Italian Parliament delivered a majority and a minority report: Commissione parlamentare di Inchiesta sulle cause di occultamento dei crimini nazifascisti, Relazione Finale, XIV Legislatura, Doc. XXIII, n. 18, approved on 08.02.2006, available at http://www.senato.it/service/PDF/PDFServer/BGT/301476.pdf; Commissione parlamentare di Inchiesta sulle cause di occultamento dei crimini nazifascisti, Relazione di Minoranza, XIV Legislatura, Doc. XXIII, n. 18-bis, presented 24.01.2006, available at http://www.senato.it/service/PDF/PDFServer/BGT/203175.pdf. This also resulted in a new judicial phase. It has nonetheless to be noted that the new judicial phase related only to crimes committed by German perpetrators (on the basis of who was still alive at the time). As for the crimes committed by Italian Fascists, their criminal persecutions ended in the 1940s with the application of amnesty laws (among them the so-called Togliatti Amnesty). These amnesties have never been questioned, not even after the discovery of 1994. On this issue, see Stramaccioni 2016; Giustolisi 2004; Franzinelli 2002; Vassalli 1997, pp. 228 et seq.; Pezzino 2012; Pezzino 2018. For a legal analysis, see Caroli 2017, p. 95 et seq.; Fornasari 2015; Buzzelli et al. 2012; Fronza 2009; Vassalli 1997, p. 228 et seq.

[133] The examples could be many. Probably the major example is still the Nuremberg trial, whose selectivity and reconstruction of historical events conditioned our view of Nazism and the Second World War. See also for further references Baldissara 2016; Maguire 2001, pp. 159 and ff.

this produces is a judicial truth enshrined by the judgment, and it projects the image of the events through a much different lens than that of historical research, which in many ways can be seen as a distorting mirror.

This suggests that the reconstruction of historical events should not be delegated only to criminal law. In the search for factual truth and collective history, other avenues or alternatives should be explored that do not compel the court to carry out this task on its own. These could be truth commissions,[134] 'truth trials' ('*juicios por la verdad*')[135] or mechanisms that do not operate with a retributive logic. In this regard, the Colombian case is a prime example which demonstrates that criminal justice cannot alone determine the memory of crimes.[136]

The mosaic of transitional processes and mechanisms is more complex than a judgment on guilt or innocence and cannot be reduced to a criminal trial. Indeed, it is an important piece of the mosaic, but it is one of many that are needed so that the tragic events of the past cease to cast their shadow on the present.

In addition and prior to the conviction of the perpetrators of crimes, a collective process is necessary which cannot stem only from an external source no matter how authoritative it may be, such as the judiciary. This process evolves in a horizontal manner and creates an interaction that the courtroom can support but not replace. Achieving a collective memory, constructed in an open and horizontal way without entrusting it to an external authority and without shortcuts is indeed fundamental for reconciling conflicting parties or, at the very least, beginning to resolve open hostility and rebuilding a new political body. Doing so leads to creating the foundation for determining not only individual criminal responsibility but also political and social accountability.[137]

---

[134] See Ambos 2009, pp. 19–86; Freeman 2006, p. 11 et seq. and the table at pp. 317–325, Stahn 2005, pp. 425–466 and the literature quoted in footnote 83, Chapter 1.

[135] On the *juicios por la verdad*, see Garibian 2014; Maculan and Pastor 2013.

[136] The *Ley de Justicia y* Paz (Ley 975/2005) and the *Sistema Integral para la Verdad, Justicia, Reparación y No Repetición* as a result of the Agreement recently signed between the Colombian Government and the guerrilla group FARC-EP. The Agreement entails a complex, original and bold transitional project, which envisages a combination of criminal and extra-judicial mechanisms in order to assess the truth and reconstruct the truth. Within the framework of the *Ley de Justicia y Paz,* the *Grupo Nacional de Memoria Histórica* was established and is composed of independent experts given the task to construct a comprehensive and impartial narration of the Colombian armed conflict. This entity, which in 2011 was replaced by the *Centro Nacional de Memoria Histórica*, is still active and has published numerous reports on armed conflict and specific victimization experiences, thereby contributing to the knowledge of this prolonged period of violence. The *Sistema Integral* provides for the creation of a *Comisión para el exclarecimiento de la verdad, convivencia y la no repetición* and is also composed of independent experts, expressly separated from the criminal courts. It is entrusted with the task of investigating the causes and the dynamics of armed conflict utilising social science methodologies. For a more in-depth analysis, see *The search for peace with justice and human rights in Colombia*, Report of the Fifth International Caravana of Jurists to Colombia, November 2016. See Gil Gil and Maculan 2017a; Gutiérrez Ramírez and Rodríguez 2016, pp. 40–60; Gil Gil and Maculan 2017b, p. 311 et seq.

[137] See Lollini 2011.

In criminal trials, where the subjects are international crimes and historical denialism, the judicial ritual risks being confused with the historical one, thereby blurring the differences between the two. Trials regarding highly significant historical events and the gathering of documentation and witnesses are certainly important sources historians can use in their work, but their primary purpose is different. They are intended to determine the criminal liability of individuals. Conversely, historical verification aims to reconstruct the facts in all of their extreme complexity, the reasons and also the political and economic dynamics of the same conflict. A conviction of a Nazi official in a criminal court is not needed in order to affirm German responsibility in the massacres of occupied Italy. Compared to the trial, historical research describes them much more thoroughly and answers many more questions about some of those directly responsible for massacres.

For these reasons, historical investigation on significant historical events cannot and must not end in the courtroom. Tribunals are not the best nor the most effective places for the reconstruction of the past that history requires. The task of the criminal trial is identifying individual responsibility for specific crimes, through the characteristics of the public hearing and the assessment of facts in a complex model.

This assertion plays a significant role with respect to historical research, most importantly due to the strong symbolic nature of the public hearing, the trial and the sentence to establish the meaning of those events and to distinguish between victims and victimisers.

The judgment is able to sanctify, through punishment, the significance of events that are fundamental for historical collective memory. However, the primary purpose of a criminal trial cannot be to 'master' the past, as this runs the risk of introducing dangerous obstacles for both law and the historical method.

3.4.1 Enshrining Memory

In addition to classical critical issues related to speech crimes, the offence of denialism has its own complexities regarding the intersection of the criminal trial and historical reconstruction, as well as the interference with formation of collective memories, such as the ethically significant common memory of past experience. These are precisely what we have defined as the areas of conflict between law and history.

As previously mentioned, this occurs when a judicial body ascertains criminal responsibility and simultaneously takes on the additional role as a factory of memory of significant historical events for a community. This occurs through the symbolic power of the judgment, the determination of the events, their characterisation, the responsibilities this entails and the punishment that unequivocally determines perpetrators and victims.

Indeed, the trial and judgment are one of the strongest vehicles for certifying events as worthy of historical collective memory. To establish which events must be remembered, it is first necessary to recognise and then determine the meaning of the events as they become etched in memory through the determination of responsibility and the resulting punishments.

There are many examples confirming this connection, no matter where the trials were celebrated or whether they have or have not had controversial outcomes and relevance. The importance of trials such as the Nuremberg and Eichmann trials in establishing the scope and extent of the crimes of the Nazi regime within collective memory can hardly be underestimated. Likewise, in more recent times, the International Criminal Tribunals for Bosnia and Rwanda regarding the atrocities committed in those countries, which today form part of public domain.

In this context, the judicial ritual is a *place of memory* and the judges are crucial actors in consolidating and enshrining a historical collective memory.

The criminal process acquires a different function and inscribes a definitive historical narrative with the authority of the court, which is a theatre of the word (and therefore a public place): the only one in which the full meaning of memory is maintained and in which it is enshrined as immutable. Places where the spoken word and the outcome of the debate have, by definition, consequences of the utmost seriousness: conviction and acquittal. Therefore, these are places which emanate an authoritative, definitive word that obligates: perhaps the only one in the collective imagination where what is said retains a profoundly compelling and compulsory significance and is permanently certified by the criminal trial, sentence and punishment inflicted.[138]

More than any other mechanism, criminal law satisfies the demands of narration and consolidation of mnemonic frameworks. They can no longer be challenged. Criminal punishment related to events of historical significance entails defining the meaning of certain facts and codifying them in memory. The criminal trial recognises, and the judgment, which is irrevocable, solidifies the events. They are thereby withdrawn from that fluid dimension of memory and historical reconstruction.[139]

As has been demonstrated through the analysis of the legislation and jurisprudence on historical denialism, the current tendency is to resort to criminal justice for manufacturing memory. Criminal law is the preferred tool: it is powerful on a symbolic level; it is simple and creates order within complexity at the cost of being reductive; and it frames the facts, recognises them and elevates them to the status of a crime. The criminal trial certifies a fixed narrative of founding events, making them a cornerstone deemed necessary for our societies.

Consequently, through law and the criminal court the principle of *res judicata* appears to be a central element in the map of the politics of collective memory.[140] *Res judicata* is a word that imposes a 'truth' which, due to the *auctoritas* of its

---

[138] Highlighting the divergence between historical and judicial approaches, see Ginzburg 1991, pp. 108–110.

[139] Ginzburg note that evidence (in the legal sense) is never sufficient protection from the forces that threaten to erode the memory of the Holocaust. See Ginzburg 1991.

[140] 'On the contrary, if historical knowledge is tangible it is no longer knowledge. Therefore, we should all fear the contemporary tendency of a forced reconstruction of the past through criminal judgment', Donini 2009, p. 183.

origin, cannot be challenged. In this sense, to borrow the expression of Francois Ost, the law and the trial become guardians and witnesses of collective memory.[141]

3.4.2 Manufacturing Memory

This landscape of public policies on historical memory has several implications, both internally (the legal framework) and externally (in particular regarding historians).

In the words of the ECtHR, the tribunal is assigned with the task of 'establishing historical facts', which brings with it a number of risks, including transforming the judge (or possibly even the legislator) into a judge of history.[142]

However, the law and the criminal trial employ a very peculiar language and logic which influence two divergent means of encompassing these elements: the restrictive approach of the judicial field and the potentially unlimited approach of the field of history.

This stems from the rules governing judicial decisions. To name a few, the principle *in dubio pro reo*, the regulatory and exclusionary mechanisms of obtaining evidence used in the trial, oral proceedings and respect for cross-examination as an epistemological basis for a just and socially acceptable decision, respectful timeframes with regard to the principle of reasonable duration of the trial and, again, the rules on the use of legal evidence (evidence that is used in the reconstruction of facts is not used for the protection of other values in accordance with the fair trial principle). Finally, the need for an obligatory conclusion that chooses between two alternatives: affirmation of guilt or proclamation of innocence. In either case, the judgment is final.

Historical judgment is an open evaluation which permits, and indeed requires, review of the interpretation of the facts already given in an endless process of re-reading the facts. This is not possible for a judge. The same dialectic of memory and forgetting has no predetermined chronological boundaries. No historian has been prohibited from using unlawfully obtained evidence. The past is never something captured in time and immutable and can always be re-read.

---

[141] Ost 1999, p. 44.

[142] On the dangers and risks of entrusting courts with a decision on a matter of history and not of law, see Vidal-Naquet 1981, p. 183. On the differences and similarities between juridical method and historical method, see on the historical perspective: Ginzburg 1991, 2000; on the legal perspective: Calamandrei 1939, p. 105 et seq.; Calamandrei 1957, p. 120 et seq.; Capograssi 1959; Jean 2009; Stolleis 2000; critical on the overlapping of the figures of the judge and of the historian: Taruffo 1992, p. 310 et seq.; Taruffo 1967, p. 438 et seq.; Garapon 2002; Thomas 1998. Stressing the typical functions of criminal law, different from those of the historical research: Pastor 2010; Jean 2009; Costa 2006, pp. 158–181; Donini 2009. Beyond the differences, some common points exist between the figures of the historian and of the judge: see Ginzburg 2000, p. 66; Resta and Zencovich 2012, p. 93 et seq.; Ferrajoli 2009, p. 26; Ricoeur 2000, p. 413 et seq.; Rosoni 1995. See also Cajani 2017.

With reference to the offence of historical denialism, the intermingling of the judicial and historical spheres is especially pronounced and can create dangerous distortions. For the historian, historical reconstruction becomes legal truth.[143] This runs the risk of turning a truth that is fundamental to historical research into an official truth at any given time and according to any given interpretative hypotheses.[144] As a result, an official truth endorses the idea of only one historical school and a 'definitive' reconstruction of the facts.[145]

The judge's evaluation focuses not so much on the reconstruction of the facts but on the examination of statements. Indeed, the judgment is on the actual denial, minimisation or justification of those events. Even if completely shared, defined and definitive, criminal law cannot protect an interpretation, nor can it vanquish statements that call it into question, since in this specific case, the law defends an ideological position. It does not seem acceptable to identify a protected interest in only *one* historical interpretation among infinite possible interpretations. Thus, only in the event that such assertions attack the interests or rights of others, or when they harm a group, can they be punishable. There is no definitive history and therefore we cannot expect it to come from the judgments which, by definition, have the authority of *res judicata*.[146]

Furthermore, in criminal trials on historical denialism the historian's own field is invaded by the judicial process. Indeed, the judge delineates 'historically established facts', therefore declaring certain parts of history no longer subject to discussion.

Beyond having effects on historical research, this can cause complications within the criminal trial, strongly influencing the dynamic of the proceedings for the purpose of reconstructing and narrating history. Quite the opposite of the intended institutional objective, which is to determine individual responsibility based on clearly identified facts.[147]

Here new conflicts emerge. Due to their symbolic nature, criminal trials with this scope must transmit a merely symbolic message that adheres to the victim's demands for justice but also respond to the strong emotion that these events provoke within public opinion. This emotion undoubtedly has an influence on the results, so much so as to create the danger of a judicial decision compressed into an exemplary punitive instance which precedes any verification. On the other hand, it is also the very historical significance of the judicial decision that inevitably ensures

---

[143] Vidal-Naquet, *Interview* in *Le Quotidien de Paris*, 9 May 1998.

[144] 'Doubting the existence of the Holocaust should not be prohibited with a law because historical truth should never be transformed into official truth': Ginzburg 2001, p. 1.

[145] Vidal-Naquet 1981, p. 183.

[146] Donini 2009, p. 186.

[147] Vidal Naquet highlights that the judicial instrument can be used and in this regard it refers to the rules on defamation and laws against racist activities; however, the article states that the condition must be to never ask the Tribunals to rule on a point concerning history, but only on law. Vidal Naquet 1981, p. 183.

that victims' rights are taken into account as well as their participation in the hearing.

However, the objective of the criminal trial should be to contain and isolate the punishment from the victim, in line with the core judicial value aimed at curbing violence.[148] The transformation of the judicial instrument into a *factory of memory* results in the over expansion of scope, which can lead to an internal vicious circle and a reconfiguration of ethics within criminal law in contrast to the liberal model that should guide it.

Finally, there is an additional issue which exposes the profound differences between historical research and criminal law.

The results of historical research, whether more academically and methodologically undisputable or put forth by enthusiasts, amateurs or activists who seek to validate predetermined theories, are presented as a special form of public discourse communicated through conferences, writings and general publications. Therefore, in their broadest sense they constitute the expression of ideas in public space.

With the criminalisation of historical denialism, historical research is brought into the courtroom, and in a quest to defend free speech it ends up almost invariably appealing to the broader principle of free speech. This is even more so if its credibility status is weak, as in the case of the more radical forms of revisionism and historical denialism, leading to the same dynamics of punishing content of a conceptual nature which, as such, is still considered a form of expression.

Within denialism trials, the essential characteristics lie somewhere between the never definitively resolved risks of the ethical tendency of law, on the one hand, and, on the other, defining conduct with the capability to harm and incite which clearly defines the offence. This reinforces the defence's 'natural attraction' to the broader protection of freedom of expression as they are to benefit if their statements or actions cannot be definitively defined as criminal. We have seen this dynamic at play in the *Perinçek* case and, with opposite results, in the *Garaudy* case.

When faced with the denialism of the founding memory of a democratic system, it should be mentioned that, although not immediately apparent but present and active, criminal law is only *one* of the ways which can be used to dealing with and not necessarily the most effective.

References

Ader B (2012) L'état de la jurisprudence sur la notion de négation depuis la loi Gayssot. Légipresse 293:236–248

Algan B (2008) The Brand New Version of Article 301 of Turkish Penal Code and the Future of Freedom of Expression Cases in Turkey. German Law Journal 9:2237–2252

[148] See Garapon 1995.

Ambos K (2009) The Legal Framework of Transitional Justice: A Systematic Study with a Special Focus on the Role of the ICC. In: Ambos K et al. (eds) Building a Future on Peace and Justice: Studies on Transitional Justice, Peace and Development. Springer, Berlin, pp 19–86

Ambos K (2014) Treatise on International Criminal Law. Volume II: The Crimes and Sentencing. Oxford University Press, Oxford

Arslan A, Berti F, De Stefani P (eds) (2017) Il paese perduto. A cent'anni dal genocidio armeno. Edizioni Angelo Guerini, Milan

Baldissara L (2016) Politiche della memoria e spazio del ricordo in Europa. Il Mulino, Bologna, 1:6–20

Bartole S, De Sena P, Zagrebelsky V (2012) Commentario breve alla Convenzione europea dei diritti dell'uomo. Giuffré, Milan

Baruch MO (2013) Des lois indignes? Les historiens, la politique et le droit. Tallandier, Paris

Belavusau U (2016) Introductory Note to *Perinçek v. Switzerland* (2015): Judgment of the Grand Chamber (ECtHR). International Legal Materials 55:627–629

Brunet F (2012) De la censure constitutionnelle de la loi "visant à réprimer la contestation de l'existence des génocides reconnus par la loi". Revue de science criminelle et de droit pénal comparé 2:343–354

Buyse A (2014) Dangerous Expressions: The ECHR, Violence and Free Speech. International and Comparative Law Quarterly 63:491–503

Buzzelli S, De Paolis M, Speranzoni A (2012) La ricostruzione giudiziale dei crimini nazifascisti in Italia. Questioni preliminari. Giappichelli, Turin

Cajani L (2017) La storia nel mirino del diritto penale. Diritto pubblico Comparato ed Europeo Online, no. 1, 25

Calamandrei P (1939) Il giudice e lo storico. Rivista di diritto processuale civile XVII:105–128

Calamandrei P (1957) Verità e verosimiglianza nel processo civile. In: Studi sul processo civile IV. Cedam, Padua, pp 115–132

Camby JP (2012) La loi et le négationnisme: de l'exploitation de l'histoire au droit au débat sur l'histoire. Les Petites Affiches 70:11–22

Capograssi G (1959) Giudizio, processo, scienza, verità. In: Capograssi G, Opere, vol. V. Giuffrè, Milan, pp 51–76

Caroli P (2015) La Corte europea in tema di offese pubbliche contro gli ebrei. Diritto penale contemporaneo online http://www.penalecontemporaneo.it/d/4368-la-corte-europea-in-tema-di-offese-pubbliche-contro-gli-ebrei. Accessed 16 July 2017

Caroli P (2017) La giustizia di transizione in Italia. L'esperienza dopo la seconda guerra mondiale. http://eprints-phd.biblio.unitn.it/1981/1/Paolo_Caroli_-_Tesi_dottorato_.pdf. Accessed 13 August 2017

Cassese A (2002) Genocide. In: Cassese A, Gaeta P, Jones JRWD (eds) The Rome Statute of the International Criminal Court: A Commentary. Oxford University Press, Oxford, pp 335–351

Cohen-Jonathan G (1999) L'apologie de Pétain devant la Cour européenne des droits de l'homme. Revue universelle des droits de l'homme 38:366–386

Corboz B (2002) Les infractions en droit suisse. Volume II. Staempfli, Bern

Cortese F (2016) What can the Perinçek case teach? DPCE online http://www.dpceonline.it/index.php/dpceonline/article/view/93. Accessed 16 July 2017

Costa P (2006) In Search of Legal Texts: Which Texts for Which Historian? In: Michalsen D (ed) Reading Past Legal Texts. Unipax, Oslo, pp 158–181

Costa-Lascoux J (1976) La Loi du 1. juillet 1972 et la protection pénale des immigrés contre la discrimination raciale. Droit social 5:181–187

Couvrat P (1993) Les infractions contre les personnes dans le nouveau Code Pénal. Revue de Science Criminelle et de Droit Comparé 3:469–480

Danti-Juan M (2012) Contestation de l'existence d'un génocide. Revue pénitentiaire et de droit pénal 2:399–402

Decoeur H (2014) The Judgment of the European Court of Human Rights in Perinçek v. Switzerland: Reducing Genocide to Law. Cambridge Journal of International and Comparative Law

Della Morte G (2016) When is a criminal prohibition of genocide denial justified? The *Perinçek* Case and the risk of a double standard. Questions of International Law, online: http://www.qil-qdi.org/criminal-prohibition-genocide-denial-justified-perincek-case-risk-double-standard/. Accessed 15 September 2017

Delmas-Marty M, Fouchard I, Fronza E, Neyret L (2013) Le crime contre l'humanité. PUF, Paris

Derieux E (2012) Sanction de la contestation de génocides et garantie de la liberté d'expression. Revue Lamy Droit de l'Immatériel 80:6–8

Donini M (2009) La gestione penale del passaggio dal Fascismo alla democrazia in Italia. Appunti sulla memoria storica e l'elaborazione del passato 'mediante il diritto penale'. Materiali per una storia della cultura giuridica 1:183–216

Droin N (2010) Les limitations à la liberté d'expression dans la loi sur la presse du 29 juillet 1881 - Disparition, permanence et résurgence du délit d'opinion. Fondation Varenne, Collection de Thèses no. 35, Paris

Droin N (2014) État des lieux de la répression du négationnisme en France et en droit comparé. Revue Trimestrielle des Droits de l'Homme 98:363–394

Dubuisson F (2007) L'incrimination générique du négationnisme est-elle conciliable avec le droit à la liberté d'expression. Revue de Droit Université Libre de Bruxelles 35:135–195

Feldman JP (1998) Peut-on dire impunément n'importe quoi sur la Shoah? Revue de droit international et de droit comparé 229–271

Ferrajoli L (1989) Diritto e ragione. Teoria del garantismo penale. Laterza, Bari

Ferrajoli L (2009) Diritto e ragione. Teoria del garantismo penale. Laterza, Bari

Fornasari G (2015) Giustizia di transizione. Enciclopedia del Diritto. Annali VIII:547–570

Fraisseix P (2006) Le droit mémoriel. Revue française de droit constitutionnel 3

Francillon J (2010) Questions prioritaires de constitutionnalité en matière d'infractions de presse (délits d'apologie de crimes de guerre, de contestation de l'existence de crimes l'humanité, et de diffamation), observations à propos de Crim. 2 et 19 mars 2010, n° 09-81.238 09-81.027, et 7 mai 2010, n° 09-80.774. Revue Sciences criminelles et Droit Comparé 3:640–654

Francillon J (2012) Pénalisation de la contestation de l'existence d'un génocide reconnu par la loi. Revue de science criminelle et de droit pénal comparé 1:179–182

Francillon J (2013a) Apologie de crimes contre l'humanité. Absence de portée normative de la "Loi Taubira" du 21 mai 2001 (Crim. 5 février 2013 no. 11-85.909). Revue de sciences criminelles et de droit comparé 1

Francillon J (2013b) Pénalisation des discours négationnistes et liberté d'expression. Mélanges offerts à Claude Bontems. L'Harmattan, Paris

Frangi M (2005) Les lois mémorielles: de l'expression de la volonté générale au législateur historien. Revue de droit public 1:241–253

Franzinelli M (2002) Le stragi nascoste, cit.; L'armadio della vergogna: impunità e rimozione dei crimini di guerra nazifascisti 1943–2001. Mondadori, Milan

Freeman M (2006) Truth Commission and Procedural fairness. Cambridge University Press, New York

Fronza E (2009) Italia. In: Ambos K, Malarino E, Elsner G (ed.) Justicia de transicion. Konrad Adenauer Stiftung, Montevideo

Fronza E (2016) Il crimine di genocidio. In: Amati E, Costi M, Fronza E, Lobba P, Maculan E, Vallini A (eds) Introduzione al diritto penale internazionale. Giappichel, Turin, pp. 323–350

Fronza E, Cortese F (2017) Il *caso Perinçek* davanti alla Corte europea dei diritti dell'uomo. Quando il giudice fa la storia. In: Arslan A, Berti F, De Stefani P (eds) Il paese perduto. A cent'anni dal genocidio armeno. Edizioni Angelo Guerini, Milan

Garapon A (1995) Bien juger: essai sur le rituel judiciaire. Odile Jacob, Paris

Garapon A (2002) Des crimes qu'on ne peut ni punir ni pardonner: pour une justice internationale. Odile Jacob, Paris

Garibian S (2006) Pour une lecture juridique des quatre lois "mémorielles". Esprit 322:1–18

Garibian S (2008) Taking Denial Seriously: Genocide Denial and Freedom of Speech in the French Law. Cardozo Journal of Conflict Resolution 9:479–488

Garibian S (2013) (Legally) binding memory? Uncertainties arising from decision no. 2012-647 DC of France's Constitutional Council'. Droit et Cultures 66:25–56

Garibian S (2014) Ghosts Also Die: Resisting Disappearance through the 'Right to the Truth' and the Juicios por la Verdad in Argentina. Journal of International Criminal Justice 12:515–538

Garibian S (2016) On the Breaking of Consensus: The Perinçek case, the Armenian Genocide and International Criminal Law

Gil Gil A, Maculan E (eds) (2017a) Colombia como nuevo modelo para la justicia de transición. Instituto Universitario General Gutiérrez Mellado, Madrid

Gil Gil A, Maculan E (2017b) La influencia de las victimas en el tratamiento juridico de la violencia colectiva. Librería Dykinson, Madrid

Ginzburg C (1991) Il giudice e lo storico. Considerazioni a margine del processo Sofri. Feltrinelli, Milan

Ginzburg C (2000) Rapporti di forza: storia, retorica, prova. Feltrinelli, Milan

Ginzburg C (2001) Beweis, Gedächtnis, Vergessen. Werkstatt Geschichte 30:50–60

Giustolisi F (2004) L'armadio della vergogna. Nutrimenti, Rome

Grandjean G (2011) La répression du négationnisme en Belgique: de la réussite législative au blocage politique. Droit et Société 1:137–160

Gunter MM (2011) Armenian History and the Question of Genocide. Palgrave Macmillan, London

Gutiérrez Ramírez LM, Rodríguez JR (2016) Una comisión de la verdad en el modelo colombiano de justicia transicional: aproximación a través de la historia reciente y la experiencia comparada. Jurídicas 10:40–60

Guyaz A (1996) L'incrimination de la discrimination raciale. Verlag, Bern

Hamon F (2012) Le Conseil constitutionnel et les lois mémorielles. Revue française de droit administratif 2:7–11

Hartog F, Baruch MO, Thomas Y, Gaudard PY (1998) Vérité judiciaire, vérité historique. Le Débat 102:4–44

Hervieu N (2014) Le négationnisme, prisme révélateur du dilemme européen face à lutte contre l'extrémisme. Revue des droits de l'homme online https://revdh.revues.org/503. Accessed 16 July 2017

Hochmann T (2011) Faurisson, "falsificateur de la jurisprudence"? Droit et Cultures 61:235–256

Hochmann T (2012) Le négationnisme face aux limites de la liberté d'expression. Étude de droit comparé. Pedone, Paris

Hochmann T (2013) Le problème des lois dites "mémorielles" sera-t-il résolu par les résolutions? La référence à l'article 34-1 de la Constitution dans le discours contemporain sur les relations entre le Parlement et l'histoire. Droit et cultures 66:57–69

Hochmann T (2016) Négationnisme: le Conseil Constitutionnel entre ange et démon. Revue des droits et libertés fondamentaux online http://www.revuedlf.com/droit-constitutionnel/negationnisme-le-conseil-constitutionnel-entre-ange-et-demon/. Accessed 16 July 2017

Hochmann T (2017) Pas de lunettes sous les oeillères: le conseil constitutionnel et le négationnisme. Revue des droits et libertés fondamentaux online http://www.revuedlf.com/droit-constitutionnel/pas-de-lunettes-sous-les-oeilleres-le-conseil-constitutionnel-et-le-negationnisme/. Accessed 16 July 2017

Jean JP (2009) Le procès et l'écriture de l'histoire. Revue de sciences humaines 9:61–74

Jouanneau B (2008) La Justice et l'Histoire face au négationnisme. Au coeur d'un procès. Fayard, Paris

Keane D (2007) Attacking Hate Speech under Article 17 of the European Convention on Human Rights. Netherlands Quarterly of Human Rights 25:641–663

Koposov N (2017) Memory Laws, Memory Wars. Cambridge University Press, Cambridge

Korman C (1989) Le délit de diffusion des idées racistes. La Semaine Juridique 50

Lapage A (2013) Le Conseil Constitutionnel ne connaitra toujours pas du délit de contestation de crimes contre l'humanité. Communication Commerce Électronique 2

Le Crom JP, Jean-Clément M (1998) (ed.) Dossier vérité historique, vérité judiciaire. Droit et Société 38:9–67

Leotta CD (2015) Profili penali del negazionismo. Riflessioni alla luce della sentenza della Corte EDU sul genocidio armeno. Cedam, Padua

Levade A, Mathieu B (2012) Le législateur ne peut fixer des vérités et en sanctionner la contestation. La Semaine juridique. Édition générale 14:680–684

Levinet M (2004) La fermeté bienvenue de la Cour européenne des droits de l'homme face au négationnisme, obs. à la décision du 24 juin 2003, Garaudy c/ France. Revue Trimestrielle des Droits de l'Homme 653–662

Lobba P (2014) A European Halt to Laws Against Genocide Denial? European Criminal Law Review 4:59–77

Lobba P (2015) Holocaust Denial before the European Court of Human Rights: Evolution of an Exceptional Regime. European Journal of International Law 26:237–253

Lollini A (2011) Constitutionalism and Transitional Justice in South Africa. Berghahn Books, Oxford

Longo S, Ubiali MC (2016) Articolo 10. In: Ubertis G, Viganò F (eds) Corte di Strasburgo e giustizia penale. Giappichelli, Turin

Luban D (2004) A Theory of Crimes Against Humanity. Yale Journal of International Law 29: 85–167

Maculan E, Pastor D (2013) El derecho a la verdad y su esercicio por medio del proceso penal. Hammurabi, Buenos Aires

Maguire (2001) Law and War: An American Story. Columbia University Press, New York

Mallet-Poujol N (2012) La loi de pénalisation du negationnisme: la censure constitutionelle ou le crépuscule des lois mémorielles. Légipresse 293:219–232

Massias F (1993) La liberté d'expression et le discours raciste ou révisionniste. Revue Trimestrielle des Droits de l'Homme 183–213

Maus D, Bougrab J (2005) Les questions de constitutionnalités posées par la loi du 29 janvier 2001. In: Maus D, Bougrab J (eds) François Luchaire, un républicain au service de la République. Publications de la Sorbonne, Paris

May L (2010) Genocide. A Normative Account. Cambridge University Press, Cambridge

Michel J (2010) Gouverner les mémoires – Les politiques mémorielles en France. PUF, Paris

Montanari M (2013) Il disegno di legge in materia di negazionismo passa all'esame dell'aula del Senato. Diritto penale contemporaneo. Online: https://www.penalecontemporaneo.it/d/2597-il-disegno-di-legge-in-materia-di-negazionismo-passa-all-esame-dell-aula-del-senato. Accessed 28 September 2017

Morange J (2009) La liberté d'expression. Bruylant, Brussels

Mouysset O (2012) Pas de nouveau délit de contestation (ou de minimisation) de l'existence de crimes contre l'humanité: suite et fin? Droit pénal 6:26–27

Niggli MA, Wiprächtiger H (ed) (2013) Strafrecht II. Article 111-392 StGB. Basler Kommentar. Helbing, Basel

Nora P (2016) Come si manipola la memoria. Lo storico, il potere, il passato. Editrice La Scuola, Brescia

Nora P, Chandernagor F (2008) Liberté pour l'histoire. CNRS éditions, Paris

O'Keefe R (2015) International Criminal Law. Oxford University Press, Oxford

Ost F (1999) Le temps du droit. Odile Jacob, Paris

Pastor D (2010) ¿Procesos penales sólo para conocer la verdad? La experiencia argentina. Revista General de Derecho Procesal 22, https://dialnet.unirioja.es/servlet/articulo?codigo=3305216. Accessed 17 November 2017

Pech L (2011) The Law of Holocaust Denial in Europe. In: Hennebel L, Hochmann T (eds) Genocide Denials and the Law. Oxford University Press, Oxford

Puig P (2012) La loi peut-elle sanctuariser l'Histoire? Revue trimestrielle de droit civil 1:78–84

Rémond R (2006) Quand l'État se mêle de l'histoire. Stock, Paris

Resta G, Zeno-Zencovich V (2012) (eds) Riparare, risarcire, ricordare. Un dialogo tra storici e giuristi. Editoriale Scientifica, Naples

Ricoeur P (2000) La mémoire, l'histoire, l'oubli. Seuil, Paris

Roets D (2004) Epilogue européen dans l'affaire Garaudy: les droits de l'homme à l'epreuve du negationnisme. Recueil Dalloz 239–254
Rosoni I (1995) Quae singula non prosunt collecta iuvant: la teoria della prova indiziaria nell'età medievale e moderna. Giuffrè, Milan
Roumelian O (1996) Un délit d'opinion au service des droits de l'homme? Petites affiches 21
Roux J (2012) Le Conseil constitutionnel et le génocide arménien: De l'a-normativité à l'inconstitutionnalité de la loi. Recueil Dalloz, 12 April 2012, no. 15, pp 987–993
Safi F (2017) A la recerche d'un fondement à l'incrimination du négationnisme. Recueil Dalloz 686–703
Salas D (2002) La justice entre histoire et mémoire. In: Jean JP, Salas D (eds) Barbie, Touvier, Papon. Des procès pour la mémoire. Autrement, Paris, pp 20–33
Schabas WA (2009) Genocide in International Law. The Crime of Crimes. Cambridge University Press, Cambridge
Schabas WA (2015) The European Convention on Human Rights. A Commentary. Oxford University Press, Oxford
Schabas WA (2016) Article 6. Genocide. In: Triffterer O, Ambos K (eds) Commentary on the Rome Statute of the International Criminal Court. Observer's Notes, Article by Article. C.H. Beck/Hart/Nomos, Munich/Oxford, pp 143–157
Stahn C (2005) The Geometry of Transitional Justice: Choices of Institutional Design. Leiden Journal of International Law 3:425–466
Stolleis M (2000) Der Historiker als Richter - der Richter als Historiker'. In: Frei N, Van Laak D, Stolleis M (eds) Geschichte vor Gericht. Historiker, Richter und die Suche nach Gerechtigkeit. Beck, Munich, pp 173–179
Stramaccioni A (2016) Crimini di guerra: Storia e memoria del caso italiano. Laterza, Bari
Taruffo M (1967) Il giudice e lo storico: considerazioni metodologiche. Rivista di diritto processuale XXII:438–465
Taruffo M (1992) La prova dei fatti giuridici. Giuffré, Milan
Ternon Y (1999) Freedom and Responsibility of the Historian. The "Lewis Affair". In: Hovannisian RG (ed) Remembrance and Denial: The Case of the Armenian Genocide. Wayne State University Press, Detroit, pp 237–248
Terry N (2017) Holocaust denial in the age of web 2.0. In: Behrens P, Jensen O, Terry N (eds) Holocaust and Genocide Denial: A Contextual Perspective. Routledge, London
Thomas Y (1998) "La vérité, le temps, le juge et l'historien". Le débat 102:17–36
Tracol X (1997) L'affaire Faurisson devant le Comité des droits de l'homme des Nations-Unies. Légipresse 141
Traverso E (2006) Il passato: istruzioni per l'uso. Storia, memoria, politica. Ombre Corte, Verona
Trechsel S, Pieth M (eds) (2012) Schweizerisches Strafgesetzbuch. Praxiskommentar. Dike, Zurich
Troper M (1999) La Loi Gayssot et la Constitution. Annales Histoire. Science sociales 6:1239–1256
van Drooghenbroeck S (2001) L'article 17 de la Convention européenne des droits de l'homme est-il indispensable? Revue Trimestrielle des Droits de l'Homme 46:552–553
Vassalli G (1997), Formula di Radbruch e diritto penale. Note sulla punizione dei "delitti di Stato" nella Germania postnazista e nella Germania postcomunista. Giuffrè, Milan
Véron M (1990) Le renforcement du dispositif répressif contre la discrimination et le racisme. Présentation des lois des 12 et 13 juillet 1990. Droit Pénal chron. 1
Verpeaux M (2007) Liberté d'expression et discours politique. Table ronde: Constitution et liberté d'expression
Vidal-Naquet P (1981) Assassins of Memory: Essays on the Denial of the Holocaust. Columbia University Press, New York
Weber M (1998) Switzerland's Anti-Racism Law. Online http://www.ihr.org/jhr/v17/v17n4p13_weber.html. Accessed 16 July 2017
Werle G, Jessberger F (2014) Principles of International Criminal Law. Oxford University Press, Oxford

Chapter 4
Criminal Law and Free Speech

Contents

Abstract This chapter focuses on the tensions between the criminal offence of historical denialism and the fundamental, yet not absolute, right to freedom of expression. A clear example of this can be found in the Holocaust denial cases involving two relevant decisions by both the German and Spanish Constitutional Courts. Setting the boundary between lawful and unlawful thoughts entails the risk of violating the cornerstone principles of criminal law, namely the legality principle, the harm principle, and the last resort principle

Keywords Free speech · harm principle · legality principle · last resort principle · German Federal Constitutional Court · Spanish Constitutional Court

4.1 'Fact' and 'Opinion': The German Federal Constitutional Court

In April 1994 the German Federal Constitutional Court (the *Bundesverfassungsgericht*, hereinafter the BVerfG) was called upon to resolve the conflict between the need for punishing Holocaust denial and the protection of the right to freedom of expression. Just a few months later, in October of the same year, the

E. Fronza, *Memory and Punishment*, International Criminal Justice Series 19,
https://doi.org/10.1007/978-94-6265-234-7_4

Parliament approved a bill introducing the crime of Holocaust denial, which largely relied upon the BVerfG's ruling.

Both this decision and the law created immediately afterward are extremely relevant in the context of this analysis. In its deliberation the Court addressed various crucial questions on the use of criminal law as a tool to deal with Holocaust Denial. Unlike the case of France, the issue of constitutionality did not arise from the application of specific criminal law provisions regarding denialism, which at that time did not even exist in the German legal system. It was indeed this judgment that served as a basis for introducing such a provision, which the Parliament did a few months later.

The BVerfG's decision highlights two underlying elements in the conflict between criminalising Holocaust denial and protecting the right to freedom of expression: on the one hand, the remarks concerning the balance of conflicting interests and their connection with the law establishing the criminal offence; on the other hand, the clash between *fact* and *opinion* with respect to the constitutional right of freedom of speech, which in many ways represents the core argument of the entire decision.[1]

4.1.1 The German Legal Framework

The German Criminal Code contains one specific provision concerning denialism, which punishes the so-called 'Auschwitz lie' ('*Auschwitzlüge*' or '*Auschwitzleugnung*'),[2] the German term used to refer to Holocaust denial.[3]

The decision of German lawmakers to introduce this offence in 1994 clearly reflects a specific historical and political background. Nevertheless, in the disparate European legal landscape on denialism, the phrasing of the provision is emblematic as it confines denialism to the Holocaust and it chooses to punish such conduct only when it is capable of disrupting public peace. Both aspects are paramount in our investigation of the crime of denialism.

[1] On the problematic issue concerning the relationship between criminal provisions prohibiting historical denialism and the fundamental right to free speech, see generally Caruso 2016; Heinze 2016; Koltay 2016; Teruel Lozano 2015a, b; Caruso 2013; Piciocchi 2013; Hochmann 2012; Maitra and McGowan 2012, pp. 24 et seq.

[2] The term Auschwitz lie (*Auschwitzlüge*) first appeared in 1973 as the title of a brochure for the book written by the German neo-Nazi Thies Christophersen on the alleged lie about the gas chambers (*Die Auschwitz-Lüge*, Kritik Verlag, Switzerland, 1978).

[3] The term 'Holocaust denial' includes all remarks questioning the existence of the other concentration camps and the other crimes committed by the Nazis.

4.1.2 From the Deckert I *to Criminal Offence*

With the Law approved on 28 October 1994—'Act amending the Criminal Code, the Code of Criminal Procedure, and Other Acts' ('*Gesetz zur Änderung des Strafgesetzbuches, der Strafprozessordnung und anderer Gesetze*')[4]—German legislators amended § 130 of the German Criminal Code (*Strafgesetzbuch*, hereinafter the StGB) (which defines the crime of 'incitement to racial hatred') and introduced a third paragraph punishing the crime of denialism.[5]

On 24 March 2005, the 'Act amending the Assemblies Act and the Criminal Code' ('*Gesetz zur Änderung des Versammlungsgesetzes und des Strafgesetzbuches*') amended § 130 StGB with a fourth paragraph. This provision punishes 'whoever, in public or at a gathering, disrupts public peace in such a way so as to offend the dignity of victims, by approving of, extolling or justifying the violent and arbitrary power of Nationalist Socialism'.[6]

Many factors led to the approval of this offence by German lawmakers. On a general note, xenophobic propaganda and violence were steadily on the rise and had been driven by the social conflict that flared up after the German reunification and the difficulties of integrating the socially diverse western and eastern parts of the country. Technological developments also facilitated the circulation of extremist ideas. On another level, the famous *Deckert I* case[7] and the ensuing debate compelled German legislators to introduce a specific offence of denialism.

---

[4] This law introduced several provisions of substantive and procedural criminal law as well as administrative measures to contrast the various forms of racism. Among the amendments to the Criminal Code, the offences of dissemination of propaganda of unconstitutional organizations, violence, and distribution of pornographic writings were involved. See. Jahn 1998.

[5] On the introduction of this offence, see Rohrßen 2009, pp. 206–210; Vormbaum 2009, p. 228 et seq. On § 130 StGB, see Salomon 2012, pp. 48–50; Hellmann and Gartner 2011, pp. 961–966; Geilen 2008; Kahn 2006, p. 163 et seq.; Von Dewitz 2006, p. 106; Brugger 2003a, b, p. 1 et seq.; Kühl 2003, p. 103 et seq.; Brugger 2002, p. 20 et seq.; Dietz 1995, p. 210; Werle 1992, p. 2530.

[6] On this amendment, see Rohrßen 2009, p. 211 et seq.; Poscher 2005, p. 1317 et seq. This provision has been subject to the review of the Federal Constitutional Court (BVerfG, Judgment, 4 November 2009, 1 BvR 2150/08). The judges reaffirmed that this provision is exceptional with respect to the right to freedom of thought, provided for by Article 5 of the German Constitution, in line with the decisions no. 369/04, 370/04, 371/04, issued by the Court on 4 February 2010 (BVerfG, Decisions, 4 February 2010, nn. 369/04, 370/04, 371/04) which had stated that personal opinions, besides their intrinsic value and correctness, are protected under the German Constitution and must be balanced with other constitutional rights, such as human dignity. According to the established case law of the Court, human dignity shall indeed prevail over the right to freedom of speech, in case the exercise of the latter ends up harming the former. In this respect, see the decision issued in 1975: BVerfG, Decision, 25 February 1975, 39, 1 (67).

[7] See Federal Court of Justice (*Bundesgerichtshof*, hereinafter the BGH), Judgment, 15 March 1994, BGHSt no. 40/97, in *Neue Juristische Wochenschrift*, 1994, 1421. The Court annulled the decision that had convicted Mr. Deckert for the crime provided for by §130 and referred the matter to the lower Court. According to the BGH there were no factual elements proving that Holocaust denial could harm the dignity of the Jewish German People.

Indeed, in 1991 Günther Deckert, at the time president of the *National Partei Deutschland*,[8] had invited Fred Leuchter, the well-known denier of the gas chambers, to give a speech at a conference in Wertheim, Germany. Mr. Deckert served as interpreter during the conference, showing his clear support of the theories expounded by Mr. Leuchter. As a result, both were immediately accused of having committed the violation of espousing racist propaganda. The following year, a criminal trial was held against Mr. Deckert alone since Mr. Leuchter had already returned to the United States. The defendant was convicted of defamation and incitement to racial hatred, under § 130 of the German Criminal Code, but was then acquitted by the Federal Court of Justice (*Bundesgerichtshof*, hereinafter the BGH) on 15 March 1994. The decision stated that publishing opinions expressed by others on Holocaust denial could not qualify as incitement to racial hatred.[9] It was therefore the judges' opinion that § 130 of the StGB, in force at the time, was not applicable to the defendant.[10]

The decision received much criticism based on the fear that racist and neo-Nazi propaganda could not be punished under the legal framework.[11]

4.1.3 The Law of 28 October 1994

Eager to send a message to the public, in 1994 the Parliament added a third paragraph to § 130 which criminalises instigation to racial hatred ('*Volksverhetzung*'). The new provision penalizes the act of praising, approving or belittling the crimes systematically perpetrated under the Nazi regime.[12]

Prior to this change, whoever publically expressed denialist opinions could be punished for the crime of insult and defamation (§ 185, § 194 para 1, Subparagraph 2 StGB),[13] defamation of the memory of the deceased (§ 189 StGB) and instigation to racial hatred (§ 130 StGB). Nevertheless, the increasing invulnerability of Holocaust denial (which the *Deckert* case seemed to prove) and the ever-more pervasive dissemination of such theories showed just how inadequate these provisions were for effectively limiting the phenomenon.

Indeed, curtailing similar episodes had largely relied upon the offence of instigation to social hatred provided for by §130 StGB among the public-order crimes. Before the 1994 reform, this provision had proven to be ineffective since it was

---

[8] At that time, the NPD had reached 5% in the elections and had been able to appoint Mr. Deckert at the German Bundestag.

[9] BGH 1994, above n 5, 1421.

[10] On the *Deckert* case, see Hochmann 2012, pp. 361–364; Wandres 2000, p. 116 et seq.

[11] Critical of this decision, see Beisel 1995, p. 997.

[12] See Wandres 2000, pp. 276–303; Huster 1996, p. 487; Beisel 1995, p. 998; Stein 1986, p. 277.

[13] Indeed, besides the existing forms of insult and defamation, in 1985 § 194 StGB was introduced, punishing whoever 'insults the memory of the victims of Nationalist Socialism'.

designed to protect public order and it focused on certain types of attacks on human dignity that were punishable only if they adhered to each of the law's specifications.[14] Acts of denying or belittling the Holocaust rarely contained all of these elements.[15]

In particular, the provision could not be used against the act of so-called 'simple' or 'mere' Holocaust denial ('*einfache Auschwitzlüge*') or in the case of offensive statements.[16] Similarly, the offence provided by § 131 StGB on the 'depiction of violence' ('*Gewaltdarstellung*') could not apply as this did not translate into cruel or inhuman conduct as required under this provision.

Apart from this particular legal framework, a decisive push towards the criminalisation of Holocaust denial—'also in order to facilitate the application of §130 and §131 StGB and to reinforce their preventive effect'[17]—came from the decisions of the Federal Court of Justice and the Federal Constitutional Court.[18] In particular, the BVerfG contributed significantly to the debate regarding the appropriateness of the criminalisation of this phenomenon. Indeed, a few months before the offence was introduced, the Court had ruled that Holocaust denial did not enjoy the protection of the freedom of expression provided in Article 5 of the German Constitution.[19]

[14] This provision punished those who 'in a manner which is capable of disturbing public peace, attacks others' human dignity, by inciting to hatred against parts of the population, to violence or arbitrary actions, by insulting, maliciously defaming, or slandering them'.

[15] § 130 StGB, the general provision against racial discrimination, includes the prohibition of any written material inciting racial hatred, previously provided for by § 131 StGB.

[16] There is a distinction, introduced in Germany, between simple denialism and qualified denialism. 'Simple' historical denialism (*blosse Auschwitzlüge*), which is punished without any other additional elements being required and consists of demonstrating one's own historical conviction without incitement to violence or intolerance (for example the Romanian Law of 13 March 2002). 'Qualified' historical denialism (*qualifizierte Auschwitzlüge*), which is punished only if an inciteful element is present (for example, in Germany, Italy and Spain). The same paradigm of criminalisation has been adopted by the EU Framework Decision. See Hochmann 2012, p. 24 et seq.; Brugger 2005, p. 15; Wandres 2000, p. 96 et seq.

[17] In this sense the German Bundestag, in German Bundestag Document (*Bundestagsdrucksache*), 12/6853, 24.

[18] See, for example, BGHZ (*Entscheidungen des Bundesgerichtshofes in Zivilsachen*), 75, 1979, 160, 161 (BGH, 18 September 1979, no. 140/78) ('*The Zionist Swindle Case*').

[19] See BVerfG, Judgment, 13 April 1994, no. 23/94, in *Neue Juristische Wochenschrift*, 1994. The Federal Constitutional Court argues that the act of questioning the *Holocaust* is a false representation of history ('*falsche geschichtliche Darstellung*') and is therefore in violation of the fundamental right to freedom of thought. For this reason, in the BVerfG's established case law, the third paragraph of § 130 represents an exception to § 5 of the German Constitution.

4.1.4 Punishable Acts

The third paragraph of § 130 StGB[20] introduced in autumn 1994 had thus been preceded by two judicial decisions: in March of that year, the BGH stated that denialism could not be punished under the legal framework in force during that time; the following month, the BVerfG laid the foundation for the offence by ruling that punishing Holocaust denial was not a breach of constitutional guarantees.

As for the description of the conduct, the German Criminal Code adopts a particularly broad definition of denialism as it criminalises denial, belittlement (considering both quality and quantity)[21] and praise[22] of the Holocaust. As a result, the provision ends up punishing any person pertaining to the revisionist movement who challenges the existence of the Holocaust through the results of his or her research.[23]

The offence is punished with imprisonment—from one to five years—and with a criminal fine.

In this way, the law seeks to combat the growing tendency of trivialising the criminal acts perpetrated by the Nazi regime by denying their existence or supporting neo-Nazi ideology or racist purposes in general, which disturbs the peace and 'poisons' the political discourse.

---

[20] See Toma 2014; Matuschek 2012; Weiler 2012; Hörnle 2010, p. 215 et seq.; Zabel 2010, p. 834 et seq.; Von Dewitz 2006. See also the following commentaries on the Criminal Code: Fischer 2017, p. 2002; Hörnle 2015, p. 619 et seq.; Sternberg-Lieben 2014, p. 1533; Von Bubnoff 2009, p. 445.

[21] Fischer 2017, p. 1014. See Sternberg-Lieben 2014, p. 1533. Quantitative belittlement may consist, for example, of reducing the number of Jews killed. Qualitative belittlement may instead consist of saying that the Jewish genocide was not so bad. The offence also covers whoever puts forward racially-based 'good reasons' or 'needs' for the perpetration of the Holocaust, or that describe the crimes of the Nazi as inevitable military or police actions. Belittlement includes raising doubts.

[22] For this offence to be perpetrated it is enough to portray these facts as '*displeasing, but necessary*', Fischer 2017, p. 1015.

[23] On the application of § 130, 3rd para in the case law, see Fischer 2017, p. 1014; Graf 2013; see also the website: https://dejure.org/dienste/lex/StGB/130/1.html. On the issues raised by the perpetration of these crimes through the use of internet, see, with respect to the decision of the BGH, *Convicts Foreigner for Internet Posted Incitement to Racial Hatred*, available at http://www.germanlawjournal.com/article.php?id=67; see also Hörnle 2001, p. 624; Morozinis 2011, p. 475 et seq. On the problems of the application of German criminal law to denialist conducts committed through Internet, see Safferling 2011, pp. 18 and ff.; Jessberger 2001.

Concerning the case law, see, among others, Regional Court of Regensburg, Judgment, 23 September 2013, 4 Ns 102 Js 1410/2009, Higher Regional Court of Brandenburg, Beschluss vom, Judgment, 16 December 2015, 1 Ws 174/15; BGH, Judgment, 3 May 2016, 3 StR 449/15, BGH, Judgment, 27 July 2016, 3 StR 149/16 (LG Hannover). The most debated case in the public opinion relates to Ursula Haverbeck-Wetzel, a 89-year old revisionist, who was convicted many times; recently, she was sentenced by the Amtsgericht Hamburg in 2015, by the Amtsgericht Velden in 2016 and by the Amtsgericht Detmold in 2017.

Today, this paragraph punishes with up to five years imprisonment 'whoever, in public or at a gathering, praises (*billigt*), denies (*leugnet*) or belittles (*verharmlost*) the acts perpetrated during the Nationalist Social Regime that are described in the first Paragraph of § 6 of the German Code of Crimes against International Law (the *Völkerstrafgesetzbuch*, hereinafter the VStGB),[24] in such a way as to disrupt the public peace.'[25]

4.1.5 Scope

Extending punishment to mere forms of belittlement has been compensated by introducing additional requirements in the third paragraph of §130 StGB which limit the scope of the criminalised conduct.

First of all, the offence is applicable to denial of the criminal acts perpetrated under Nazi rule. In this respect, the German crime of denialism does not seek to punish the public and unambiguous denial of genocides or crimes against humanity in general—as is instead provided by French law.

The acts referred to by §130 StGB are the crimes committed by the German National Socialist Regime,[26] namely those that fall under the description provided for by § 6 of the German Code of Crimes against International Law, with respect to both the *actus reus* and the *mens rea*. The offence does not refer exclusively to the Jewish genocide[27] organised by the German government, but it also includes single actions perpetrated against specific individuals because they are members of a minority—as per § 6, para 1 VStGB—and not for solely personal reasons.

In addition to the persecution of Jewish people, §130 StGB includes any similar act perpetrated against other groups or ethnic minorities, such as the Sinti or the Roma.

On the contrary, the provision does not contemplate punishment for the denial, belittlement or praise of other particularly atrocious criminal acts, such as the Nazi '*Euthanasieaktionen*' or the enforced sterilisation of disabled people committed

[24] The German Code of Crimes against International Law entered into force on 30 June 2002. See *Bundesministerium der Justiz* (Hrsg.), *Arbeitsentwurf eines Gesetzes zur Einführung des Völkerstrafgesetzbuchs mit Begrüdung*; Werle and Jessberger 2014, p. 151 et seq. See also Satzger 2002, p. 261; Kress 2009. Before 2002, the provisions referred to are described in the first Paragraph of § 220a StGB ('*Völkermord*', Genocide). See Werle and Jessberger 2002.

[25] The StGB decided not to extend the scope of these acts to other genocides or serious crimes. Fischer 2017, p. 1014. See Hellmann and Gartner 2011, p. 961 et seq.

[26] The expression 'under the National Socialist Regime' ('*unter der nazionalsozialistischen Herrschaft*') refers to the time when the Nazis were in power, that is, from 1933 to 1945.

[27] Critical of this limitation Von Bubnoff 2009, p. 445.

under Nazi rule. These crimes do not meet the legal requirement of the offence because the victims (for example the disabled) do not qualify as a 'racial, national, religious or ethnic group' as provided for by § 6, para 1 VStGB.

4.1.6 Public Nature and Potential to Disturb the Public Peace

Two additional requirements have been introduced in order to limit the scope of the application of the offence.

First, Holocaust denial must take place *publicly*, that is, the conduct must be performed in public or at a gathering, no matter how limited the number of participants. However, this condition is not met when the participants of a small gathering are immune to expressions of Holocaust denial and there is no chance that the ideas in question reach a broader audience.[28]

The second legal requirement is that the conduct is capable of disturbing public peace,[29] meaning both the condition of safety and the feeling of security of the population. Indeed, the fact that this behaviour is performed publicly generally leads to the assumption that it fulfils a condition to disturb public peace.

'Public peace', mentioned in several provisions of the Criminal Code (§§ 126, 130, 140, 166), is primarily defined as the situation in which citizens feel their rights and legitimate interests are—and will be—protected under the legal system. This subjective conception of public peace is based on the citizens' feeling of public safety. A different interpretation defines public peace to be an objective situation characterised by the absence of violence among social classes. Such an interpretation does not change the overall structure of the offence, which still punishes the mere endangerment of the protected legal interest, though the level of endangerment required in this case is not merely abstract but rather potential or concrete.

Although the offences of Holocaust denial primarily aim at protecting the public peace, against this background scholars believe that additional interests fall under the scope of its protection.[30]

Legal scholarship has pointed out that if the offence is said to protect public peace, then the act of denying past crimes cannot be considered automatically dangerous for public safety. Indeed, such an exception to Article 5 of the German Constitution would require the unlawful statements to entail the actual risk of violent attacks against citizens or individuals. Scholars also argue that the offence

[28] Fischer 2017, p. 1010.

[29] Fischer 2011, pp. 1119–1141; Fischer 1986.

[30] Therefore, § 130 StGB reverses the burden of proof concerning conduct that would already be punishable under § 140, 2nd para. StGB, with the denial that would depend on the underlying intention of the perpetrator. See Fischer 2017, p. 1013. On the protected legal interests mentioned (human dignity, personal rights, and public peace) with respect to this offence, see Knauer 2014; Glet 2011; Jacobi 2010; Guenther 2000.

does not protect historical truth on the grounds that historical facts are unquestionable, as this very assumption would be difficult to prove. From this perspective, the offence does not punish the mere misconception of historical facts, but rather a negation that lacks a serious critical background and feigns a mistake to conceal the implicit intention of praising or belittling such crimes.

As a result, the punishable conduct of harming or endangering public peace must be linked to another element of the offence of instigation to racial hatred (former § 130 StGB): the direct violation of the interests of individuals. This happens, for instance, when the conduct targets a part of the population or a *national*, *racial*, *religious* or *ethnic* minority with such intensity as to harm their personal dignity. However, it is unclear what meaning the concept of 'personal dignity' has in practice, and especially whether it refers to the public in general, to which the ethnic or religious group the victims belong, or rather to the smaller group of Holocaust survivors and their family members. In this last case, the scope of the offence would be to protect the 'demand for respect' ('*Achtungsanspruch*') of those who perished during the Holocaust, the survivors and their relatives. Should this *not* be the case, the offence would then seek to protect a broad notion of human dignity, which would include the right of the individual not to have his or her identity vilified. This would imply, of course, that being part of the group targeted by the unlawful conduct is fundamental to the development of the victim's identity. Lastly, according to some scholarship and certain case law, the offence of Holocaust denial also aims to protect political discourse from any form of potential 'poisoning' as the case would be whenever racist objectives or Nazi ideology appear to be acceptable. In light of this, the ability of the conduct to harm ultimately depends on which interest the offence is intended to protect.

Of course, an assessment of this capacity must focus on the disturbance of public peace. The evaluation should consider the content of the unlawful statements, the time, the place and the way they have been expressed, as well as all other aspects involved in the action.[31]

However, it has been argued that the offence does not require the protected interest to be harmed or endangered in practice, as its mere potential endangerment is enough to necessitate punishment. Another interpretation suggests that the offence combines abstract and real endangerment,[32] as the unlawful conduct should not actually endanger but rather be able to endanger in practice public peace. From this perspective, and unlike previous interpretations, the assessment should be based on concrete past circumstances that have actually disturbed the public peace, such as the content of the opinions being expressed, their time and place.

As discussed above, part of the scholarship argues that the crime of Holocaust denial seeks to prevent the 'poisoning' of political discourse, thereby punishing all conduct capable of producing such an effect. Those who believe that such endangerment should be assessed in practice further suggest that said assessment should

---

[31] Fischer 2017, p. 1017. See also Krauß 2009, p. 501.

[32] Miebach et al. 2012, p. 652. On this aspect, see for instance also Zabel 2010, p. 845 note 55.

consider the current intellectual environment and its sensitivity to these types of opinions.[33] For instance, if the Holocaust were called into question, the seriousness of the arguments put forth should be evaluated according to whether they are, or are not, insubstantial propaganda and whether they dispute minor events, or instead they challenge the actual extermination of the Jewish people.

Considering the above, it is hard to determine if the introduction of this requirement—the disturbance of public peace—is effective in limiting denialism and preventing that mere personal opinions be subject to punishment. This ultimately depends on what level of endangerment—merely abstract, potential or concrete—the offence is thought to require. Nonetheless, whatever the endangerment may be, many have questioned whether such a requirement can prevent the improper expansion of the offence,[34] in addition to considering how the feeling of social insecurity might end up influencing the judge's assessment.

4.1.7 The Federal Constitutional Court Decision

The Federal Constitutional Court decision issued on 13 April 1994 ruled that a legislative act limiting the right to freedom of expression in order to punish the so-called 'Auschwitz lie' is legitimate under German constitutional law.[35]

As discussed above, this ruling was issued *before* German lawmakers introduced the third paragraph of § 130 StGB for punishing Holocaust denial. Nevertheless, this decision is an important precedent frequently referred to by foreign courts and is a fundamental ruling on the balance of legal interests and fundamental rights harmed by denialism. Indeed, it outlines like no other judgment the complexity and problems inherent in this form of criminalisation.

The arguments made by the Court in order to substantiate the compatibility between the punishment of the so-called 'Auschwitz lie' and the constitutional right to freedom of speech are extremely important in the ongoing discussion on the criminalisation of denialism. Indeed, alongside their reflection on the balance of conflicting interests, which can only justify limiting a right as fundamental as the freedom of expression, the judges of the BVerfG investigate the distinction between

---

[33] Among the relevant circumstances: repeating xenophobic words in a menacing manner at a gathering of right-wing extremist or hanging a xenophobic pamphlet in a migration office (Krauß 2009, p. 457). Other elements concerning the targeted group must be assessed, as its level of homogeneity, its distinctive traits, and its level of social integration at the time. It is also necessary to consider the sensitivity of the public opinion to xenophobic, neo-Nazi or racist ideas in a particular moment in time or in certain sectors of the population, or the recognizable peculiarity of the person being targeted (as certain distinctive traits of the Jewish people), *ibid.*, 482.

[34] Fischer 2017, p. 1005.

[35] See BverfG, 13 April 1994, no. 23/94, above n 17, p. 1779. See Grimm 2009, p. 557 et seq.; Visconti 2008; Brugger 2005, pp. 1–21; Haupt 2005; Brugger 2002; Finer et al. 1995, p. 35 et seq.

'expressing an opinion' and 'stating a fact' and the role played by the latter in the development of the former.

The risk arises here that Holocaust denial could be translated into the criminalisation of mere ideas. In this respect, the Court chose to address the dilemma from within the limits of freedom of expression and to analyse the elements characterising this right and its development. As we shall see later, this allowed the Court to discuss the defining elements of denialism outside these limits and to use external criteria in their analysis.

The judgment of the BVerfG originated from an appeal against an administrative decision that had lingered over the tension between the freedom of speech and the use of criminal law. Specifically, the municipality of Munich had taken pre-emptive measures to restrict the right to freedom of speech on the occasion of a conference organised by the National Democratic Party[36] on the responsibilities of Germany during World War II. The well-known denier David Irving had been invited to give a speech at the conference and was likely to negate the extermination of the Jewish people.[37] As a consequence, the competent authority issued the permit for holding the conference on the condition that the organisers expressly made sure that no opinion denying the Holocaust would be expressed. The very content of this request, in many ways quite unusual, demonstrate the urgency on the part of public authorities—and lawmakers—to monitor these phenomena.

From a practical—and formal—point of view, both the request and the subsequent decision of the authorities had a clearly preventive implication. The prohibitive measure was based on the assumption that a crime could potentially be perpetrated even if someone had not actually been caught in the act, which, for example, would have justified the order to cancel the gathering. Nevertheless, the appeal brought before the Court did not focus on this particular aspect of the administrative measure.

The appellant did not question the risk that opinions denying the Holocaust would be expressed at the conference, but challenged the constitutionality of this type of restriction in general. They alleged that the fundamental right to freedom of expression, provided for by Article 5 of the German Constitution, had been violated by the provisions of the law on meetings and demonstrations (§5, no. 4) and by the provisions of the Criminal Code that had been applied.[38]

The appellant further claimed that the right to freedom of speech outranked in importance and overruled the right to personality, which the Federal Constitutional Court believed had been violated by the denial of Holocaust.

---

[36] *Nationaldemokratische Partei Deutschland*: an extremist right-wing party, consisting in part of neo-Nazi supporters.

[37] The administrative authorities, through the reference to the case law of the Tribunals of first instance, have qualified the Holocaust denial as an insult to the Jewish people.

[38] According to the appellant, these provisions would ultimately prevent an undesirable discussion on modern history and suppress historical research on the most recent events of the German history, thereby frustrating the exercise of a fundamental right.

Although the contested administrative measure had restricted the right to freedom of assembly, against this background the BVerfG settled the case by referring to the right to freedom of speech and ruling that the act of denying the extermination of the Jewish people under Nazi rule did not fall under the scope of Article 5 of the Constitution.[39]

4.1.7.1 'Fact' and 'Opinion', Objectivity and Subjectivity

In its reasoning, the BVerfG distinguished between *fact* and *opinion*. The protection provided for by the German Constitution extends to both the *expression of an opinion* ('*Meinungsäußerung*'), which is defined by the subjective connection existing between an individual and the content of his or her statement, and the *assertion of a fact* ('*Tatsachenbehauptungen*'), which is characterised by the objective relationship between the statement and the reality it refers to. In the Court's reasoning, the assertion of a fact enjoys a different degree of legal protection compared to the expression of an opinion, as the former is guaranteed only insofar as it serves as the basis for the development of an opinion.

Whenever the assertion of a fact is imprecise or otherwise intentionally or verifiably false, and cannot therefore serve the purpose of developing personal opinions, then it *no longer falls under* the scope of protection ensured by the German Constitution. Only if the distinction between assertion and opinion is impossible, or it is too complicated, a statement should be considered as the expression of a personal opinion, and thus this fundamental right may not be subject to excessive limitations.[40]

The Court cites general norms allowing the restriction of the right to freedom of speech and reiterates the importance of balancing the fundamental right being restricted and the interest being protected.

In this respect, the BVerfG recognises that the right to freedom of speech does not always outrank the protection of personality. It is instead the latter that generally overrules the former[41] because the violation of personality rights is usually more detrimental than the restriction of the right to freedom of expression. Furthermore, when the facts being asserted are verifiably false—as in the case pending before the Court—the right to freedom of speech is generally superseded by the protection of personality rights.

---

[39] The Federal Constitutional Court considers the offence of Holocaust denial though the lens of §5, 2nd para. of the German Constitution, as a form of exception-limitation to the right to freedom of speech. The violation of Article 5 depends on whether the balance between the right to freedom of speech and the harmed legal interest refers to the *statement of a fact* or the *expression of an opinion.*

[40] Decision of the BVerfG (*Entscheidungen des Bundesverfassungsgerichts*), 61, 1 (9); 85, 1 (15 et seq.).

[41] See BVerfG, point no. II of the decision: BVerfGE 61, 1 [8 f.]; 85, 1 [17].

The Court also argues that a statement denying the Holocaust is not to be qualified as the expression of a personal opinion but as the *assertion of a fact*, which enjoys legal protection only insofar as it actually leads to the development of a personal opinion. This is, of course, not the case for any statement denying the Holocaust because such an assertion is verifiably false.

The criminalisation of denialism is thus legitimate for two reasons. On the one hand, the denial of crimes perpetrated under Nazi rule harms personality rights and is therefore more detrimental than restricting freedom of speech in this case. On the other hand, any statement denying the Holocaust is unmistakably false and falls therefore outside the scope of protection ensured by the right to freedom of speech.

As a result, the BVerfG concludes that denialism must be qualified as a form of insult and therefore punished according to § 185 StGB and § 194 para. 2 StGB for the resulting violation of right to personality.

The judgment thus established the legitimacy of a legislative act limiting the right to freedom of speech and set the 'weighting rules' to be applied when balancing fundamental rights and the use of criminal law. Criminalisation may be limited by the balance with personality rights and by the possibility for the defendant to prove the truthfulness of the facts referred to in his or her statement.[42]

4.1.7.2 The 'Truth of Facts'?

This judgment raises a crucial issue: the BVerfG's decision requires viable criteria for distinguishing between facts and opinions, but it also entails the risk of excessively limiting freedom of speech. Even more so when the truth of the facts being referred to is the parameter for distinguishing an *opinion* ('Meinungausserung'), which is protected under the Constitution, from an *assertion of a fact* ('Tatsachebehauptung'), which instead is considered an expression of freedom of speech insofar as it serves as a basis for the development of an opinion.

For this reason, under the German constitutional system, the assertion of a fact does not enjoy the same degree of protection as the expression of an opinion because the legal protection of the former depends on the assessment of the 'truth'. Whenever the facts being referred to are false no protection is guaranteed.

Is it not dangerous that this decision is based on assessing the actual 'truth'? What instruments can a judge use to ascertain that a historical fact is indeed true? Such criteria pertain to the very delicate area of speech crimes, an expression that portends the numerous problems that are bound to arise.

---

[42] On this very problematic issue, see generally the book of the Italian constitutional lawyer Bin 1992, p. 32 et seq.; on the conflicts between free speech and human dignity, see also Tesauro 2013, p. 50 et seq.

4.1.7.3 Historical and Judicial 'Truth'

Aside from the complexity of ascertaining the truth, the Court also seems to disregard the difference between historical and judicial truth, with only the latter being the result of legal proceedings.

As mentioned, the judicial truth and its characteristics have been the subject of various in-depth studies which are too numerous to cite here. For the sake of brevity, consider it sufficient to emphasise that the scope of validity of judicial truth and its ability to answer specific questions are limited by the legal consequences of *res judicata* and its definite and indisputable nature.

Historical truth—as discussed above—is instead the result of diverse social processes, which by definition are free from any form of limitation, except for the methodology shared by historians in a particular moment in time. Such methodology provides different answers because it responds to different questions, and it reflects the *meaning* acquired by a *series of events*. Unlike judicial truth, historical truth is never definitive because society, which constantly analyses the past, keeps evolving and thus continually faces new challenges. Likewise, the answers that history gives ultimately depend on the perspective adopted—and the problems faced—by the persons asking the questions.

The clearly defined and formalised rules of judicial findings are designed to establish facts correctly in order to reach an undisputable verdict (although their inherent shortcomings have been outlined by scholars). They could hardly be more antithetical to the essence of history, which leads to inherently contradictory and diverse findings whereby the overall meaning of a historical event determines, *ex post*, which facts are relevant for its description.

Whereas the law aims to establish a clearly defined, unambiguous and necessarily definitive truth—a form of *singular* truth—history addresses our past from different angles and using diverse techniques. It answers disparate questions and therefore suggests historical descriptions and causal links that are continuously challenged and translated into an intrinsically *plural* truth.

4.2 'Fact' and 'Value': The Spanish Constitutional Court

4.2.1 The Spanish Legal Framework

A few years after the approval of the French law and immediately after the aforementioned German legislation, Spanish lawmakers introduced an autonomous offence of denialism into the Criminal Code as a response to the growth of this phenomenon in Spain and the widespread indignation of public opinion.

The description of the defining elements of the offence and of the procedure that led to its approval is imperative in order to examine the decision of the Constitutional Court, which declared the provision partially unconstitutional.

Indeed, this ruling is crucial for this investigation in light of the reasoning put forward by the Court. Faced with the question of the compatibility of the offence of denialism and the right to freedom of speech, the Spanish Constitutional Court stressed the importance of the latter for any democratic legal system and declared the former partially unconstitutional by distinguishing 'facts' from 'values', as opposed to 'facts' and 'opinions' in the case of the BVerfG.

4.2.1.1 *Ley Orgánica* of 11 May 1995

The offence of denialism was introduced into the Spanish Criminal Code in 1995, after some disturbing Holocaust denial cases (like the notorious *Makoki* and *Friedman* cases) had sparked fierce debate.[43] At the time, the need for a criminal law response to counteract this phenomenon was widespread and, although the new Spanish Criminal Code (Organic Law no. 4 of 11 May 1995) was being approved, legislators nevertheless decided to introduce a new offence.[44] The approval of the provision was the result of a long process. Politicians and the media were enthusiastic about it, while legal scholars expressed open scepticism.[45] The process began in 1993 and shed light on the inadequacies of the Spanish criminal law system.[46]

It all began with the case of Violeta Friedman, an Auschwitz survivor who had filed a claim against León Degrelle for violating her right to dignity and honour. Mr. Degrelle, a former high-ranking official of the SS, had given an interview in the magazine *Tiempo* in which he openly justified the persecution of the Jewish people perpetrated by the Nazis and questioned the existence of the gas chambers. The courts of first and second instance, as well as the Supreme Court of Spain, all dismissed the complaint on the grounds that the applicant lacked *locus standi* because the defendant had not directly harmed Mrs. Friedman's personality rights, and considered that the contested statements were the expression of the right to freedom of speech guaranteed under the Spanish Constitution.[47]

[43] On the judicial precedents that played a role in the introduction of the criminal offence, see Rodríguez Montañés 2012, p. 305. The Constitutional Court had rejected the claim filed by the director of the publishing house *Makoki* against his conviction for insult against the Jewish people, after he published the French comic book 'Hitler=SS'). On the *Makoki case*, see Martínez Sospedra 1993, p. 5785.

[44] The Criminal Code in force at the time had been approved with Decree no. 3096 of 1973, thus before the end of Franco's regime and the democratic transition.

[45] See Bilbao Ubillos 2009, p. 314.

[46] Constitutional Court of Spain, Judgment, 11 November 1991, no. 214/1991, in *Jurisprudencia Constitucional*, 31, 444 et seq.

[47] Court of First Instance number 6 of Madrid (*Juzgado de Primera Instancia núm. 6 de Madrid*), Judgment, 16 June 1986, no. 1284/85; Regional Court of Madrid (*Audiencia Territorial de Madrid*), First Chamber, Judgment, 9 February 1988, Appeal no. 572/86; Supreme Court of Spain, First Chamber, Judgment, 5 December 1989, Appeal no. 771/88.

The Constitutional Court of Spain instead ruled in favour of the *recurso de amparo* raised by Mrs. Friedman. The Court stated that the dignity and honour of an individual can be harmed by an insult to the social group he or she belongs to and that the right to freedom of speech and expression does not include racist or xenophobic statements that offend human dignity. This case demonstrated how much Spain lacked a proper legal framework for dealing with Holocaust denial. Indeed, the Friedman case and similar episodes that followed compelled politicians to send a clear and symbolic message, demonstrating unanimous intention to fight against the growth of Holocaust denial or other racist remarks—even with the use of criminal law.[48] Such a commitment was felt all the more keenly in a country like Spain, which under Franco's regime had welcomed thousands of Nazi and fascist war criminals, the most famous and active of whom was indeed Mr. Degrelle.

Therefore, in May 1995, the new offence of denial of crimes of genocide ('*Apología de los delitos de genocidio*') was introduced into the Spanish legal system under Article 137-(b) of the Criminal Code.

The provision stated:

> The denial of the offences provided for by the previous provision shall be subject to a penalty lower by two degrees than the one provided for therein.
>
> Denial consists of the expression, before a group of individuals or by any other means of communication, of ideas or doctrines that extol, deny, belittle or justify the crimes provided for by the previous provision, that glorify the perpetrator thereof, or that aim at establishing or reinstating regimes or institutions that protect practices that generate crimes of genocide, insofar as the nature and circumstances of these conducts are such as to constitute direct incitement to commit an offence.

This provision included a particularly wide range of punishable conducts and the requirements that the unlawful conducts translate into direct incitement to commit a crime. It remained in force for only one year because a few months after its introduction the Organic Law establishing the new Spanish Criminal Code was approved on 23 November 1995 and entered into force on 24 May 1996.

4.2.1.2 The 1995 Reform of the Criminal Code

The 1995 reform introduced the crime of genocide in Article 607 of the Spanish Criminal Code.[49] While the first paragraph of the provision defines the offence of genocide, the second paragraph describes a specific offence that punishes the denial of genocide, in a broad sense the act of 'denying' or 'justifying' its perpetration.

---

[48] See Landa Gorostiza 2001, p. 102.

[49] See Bilbao Ubillos 2009, pp. 318–319.

This provision is located in Title XXIV of the Criminal Code regarding 'crimes against the international community' and under Chapter II regarding 'crimes of genocide.'[50]

The provision reads:

> Diffusion by any means of ideas or doctrines that deny or justify the crimes defined in the preceding Section of this Article, or that aim to reinstate regimes or institutions that protect practices that generate these shall be punished with a sentence of imprisonment from one to two years.[51]

This norm carefully defines the punishable conduct, which is limited to the acts of denying or justifying crimes of genocide, and leaves out all reference to mere belittlement of the same. Furthermore, the unlawful conduct is punished regardless of its ability to actually humiliate, harass or provoke the victims of the offences being referred to: the mere diffusion of such ideas or doctrines is sufficient for issuing punishment.

In this respect, although only two years had passed since the previous reform, the offence is considerably different from the one provided for by Article 137-b of the former Criminal Code, which required the unlawful conduct be capable of incitement to commit a crime.

A debate arose among legal scholars on both the interests that the new offence sought to protect and on its relationship with other Criminal Code provisions, namely Article 510 (punishing incitement to hate or violence against social groups or associations),[52] Article 615 (punishing the provocation, conspiracy and solicitation to commit a genocide)[53] and Article 18 (punishing the unlawful defence of a criminal act).

Indeed, an issue that sparked controversy and led to rather contradictory judicial decisions was the application of the offence along with other provisions of the Spanish Criminal Code. In particular, the question arose as to whether the act defined in the second paragraph of Article 607 could be qualified as defence of a criminal act, thereby also falling under the scope of application of Article 18 of the Criminal Code. This interpretation put forward by some scholars implied that the unlawful conduct could be punished only insofar as it translated into a direct incitement to commit a crime, a requirement that had to be ascertained in light of

[50] Manzanares Samaniego 2016; Gómez Tomillo 2011; Fernández Hernández 2010, pp. 533–536; Quintero Olivares and Valle-Muniz 2008; García Arán 2004, p. 2688 et seq.; Landa Gorostiza 2003, pp. 105–119.

[51] See Gascón Cuenca 2016; Rodríguez Montañés 2012.

[52] Article 510 of the Criminal Code states: '1. Those who provoke discrimination, hate or violence against groups or associations due to racist, anti-Semitic reasons or any other reason related to ideology, religion or belief, family situation, belonging to an ethnic group or race, national origin, gender, sexual preference, illness or handicap, shall be punished with a sentence of imprisonment from one to three years and a fine from six to twelve months'.

[53] Article 615 provides: 'Provocation, conspiracy and solicitation to commit the crimes foreseen in the preceding Chapters of this Title shall be punished with the penalty lower by one or two degrees to which the actual crime is subject'.

the circumstances of the action (being perpetrated against a group of individuals or by any other suitable means of propaganda) and of its content (denying or praising genocides).[54]

Such an interpretation limits the scope of Article 607, para. 2 so that its application is more consistent with the right to freedom of speech guaranteed under the Spanish Constitution. It also tends to disregard the provision's actual wording and the structural differences between this offence and the act of defending a criminal act. Unlike its predecessor, the offence introduced in 1995 does not require the conduct to be capable of incitement to commit a crime, but rather consists in the expressed denial or justification of a genocide's perpetration—that is, the mere dissemination of ideas.[55]

Furthermore, the distinction between direct and indirect incitement has been a constant reference point for Spanish case law in distinguishing the offence provided by Article 607, para. 2 from the crimes of conspiracy and encouragement to commit a genocide (Article 615) and from the crime of incitement to racial hatred and discrimination (Article 510). Both offences, especially the latter, share with the crime of genocide denial the problem of imposing limits on the right to freedom of speech.

In this respect, the Supreme Court has systematically interpreted criminal offences concerning xenophobia and discrimination and it maintains that Articles 615 and 510 of the Criminal Code punish the *direct* incitement to commit, respectively, genocide and discriminatory acts.[56] Both provisions require that the crimes being condoned must be sufficiently defined, that the incitement be heard by participants or bystanders, be public and actually be able to convince the listeners. Denialism is instead a form of *indirect* incitement that is not necessarily perpetrated in public and it is punished insofar as it generates a general sentiment that entails the *certain* risk of acts of hatred, discrimination or violence being committed. The certain nature of such risk results from the specific context in which these ideas are expressed, that is, the Spanish social context with its recent history of fascism and racism, which is therefore particularly susceptible to anti-Semitic ideas and to racial hatred.

In this respect, the preventive nature of the offence provided for by Article 607, para 2 is justified—and is itself influenced—by the marked danger that genocide denial is able to engender in a particular *context of crisis*.[57] Hence the context must be assessed for determining whether restricting the right to freedom or speech is legitimate.

However, the text of the provision was amended after a 2007 Constitutional Court judgment. The Court stated that the act of denying a genocide could no

---

[54] See for example Fernández Hernández 2010; Vives Antòn et al. 2008, p. 1150.

[55] This crime is also a speech crime, criticized for this reason by several authors: Teruel Lozano 2015a, b, pp. 530 and ff.; Ramos Vázquez 2009, p. 122; Feijoo Sánchez 1998, p. 2267.

[56] Spanish Supreme Court, *Librería Kalki*, Judgment, 12 April 2011, no. 259/2011.

[57] *Ibid.*

longer be a criminal offence as it encroached upon the right to freedom of speech guaranteed under the Spanish Constitution, whereas the act of justifying genocide could remain subject to punishment because it was deemed able to potentially incite others to commit this form of criminal act. The abovementioned decision will be subject to thorough analysis in the following sections, as it truly exemplifies the complexity of criminalising these forms of expression. As a general note, the case of Spain also demonstrates the conflict between the offence of denialism and the right to freedom of speech, which none of the various wordings of the offence seem to be able to prevent.

4.2.1.3 The 2015 Reform of the Criminal Code

The Spanish legal framework on genocide denial was amended again by the 2015 reform of the Criminal Code.[58] This new set of regulations introduced significant changes to criminal sanctions and to several other crucial aspects of criminal law, in addition to substantially redefining the provisions on genocide denial.[59]

The legislative proposal specifies that the amendment was dictated by the need to implement the EU Framework Decision on Holocaust denial and ensure that the legal framework align with the 2007 decision of the Constitutional Court. Indeed, the Court had ruled that the provision was legitimate insofar as the punished conduct translated into an incitement to hostility and hatred against social minorities.

The most important innovation is the relocation of denialism within the Criminal Code under Article 510, which also defines the offence of incitement to racial and social discrimination. This provision now punishes the act of inciting hatred, hostility, discrimination or violence (letter a), the production and distribution of materials for this purpose (letter b), the actual crime of genocide denial (letter c), the violation of human dignity by means of humiliation or disdain (letter a) and the public justification or praise of offences committed for anti-Semitic or racist reasons. The use of technological means that render the unlawful statements accessible to a large audience constitutes an aggravating circumstance if capable of disturbing public peace or if the perpetrator is a member of a criminal organisation (paras 3 and 4 of Article 510).[60]

As for the offence of genocide denial, the reform re-establishes the crime of denying genocides, which had been declared unconstitutional by the Constitutional Court, as well as the crime of belittling or praising genocides, which had appeared in Article 137-*bis* of the previous Spanish Criminal Code but had been left out of

[58] For a detailed analysis of the provision, see Alastuey Dobón 2016; Bernal del Castillo 2016. For an analysis from a criminal - constitutional perspective, see Teruel Lozano 2015a, b.

[59] Morales Prats and Quintero Olivares 2016; Sánchez Melgar 2016; Bidasolo et al. 2015.

[60] On Article 510 of the Criminal Code, see de Pablo Serrano and Tapia Ballesteros 2017; Dolz Lago 2016; Teruel Lozano 2015a, pp. 1–51.

the second paragraph of Article 607. The act of justifying is punished under the second paragraph of the provision when it refers to crimes perpetrated against a social minority for anti-Semitic or racist reasons, but is not included in reference to international crimes.

Under the new provision, denial, belittlement and praise extend to other categories of international crimes, namely crimes against humanity and war crimes. The provision covers unlawful motives that had not been considered before, such as the perpetration of crimes based on nationality, sexual orientation and disability. Lastly, the provision specifies that the unlawful conduct must be perpetrated against a social group, or a part or member of the same.

While these amendments serve the purpose of extending the offence's scope of application, the provision requires the propensity of the punished conduct to create a 'climate' of hatred, distrust or discrimination against the victims, thereby limiting the range of criminalisation. Nevertheless, the wording of the provision appears to be broader than the requirement of the 'ability to incite' mentioned in the 1973 Criminal Code and referred to by the 2007 Constitutional Court decision. In this respect, contrary to the reasoning of the proposal, the amendments to the crime of genocide denial do not entirely reflect the abovementioned ruling but rather introduce certain elements contradicting this decision.

Finally, in line with the overall approach of the Reform, the maximum levels of sanctions have been raised from three to four years of imprisonment, in addition to a monetary sanction.

4.2.2 The Decision of the Constitutional Court

The Constitutional Court decision issued on 7 November 2007 (which declared the offence of genocide denial provided by the second paragraph of Article 607 partially unconstitutional) is relevant to this analysis.

The very decision to declare the crime of denialism unconstitutional seems to contradict the predominant view amongst scholars,[61] which tends to advocate the constitutionality of the offence. The judgment also presents various arguments that invite reflection on the most critical aspects of criminalising denialism, especially on the constraints that may be imposed upon the right to freedom of speech through criminal law.

Indeed, the entire decision is based on the distinction between *denying* and *justifying*. The former consists in contesting the existence of a fact, a sort of yes/no statement: a *question of fact*. The latter consists of the appraisal of the positive or negative significance of a fact, the existence of which is not called into question. In this respect, such an appraisal compares good and evil and is therefore a *question of value*.

[61] This aspect is emphasised also by Bilbao Ubillos 2009, p. 299.

The distinction between 'fact' and 'value' is indeed the hallmark of this decision, reverberating at various levels and raising critical questions. It also establishes a peculiar relationship with the right to freedom of speech, which is seen as the founding element of democratic legal systems.

The importance attached to the rulings of the European Court of Human Rights, to which the Spanish judges frequently refer, is another extremely important feature of the ruling.

Called upon to address the compatibility of the constitutional right to freedom of speech and Article 607, para 2 of the Spanish Criminal Code,[62] the Constitutional Court declared the provision partially unconstitutional for punishing the act of 'denying' genocides because it encroached upon the right to freedom of thought provided for by Article 20 of the Constitution. However, the Court also ruled that the act of 'justifying' genocides could instead be subject to punishment if it translated into direct incitement to perpetrate genocide.

4.2.2.1 Denial Not Necessarily Inciting Hatred: The *Varela* Case

The issue of the constitutionality of Article 607, para. 2 was raised during the judgment on the appeal against Pedro Varela in the *Libreria Europa* case. On 16 November 1998, Criminal Court number 3 of Barcelona sentenced Mr. Varela, the owner of the internationally-known bookshop *Libreria Europa*, for distributing books, publications and other materials with anti-Semitic and discriminatory content insulting the Jewish community. Mr. Varela was convicted and sentenced to two years of imprisonment for repeated genocide denial (Article 607, para. 2) and to another three years of imprisonment plus a fine for repeated incitement to discrimination, hatred and violence against groups or associations on racist or anti-Semitic grounds (Article 510).[63]

In its ruling, the First Instance Court pointed out that Holocaust denial is different from—and more serious than—the act of questioning the existence of a historical fact because it creates a climate of hostility and disdain against the Jewish community, which can later translate into violent acts or active forms of discrimination.[64]

The defendant then filed an appeal against this decision, claiming that the legal interest allegedly violated by his conduct could not be protected under criminal law as it was abstract in nature and it encroached upon the right to freedom of speech,

[62] This decision was not taken unanimously (see the dissenting opinions, annexed to the judgment). On this ruling, see Ramos Vázquez 2009, pp. 120–137; de la Rosa Cortina 2007, p. 6842; Landa Gorostiza 1999, p. 709.

[63] On the decision issued in the *Varela* case (or *Libreria Europa* case), see Bilbao Ubillos 2009, pp. 323–328; Català and Pérez 2007, p. 181; Landa Gorostiza 1999, pp. 691–692. On Article 510 of the Spanish Criminal Code, see Landa Gorostiza 2012. See also de Pablo Serrano 2017, p. 8911; Bernal del Castillo 2016.

[64] Provincial Court of Barcelona (section 3), 5 March 2008.

thereby violating Article 20, para. 1 of the Spanish Constitution (‘*Antecedente de hecho n. 3*’). The appellant therefore asked the Court to raise the issue of constitutionality concerning the offences for which he had been charged and their violation of the constitutional provisions on the right to freedom of speech.

The Third Chamber of the Provincial Court of Barcelona partially upheld the request and in February 2002 issued Act no. 5152-2000 questioning the constitutionality of Article 607, para. 2. In its ruling, the Provincial Court maintained that the legal interest protected by this provision could not be guaranteed through criminal law, that the offence unlawfully restricted the right to freedom of speech and that this constitutional right could only be restricted to protect an equally important fundamental right. The Court also added that the Spanish Criminal Code already ensured an adequate punitive response against any discriminatory act, which could also include denialism.[65]

The case was settled seven years later by the *Plenum* of the Constitutional Court with decision no. 235/2007 issued on 7 November,[66] which partially upheld the observations raised by appellant.[67] The decision stated that Article 607, para. 2 of the Criminal Code was in violation of the Spanish Constitution insofar as it punished the act of ‘denying’ genocides.[68]

The verdict was far from being a foregone conclusion, and the Court’s reasoning eloquently expresses the difficulties of criminalising denialism.

4.2.2.2 Denial Is Lawful

The Constitutional Court starts by stressing the importance of the right to freedom of speech,[69] which lies at the foundation of the Spanish constitutional system. For this reason, freedom of speech is not simply an individual right, but rather a necessary precondition for the exercise of other rights that pertain to the functioning of a democratic legal system.

It follows by reason that the exercise of this right should be guaranteed even when it translates into opinions that might appear disturbing, unsettling, dangerous or incorrect considering the pluralistic character of modern societies. This constitutional right even extends to opinions that are against the very essence of the Constitution as long as they do not encroach upon other equally important

---

[65] This norm is constitutionally legitimate according to Martínez Sospedra 2000, p. 99 et seq. *Contra* Feijoo Sánchez 1998.

[66] Constitutional Court of Spain, Judgment, 7 November 2007, no. 235/2007, BOE-T-2007-21161, in *BOE no. 295*, 10 December 2007, 42–59.

[67] Criticising this judgment: Suárez Espino 2008, p. 1 et seq.; Català and Pérez 2007, p. 181 et seq. With a more positive opinion, see Lascuráin Sánchez 2010, p. 1 et seq.; Ramós Vazquez 2009, p. 120 et seq. (who argues that the punishment of the act of justifying should also have been declared unconstitutional); Salvador Coderch and Rubi Puig 2008, p. 1 et seq.

[68] Bilbao Ubillos 2009, p. 299, who qualifies the decision of the Constitutional Court as ‘*correcta*’.

[69] Constitutional Court of Spain, Judgment 235/2007, above n 63, 48.

constitutional rights, and only in this case shall the right to freedom of speech be limited and the resulting violations be punished as a criminal offence.

The question remains as to whether the dissemination of opinions that deny or justify the perpetration of genocide encroaches upon constitutional rights and can therefore be punished. In this respect, the Constitutional Court makes reference to its own 1991 judgment which established that opinions concerning historical facts were guaranteed under the constitutional right to freedom of speech classified as 'subjective views on historical facts'.[70] Against this clear-cut background, the Court acknowledges that 'the recognition accorded by the Constitution to human dignity defines the framework within which constitutional rights shall be exercised and, in light thereof, the act of praising those who commit genocide, through the glorification of their image and the justification of their actions, shall not enjoy constitutional protection whenever it entails the humiliation of the victims (STC 176/1995, 11 December, FJ 5)'.[71] The Court therefore rules that limitations on the right to freedom of speech shall ultimately coincide with those established by the European Court of Human Rights (ECtHR) with reference to the second paragraph of Article 10 of the European Convention on Human Rights (ECHR).[72]

From a different angle, the decision also underlines that the second paragraph of Article 607 of the Criminal Code criminalises the mere diffusion of ideas without the existence of a violation of other constitutional rights. It therefore punishes acts that are inherently guaranteed by the constitutional rights to freedom of speech (Article 20, para 1 of the Spanish Constitution) and to freedom of conscience (Article 16 of the Spanish Constitution). For this reason, the Spanish Constitution does not allow lawmakers to punish the diffusion of these ideas, no matter how despicable they may be.[73] The only possible exception to this general principle is in the case that the right to freedom of speech degenerates into 'hate speech',[74] which the Spanish Constitutional Court—using ECtHR case law as a reference[75]—describes as incitement to violence against citizens or against racial or social groups.

After these remarks, the Constitutional Court assesses the constitutionality of the criminal provision in question by referring to a broader legal framework, which includes Articles 615 and 510 of the Criminal Code (implementing the Genocide Convention), as well as the offences against dignity and the other provisions regarding the exercise of fundamental rights. With respect to unlawful conduct, the Court stresses the difference between 'denying' and 'justifying', which later

[70] *Ibid.*, 49.

[71] *Ibid.*, 46.

[72] Critical of the interpretation provided for by the case law of the ECHR, see also Pech 2011, p. 209. In this sense, see also Cuerda Arnau 2008, p. 88, who speaks about a '*trasposición inadecuada*'.

[73] Constitutional Court of Spain, Judgment 235/2007, above n 63, 50 (*Fundamento Juridico*, para 6).

[74] On this particular aspect, see later in this paragraph.

[75] 'Hate speech' is defined by referring to the judgment of the ECHR, *Erdogdu v. Turkey*, Judgment, 8 July 1999, Applications no. 25067/94 and 25068/94.

becomes the fundamental reference point in its reasoning when establishing the criminal relevance of this conduct: while denial falls under the scope of application of the right to freedom of speech, justification is subject to criminal punishment.

'Justification does not imply that the existence of a given genocide is radically denied, but rather that it is minimised or that its perpetration is said to be lawful, provided that the perpetrators are clearly identified'. Therefore, its criminalisation is constitutionally legitimate insofar as this conduct translates into an indirect incitement to commit violence against social groups or into disdain for the victims of genocides.[76]

In order to reassert its interpretation that qualifies the conduct punished by Article 607, para. 2 as a form of indirect incitement, the Court makes reference to the EU Framework Decision, which at the time (April 2006) was still in force. According to the judges' understanding, their interpretation was indeed 'perfectly consistent' with the EU Framework Decision proposal (FJ 9), which, nonetheless punishes both denial and justification of genocides.

Another crucial aspect of the Court's reasoning is the possibility that denial be qualified as 'hate speech', which the ECtHR describes as a form of expression of ideas, personal views and opinions that does not fall under the scope of application of Article 10 of the ECHR, 'because, in light of its character, it translates into a direct incitement to violence against citizens of certain racial groups or religious beliefs'.

In principle, the mere denial of crimes of genocide appears to fall outside this category as 'the conduct consists of simply denying a genocide' and cannot therefore be qualified as 'a form of "hate speech"'. Indeed, 'the mere act of expressing personal views on the existence of certain facts, without commenting on their moral correctness or their lawfulness, falls under the scope of the right to scientific freedom', which under the Spanish Constitution enjoys an even stronger protection than the right to freedom of speech and freedom of information.[77]

In this respect, not only is a statement *about a fact* lawful, but it is actually protected twice: under the right to freedom of speech and again under the right to freedom of historical research.

To support this assertion, the Constitutional Court refers to its decision no. 43 of 23 March 2004, which states that historical research 'is inherently controversial and questionable, for it draws upon assertions and judgments that can never be qualified as objectively right or wrong'. In the eyes of the Court, the 'intrinsic uncertainty of the historical debate' is an element to be valued and protected under the law 'as it plays a fundamental role in the development of an historical conscience fitting the dignity of the citizens of a free and democratic society'.[78]

---

[76] Unlike the types of provocation and condoning that both require direct instigation as contained in the general part of the Code. See Article 18 of the Spanish Criminal Code and Astacio Cabrera 2011; Batista Gonzáles 1997, pp. 63–68.

[77] Constitutional Court of Spain, Judgment 235/2007, above n 63, 47.

[78] *Ibid.*, 48 (*Fundamento Juridico*, para 4).

According to the line of argument followed in this decision, *mere denial* is criminally harmless ('*penalmente inane*') compared to other conduct that implies moral sympathy for a criminal act and promotes it through positive assessment.

Additionally, the constitutional judges point out that Article 607, para. 2 does not require 'denial' to create—or have the ability to create—a climate of social hostility against the victims of the genocide being called into question. Criminalisation of such conduct is therefore unconstitutional also in this perspective. Indeed, the conduct would not even potentially endanger the interests that the offence seeks to protect, and thus its criminalisation violates Article 20, para. 1 of the Spanish Constitution.[79]

The Court argues that the conduct in question does not justify the use of criminal law 'as it is unable to put even in potential danger the interests protected under the offence and its criminalisation thus encroaches upon the right to freedom of speech' (Article 20, para. 1 of the Constitution).

With reference to the criminal acts committed during World War II, the public prosecutor in charge of the *Varela* case underlined that decisions no. 241/1990 (the abovementioned *Friedman* case) and no. 176/199[80] of the Constitutional Court had already pointed out that the right to freedom of speech is not unlimited. These cases also distinguished between 'the expression of the mere remarks, doubts or opinions on the Jewish Holocaust that can go as far as to deny the existence of the Holocaust and still fall under the scope of application of the right to freedom of speech, however despicable they may appear to be' and 'the expression of offensive statements, which do not merely raise doubts about the existence of the Jewish persecution or of any other killing, but rather make allegations that insult and discredit the victims of such acts and therefore fall outside the scope of Article 20, 1st para. letter a) of the Spanish Constitution'.

Lastly, the Constitutional Court argued that although the distribution of publications questioning the existence of the Holocaust could endanger protected legal interests, the legitimacy of its punishment would still have to be reviewed under the lens of the proportionality principle because 'such a broad restriction of these fundamental freedoms may not be justified for merely preventive or security-oriented reasons'.[81]

4.2.2.3 Justification Is Unlawful

The Constitutional Court put forward rather different arguments and reached the opposite conclusion about 'justifying genocides', which is indeed the expression of

---

[79] Article 20, para. 1 of the Constitution establishes the right to 'freely express and spread thoughts, ideas and opinions through words, works or any other means of communication'.

[80] See Gil Gil and Maculan 2016, p. 345 et seq.

[81] Constitutional Court of Spain, 16 December 1987, no. 199/1987 (*Fundamento Juridico*, para 12).

a *value judgment* of the crime that the perpetrator expresses in order to create a climate of hostility against the members of the social groups targeted by the genocide. Any doctrine justifying such acts can therefore be qualified as actual 'hate speech'.[82]

In its ruling,[83] the Constitutional Court specified that criminalising the dissemination of ideas justifying genocides as an expression of hate speech is in line with the most recent international legal instruments. In particular, the Court refers to Article 1 of what was then the EU Framework Decision proposal, which required Member States to punish whoever condoned, denied or trivialised crimes of genocide whenever this conduct was carried out 'in a manner likely to incite to violence or hatred against such a group or a member of such a group'.

The Court argues that the legislator is entitled to criminalise such forms of 'justification' if they are expressed in public[84] and translate into an indirect incitement[85] to perpetrate genocide, a particularly repugnant crime that undermines the very existence of society.[86] In other words, the act of justifying a crime as abominable as genocide must be able to endanger, at least in theory, the protected legal interest. The assessment of whether it does should consider the circumstances of the action,[87] and in particular the content of the opinions being expressed, the time and place, the nature of the incitement, its intended audience and the way it was expressed. Indeed, an isolated action is unable to create a climate of violence and hostility against genocide victims or their social group which could lead to the perpetration of discriminatory acts.[88] The punishment of the unlawful conduct therefore depends on its actual ability—in light of its content and its circumstances—to become an indirect incitement to commit genocide.[89]

The Court outlines the distinction between 'denial' and 'justification' based on the dichotomy of 'fact' and 'value', which becomes the centrepiece of its reasoning and final verdict. It is the basis for defining the boundaries of legitimately using criminal law and for reaffirming that 'justification' must be interpreted as a form of

---

[82] On the hate speech phenomenon in Spain, see de Pablo Serrano and Tapia Ballesteros 2017; Revenga Sánchez 2015.

[83] Constitutional Court of Spain, Judgment 235/2007, above n 63, 52 (*Fundamento Juridico*, para 9).

[84] Or at least in such a way so as to allow a considerable number of people to have access to the opinions being expressed: Constitutional Court of Spain, Judgment 235/2007, above n 63, 52 (*Fundamento Juridico*, para 8).

[85] See Cueva Fernández 2012, p. 105.

[86] *Fundamento Juridico* 9 of the decision. On the inconsistencies of this ruling, see Ramos Vázquez 2009.

[87] Constitutional Court of Spain, Judgment 235/2007, above n 63, 52 (*Fundamento Juridico*, para 8), where the Tribunal addresses the question as to whether the endangerment of the legal interest required by offence is abstract or concrete and as to how it should be assessed.

[88] See the ruling of the Provincial Court of Barcelona (Section 2) issued on 26 April 2010, FD 6, which upheld the conviction of Mr Varela for the crime provided for by Article 607, 2nd para of the Criminal Code.

[89] Landa Gorostiza 2012, pp. 314–315, when examining the decision no. 259 of 11 April 2011.

indirect incitement. In brief, according to the Constitutional Court, justifying genocide infringes upon rights and freedoms protected under the Spanish Constitution, whereas denying such genocide does not because it contains no value judgment.

4.2.2.4 A Viable Distinction?

The question remains as to whether the distinction between denying and justifying is actually viable.[90] Indeed, for it to be applicable, both types of conduct would have to endanger the same legal interest and entail a similar level of endangerment. Justification of genocide does not seem to require a higher level of endangerment than denial of genocide, so the distinction between indirect danger and incitement to commit genocide would apply to the latter as well. It is precisely this particular distinction which lies at the very heart of the Constitutional Court's reasoning (which also refers to the EU Framework Decision) and is central to the entire discussion concerning the criminalisation of denialism. In fact, the debate does not focus on the legitimacy of criminalising denial, but rather on distinguishing which conduct can be punished and which cannot.[91]

Following the very same line of reasoning, the Constitutional Court could have also argued that criminalising the justification of genocides was unconstitutional. This conclusion, however, would have called into question the legitimacy of punishing the justification of terrorism (provided for by Article 578 of the Criminal Code), which instead could not be challenged.[92]

4.2.2.5 The *Librería Kalki* Case

After the 2007 decision of the Constitutional Court, Article 607, para. 2 of the Criminal Code remained virtually unapplied.

To this end, it is worth mentioning the decision issued in the *Libreria Kalki*[93] case by the Supreme Court, which acquitted the defendants and expressly referred to the Constitutional Court's judgment on the second paragraph of Article 607.

[90] See the four dissenting opinions. Bifulco defines as 'arduous' the possibility of distinguishing between denial and justification, see Bifulco 2012, p. 45. On such distinction, see also Landa Gorostiza 2012, pp. 314–315; Caruso 2008, p. 636.

[91] Ramos Vázquez 2009.

[92] On this offence and the relationship between Articles 578 and 607, 2nd para of the Criminal Code, see Ramos Vázquez 2008a, pp. 771–795; Ramos Vázquez 2008b, pp. 371–392. On Article 578 1st para of the judgment of the Supreme Court of Spain, Criminal Chamber, *Luciano Varela Castro*, Judgment, 25 May 2017, no. 378/2017, in particular point 4 of the decision. On Article 578 of the Criminal Code, see the judgment of the Supreme Court of Spain, Criminal Chamber, *Luciano Varela Castro*, Judgment, 25 May 2017, no. 378/2017, para 4.

[93] Supreme Court of Spain, Judgment, 12 April 2011, no. 259.

The Court reaffirmed that the conduct punished by this provision must be 'an indirect incitement to commit a genocide' or an instigation to hatred against certain racial, ethnic, religious or national groups 'so as to entail the certain risk of creating a climate of violence and hostility' and that the act of mere denial cannot be subject to punishment.

The Supreme Court also specified that the legal interest protected by the offence is harmed 'whenever the author resorts to means that enable widespread and public access to the opinions expressed, that can reach and impact upon a large number of people, but also that appear to be able—due to the content of the message and the circumstances of its diffusion—to influence the opinions and the actions of the audience in a direction which is detrimental for such interests. It is not the mere diffusion of opinions that is being punished, but rather the diffusion of ideas so as to create an actual danger for the protected legal interest.'[94]

In the Court's opinion, this particular requirement was lacking in the case brought before it. Indeed, according to the judges, the act of owning or selling certain books (which, by the way, could also be found in the Spanish National Library) cannot be qualified as an indirect incitement to commit genocide.

References

Alastuey Dobón C (2016) Discurso del odio y negacionismo en la reforma del código penal de 2015. Revista Electrónica de Ciencia Penal y Criminología 18–14

Astacio Cabrera JG (2011) Tratamiento jurídico-penal de la apología del terrorismo. Universidad de Granada, Granada

Batista Gonzáles MP (1997) Provocación y apología. El art. 18 del nuevo Código Penal. Revista de la Facultad de Derecho de la Universidad Complutense 88:63–68

Beisel D (1995) Die Strafbarkeit der Auschwitzlüge. Neue Juristische Wochenschrift 997–1000

Bernal del Castillo J (2016) La justificación y enaltecimiento del genocidio en la Reforma del Código Penal de 2015. InDret 2

Bidasolo MC et al. (2015) Comntarios al código penal. Tirant, Madrid

Bifulco D (2012) Negare l'evidenza, Diritto e storia di fronte alla 'menzogna' di Auschwitz. Franco Angeli, Milan

Bilbao Ubillos JM (2009) La negación de un genocidio no es una conducta punible (comentario *de la* STC 235/2007). Revista Española de Derecho Constitucional 85:314–328

Bin R (1992) Diritti e argomenti. Il bilanciamento degli interessi nella giurisprudenza costituzionale. Giuffrè, Milan

Brugger W (2002) The Treatment of Hate Speech in German Constitutional Law (part 1). German Law Journal 3:1–44

Brugger W (2003a) The Treatment of Hate Speech in German Constitutional Law (part 1). German Law Journal 4:1–22

Brugger W (2003b) The Treatment of Hate Speech in German Constitutional Law (part 2). German Law Journal 4:23–44

Brugger W (2005) Ban on or Protection of Hate Speech? Some Observations Based on German and American Law. Tulane European and Civil Law Forum 17:1–21

[94] Constitutional Court, Judgment 235/2007, cit., 52 (*Fundamento Juridico*, para 9).

Caruso C (2008) Tra il negare e l'istigare c'è di mezzo il giustificare: su una decisione del tribunale Costituzionale spagnolo. Quaderni Costituzionali 3:635–639

Caruso C (2013) La libertà di espressione in azione. Contributo a una teoria costituzionale del discorso pubblico. Bononia University Press, Bologna

Caruso C (2016) Tolleranza per gli intolleranti? Una ragionevole apologia della libertà di espressione. DPCE online 1:99–114

Català A, Pérez Z (2007) La negación del holocausto. A propósito de la STC 235/2007, de 7 de noviembre de 2007. Revista Europea de Derechos Fundamentales 10:181–196

Cuerda Arnau ML (2008) Terrorismo y libertades políticas, Teoría & Derecho. Revista de Pensamiento Jurídico (El Estado de Derecho Frente a la amenaza del nuevo terrorismo) 3: 61–97

Cueva Fernández R (2012) A propósito de la Sentencia del Tribunal Supremo 259/2011: Discurso del odio, incitación y derecho al honor colectivo. ¿Una nueva vuelta de tuerca contra la prohibición del hate speech? Eunomia 99–108

de la Rosa Cortina JM (2007) Negacionismo y revisionismo del genocidio: perspectiva penal y constitucional. Diario La Ley 6842

de Pablo Serrano A (2017) Límites jurídico-penales del discurso (puro) del odio. Sociedad del desprecio y discurso del odio. In: Alonso L, Vàzquez V (eds) Sobre la libertad de expresión y el discurso del odio. Textos críticos, Athenaica, Seville, pp 145–165

de Pablo Serrano A, Tapia Ballesteros P (2017) Discurso del odio: problemas en la delimitación del bien jurídico y en la nueva configuración del tipo penal. Diario La Ley 8911

Dietz S (1995) Die Lüge von der "Auschwitzlüge" - Wie weit reicht das Recht auf Meinungsäußerung? Kritische Justiz 28:210–222

Dolz Lago MJ (2016) Oído a los delitos de odio (algunas cuestiones claves sobre la reforma del art. 510 CP por LO 1/2015. Diario La Ley 8712

Feijoo Sánchez BJ (1998) Reflexiones sobre los delitos de genocidio (art. 607 del Código Penal). La Ley 6:2267–2284

Fernández Hernández A (2010) Delito de genocidio (art. 607). In: Álvarez Garcia FJ, Gonzáles Cussac JL (eds) Comentarios a la Reforma Penal de 2010. Tirant lo Blanc, Valencia, pp 533–536

Finer SE, Bogdanor V, Rudden B (1995) Comparing Constitutions. Clarendon Press, Chicago

Fischer T (1986) Öffentlicher Friede und Gedankenäußerung. Dissertation, Würzburg University

Fischer T (2011) Störung des Öffentlichen Friedens (§ 130 Abs. 4 StGB): Strafwürdigkeit als Tatbestandsmerkmal. Zugleich eine Besprechung von BVerfG, Beschl. vom 4. November 2009 - 1 BvR 2150/08. In: Paeffgen HU (ed) Strafrechtswissenschaft als Analyse und Konstruktion. Festschrift für Ingeborg Puppe zum 70. Geburtstag, Duncker & Humblot, Berlin, pp 1119–1141

Fischer T (2017) Strafgesetzbuch und Nebengesetze, § 130 StGB. Beck, Munich

García Arán M (2004) Artículo 607. In: Córdoba R, García Arán M (eds) Comentarios al Código penal, Parte especial, Tomo II. Marcial Pons, Madrid, pp 2688–2703

Gascón Cuenca A (2016) El discurso del odio en el ordenamiento jurídico español: su adecuación a los estándares internacionales de *protección*. Aranzadi, Pamplona

Geilen G (2008) Unvorsätzliche "Auschwitzlüge"? Bemerkungen zu § 130 Abs. 3 StGB. Festschrift für Rolf Dietrich. Herzberg

Gil Gil A, Maculan E (ed.) (2016) Derecho penal internacional. Libreria Dykinson, Madrid

Glet A (2011) Sozialkonstruktion und strafrechtliche Verfolgung von Hasskriminalität in Deutschland. Dissertation, Berlin

Gómez Tomillo M (ed) (2011) Comentarios al Código Penal. Lex Nova, Valladolid

Graf JP (2013) BGH-Rechsprechung Strafrecht 2012–2013: die wichtigsten Entscheidungen mit Erläuterung und Praxishinweisen. De Gruyter, Berlin

Grimm D (2009) The Holocaust Denial Decision of the Federal Constitutional Court of Germany. In: Hare I, Weinstein J (eds) Extreme Speech and Democracy. Oxford University Press, Oxford, pp 557–561

Guenther K (2000) The Denial of Holocaust: Employing criminal law to combat Antisemitism. Tel Aviv University Studies in Law 15:51–66

Haupt CE (2005) Regulating Hate Speech - Damned If You Do and Damned If You Don't: Lessons Learned from Comparing The German and U.S. Approaches. Boston University International Law Journal 23:299–336

Heinze E (2016) Hate speech and democratic citizenship. Oxford University Press, Oxford

Hellmann M, Gartner J (2011) Neues beim Volksverhetzungstatbestand - Europäische Vorgaben und ihre Umsetzung. Neue Juristische Wochenschrift 961–966

Hochmann T (2012) Le négationnisme face aux limites de la liberté d'expression. Etude de droit comparé. Pedone, Paris

Hörnle T (2001) Anmerkungen zu BGH NJW 2001, 624. Neue Zeitschrift für Strafrecht: 310–311

Hörnle T (2010) Strafe als Reaktion auf grob anstößiges Verhalten am Beispiel von Bekenntnisbeschimpfungen und Holocaust-Leugnen (§§ 166, 130 Abs. 3 StGB). In: Rosenau H, Kim S (eds) Straftheorie und Strafgerechtigkeit. Deutsch-Japanischer Strafrechtsdialog. Peter Lang, Frankfurt am Main/Berlin/Bern.Brussels.New York/Oxford/ Vienna: 215–229

Hörnle T (2015) Theories of Criminalization. In: Dubber MD, Hörnle T (eds) The Oxford Handbook of Criminal Law. Oxford University Press, Oxford, pp 301–314

Huster S (1996) Das Verbot der "Auschwitzlüge", die Meinungsfreiheit und das Bundesverfassungsgericht. Neue Juristische Wochenschrift: 487–491

Jacobi K (2010) Das Ziel des Rechtsgüterschutzes bei der Volksverhetzung. Universität Köln

Jessberger F (2001) Anmerkung zur Entscheidung des Bundesgerichtshofs vom 12. Dezember 2000, 1 StR 184/00 (Verbreitung der Auschwitzlüge im Internet). Juristiche Rundschau. 492–435

Jahn J (1998) Strafrechtliche Mittel gegen Rechtsextremismus: die Änderungen der §§ 130 und 86a StGB als Reaktion auf fremdenfeindliche Gewalt im Licht der Geschichte des politischen Strafrechts in Deutschland. Frankfurt am Main/Berlin/Bern/New York/Paris/Vienna

Kahn RA (2006) Cross-Burning, Holocaust Denial and the Development of Hate Speech Law in the United States and Germany. University of Detroit Mercy Law Review 1:163–194

Knauer F (2014) Der Schutz der Menschenwürde im Strafrecht. ZStW 126:305–336

Koltay A (2016) Comparative Perspectives on the Fundamental Freedom of Expression. Wolters-Kluwer, Alphen aan den Rijn

Krauß M (2009) Leipziger Kommentar Strafgesetzbuch: StGB Band 5: §§ 110-145d. De Gruyter, Berlin

Kress C (2009) Vom Nutzen eines deutschen Völkerstrafgesetzbuchs. Nomos, Baden-Baden

Kühl K (2003) Auschwitz-Leugnen als strafbare Volksverhetzung? In: Bernsmann K, Ulsenheimer (eds) Bochumer Beiträge zu aktuellen Strafrechtsthemen. Vorträge anläßlich des Symposions zum 70. Geburtstag von Gerd Geilen am 12./13.10.2001. Cologne, pp 103–119

Landa Gorostiza JM (1999) La llamada "mentira de Auschwitz" y el "delito de provocación" a la luz del "caso Varela": una oportunidad perdida para la cuestión de inconstitucionalidad. Actualidad Penal 36:691–692

Landa Gorostiza JM (2001) La política criminal contra la xenofobia y las tendencias expansionistas del derecho penal. Comares, Granada

Landa Gorostiza JM (2003) Nuevos crímenes contra la humanidad: el nuevo delito de lesa humanidad (artículo 607 Bis CP 1995) desde una perspectiva intrasistemàtica. In: Eguzkilore: Cuaderno del Instituto Vasco de Criminología 17:105–119

Landa Gorostiza JM (2012) Incitación al odio: evolución jurisprudencial (1995–2011) *del* art. 510 CP *y* propuesta de lege lata, (A la vez un comentario a la STS 259/2011 —librería Kalki— y a la STC 235/2007). Revista de Derecho Penal y Criminología 7:297–346

Lascuráin Sánchez JA (2010) La libertad de expresión tenía un precio. Revista Aranzadi Doctrinal 6:69–78

Maitra I, McGowan MK (eds) (2012) Speech and Harm: Controversies Over Free Speech. Oxford University Press, Oxford

Manzanares Samaniego J (2016) Código penal, 2 volúmenes. Comentarios y jurisprudencia. Librería Dykinson, Madrid

Martínez Sospedra M (1993) No todas las ideas son respetables. Racismo y nacionalsocialismo en el Estado constitucional democràtico. Acerca de la STC 214/1991, de 11 de noviembre. Revista General de Derecho 585:5785–5804

Martínez Sospedra M (2000) Aplastar la serpiente en el huevo. Acerca de la cuestión de inconstitucionalidad promovida contra el artículo 607.2 del CP. Revista general de Derecho 664:99–116

Matuschek M (2012) Erinnerungsstrafrecht. Eine Neubegründung des Verbots der Holocaustleugnung auf rechtsvergleichender und sozialphilosophischer Grundlage. Duncker & Humblot, Berlin

Miebach K et al. (2012) Münchener Kommentar zum Strafgesetzbuch: StGB Band 3: §§ 80-184g StGB. Beck, Munich

Morales Prats F, Quintero Olivares G (ed.) (2016) Comentarios al código penal españo. 2 volúmenes. Aranzadi, Madrid

Morozinis I (2011) Die Strafbarkeit der "Auschwitzlüge" im Internet, insbesondere im Hinblick auf "Streaming-Videos". Goltdammer's Archiv für Strafrecht 8:475–487

Pech L (2011) The Law of Holocaust Denial in Europe. In: Hennebel L, Hochmann T (eds) Genocide Denials and the Law. Oxford University Press, Oxford, pp 185–284

Piciocchi C (2013) La dignità come rappresentazione giuridica della condizione umana. Cedam, Padua

Poscher R (2005) Neue Rechtgrundlagen gegen rechtsextremistische Versammlungen. Neue Juristische Wochenschrift 1316–1319

Quintero Olivares G, Valle-Muniz JA (2008) Comentarios al nuevo Código Penal. Aranzadi, Pamplona

Ramos Vázquez JA (2008a) Presente y futuro del delito de enaltecimiento y justificación del terrorismo. Anuario da Facultade de Dereito da Universidade da Coruña 12:771–795

Ramos Vázquez AJ (2008b) Sobre la peculiar lógica de los procesos por terrorismo (las paradojas de la absolución de Otegui). In: Puente A, Zapico Barbeito M, Rodríguez Moro L (eds) Criminalidad organizada, terrorismo e inmigración. Retos contemporáneos de la política criminal. Comares, Granada, pp 371–392

Ramos Vázquez JA (2009) La declaración de inconstitucionalidad del delito de "negacionismo". Revista Penal 23:120–137

Revenga Sánchez M (ed) (2015) Libertad de expresión y discursos del odio. Universidad de Alcalá/Defensor del Pueblo, Madrid

Rodríguez Montañés T (2012) Libertad de expresión, discurso extremo y delito. Una aproximación desde la Constitución a las fronteras del Derecho penal. Tirant lo Blanch, Valencia

Rohrßen B (2009) Von der "Anreizung zum Klassenkampf" zur "Volksverhetzung" (§ 130 StGB). Reformdiskussion und Gesetzgebung seit dem 19. Jahrhundert. Walter de Gruyter, Berlin

Safferling C (2011) Internationales Strafrecht: Strafanwendungsrecht – Völkerstrafrecht - Europäisches Strafrecht. Springer, Berlin

Salomon TR (2012) Meinungsfreiheit und die Strafbarkeit des Negationismus. Zeitschrift für Rechtspolitik 48–50

Salvador Coderch P, Rubi Puig A (2008) Genocide - Denial and Freedom of Speech. Comments on the Spanish Constitucional Court's Judgment 235/2007, November 7th. InDret 4

Sánchez Melgar J (2016) Código penal. Comentarios y jurisprudencia. Sepin, Madrid

Satzger H (2002) German Criminal Law and the Rome Statute – A Critical Analysis of the New German Code of Crimes against International Law. International Criminal Law Review 2:261–282

Stein E (1986) History Against Free Speech: The New German Law Against the "Auschwitz" – and Other – "Lies". Michigan Law Review 85:277–324

Sternberg-Lieben D (2014) § 130 StGB. In: Schönke A, Schröder H (ed.) Strafgesetzbuch. Kommentar 29. Auflage. Beck, Munich, pp 1533–1557

Suárez Espino ML (2008) Comentario a la STC 235/2007, de 7 de noviembre, por la que se declara la inconstitucionalidad del delito de negación de genocidio. InDret 2

Teruel Lozano GM (2015a) La libertad de expresión a los delitos de negacionismo y de provocación al odio y a la violencia: sombras sin luces en la reforma del código penal. Revista para el análisis del derecho 4:1–51

Teruel Lozano GM (2015b) La lucha del Derecho contra el negacionismo: una peligrosa frontera. Estudio constitucional de los límites penales a la libertad de expresión en un ordenamiento abierto y personalista. Centro de Estudios Políticos y Constitucionales, Madrid

Tesauro A (2013) Riflessioni in tema di dignità umana, bilanciamento e propaganda razzista. Giappichelli, Turin

Toma J (2014) Zur Strafbarkeit und Strafwürdigkeit des Billigens, Leugnens und Verharmlosens von Völkermord und Menschlichkeitsverbrechen. Kovač, Hamburg

Turienzo Fernández A (2015) El delito de negación del holocausto (Holocaust Denial) (Auschwitzlüge). InDret Vol. 1

Visconti C (2008) Aspetti penalistici del discorso pubblico. Giappichelli, Turin

Vives Antòn TS et al. (2008) Derecho Penal. Parte especial. Tirant lo Blanc, Valencia

Von Bubnoff E (2009) § 130 StGB. In: Laufhütte HW, Rissing-van SR, Tiedemann K (eds) Strafgesetzbuch. Leipziger Kommentar. De Gruyter Recht, Berlin, pp 445–472

Von Dewitz C (2006) NS-Gedankengut und Strafrecht - Die §§ 86, 86a StGB und § 130 StGB zwischen der Abwehr neonazistischer Gefahren und symbolischem Strafrecht, in Strafrechtliche Forschungsberichte aus dem Max-Planck-Institutes für ausländisches und internationales Strafrecht, Band S. Duncker & Humblot, Berlin

Vormbaum T (2009) Einführung in die moderne Strafrechtsgeschichte. Springer, Berlin

Wandres T (2000) Die Strafbarkeit des Auschwitz-Leugnens. Duncker & Humblot, Berlin

Weiler B (2012) Der Tatbestand "Volksverhetzung" im europäischen Vergleich: zugleich ein Beitrag zur Frage der Verfassungsmäßigkeit des § 130 Abs. 3 und 4 StGB. Kovač, Hamburg

Werle G (1992) Der Holocaust als Gegenstand der bundesdeutschen Strafjustiz. Neue Juristische Wochenschrift 2529–2535

Werle G, Jessberger F (2002) International Criminal Justice is Coming Home: The New German Code of Crimes against International Law. Criminal Law Forum 13:191–223

Werle G Jessberger F (2014) Principles of International Criminal Law. Oxford University Press, Oxford

Zabel B (2010) Soll das Strafrecht Erinnerungen schützen? Zeitschrift für die Gesamte Strafrechtswissenschaft 122:834–853

Chapter 5
Conclusion

Contents

Abstract The conclusive chapter presents the findings of the comparative study undertaken in this book. The study of the criminal offence of historical denialism is paradigmatic of some trends of the modern criminal law. The recourse to criminal law and the trial to protect and forge collective historical memory demonstrates that human rights are now at the centre of a new ethical pact. This has supplanted the original pact against the Holocaust, the foundational event of the European identity. Yet this process has shown that, paradoxically, there is no common European memory. Rather, different domestic legislations implementing the EU Framework Decision correspond to different historical memories. Moreover, criminalisation jeopardises the tenets of the liberal approach of criminal law and unveils a widespread trend towards the juridification of memory and remembering. Therefore, politics and history, which should be the prime actors of collective memory, are somehow marginalised by criminal law. Criminal law on the contrary, is proving to be neither the most adequate nor the most effective remedy.

Keywords warden of memory · symbolic criminal law · manifest and latent functions · ethical pact · public sphere

5.1 Criminal Law as a Warden of Memory

The previous chapter explored several aspects of the conflict between criminal law and free speech associated with the criminalization of historical denialism. The following pages will focus on one of the most important elements of the genesis and genetics of the crime of historical denialism: its *symbolic* nature.

E. Fronza, *Memory and Punishment*, International Criminal Justice Series 19,
https://doi.org/10.1007/978-94-6265-234-7_5

In the case of historical denialism, criminal law is used to counteract this insidious phenomenon that offends public opinion and to protect the collective memory of historical facts that society considers significant. The criminalisation of denialism is part of a broader movement (or, more precisely, a pathology) in which the use of criminal law is expanded across various fields in response to society's sense of insecurity and loss as traditional points of reference change or are challenged.[1] In the face of this change, society turns to the legislator and the judge for protection. Criminal Law is expected to step into thwart the mutable and chaotic nature of practices which threaten to reshape or confuse significant events considered cornerstones of our societies. It is as if a final court decision has the power to negate the plural and fluid qualities of time. It seems like an effort to fortify the 'signposts' of collective experience of the violent past when faced with a simplistic approach trying to bury them.

The concept of symbolic criminal law here is used in its purely negative sense,[2] that is, a rhetorical law lacking effectiveness directed towards political and electoral consensus.[3] As such, criminal provisions are not expected by definition to achieve their express purpose of combating the phenomenon in question. Rather, the use of criminal law tends primarily to reassure public opinion and, in specific cases, to strengthen the collective memory around a universe of common founding values. In this way, it is mostly the power of criminal law that is exploited in terms of symbolic communication, with the tribunal and judicial ritual becoming a battleground between ethical and social conceptions. In light of the primarily political objectives, these types of provisions actually go beyond the specific scope of the usual protection via criminal law.

This kind of legal intervention is one in which the effective function is secondary to the merely symbolic function of criminal law in protecting the founding values of communities. The dominance of the declarative message and the recipient (not the person who committed a crime but the public opinion) runs the risk of dangerous consequences. This is a common trend in other sectors where criminal law is called upon to intervene, such as the provisions punishing online child pornography or condoning terrorism.[4]

---

[1] See Silva Sánchez 2001; concerning overcriminalization, see Husak 2007.

[2] In English literature this function of criminal law is often described as 'expressive criminal law'. On this political criminal tendency at a national level, see Feinberg 1974, pp. 98–118; within hate crimes legislation, see Beale 2000, pp. 1227–1254. On the significance of the symbolic function at the EU level, see, even for further references, Elholm and Colson 2016, pp. 48–64.

[3] In the vast existing literature on this negative connotation, among others, see Hassemer 1989, p. 553 et seq.; Noll 1981, p. 347 et seq. See also Ashworth and Horder 2013, chapter II; Pulitanò 2013, pp. 123–146; Fiandaca 2013, pp. 95–121; Salas 2013; Oliver and Marion 2010, p. 397 et seq.; Hassemer 2008, p. 93 et seq.; Bonini 2003, pp. 491–534; Díez Ripollés 2003; Harcourt 2002, pp. 145–172; Paliero 1990; Baratta 1990, pp. 19–31; Bricola 1984, p. 3 et seq.; Bricola 1981, pp. 445–460. On the risks of the prevalence of the symbolic functions, see Pavarini 2006b, p. 1019; Lazerges 2004, pp. 194–202; Baratta 1989, pp. 19 et seq.; van de Kerchove 1987, pp. 317–351.

[4] See Bird 2015, pp. 161–177; Tondini 2007.

This does not mean that the criminal provision itself is not applied. On the contrary, laws regarding denialism have been applied nationally and regionally as this research demonstrates. This is fundamental for the symbolic function of law, which is interconnected with the criminal trial and the punishment issued. Law has an evocative power and the punishment applied through the judgment has the objective to definitively reaffirm the universe of values attacked by denialist statements. For electoral support or for satisfying public opinion, as is noted, lawmakers often employ criminal laws 'justifying' their use for reasons of security and peace of mind. This, however, is not a rational motivation directed towards the consequences of the application of the law but to the illogical consequences of the scope of the law. Indeed, the specific protection of emotions constitutes an incongruous example of criminal law geared towards the irrationality of functions'.[5]

In this way, criminal law acts with a merely symbolic purpose to protect and reconstruct a collective identity and also seeks to reinforce the collective memory of significant events of which it is an integral part. Consequently, criminal law, at national and international level, becomes more *the bearer of a message* rather than the warden of interests deserving protection.

5.2 The Reversal of Manifest and Latent Functions

Criminal provisions punishing historical denialism belong to the category of symbolic legislative intervention.[6] This concept is understood to have a more negative meaning. Within this criminal policy the intention of the legislator is to have an announcement effect and to maximize its media impact, rather than to tackle actual problems or to modify legal situations.[7] Far from being exceptional, examples of symbolic criminal legislation can be found both at the national and the European level.

In these cases, penalisation has a purpose other than the one it primarily claims to have, namely pursuing *latent* functions which, in facts, prevail to the one explicitly declared. Such legislation thus becomes *a gesture*, a mere symbol, which

[5] Donini 2008, p. 1560 et seq.

[6] Concerning the view that the offence of historical denialism belongs to a symbolic paradigm, see Cavaliere 2016, pp. 999–1015; Fronza 2015, p. 653; Lobba 2011; Donini 2008, p. 1546 et seq.; Canestrari 2006, p. 149; Roxin 2006, p. 731. See also Paliero 2016, p. 1150 ('Perché ciò che si tutela non può che essere un valore, proprio perché l'opzione punitiva ha significato identitario e cioè serve unicamente ad affermare in modo simbolico-tabuistico il clima di valori maggioritario versus quello minoritario dissenziente'); Teruel Lozano 2015, p. 526 et seq.; Manes 2007, p. 782 et seq.; Romano 2007; Hörnle 2005, p. 315 et seq. On human dignity as protected legal interest, see Caputo 2014; Bifulco 2012, p. 89 et seq.; Visconti 2008, p. 153 et seq. Concerning the protected interest by the offence of historical denialism as instrumental to 'European identity', see Sotis 2007, p. 98; see also from a legal philosophy perspective Waldron 2012; Baker and Zhao 2013, pp. 621–656. On the EU Framework Decision of 2008 as the clearest example of an EU criminal law measure adopted for expressive purposes, see Turner 2012, pp. 555–583; see also Paliero 2016, pp. 1154–1191; Fletcher et al. 2008, p. 194 et seq.; Hildebrandt 2007, pp. 57–78. See also Bazyler 2016.

[7] Elholm and Colson 2016, p. 52.

distinguishes friend from foe and responds to the public opinion's demands for reassurance, support and protection of the collective identity and values and to reinforce the public memory. In establishing their merely symbolic significance a broad social consensus forms around a set of values and events considered indisputable and deeply meaningful.

Hence a discrepancy is created between *overt* and *latent* functions of the crime whereby the latter prevails over the former.[8] The true objectives of criminalisation are different from those originally intended, resulting in a contradictory *duplication* of messages:[9] an overt one for the deniers and a latent one for public opinion. Public pressure is a decisive factor here. As a reaction to denialist statements, society is offended by the upending of the foundational values. Public opinion needs a clear and firm gesture confirming shared commitment to the values expressed in national constitutions and collective memory. That gesture is made through criminal law and criminal trials.

When attributed with a symbolic function the criminal offence becomes problematic as it is adopted on the basis of its symbolic value amidst a clash between different ethical and social conceptions. There is a shift in objectives which places political ends before the specific and limited purposes of criminal legislation and trials. This creates potential negative repercussions for criminal law and its general function to uphold legality and the harm principle. The veracity of the Holocaust and genocides or crimes against humanity specified in these provisions is an element that imbues symbolic legislation with a high degree of legitimacy.[10] Social consensus alone, however widespread and morally significant, cannot alone legitimise the criminalisation of conducts of denialism. According to the *ultima ratio* principle, criminal sanctions must be applied only when they are essential and based on the principles of subsidiarity, necessity and proportionality, and in all cases they must be considered as a last resort after a preliminary analysis of costs and benefits. In other words an act can be criminalised only if all other measures (legal and otherwise) have proved insufficient to safeguard a fundamental interest.

In the phase of opting for criminalisation, the legislator should always select the punishment indicated by social consensus, thereby acting as the 'judge of public opinion', an inherent responsibility of those s in elected representative offices.[11] Therefore, in cases where an interest is *not* considered worthy of protection under criminal law, or it is difficult to verify if protected interests are armed, the legislator must resist demands for punishment. The legislator should resist the pressure exerted by social consensus and refuse to create a crime that would not be effective or that

---

[8] On the function of deceit (*Täuschungsfunktion*) of symbolic criminal law, see Hassemer 1989, p. 555 et seq.

[9] Paliero 1990, pp. 539–541.

[10] See Garland 2002, pp. 160–189; Paliero 1993, p. 184 et seq.

[11] Paliero 1992. Emphasises how 'all populist responses (…) tend to be emotional, regressive', Ceretti 2004. On penal populism, see Palazzo 2016; Fiandaca 2013, p. 97; Pulitanò 2013, p. 125 et seq.; Salas 2013. There is a risk of the use of criminal sanctions for political aims; the punishment of historical denialism is one of the examples, see Manes 2012, p. 855.

has a primarily symbolic function. An offence in which messages and functions are duplicated has inevitable consequences for the rights of the accused and threatens the fundamental principles of a constitutionally-oriented criminal law.[12]

By accommodating the emotional impulse to punish stemming from public opinion and politics when fundamental values appear to be violated, a criminal response is employed because it is considered the maximum expression of law. This is because criminal law is viewed as having an inherently prestigious[13] and magical nature—as an instrument that can assuage anger, the rational component of which is so limited that its 'main if not exclusive function is exorcism'.[14] Criminalisation may also be considered an instrument of salvation,[15] which focuses on the immediate effect of collective reassurance created by the symbolic provision, the trial and the punishment rather than weighing its consequences.

The objective of conveying a message through a criminal offence is a common feature of the legislation regarding denialism both at the European and the national level. By adhering to the belief that criminal prosecution is 'magical',[16] the criminal offence aims to affirm founding values called into question by denialist statements. In the specific case of EU law, it should be noted that the European Union adds another and more general message about the protection and construction of a common European identity through respect for human rights and the collective memory of their grave violations.[17] The denial of the Holocaust was the focus of the 'original' offence of denialism and, thus, for the European legislator it acquires a crucial value with respect to all other gross violations of human rights, constituting a warning in the face of which one cannot remain silent.

This symbolic nature of the crime reaches a critical point during criminal trials, which are transformed into 'arenas of memory'. Initially, with the prosecution of the defendant, and afterwards with the imprimatur of a judgment as the guardian that pronounces the 'indisputable' truth thus protected by the criminal offence. Thus, in this process, the deniers will be punished, their ideas become stigmatised by the judgment and collective identity and core values will be affirmed with authoritative recognition.[18]

However, as mentioned before, this choice generates conflict with historical research and diverges from general principles of a liberal criminal approach.

[12] On a constitutional approach to criminal law, the Italian experience has been paradigmatic, see Canestrari et al. 2007, p. 93 et seq.; Palazzo 1985, p. 545; Manes 2005; Donini 2009, p. 421 et seq.; Donini 2003; Donini 2001a, p. 65 et seq.; Donini 2001b, p. 29 et seq.; Bricola 1973, p. 3 et seq. For the importance of this approach abroad, see Hassemer 2009; Puig and Queralt Jiménez 2010. In English literature, see Berger 2014, pp. 422–444; Fletcher 1998. Concerning the reception of this approach at the European level, see Donini 2012, pp. 51–74; Herlin-Karnell 2012. On criminal law as a science of fundamental guarantees, see Donini 2017.

[13] Stortoni 1994, p. 14 et seq.

[14] Delmas-Marty 1985, 170

[15] Gamberini 2005.

[16] Delmas-Marty 1985.

[17] Sotis 2007, p. 94 et seq.; see also Hildebrandt 2007, pp. 57–78.

[18] On the trial as a 'ritual' (rite), see Garapon 1985, pp. 138 et seq.

Moreover, by the prosecution and the trial becoming part of the symbolic paradigm in the sense delineated above, this dynamic of criminalisation brings with it other risky deviations.

5.3 The Return of Ethics?

The offence of denialism is seen as an *act of memory* that connects two temporal dimensions: the past, to be remembered in all its significance; and the future, which must in turn be founded on the same core values being challenged by the denier's assertions. In this way, the crime takes on a foundational function for the community.[19] However, in order to fulfil this task, the law and criminal trials move into a terrain that is emotional and value-driven. The official narrative of historical memory is seen as worthy of criminal protection because it is considered an indicator of the universe of values that should guide our society.

This is a dangerous transition because it involves using a criminal provision in a manner contrary to the logic inherent in the right that society seeks to protect: a world in which criminal law steps in before any real risk or harm is perceived, prosecutes ideas and punishes a type of offender more than an actual offence. As previously mentioned, this is why denialist offences that are merely symbolic and express a reassuring message to the public opinion seem to contradict some of the tenets of criminal law, in particular the principles of legality and the harm principle. Conducts to be punished should be immediately offensive and not simply create a risk of a subsequent offence.[20]

Maintaining these fundamental guarantees distinguishes laws that punish an 'enemy' that is such by nature ('criminal law of the enemy')[21] from laws that

[19] There are many examples that support the assumption that memory of historical events is related to the political scenario of the present and the ethical pact that should be the basis of our communities in the future. A very recent example is the vandalization and removal of Confederate monuments in the USA after the episode of racial violence in Charlottesville in August 2017: http://edition.cnn.com/2017/08/18/us/monuments-memorials-vandalized-charlottesville/index.html; http://edition.cnn.com/2017/08/15/us/confederate-memorial-removal-us-trnd/index.html; https://www.washingtonpost.com/news/morning-mix/wp/2017/08/31/in-los-angeles-columbus-day-is-toppled-like-a-confederate-statute/?utm_term=.c10147c1c978.

[20] Ashworth and Horder 2013, p. 38.

[21] The concept of 'criminal law of the enemy' ('Feindstrafrecht' in German) can be traced back to Karl Schmitt. More recently, it has been revisited in the works of the German law professor Gunther Jakobs, who first used the concept with reference to the phenomenon of international terrorism during a conference in Berlin in 1999 about German criminal science. On the theory of this author, see Jakobs 2006; Jakobs 2005a, p. 247 et seq.; Jakobs 2005b, p. 839 et seq.; Jakobs 2003, p. 41 et seq.; Jakobs 2000, p. 47 et seq.; Jakobs 1997; Jakobs 1995, p. 843 et seq.; Jakobs 1985, p. 751 et seq. On the debate concerning the theory of Gunther Jakobs, among numerous works, see Ohana 2014; Morguet 2009; Cancio Meliá and Jara 2006; Cancio Meliá 2005, pp. 267–289; Cancio Meliá and Jakobs 2003, 57–102. See also Cancio Meliá 2010; Donini 2007a, p. 79 et seq.; Donini 2007b, p. 131 et seq.; Donini and Papa 2007; Ambos 2006, p. 1 et seq.; Pavarini 2006a, p. 7 et seq.;

punish a criminal defined as such by acts ('criminal law of the citizen'). It is useful to briefly focus on the theoretical framework of these potentially dangerous legal iterations. The theory distinguishes between 'person', understood as an abstract concept associated with duties and rights that constitute the status of a citizen, and 'individual', considered as a subject of flesh and bone who forms relationships with others and with public authorities. The latter has the rights of the person only if he or she complies with the laws of social cohabitation. Therefore, those who systematically violate the norms, refuse to recognise themselves as part of the social pact and do not give guarantees of loyalty to the rule of law have no right to be treated as a 'person' and will be considered an 'enemy'. Hence, the distinction between criminal law of the citizen (*Bürgerstrafrecht*) and criminal law of the enemy (*Feindstrafrecht*), different and characterized by exceptional measures to protect society from those who do not accept 'shared common values'. Such a criminal political framework focuses on the actions of the criminal and not the offence. It deviates from a pure liberal criminal law model, incorporating policies based on prevention and a decrease of guarantees which express a certain political vision of society in response to phenomena considered to be pernicious.

Therefore, a liberal criminal law should never punish for not being faithful to certain values (even if shared by the majority, enshrined in a judgment) nor for not accepting and sharing them as truth. When a legal system uses criminal law to protect a foundational moment, to develop a historical narrative or an established historical truth, it is intervening in the sphere of values with the risk of suppressing ideas and not actions. It turns into a more political than judicial ritual where the protection of values is no longer mediated in a rational legal framework defined by and founded on essential guarantees.[22]

The dialectic between law and values is complex. Values, of course, are protected and promoted by criminal law. However, the latter cannot become an instrument for determining individual criminal responsibility while at the same time symbolically conferring upon founding values a repressive function which overlaps with those considered politically ethical.

In other words, the problem is not the evocative character and symbolic function that criminal laws generally have on their own. Indeed, these inherent characteristics have always been present and used by the legislator and the judge alike within their respective fields. The problem arises when the symbolic and narrative dimensions[23] prevail over that which is prescriptive, creating a situation in which all guarantees are not fully respected. Directed first against the offender and then

Zaffaroni 2006; Aponte 2005; Muñoz Conde 2005, pp. 123–137; Aponte 2004; Prittwitz 2004, p. 107 et seq.; Vormbaum 1995, p. 734 et seq. On the friend/enemy relationship, see Schmitt 2005, especially pp. 66–95; Schmitt 1972, 1981; see also Plessner 2006, p. 101 et seq. On the concept of *Verfeidung* and on the difference between Schmitt and Plessner with regard to the friend/enemy duo, see Hörnle 2015, Chapter 30; Accarino 2006, pp. 15–22; Portinaro 1992.

[22] On political justice as justice which pursues political ends, also for the appropriate bibliographic references, see Portinaro 1996, XII–XV.

[23] Garapon 2002.

against the facts, the symbolic dimension of law inevitably influences the measures taken and potentially opens a door for a return to authoritarian models.

The universe of values, on the one hand, and the lack of respect for some individuals of a set of founding values, on the other hand, do not sufficiently justify punishing these behaviours. Unless one accepts the cost of punishing *ideas* and a certain type of offender—a dangerous person—rather than punishing a criminal *act*. Criminal law cannot intervene to authoritatively protect historical memory without abandoning a liberal criminal law approach.

In other words, here the protection of fundamental rights as a *founding moment* depends on the compression of the same fundamental rights which are its basis and scope. There must be a core of fundamental rights that is not abandoned. We have a cultural and judicial tradition that has made freedom of expression one of its core components, even if it is conflictual or pluralistic. Freedom of strictly innocuous thoughts would be unnecessary. If the risk (of truly free speech) is not accepted, then we live in danger of atrophy.[24] Indeed, criminal law should have a minimal role and constitute a last resort mean which does not outstep the limits of law and averts a belligerent approach as well as a dangerous fusion of politics and justice. It is therefore right for the legislator to refrain from using criminal law in these areas. Fundamental rights, of which freedom of expression is part, must be the last frontier. After all, criminal law and fundamental guarantees are interrelated. If one becomes distorted, then so does the other.

The risk is that the crime of historical denialism provides immediate and emotional protection, and the combination therein of law and ethics seems ominous. It is a harbinger of a dangerous 'politicisation and ethicalization' of the criminal legislation,[25] creating the aforementioned dangerous confusion between law and politics.

Politics and law are two paradigms for regulating the coexistence of human beings in all their plurality, and between them there is a delicate equilibrium always on the verge of imbalance. In general, politics precedes and exceeds law as a self-regulating instrument of a pluralistic society of human beings, and in liberal societies politics tends to manifest itself in activities geared toward public rules. These are rules that govern the daily interaction of citizens, define how they should function, allow them to resolve the conflicts that arise within the public sphere,[26] and permit them to settle those same conflicts via legislative regulation.

However, for this to occur the reciprocal implication must not cause one to take precedence over another. Politics must act through the production of norms and refuse to directly confront its internal conflicts into the public sphere. Law must

---

[24] Gamberini 2013.

[25] That is a return to an ethical trend: in this case, the risk is to punish only an immoral behavior. See Donini 2004, p. 18; see also Cadoppi 2010. On a criminal system protecting sacred values as a paternalistic system (so inconsistent with democratic principles), see Fiore 2002, p. 14; see also Anderheiden et al. 2006; and the critical view of Gamberini 1973, p. 671 et seq.; Hörnle 2005; Canestrari 2006, p. 139 et seq.

[26] Public sphere means the collective space, both physical and virtual, within which free expression and political action are practiced. See Arendt 1998.

accept the innovative potential and the inherent freedom of politics because hyper-regulation would interrupt the resolution of conflicts and would only result in them exploding outside their formally established field. In other words, the threshold between politics and law must be clearly perceptible and respected by both sides, without one invading the other and undermining their different objectives and means of functioning.

As previously mentioned, altering this balance at the judicial level could introduce a severe discontinuity of fundamental principles of a liberal criminal approach. Placing punishment at the centre of the politics of memory and opting for over-criminalisation, can lead to emotions invading law and the criminal trials.

In the words of the Italian political scientist Carlo Galli there is:

> '[A]n innate and structural shared kinship of law and politics, in the sense that the law is established by a politics that cannot but be 'law-oriented', although it precedes and extends beyond it. This moment of co-implication may be defined as "political" if the term connotes the conflict's last chance, which also demonstrates a morphogenetic capacity, that is, the ability to produce from the conflict a (temporary and incomplete) neutralization of a "political" form that is simultaneously legal "order". The law's natal relationship to politics (better yet, the "political"), (…), constantly subjects the law to deformation, when the precarious and historically mutable balance between formalised law and institutionalised politics established by the modern age is undermined. In other words, when the "political" upsets "politics".'[27]

Considering this dialectic and the co-implication of law and politics, other means of countering historical denialism without recourse to criminal punishment must be taken into consideration.

5.4 An Attack on the Ethical Pact

We have observed how the decision to punish historical denialism entails a significant infringement upon the fundamental right to freedom of expression, as well as upon the field of historical research.

In addition to these distortions, there is the intervention of criminal prosecution to provide a mainly symbolic 'solution' driven by the emotional need for punishment. The main aim of punishing denialism is to reassure the public opinion and to protect founding values. When it prevails, this merely symbolic and value-centred dimension implies a political overexposure of criminal law.

This is not an isolated case. Laws like these, which focus on criminalising dangerous *thoughts* (and not criminal *acts*), tend to expand the criminal law paradigm and make it more subjective, thereby detaching it from objective criteria and forcing it to take on an emotional connotation.

However, the specificities of criminal law raise serious doubts about the use of these offences, their effectiveness and, ultimately, their legitimacy. Even with

[27] Galli 2007.

respect to the principles of legality, the harm principle and those which constitute the foundation (and the limits) of liberal criminal law.

In the face of phenomena like historical denialism, we certainly need to react, but the question is whether the resort to criminal prosecution is the most appropriate choice. As the French philosopher Pierre-André Taguieff claims, '[T]o overcome racism and persuade its supporters there is no need to fight against racism. We need to return to the only true pedagogy, that of the example: demonstrate successful types of existence without racism, and without its antagonist double, anti-racism.'[28] Taguieff's words, combined with the conflicts and malfunctioning demonstrated through this research on legislation and case law, emphasise the need to counteract denialism by using methods of political action, and not at the judicial and the criminal level.

The legislation that criminalises denialist statements puts the criminal lawyer in a paradoxical situation. On the one hand, the danger and gravity of these pernicious statements are evident; while, on the other hand, the question is whether stopping or even containing the spread of this phenomenon via criminal law is necessary, opportune and effective.

After the end of World War II, the new constitutions of various European states and a set of international legal instruments formalised the firm rejection of the atrocities that occurred during the conflict and the hyper-authoritarian, racial, hierarchical and divisive ideologies that were its root cause, thereby enshrining acceptance of the founding values of the new democratic systems. These values are the result of the reaction to the destructive ideas of the murderous totalitarian regimes and they are a hallmark of the post-war period, as such they have been incorporated in the entire ethical and legal system that developed from 1945 onwards (constitutions, national legislation and international documents, both binding and non-binding).

Denialist statements negate the facts that triggered this reaction and therefore reject the ethical-political paradigm that arose after World War II. This phenomenon indeed strikes at the connective tissue of contemporary societies, that is, the *ethical pact* of unconditionally rejecting the ideologies and actions that dragged Europe into the horror of war and totalitarianism. The historical experience is the constituent moment which continues to live on in individuals and communities in the form of collective memory. The intended meaning of the locution 'ethical pact' as utilised here is a shared commitment to uniformly interpret a founding event: the Nazi genocide, which significantly contributed to changing the essential values and foundations of numerous national constitutions and the international legal system as a whole which imbue it and manifest a social compact that arises from a shared experience resulting in a collective memory and a desire not to go down that road again. The founding values of democratic societies look to it as a collective historical heritage and consider it a critical warning. This is proven by the offence of historical denialism, which is limited —in most cases, at least originally—to the denial of the Holocaust. Therefore, racism and denialism shake the ethical and legal foundations of post-war reconstruction.

[28] Taguieff 2001. See also related works by René Girard on mimetic theory, Girard 1987.

Today the crime of historical denialism also includes violations of the memory of more recent international crimes, broadening the protected mnemonic framework to include the present. The protection of the ethical pact transitions from having as its centre the founding event (the Holocaust) to encompassing mass atrocities of human rights in which we see the same dynamics that led to the tragedy of totalitarianism and that we are collectively committed to reject.

As a result, the defence of this fundamental ethical pact is expressed not only by prosecuting direct violations of human rights, but also by combating the questioning of the founding values they represent, whether serious violations of the past (the Holocaust, the Armenian genocide) or more recent ones (Rwandan genocide, ethnic cleansing in the former Yugoslavia).

In this sense, both the memory of the most tragic period of the 20th century, between 1914 and 1945, as well as the memory of the most serious episodes of human rights violations 'defined as such by the Statute of the International Criminal Court' have a precise and decisive public scope and do not represent a mere cultural fact. They are thus cornerstones of the political sphere.

Denialists are aware of the scope of this memory and its significance to the integral genetic components of liberal societies. They utilise freedom of speech in all its subversive and rhetorical potential in order to combat and overthrow the foundations of that ethical pact through its very connection to this collective historical memory: this, and nothing else, is the real and primary objective of their actions.

Not only the jurisprudence of the European Court of Human Rights seems to be aware of the subversive effect of denialist assertions—which affirms that denialist statements are in opposition to the founding ideas of the European Convention—but so does the European Union. Its Framework Decision provides that these acts constitute direct violations of the principles of liberty, democracy and respect for human rights. These are the core principles upon which the European Union is founded and the roots of which are embedded in the collective historical heritage of the tragic events shared by Member States, in particular the founding members.

However, the analysis of the legislation and case law examined in this study sheds light on various problematic implications of choosing criminal law as the primary mean to contrast historical denialism. The decision to judicially fix and protect historical memory through criminal prosecution creates conflict with the freedom of historical research, the freedom of expression and—given the value-related terrain inherent in criminal law—the foundations of positive law. Entering the sphere of values leads to another problematic area: the relationship between the sphere of law and that of pure politics, the balance of which ends up being threatened.

5.5 In Defence of the Non-Criminal Protection of History

The criminalisation of historical denialism raises very complex questions. The problem that arises with its spread and which justifies the social alarm it provokes must be considered first of all *political*.

The phenomenon of denialism rejects the ethical code of historical research to which it claims to belong, and at the same time claims freedom of speech, thereby deliberately seeking to destroy the foundations upon which democratic systems are based (pluralism, tolerance and equality). It is the significance of the narrative construction of tragic events which is called into question and with it the values transmitted to us by that experience.

Denialism typically begins with circumstances or facts separated from the context through which it seeks to demonstrate, or at least presuppose, inaccuracies or groundlessness. Immediately, doubts about one or more details lead to purported invalidation or 'falsification' (in the scientific sense of the term) of the entire historical reconstruction and, as a result, of its meaning. However, this presumed accuracy is a betrayal of historical research with the pretence that in this field the individual parts prevail over the big picture and the overall phenomena are being reconstructed.

To give some examples: in addition to Auschwitz and the immense impact of the discovery of the extermination camps in 1945, it has emerged that systematic executions carried out by simple 'police actions' or acts of war including roundups behind the frontlines also weigh heavily on the totality of the Holocaust. Today we are able to distinguish between different kinds of camps—detention, work and extermination—and therefore some do not demonstrate the traits of an extermination camp. Within extermination we encounter other categories, such as the significant number of Soviet prisoners of war who were subject to systematic execution just like the deportees of Jewish origin. However, surprising circumstances still emerge, such as those narrated by Jorge Semprun about a library at Buchenwald to which some deportees were granted access.[29]

These and other similar facts offer a more complex picture and can surprise those who have only a basic knowledge of such events, but they do not undermine in any way the essence of the genocidal policies deliberately pursued by the Third Reich, the moral significance that this historical knowledge has for us and the consequences which oblige us to take an ethical stance. There is not even a change in the view of the substantial differences between our universal values and ideologies grounded in the idea of victory, achieved by marching with spiked boots over piles of the dead, as summarised in a famous judgment by anti-fascist playwright Bertolt Brecht. This is exactly the opposite of what the denialists proclaim, identifying individual and seemingly dissonant circumstances to dismiss the significance of the entire reconstruction, thus seeking to obscure and erase the cautionary message it

[29] Semprun 2005.

contains as well as the founding collective memory of the ethical pact underlying democratic institutions.

Therefore, historical denialism pertains more to an ethical-political rather than penal-legal realm. Denialism attacks the constituent moment of democracy far more than its constituted components: the institutions.

In question here is whether the moment of the creation of a given political framework is constituent. It is both a moment earlier in time—such as the memory of the Holocaust, the Resistance and the fight against fascism for countries such as France and Italy—and an internal moment—as politics and institutions cannot 'live' if they lack support and participation, if citizens do not take ownership of the values that the law represents or do not transform them into collective behaviour. Denialism claims that moment was not a severely painful experience involving hundreds of millions of people, but only a spurious myth, a pure invention of the winners (and victims) at the time who are no different from the losers. As a consequence, it is asserted as a fabrication to be abandoned, and denialism thus attacks fundamental values—human rights—to demolish the entire construction.

The attack of deniers is deep, serious and has the potential to harm or undermine the ethical pact, but criminal law, which we commonly believe to be the most powerful weapon society possesses for countering these threats and to which we attribute an almost *magical* power of determination, in the end has many drawbacks. In fact, there are strong misgivings about whether it is the most appropriate means for addressing the phenomenon at hand. In many ways it seems to be a shortcut that could damage some of the same interests we seek to protect by subverting the original purpose of criminal law and bringing other new conflicts into play. This tension is related to the freedom of research, to the right to free speech or to the principles of liberal criminal law and involve aspects that are all, just like foundational memories, pre-conditions for the proper functioning of the open, plural and democratic societies we seek to protect.

Thus, the issue is not whether or not to punish denialism, but rather with which mechanisms, or whether to only punish it when it is likely to incite to violence or hatred or in its pure form. With denialism it appears problematic to produce criminal laws, impose an 'official' version of historical truth using legal means and ask that it be enshrined in historical awareness through a criminal trial and a judgement. The truth is the truth and has no need to be a legal truth. On the contrary, by becoming a legal truth it could eventually be manipulated for some other end.[30]

Referring to a rhetorical question asked by Yoseph Hayim Yerushalmy, the Italian historian Carlo Ginzburg said in his essay on 'Uses of Forgetting':

> Is it reasonable to think that the opposite of 'forgetting' is not 'memory' but justice?[31]

[30] Vidal-Naquet, interview, in *Le Quotidien de Paris*, 9 May 1998.

[31] Yerushalmy 1990, p. 24; Baer and Sznaider 2017.

Ginzburg argues that when forgetting is pitted against the justice system, the former is the victor.[32]

Criminal prosecution of denialism risks becoming a false solution or a shortcut that could ironically follow the same path of the wrong it seeks to counter, with the added danger of turning deniers into martyrs of freedom of expression and leading to renewed propagation of their falsehoods.[33] The mechanisms of victimisation have always been part of the strategy in question: the claims of denialists (especially denial of the gas chambers and the Holocaust) are not only presented as statements of truth complying with historical reality, but also as those that have been censored and repudiated because they unmask (according to them) a fraudulent official history. Therefore, relying solely on punishment of such theories may be counterproductive because it may very well generate more consensus around the phenomenon that is being disputed. Indeed, it may have the opposite effect of creating more visibility for those claims.

Moreover, there are other existing offences that can apply to such acts. As a result, creating new ones is not necessary, especially considering the fundamental principle of *ultima ratio*, which dictates the use of criminal law as a last resort. Incitement is already punished. It is therefore not necessary to introduce a new criminal offence. According to the harm principle, if denialist statements do not meet the minimum threshold required for incitement they will not be relevant to criminal law.

The criminalisation of denialism, at national and international level, shows that criminal trials are asked to *sanction* (*sanctum facere*) and *to pass judgement on the significance* of historical events that must be kept alive—that we still consider an integral part of our present. The criminal trial takes events of the past, produces knowledge and a representation of them (which is legitimate) and defines their meaning in a way that ends discussion on the matter.[34] Therefore, it is perceived as an instrument endowed with the *auctoritas* and immutability for officially and permanently imposing historical and relevant facts. Criminal law, including prosecution and trial, thereby becomes an *arbiter* of what from our past continues to be a part of the present and what does not (or, in the words of the Italian historian Enzo Traverso, what is *strong* and what is *weak*).[35]

It is in this sense that criminal law intervenes in the relationship between past and present. When we speak about moments of the past that must remain a constitutive part of the present, we refer to normal aspects of our daily experience, though they may not always be perceived as such: they define the present setting it apart from mere immediacy.

---

[32] Ginzburg 2001.

[33] Vidal-Naquet 1995. Deniers are socially marginalised figures who are reinforced by each sentence handed down to them, as is demonstrated in various trials, such as that of Irving and Garaudy, as well as the German internet provider's block of the *Zündel* website.

[34] Highlights that history is constantly rewritten while law is rather more restricted. Ricoeur 2000, p. 647. Legal time is not only linear but it is also limited: it runs during the trial and ends with the pronouncement of the final judgment, see Delmas-Marty 2004, p. 193.

[35] Traverso 2006, p. 51.

Our actions are not determined in a linear way based on a simple cause and effect relationship ordered chronologically through time. Instead, they are the result of a process that is as conscious as it is instinctive. To use a metaphor, we use a 'map' for navigating, understanding and acting upon choices. At the centre of the map is the current situation, with its problems and possibilities, and to define its coordinates are surrounding circumstances and events of the past that we view as experiences in the full sense of the term, as well as a potential representation of the future which can be influenced by our conduct.

Understanding the situation in which we find ourselves and reflecting on the effect of our actions in order to decide what to do, inevitably means looking toward the future. Then we try to imagine possible developments based on our personal experience and education, in relation to those moments and aspects of the past that we are aware of, as well as on other events of the past that have significant connections with what involves us now, and that through comparison can provide indications about possible current developments. Thus, both the past and the future, or rather, certain aspects of both in relation to each other, are part of our 'now': they are *present* in a full sense. The historical past, like our experience, encircles us, and we, in the words of the philosopher Walter Benjamin,[36] perceive it in the connections that permit us to shape our actions in the present in the same way as we see the stars forming constellations that create relationships with each other in the night sky.

In this sense, the moment criminal law becomes an arbiter of our vision and narrative of the past, it also acquires a nascent monopoly on *how much* of it *is able to act in the present*, and thus confers upon law the ability, and responsibility, *to select* what of our past pertains to us. Consequently, criminal law acts as a 'court of last resort' of memory, specifically with respect to its presence in our decisions, thereby determining its *political* significance. In other words, according to an expression of the Italian criminal lawyer Giuliano Vassalli, it renders evident the 'primordial, essential'[37] role of criminal law with respect to the values and founding principles of a state's structure and ethical-constitutional character.

The criminal trial, in this instance, is much more than a simple declaration of individual criminal responsibility. It becomes a *space of memory*, or a bridge between past and future, because it judges past events, but under the protection of a new regime. In this way, the criminal trial becomes a stage where new political values and a new relationship between citizens and power are enacted. The narrative of the trial is thus inscribed within another narrative: that of politics, where it erupts with all its evocative power, determination and the 'solidity' of its judgment.

The Medusa of complexity once again rears its head. If a criminal trial ascertains the facts and establishes individual responsibility for mass atrocities, it determines what from the past can remain active and organises memory and forgetting, establishing the *instituant* and the *institué* require intervention that pertains to

---

[36] Benjamin 1997.

[37] Regarding anti-fascist legislation, see Vassalli 2001, p. 215.

politics. It can only be fleshed out within the public space with collective consensus.

In a moment when bearings become fluid and muddled, we must respond to establish the founding values we wish to share. However, a specific offence punishing denialist proclamations does not appear, for all the above reasons, appropriate, effective or legitimate for countering these phenomena. Indeed, it could lead to ominous deficiencies in the fields of law and history.[38]

Concluding this reflection on *how* to respond to the pernicious phenomena of denialism, I believe that criminal law is not the most appropriate instrument to counteract them. In addition to the reasons previously stated (the necessary respect of the legality and harm principles in limiting a fundamental right such as free speech), I put forth the argument that penalization of historical denialism may even be counterproductive in that it results in a broader dissemination of denialist statements. This is even more true considering that denialism and sacralization feed on each other.[39]

Moreover, it is not a function of criminal law to counteract phenomena that play out on a strictly political-foundational level.[40] In the words of the German criminal lawyer Claus Roxin, 'the historical truth as such should be able to affirm itself without criminal law.'[41]

---

[38] For a critique of this trend of establishing a unique truth in court, see Traverso 2006, p. 116. Traverso concludes that this process has the perverse effect of transforming deniers into victims of censorship and defenders of free speech.

[39] See Pisanty 2012, p. 40; in her view denialism draws its lifeblood from sacred prohibitions like a plant that feeds on herbicides. See also Paliero 2016.

[40] This critical view is shared by many lawyers. Amongst others, see Pulitanò 2015; Loytomaki 2014; Fronza and Gamberini 2013; Donini 2008; Canestrari 2006; Roxin 2006; Stortoni 2002, p. 41; see also, in Italian: *Appello camere penali*, '*Al negazionismo si risponde con le armi della cultura non con quelle del diritto penale*', 16 October 2013. Also Ronald Dworkin states: 'They (deniers) are delighted with trials turning on speech because these provide brilliant forums for their views - the Munich trial of Ewald Althans, another Holocaust denier, featured hours of videos of Hitler's speeches and other neo-Nazi propaganda'. See Dworkin, Should wrong opinions be banned? in *The Independent*, 28 May 1995. This position, according to this article, that it is not a task of law to deal with the 'assassins of memory', is also very common among historians: see, for instance: Ginzburg, La storia non si arrende alla fiction dei negazionisti, in *Corriere della Sera*, 27 November 2008, p. 45); Ginzburg, *Perché è un errore punire i negazionisti*, Interview by Simonetta Fiori, 22 October 2013; Flores, Tra negazionismo e verità di Stato, in *rivista Il Mulino*, 2 May 2016; Flores, Opinione o istigazione? Marcello Flores contro la legge contro il negazionismo, Interview by Barbara Bertocin, in *Una Città*, 2013; Prosperi, Se le bugie negazioniste diventeranno un reato, in *La Repubblica*, 16 October 2010. See Ginzburg 1991; Nora 2016; Cajani 2011; Traverso, La fabbrica europea dell'Olocausto, interview by Iaia Vantaggiato, in *Il Manifesto*, 11 November 2005. See also the Appeals promoted by the historians: in Italy an Appeal was launched against the ban of historical denialism 'Contro il negazionismo per la libertà della ricerca storica', 22 January 2007, in *L'Unità*, 23 January 2007, p. 27; and in France see '*Liberté pour l'histoire!*, *Libération*, 13 December 2005. See also the articles published in the special issue on the *Criminalizzazione del dissenso*, Rivista di diritto e procedura penale 2016.

[41] Roxin 2006, p. 731.

It is therefore necessary to react 'against the agents of forgetting, against those who shred documents, against the assassins of memory and 'editors' of encyclopaedias, against the conspirators of silence, against those (...) who can erase a man from a photograph in such a way that only the hat remains',[42] who therefore attack on an ideological level, bending and rewriting reality according to their needs and their goals.

The response can only be on a political level. What is needed is a clear public display of founding values that historical collective memory preserves[43] and which transmits the choices between just and unjust that it calls us to make by showing us the consequences of similar choices made by those who have lived before us. This is more important than punishing opponents of democracy whose primary weapon is lying.

As a result, counteracting denialism means sustaining a process that is not as readily visible and not as stigmatising as criminal prosecution, but certainly deeper, more effective and hence more legitimate: the *long road* of politics and education, the vast open spaces of the public sphere, and not the narrow confines of criminal courtrooms and laws.

References

Accarino B (2006) Premessa. In: Plessner H (1931) Potere e natura umana (tr. into Italian by Accarino B, Casanova N of Power and Human Nature). Feltrinelli, Milan, pp 15–22

Ambos K (2006) Feindstrafrecht. Rivista penale svizzera 124:1–32

Anderheiden M et al. (eds) (2006) Paternalismus und Recht. In memoriam Angela Augustin (1968–2004). Mohr Siebeck, Tübingen

Aponte A (2004) Krieg und Feindstrafrecht. Überlegungen zum 'effizienten' Feindstrafrecht anhand der Situation in Kolumbien. Baden-Baden, Munich

Aponte A (2005) ¿Derecho penal del enemigo o derecho penal del ciudadano? Bogota

Arendt H (1998) The Human Condition. University of Chicago Press, Chicago

Ash TG (2016) Free Speech: Ten Principles for a Connected World. Atlantic Books, London

Ashworth A, Horder J (2013) Principles of Criminal Law. Oxford University Press, Oxford

Baer A, Sznaider N (2017) Memory and Forgetting in the Post-Holocaust Era: The Ethics of Never Again. Routledge, London/New York

Baker DJ, Zhao LX (2013) The normativity of using prison to control hate speech: the hollowness of Waldron's theory. New Criminal Law Review 4:621–656

Baratta A (1989) Funzioni strumentali e funzioni simboliche del diritto penale. Lineamenti di una teoria del bene giuridico. Studi in memoria di Giovanni Tarello, volume II. Giuffrè, Milan

Baratta A (1990) Legittimazione strumentale e funzione simbolica del sistema punitivo. Per un uso "alternativo" del diritto penale. Difesa penale 29:19–31

Bazyler M (2016) Holocaust, Genocide, and the Law: A Quest for Justice in a Post-Holocaust World. Oxford University Press, Oxford

Beale SS (2000) Federalizing Hate Crimes: Symbolic Politics, Expressive Law, or Tool for Criminal Enforcement? Boston University Law Review 80:1227–1254

[42] See Yerushalmy 1990, pp. 23–24.

[43] On 'politics of memory' and the necessity of public debate, see Ash 2016, part II no. 3.

Benjamin W (1997) Sul concetto di storia. Einaudi, Turin
Berger BL (2014) Constitutional Principles. In: Dubber MD, Hörnle T (eds) The Oxford Handbook of Criminal Law. Oxford University Press, Oxford, pp 422–444
Bifulco D (2012) Negare l'evidenza, Diritto e storia di fronte alla 'menzogna' di Auschwitz. Franco Angeli, Milan
Bird P (2015) Virtual Child Pornography Laws and the Constraints Imposed by the First Amendment. Barry Law Review 16:161–177
Bonini S (2003) Quali spazi per una funzione simbolica del diritto penale? Indice penale 491–534
Bricola F (1973) Teoria generale del reato. Novissimo Digesto italiano XIX 3–25
Bricola F (1981) Funzione promozionale, tecnica premiale e diritto penale. Questione Criminale 445–460
Bricola F (1984) Tecniche di tutela penale e tecniche alternative di tutela. Funzioni e limiti del diritto penale. Cedam, Padua
Cadoppi A (2010) (ed) Laicità, valori e diritto penale. The Moral Limits of the Criminal Law. In ricordo di Joel Feinberg. Giuffrè, Milan
Cajani L (2011) Criminal Laws on History. The case of the European Union. Historein. How to deal with tormented pasts 3:19–29
Cancio Meliá M (2005) "Feindstrafrecht"? Zeitschrift für die gesamte Strafrechtswissenschaft 117:267–289
Cancio Meliá M (2010) Los delitos de terrorismo estructura típica e injusto. Editorial Reus, Madrid
Cancio Meliá M, Jakobs G (2003) Derecho penal del enemigo. Madrid
Cancio Meliá M, Jara G (2006) (ed.) Derecho penal del enemigo, el discurso penal de la exclusión. Edisofer, Madrid
Canestrari S (2006) Laicità e diritto penale nelle democrazie costituzionali. In: Dolcini E, Paliero CE (eds) Studi in onore di Giorgio Marinucci, I. Giuffrè, Milan, pp 149–163
Canestrari S, Cornacchia L, De Simone G (2007) Manuale di diritto penale. Parte generale. Il Mulino, Bologna
Caputo M (2014) La "menzogna di Auschwitz", le "verità" del diritto penale. La criminalizzazione del c.d. negazionismo tra ordine pubblico, dignità e senso di umanità. Diritto penale contemporaneo. Online: https://www.penalecontemporaneo.it/upload/1389084288CAPUTO%202014a.pdf. Accessed 1 October 2017
Cavaliere A (2016) La discussione intorno alla punibilità del negazionismo, i principi di offensività e libera manifestazione del pensiero e la funzione della pena. Rivista italiana di diritto e procedura penale 2:999–1015
Ceretti A (2004) Presentazione. In: Garland D (2001) (tr. into Italian by Ceretti A, Gibellini F of The Culture of Control) La cultura del controllo: crimine e ordine sociale nel mondo contemporaneo. Il Saggiatore, Milan
Delmas-Marty M (1985) Les chemins de la répression. Presses Universitaires de France, Paris
Delmas-Marty M (2004) Le relatif et l'universel. Les forces imaginantes du droit. I. Seuil, Paris
Díez Ripollés JL (2003) El Derecho Penal Simbólico Y Los Efectos De La Pena. In: Arroyo Zapatero L, Neumann U, Nieto Martín A (eds) Crítica Y Justificación Del Derecho Penal En El Cambio De Siglo. Ediciones De La Universidad De Castilla, Cuenca
Donini M (2001a) Alla ricerca di un disegno. Scritti sulle riforme penali in Italia. Cedam, Padua
Donini M (2001b) Ragioni e limiti della fondazione del diritto penale sulla Carta costituzionale. Il significato dell'esperienza italiana. Foro italiano V:29–43
Donini M (2003) Alla ricerca di un disegno. Scritti sulle riforme penali in Italia. Cedam, Padua
Donini M (2004) Il volto attuale dell'illecito penale. La democrazia penale tra differenziazione e sussidiarietà. Giuffrè, Milan
Donini M (2007a) Diritto penale del nemico. Scritti in onore di Federico Stella. Jovene, Naples
Donini M (2007b) Diritto penale penale di lotta vs diritto penale del nemico. In Gamberini A, Orlandi R (eds) Delitto politico e diritto penale del nemico. Monduzzi, Bologna
Donini M (2008) "Danno" e "offesa" nella cd. tutela penale dei sentimenti. Note su morale e sicurezza come beni giuridici, a margine della categoria dell' "offense" di Joel Feinberg. Rivista italiana di diritto e procedura penale 4

Donini M (2009) Principi costituzionali e sistema penale. Modello e programma. IUS17@unibo.it 421–437
Donini M (2012) L'eredità di Bricola e il costituzionalismo penale come metodo. Diritto penale contemporaneo 2:51–74
Donini M (2017) Massimo Pavarini e la scienza penale. Ovvero sul valore conoscitivo dell'antimoderno sentimento della compassione applicato allo studio della questione criminale. Diritto penale contemporaneo 1–20
Donini M, Papa M (eds) (2007) Diritto penale del nemico. Un dibattito internazionale. Giuffrè, Milan
Elholm T, Colson R (2016) The Symbolic Purpose of EU Criminal Law. In: Colson R, Field S (eds) EU Criminal Justice and the Challenges of Diversity: Legal Cultures in the Area of Freedom, Security and Justice. Cambridge University Press, Cambridge, pp 48–64
Feinberg J (1974) Doing and Deserving: Essays in the Theory of Responsibility. Princeton University Press. New Jersey
Fiandaca G (2013) Populismo politico e populismo giudiziario. Criminalia 95–121
Fiore C (2002) I reati di opinione. In: Moccia S (ed) Diritti dell'uomo e sistema penale. Edizioni Scientifiche Italiane, Naples
Fletcher GP (1998) Basic Concepts of Criminal Law. Oxford University Press, Oxford
Fletcher M, Lööf R, Gilmore B (2008) EU Criminal Law and Justice. Edward Elgar, Cheltenham
Fronza E (2015) Negazionismo. Enciclopedia del Diritto Annali VIII:633–658
Galli C (2007) Diritto e politica: profili teorici e politici del loro rapporto. In: Gamberini A, Orlandi R (eds) Delitto politico e diritto penale del nemico. Monduzzi, Bologna, pp 45–60
Gamberini A (1973) I "pensieri leciti" della Corte Costituzionale. Rivista italiana di diritto e procedura penale: 671 et seq.
Gamberini A (2005) Profili di diritto penale sostanziale dell'azione di contrasto al terrorismo. Relazione svolta presso la Corte di Cassazione nel 2005
Gamberini A (2013) Tutela della memoria e diritto penale: una riflessione sistematica e comparativa a partire dal reato di negazionismo. Diritto penale contemporaneo. Online: https://www.penalecontemporaneo.it/d/2716-tutela-della-memoria-e-diritto-penale-una-riflessione-sistematica-e-comparativa-a-partire-dal-reato. Accessed 2 October 2017
Garapon A (1985) L'Ane portant des reliques: essai sur le rituel judiciaire. Le Centurion, Paris
Garapon A (2002) Des crimes qu'on ne peut ni punir ni pardonner. Pour une justice internationale. Odile Jacob, Paris
Garland D (2002) Beyond the culture of control. Critical Review of International Social and Political Philosophy 7:160–189
Ginzburg C (1991) Il giudice e lo storico. Considerazioni a margine del processo Sofri. Einaudi, Turin
Ginzburg C (2001) Beweis, Gedächtnis, Vergessen. WerkstattGeschichte 30:50–60
Girard R (1987) Things hidden since the foundation of the world. Stanford University Press, California
Harcourt BE (2002) Joel Feinberg on crime and punishment: exploring the relationship between "the moral limits of the criminal law" and "the expressive function of punishment". Buffalo Criminal Law Review 145–172
Hassemer W (1989) Symbolischer Strafrecht und Rechtsgüterschutz. Neue Zeitschrift für Strafrecht 553–574
Hassemer W (2008) Das Symbolische am symbolischen Strafrecht. In: Hassemer W (ed) Strafrecht. Sein Selbstverständnis, seine Welt. BWV, Berlin
Hassemer W (2009) Warum Strafe sein muss. Ein Plädoyer. Ullstein, Berlin
Herlin-Karnell E (2012) The constitutional Dimension of European Criminal Law. Hart, Portland
Hildebrandt M (2007) European Criminal Law and European Identity. Criminal Law and Philosophy 1:57–78
Hörnle T (2005) Grob anstössiges Verhalten: strafrechtlicher Schutz von Moral, Gefühlen und Tabus. Verlag, Frankfurt am Main

Hörnle T (2015) Theories of Criminalization. In: Dubber MD, Hörnle T (eds) The Oxford Handbook of Criminal Law. Oxford University Press, Oxford
Husak D (2007) Overcriminalization: The Limits of the Criminal Law. Oxford University Press, Oxford
Jakobs G (1985) Kriminalisierung im Vorfeld einer Rechstgutverletzung. Zeitschrift für die gesamte Strafrechtswissenschaft 97
Jakobs G (1995) Das Strafrecht zwischen Funktionalismus und alteuropäischem Prinzipendenken. Zeitschrift für die gesamte Strafrechtswissenschaft 107:843–857
Jakobs G (1997) Norm, Person, Gesellschaft. Vorüberlegungen zu einer Rechtsphilosophie. Berlin
Jakobs G (2000) Das Selbsverständnis der Strafrechtswissenschaft vor der Herausforderung der Gegenwart. In: Eser A, Hassemer W, Burhardt B (eds) Die deutsche Strafrechtswissenschaft vor der Jahrtausendwende. München, pp 47–63
Jakobs G (2003) Bürgerstrafrecht und Feindstrafrecht. In: Yu V, Hsu H (eds) Foundations and Limits of Criminal Law and Criminal Procedure. An anthology in memory of Professor Fu-Tseng Hun. Taipeh, pp 41–63
Jakobs G (2005a) Individuum und Person. Zeitschrift für die gesamte Strafrechtswissenschaft 117:247–268
Jakobs G (2005b) Terroristen als Personen im Recht? Zeitschrift für die gesamte Strafrechtswissenschaft 117:839–853
Jakobs G (2006) Enemy Criminal Law? An investigation of the conditions of legality. HRRS 289–302
Lazerges C (2004) De la fonction déclarative de la loi pénale. Revue de science criminelle et de droit pénal comparé 59:194–202
Lobba P (2011) La lotta al razzismo nel diritto penale europeo dopo Lisbona. Osservazioni sulla decisione quadro 2008/913/GAI e sul reato di negazionismo. Ius17@unibo.it 107–156
Loytomaki S (2014) Law and the Politics of Memory: Confronting the Past. Routledge, London
Manes V (2005) Il principio di offensività nel diritto penale. Giappichelli, Turin
Manes V (2007) Attualità e prospettive del giudizio di ragione volezza in materia penale. Rivista italiana di diritto e procedura penale 782–798
Manes V (2012) I principi penalistici nel network multilivello: trapianto palingenesi, cross-fertilization? Rivista italiana diritto e procedura penale 1:839–874
Morguet G (2009) Feindstrafrecht – Eine kritische Analyse. Dunker & Humblot, Berlin
Muñoz Conde F (2005) De nuevo sobre el "derecho penal del enemigo". Revista Penal 16: 123–137
Noll P (1981) Symbolische Gesetzgebung. Zeitschrift für Schweizerisches Strafrecht 347–365
Nora P (2016) Come si manipola la memoria. Lo storico il potere, il passato. La Scuola, Brescia
Ohana D (2014) Günther Jakobs's "Feindstrafrecht". A Dispassionate Account. In: Dubber MD (ed) Foundational Texts in Modern Criminal Law. Oxford University Press, Oxford
Oliver WM, Marion NE (2010) Symbolic Politics, Criminal Justice Policy, and Third Political Party Platforms. Criminal Justice Policy Review 21:397–413
Palazzo FC (1985) Valori costituzionali e diritto penale (un contributo comparatistico). In Pizzorusso A, Varano V (eds) L'influenza dei valori costituzionali sui sistemi giuridici contemporanei. Giuffrè, Milan, pp 531–547
Palazzo FC (2016) Il principio di legalità tra Costituzione e suggestioni sovranazionali. Online: www.lalegislazionepenale.eu. Accessed 2 October 2017
Paliero CE (1990) Il principio di effettività nel diritto penale. Rivista italiana di diritto e procedura penale 473–492
Paliero CE (1992) Diritto penale e consenso sociale. Verso un nuovo codice penale. Milan, 184–205
Paliero CE (2016) La laicità penale alla sfida del "secolo delle paure". Rivista italiana di diritto e procedura penale 59:1154 1191
Pavarini M (2006a) La neutralizzazione degli uomini inaffidabili. La nuova disciplina della recidiva e altro ancora sulla guerra alle Unpersonen. Studi sulla Questione Criminale 2:7–21

Pavarini M (2006b) Sicurezza dalla criminalità e governo delle città. In: Dolcini E, Paliero CE (eds) Studi in onore di Giorgio Marinucci. Vol. I. Giuffrè, Milan, pp 1019–1050
Pisanty V (2012) Abusi di memoria. Negare, banalizzare, sacralizzare la Shoah. Mondadori. Milan
Plessner H (2006) Potere e natura umana. Feltrinelli. Milano
Portinaro PP (1992) Materiali per una storicizzazione della coppia amico-nemico. In: Morani M, Portinaro PP, Vitale A (eds) Amicus (Inimicus) Hostis. Le radici concettuali della conflittualità 'privata' e della conflittualità 'politica', Giuffrè, Milan
Portinaro PP (1996) Premessa. In: Demandt A (ed) Processare il nemico. Da Socrate a Norimberga. Einaudi, Turin, pp XII–XV
Prittwitz C (2004) Derecho penal del enemigo: ¿análisis crítico o programa del Derecho penal? In: Puig M, Bidasolo C, Martín G (eds) La política criminal en Europa, pp 107–123
Puig M, Queralt Jiménez JJ (eds) (2010) Constitución y principios del derecho penal: algunas bases constitucionales. Tirant lo blanch, Valencia
Pulitanò D (2013) Populismi e penale, sulla attuale situazione spirituale della giustizia penale. Criminalia 123–146
Pulitanò D (2015) Di fronte al negazionismo e al discorso d'odio. Diritto penale contemporaneo. Online: https://www.penalecontemporaneo.it/upload/1426333841PULITANO_2015.pdf. Accessed 28 September 2017
Ricoeur P (2000) La mémoire, l'histoire, l'oubli. Seuil, Paris
Romano M (2007) Principio di laicità dello Stato, religioni, norme penali. Rivista trimestrale di diritto e procedura penale 493–513
Roxin C (2006) Was darf der Staat unter Strafe stellen? Zur Legitimation von Strafdrohungen. In: Dolcini E, Paliero CE (eds) Studi in onore di Giorgio Marinucci, I. Giuffrè, Milan
Salas D (2013) La volonté de punir: essai sur le populisme pénal. Fayard, Paris
Schmitt C (1972) Le categorie del 'politico'. Bologna
Schmitt C (1981) Teoria del partigiano. Note complementari al concetto di politico. Milan
Schmitt C (2005) Un giurista davanti a se stesso. Saggi e interviste. Vicenza
Semprun J (2005) Vivrò col suo nome, morirà con il mio. Einaudi, Turin
Silva Sánchez JM (2001) La expansión del derecho penal. Civitas, Madrid
Sotis C (2007) Il diritto senza codice. Uno studio sul diritto penale europeo vigente. Giuffrè, Milan
Stortoni L (1994) Le nuove norme contro l'intolleranza: legge o proclama? Critica del Diritto 14–32
Stortoni L (2002) Diritti dell'uomo ed emergenza: (l'eredità de) gli anni di piombo. In: Moccia S (ed) Diritti dell'uomo e sistema penale. Edizioni Scientifiche Italiane, Napoli
Taguieff PA (2001) The Force of Prejudice: On Racism and Its Doubles. University of Minnesota Press, Minnesota
Teruel Lozano GM (2015) La libertad de expresión a los delitos de negacionismo y de provocación al odio y a la violencia: sombras sin luces en la reforma del código penal. Revista para el análisis del derecho 4:1–51
Tondini M (2007) Beyond the Law of the Enemy. Recovering from the Failures of the Global War on Terrorism through Law. Jura Gentium http://www.juragentium.org/topics/wlgo/cortona/en/tondini.htm. Accessed 20 August 2017
Traverso E (2006) Il passato: istruzioni per l'uso. Storia, memoria, politica. Ombre Corte, Verona
Turner JI (2012) The Expressive Dimension of EU Criminal Law. American Journal of Comparative Law 60:555–583
van de Kerchove M (1987) Les lois pénales sont-eles faites pour être appliquées? Réflexions sur les phénomènes de dissociation entre la validité formelle et l'effectivité des normes juridiques. In: Ost F, van de Kerchove M (eds) Jalons pour une théorie critique du droit. Publications des Faculté universitaires Saint-Louis, Bruxelles, pp 317–351
Vassalli G (2001) Formula di Radbruch e diritto penale. Note sulla punizione dei "delitti di Stato" nella Germania postnazista e nella Germania postcomunista. Giuffrè, Milan
Vidal-Naquet P (1995) Les Assassins de la Mémoire. "Un Eichmann de Papier" et autres essais sur le révisionnisme. Seuil, Paris

Visconti C (2008) Aspetti penalistici del discorso pubblico. Giappichelli, Turin
Vormbaum T (1995) "Politisches" Strafrecht. Zeitschrift für die gesamte Strafrechtswissenschaft 107:734–752
Waldron J (2012) The Harm in Hate Speech. Harvard University Press, Cambridge
Yerushalmy Y (1990) Usi dell'oblio. In: Yerushalmi Y, Loraux N, Mommsen H, Milner JC, Vattimo G (eds) Usi dell´oblio. Parma
Zaffaroni R (2006) El enemigo en el derecho penal. Buenos Aires

Appendix

As the present book is being published, the world press is once again focused on denialism. On the eve of Holocaust Remembrance Day 2018, the Polish Sejm approved a law on the defamation of the Polish State and Nation. The new law amends the Institute of National Remembrance Act, punishing with an imprisonment sentence of up to three years whoever claims, publicly and contrary to the facts, that the Polish Nation or the Republic of Poland is responsible or co-responsible for crimes committed by the Third Reich. Such speech is to be punished even if committed unintentionally and applies to both Polish and foreign citizens.

E. Fronza, *Memory and Punishment*, International Criminal Justice Series 19,
https://doi.org/10.1007/978-94-6265-234-7

Table of EU Legislation on Denialism

	Current criminal law provision	Amendments	Punishable conduct	Object of the punishable conduct	Additional elements of the criminal offence	Criminal sanction
Austria	Article 3 para (h) of the *National Socialism Prohibition Act* of 18 February 1947	19 March 1992	Denial, serious minimisation, approval, justification	Genocide and other crimes against humanity committed by the National-Socialist regime	Public nature of the statement	Imprisonment up to 10 years, doubled for particularly dangerous individuals
Belgium	Article 1 of the *Law tending to repress the negation, minimisation, justification or approbation of the genocide committed by the German National-Socialist regime during the Second World War* of 23 March 1995	In 1999 there was an amendment concerning the criminal sanction	Denial, trivial minimisation, approbation or justification	Genocide committed by the National-Socialist regime during the Second World War. For the definition of genocide, there is a reference to Article 2 of the *Convention on the Prevention and Punishment of the Crime of Genocide* of 9 December 1948	Public nature of the statement	• Imprisonment from 8 days to 1 year and a fine from 0.64 to 123,5 euros • Billposting or publication of the judgement in a newspaper
Bulgaria	Article 419a Criminal Code (Chapter XIV: Complementary dispositions), 13 April 2011	/	Denial, trivial minimisation, justification	Crimes against peace and crimes against humanity, as defined in Articles 407 et seq. Bulgarian Criminal Code	Risk that the conduct generates discriminatory violence and hatred	Imprisonment from 1 to 5 years
Croatia	Article 325 Criminal Code (Chapter XXX: Crimes against public order), 26 October 2011	Article 325 amended Article 174 Criminal Code, originally provided for racial discriminatory conduct	Denial, trivial minimisation, approbation	Genocide, crime of aggression, crimes against humanity and war crimes, as defined in Article 88 et seq. Croatian Criminal Code	• Public nature of the statement • Conduct must be capable of instigating violence and hatred	Imprisonment up to 3 years

(continued)

(continued)

	Current criminal law provision	Amendments	Punishable conduct	Object of the punishable conduct	Additional elements of the criminal offence	Criminal sanction
Cyprus	*Law n. 134(I) on the combat against certain forms of racism and xenophobia* of 21 October 2011	/	Denial, serious minimisation, approbation	Genocide, crimes against humanity and war crimes, as defined in Articles 6–8 of the Statute of the International Criminal Court and ascertained with a final judgement delivered by an international tribunal	Public nature of the statement	Imprisonment up to 5 years or a fine up to 10.000 euros
Czech Republic	Article 405 Criminal Code (Title XIII: War crimes, crimes against peace and crimes against humanity), 9 February 2009	Article 405 codifies Article 261 of the 2001 *Law Against Support and Dissemination of Movements Oppressing Human Rights and Freedom*	Denial, questioning, approbation and justification	• Nazi and Communist genocide and other genocides, as defined in Article 400 Criminal Code • Crimes against humanity committed by Nazis or Communists. Crimes against humanity are defined in Article 401 Criminal Code	Public nature of the statement	Imprisonment from 6 months to 3 years
Denmark						
Estonia						
Finland						

(continued)

(continued)

	Current criminal law provision	Amendments	Punishable conduct	Object of the punishable conduct	Additional elements of the criminal offence	Criminal sanction
France	Article 24 *bis* Freedom of the Press Act of 29 July 1881, introduced by Article 9 of Law no. 90-615 (*Gayssot* Act) *tending to repress all the acts of racism, antisemitism and xenophobia* of 13 July 1990	Law no. 2017-86 of 27 January 2017 Law no. 2014-1353 of 13 November 2014 Law no. 92-1336 of 16 December 1992	I Para: contestation II Para: Denial, minimisation and outrageous trivialization	Paragraph I: crimes against humanity, as defined in Article 6 of the Statute of the International Military Tribunal of Nuremberg and ascertained by a French or international court Paragraph II: international crimes as defined in Articles 6–8 of the Statute of the International Criminal Court and ascertained by a French or an international court with a judgement of conviction	Public nature of the statement	• Imprisonment up to 1 year and fine up to 45.000 euros • Publication of the judgement of conviction
Germany	Article 130(3) Criminal Code (Chapter VII: Crimes against the public order), 28 October 1994	*Gesetz zur Änderung des Versammlungsgesetzes und des Strafgesetzbuches* of 24 March 2005, which introduces Article 130(4) Criminal Code punishing whosoever publicly or in a meeting disturbs the public peace in a manner that violates the dignity of the victims by approving of, glorifying, or justifying National Socialist rule of arbitrary force shall be liable to imprisonment not exceeding three years or a fine	Denial, minimisation, approbation	National-Socialist genocide, as defined in Article 6 of the German Code of Crimes against International Law of 30 June 2002 (VStGB)	• Public nature of the statement • Conduct carried out in manner likely to disturb public order	Imprisonment up to 5 years or a fine (amount not specified)

(continued)

(continued)

	Current criminal law provision	Amendments	Punishable conduct	Object of the punishable conduct	Additional elements of the criminal offence	Criminal sanction
Greece	Article 2 of Law no. 4285 of 4 September 2014	Law no. 4285/2014 amended Law n. 927/1979 on racial discrimination	Denial, minimisation, approbation	• Holocaust and other Nazi crimes • Genocide, crimes against humanity and war crimes. The crimes are to be ascertained by a judgement of an international court or defined as such by the Greek Parliament	• Public nature of the statement • Conduct must be capable of instigating violence and hatred	• Imprisonment from 3 months to 3 years and a fine from 5.000 to 20.000 euros • Aggravating circumstance: imprisonment from 6 months to 3 years and fine from 10.000 to 25.000 euros if the fact is committed by a public official or by a public employee exercising his/her duties
Hungary	Article 333 Criminal Code (Chapter XXXII: Crimes against the public order), Law XLVIII of 2013	Law XLVIII/2013 amended Article 269c Criminal Code, introduced in 2010	Denial, calling into discussion, minimisation, justification	Genocide and crimes against humanity committed by the Nazi and Communist regime The crime of genocide and crimes against humanity are defined in Article 142 et seq. Criminal Code	Public nature of the statement	Imprisonment up to 3 years
Ireland						
Italy	Article 3 *bis* of Law no. 654 of 13 October 1975, introduced by Law no. 115 of 16 June 2016	/	Denial, apology and gross minimisation	Shoah and crimes of genocide, crimes against humanity and war crimes as defined in Articles 6–8 of the Statute of the International Criminal Court	• Denial must be object of propaganda, instigation or incitement • Real danger of diffusion	Imprisonment from 2 to 6 years

(continued)

(continued)

	Current criminal law provision	Amendments	Punishable conduct	Object of the punishable conduct	Additional elements of the criminal offence	Criminal sanction
Latvia	Article 74-1 Criminal Code (Chapter IX: Crimes against humanity and peace, war crimes and genocide), 21 May 2009	In 2012 there was an amendment regarding the criminal sanction	Denial, celebration, justification	Genocide, crimes against humanity, war crimes and crimes against peace. These crimes are defined in Article 71 et seq. Criminal Code	Public nature of the statement	Imprisonment up to 5 years or a fine (amount not specified) or conviction to community service
Lithuania	Article 170(2) Criminal Code (Public approbation of international crimes, crimes committed by USSR and by Nazi Germany against the Republic of Lithuania or its residents), introduced by Law no. 75-3792 of 2010	/	Denial, trivial minimisation, approbation	• Genocide, war crimes and crimes against humanity defined as such by national law, EU acts, Lithuanian or international courts • Nazi or Soviet aggression • Genocide, war crimes and crimes against humanity committed by Nazis and Communists against the Lithuanian territory or residents • Serious crimes committed between 1990 and 1991 in Lithuania (during the fight for independence)	• Public nature of the statement • Conduct carried out in manner likely to disturb public order or which is threatening, violent or offensive	Imprisonment up to 2 years or arrest or a fine (amount not specified)

(continued)

(continued)

	Current criminal law provision	Amendments	Punishable conduct	Object of the punishable conduct	Additional elements of the criminal offence	Criminal sanction
Luxembourg	Article 457-3 Criminal Code (Chapter VI: Racism, revisionism and other forms of discrimination), 13 February 2011	The punishable conducts are expanded by Law of 27 February 2012	Denial, minimisation, contestation, justification	• War crimes and crimes against humanity defined as such in Article 6 of the Statute of the International Military Tribunal of Nuremberg and ascertained by a Luxembourg or international court • Genocide, war crimes and crimes against humanity defined as such by Article 136 *bis* et seq. Criminal Code and ascertained by a Luxembourg or international court	Public nature of the statement	Imprisonment from 8 days to 2 years and/or a fine from 251 to 25.000 euros
Malta	Article 82b Criminal Code (Title II: Crimes against public order), 3 November 2009	/	Denial, trivial minimisation, approbation	Genocide, war crimes and crimes against humanity as defined by the Criminal Code, committed against a group of people or a member of a group identified on the basis of race, colour, religion or ethnical or national origin	• Public nature of the statement • Conduct must be capable of instigating violence and hatred • Conduct carried out in a manner likely to disturb public order or which is threatening, violent or offensive	Imprisonment from 8 months to 2 years

(continued)

(continued)

	Current criminal law provision	Amendments	Punishable conduct	Object of the punishable conduct	Additional elements of the criminal offence	Criminal sanction
Netherlands						
Poland	Article 55 of the *Act on the Institute of National Remembrance - Commission for the Prosecution of Crimes against the Polish Nation* of 18 December 1998	/	Denial	• Nazi and communist crimes and other war crimes, crimes against humanity and crimes against peace committed against Polish citizens or other nationalities between 1 September 1939 and 31 December 1989 • Other repressive measures committed because of political motives by the judiciary or by the persons that acted on the basis of orders of public prosecutors or judges as provided by the 23 February 1991 Law	Public nature of the statement	Imprisonment up to 3 years
Portugal	Article 240 (Chapter II: Crimes against humanity), 2 September 1998	Law no. 57 of 4 September 2007	Denial	War crimes, crimes against peace and crimes against humanity. These crimes are defined by Article 239 et seq. Criminal Code	• Public nature of the statement • Conduct is carried out in manner likely to incite or encourage hatred and discrimination	Imprisonment from 6 months to 5 years

(continued)

(continued)

	Current criminal law provision	Amendments	Punishable conduct	Object of the punishable conduct	Additional elements of the criminal offence	Criminal sanction
Romania	Article 6 of Decree no. 669 of 22 July 2015	Emergency Ordinance of 14 March 2002; the ordinance was converted into law on 6 May 2006	Denial, contestation, approbation, justification and minimisation	Genocide and crimes against humanity	Public nature of the statement	Imprisonment from 6 months to 6 years
Slovakia	Article 424-a Criminal Code (Chapter XII: Crimes against peace and crimes against humanity, terrorism, fundamentalism and war crimes), 20 May 2005	The Criminal Code entered into force on 1 January 2006	Denial, trivial minimisation	• Genocide, war crimes and crimes against humanity as defined by Articles 6–8 of the Statute of the International Criminal Court • War crimes, crimes against peace and crimes against humanity as defined by Article 6 of the Statute of the International Military Tribunal of Nuremberg	• Public nature of the statement • Conduct addressed to an individual or a group of persons because of their race, religion, ethnicity, nationality	Imprisonment from 1 to 3 years

(continued)

(continued)

	Current criminal law provision	Amendments	Punishable conduct	Object of the punishable conduct	Additional elements of the criminal offence	Criminal sanction
Slovenia	Article 297 Criminal Code (Chapter XXIX: Crimes against public order), 2 November 2011	In 2008 Article 297 Criminal Code already punished the incitement to hatred	Denial, justification, approbation, derision, defence	• Genocide, Holocaust, war crimes, crimes against humanity, crime of aggression • Other crimes against humanity defined as such by the Slovenian legal system Such crimes are defined in Article 100 et seq. Criminal Code. For the definition of the crime of aggression there is a reference to international law	Public nature of the statement	Imprisonment up to 2 years
Spain	Article 510(1)(c) Criminal Code (Chapter IV: Crimes regarding the exercise of fundamental rights and public freedoms), Organic Law no. 10/1995 of 23 November 1995	Organic Law no. 1 of 30 March 2015 Judgement of the Constitutional Court of 7 November 2007	Denial, trivial minimisation, exaltation	Genocide, crimes against humanity, war crimes against protected persons and goods	• Public nature of the statement • Conduct carried out in manner likely to indirectly instigate the commission of a genocide	Imprisonment from 1 to 2 years
Sweden						
United Kingdom						

Bibliography

Abregú M (1996) La tutela judicial del derecho a la verdad en la Argentina. Revista Instituto Interamericano de derechos humanos 24:11–41

Accarino B (2006) Premessa. In: Plessner H, Potere e natura umana. Feltrinelli, Milan, pp 15–22

Ader B (2012) L'état de la jurisprudence sur la notion de négation depuis la loi Gayssot. Légipresse 293:236–254

Adjemian B (2012) Le débat inachevé des historiens français sur les «lois mémorielles» et la pénalisation du négationnisme: retour sur une décennie de controverse. Etudes arméniennes contemporaines 15:9–34

Alastuey Dobón C (2016) Discurso del odio y negacionismo en la reforma del código penal de 2015. Revista Electrónica de Ciencia Penal y Criminología 18-14

Algan B (2008) The Brand New Version of Article 301 of Turkish Penal Code and the Future of Freedom of Expression Cases in Turkey. German Law Journal 9:2237–2252

Alix J (2010) Terrorisme et droit penal. Etude critique des incriminations terroristes. Dalloz, Paris

Alix J (2014) Réprimer la participation au terrorisme. Revue des Sciences Criminelles et de Droit Comparé 4:849–866

Alix J (2015) La répression de l'incitation au terrorisme. Gazette du Palais 55:11–33

Amati E, Costi M, Fronza E, Lobba P, Maculan E, Vallini A (2016) Introduzione al diritto penale internazionale. Giappichelli, Turin

Ambos K (2006) Feindstrafrecht. Rivista penale svizzera 124:1–30

Ambos K (2009) The Legal Framework of Transitional Justice: A Systematic Study with a Special Focus on the Role of the ICC. In: Ambos K et al. (eds) Building a Future on Peace and Justice: Studies on Transitional Justice, Peace and Development. Springer, Berlin, pp 19–86

Ambos K (2014) Treatise on International Criminal Law. Volume II: The Crimes and Sentencing. Oxford University Press, Oxford

Ambos K (2017) Derecho penal europeo. Thomson Reuters, Civitas

Ambos K, Malarino E, Elsner G (2009) (eds) Justicia de Transición. Informes de América Latina, Alemania, Italia y España. Konrad-Adenauer-Stiftung, Berlin

Ambos K, Wirth S (2002) The Current Law of Crimes Against Humanity. An Analysis of UNTAET Regulation 15/2000. Criminal Law Forum 13:1–90

Anderheiden M et al. (2006) (eds) Paternalismus und Recht. In memoriam Angela Augustin (1968–2004). Mohr Siebeck, Tübingen

Aponte A (2004) Krieg und Feindstrafrecht. Überlegungen zum 'effizienten' Feindstrafrecht anhand der Situation in Kolumbien. Baden-Baden/Munich

Aponte A (2005) ¿Derecho penal del enemigo o derecho penal del ciudadano? Bogota

Appleman JA (1954) Military Tribunals and International Crimes. Bobbs-Merrill, Indianapolis

Arendt H (1966) The origins of Totalitarianism. Harcourt, New York

Arendt H (1998) The Human Condition. University of Chicago Press, Chicago

Arslan A, Berti F, De Stefani P (2017) (eds) Il paese perduto. A cent'anni dal genocidio armeno. Edizioni Angelo Guerini, Milan

E. Fronza, *Memory and Punishment*, International Criminal Justice Series 19,
https://doi.org/10.1007/978-94-6265-234-7

Ash TG (2016) Free Speech: Ten Principles for a Connected World. Atlantic Books, London
Ashworth A, Horder J (2013) Principles of Criminal Law. Oxford University Press, Oxford
Ashworth A, Zedner L (2008) Defending the Criminal Law: Reflections on the Changing Character of Crime, Procedure, and Sanctions. Criminal Law and Philosophy 2:21–51
Assmann A (2012) Cultural Memory and Western Civilization: Functions, Media. Cambridge University Press, Cambridge
Astacio Cabrera JG (2011) Tratamiento jurídico-penal de la apología del terrorismo. Universidad de Granada, Granada
Atkins SE (2009) Holocaust Denial as an International Movement. Westport, Connecticut
Auron Y (2004) The Banality of Denial: Israel and the Armenian Genocide. Routledge, London
Baer A, Sznaider N (2017) Memory and Forgetting in the Post-Holocaust Era: The Ethics of Never Again. Routledge, London/New York
Baker DJ (2008) Constitutionalizing the Harm Principle. Criminal Justice Ethics 3–28
Baker DJ, Zhao LX (2013) The normativity of using prison to control hate speech: the hollowness of Waldron's theory. New Criminal Law Review 4:621–656
Bakircioglu O (2008) Freedom of Expression and Hate Speech. Tulsa Journal of Comparative and International Law 16:1–49
Baldissara L (2009) Il massacro. Guerra ai civili a Monte Sole. Il Mulino, Bologna
Baldissara L (2016) Politiche della memoria e spazio del ricordo in Europa. Il Mulino, Bologna, 1:6–20
Baratta A (1989) Funzioni strumentali e funzioni simboliche del diritto penale. Lineamenti di una teoria del bene giuridico. Studi in memoria di Giovanni Tarello, volume II. Giuffrè, Milan
Baratta A (1990) Legittimazione strumentale e funzione simbolica del sistema punitivo. Per un uso "alternativo" del diritto penale. Difesa penale 29:19–31
Barak-Erez D, Scharia D (2011) Freedom of Speech, Support for Terrorism, and the Challenge of Global Constitutional Law. National Security Journal 2:1–30
Barbosa Delgado FR (2012) El margen nacional de apreciación y sus límites en la libertad de expresión: análisis comparado de los sistemas europeo e interamericano de derechos humanos. Universidad Externado de Colombia, Bogota
Bargiacchi P (2008) Cenni sulle tendenze della prassi internazionale ed europea in tema di negazionismo. Rivista della cooperazione giuridica internazionale 10:70–86
Bartole S, De Sena P, Zagrebelsky V (2012) Commentario breve alla Convenzione europea dei diritti dell'uomo. Giuffré, Milan
Bartoli R (2008) Lotta al terrorismo internazionale. Tra diritto penale del nemico, jus in bello del criminale e annientamento del nemico assoluto. Giappichelli, Turin
Baruch MO (2013) Des lois indignes? Les historiens, la politique et le droit. Tallandier, Paris
Bassiouni MC (2011) Crimes Against Humanity. Historical Evolution and Contemporary Application. Cambridge University Press, New York
Bastian T (1997) Auschwitz und Auschwitzlüge. Beck, Munich
Batista Gonzáles MP (1997) Provocación y apología. El art. 18 del nuevo Código Penal. Revista de la Facultad de Derecho de la Universidad Complutense 88:63–68
Bauman Z (2000) Liquid Modernity. Polity Press, London
Bazyler M (2016) Holocaust, Genocide, and the Law: A Quest for Justice in a Post-Holocaust World. Oxford University Press, Oxford
Beale SS (2000) Federalizing Hate Crimes: Symbolic Politics, Expressive Law, or Tool for Criminal Enforcement? Boston University Law Review 80:1227–1254
Behrens P (2012) Genocide and the Question of Motives. Journal of International Criminal Justice 10:501–523
Behrens P, Jensen O, Terry N (2017) (eds) Holocaust and Genocide Denial: A Contextual Perspective. Routledge, Abingdon-on-Thames
Beisel D (1995) Die Strafbarkeit der Auschwitzlüge. Neue Juristische Wochenschrift 997–1000
Belavusau U (2013) Freedom of Speech. Routledge, London

Belavusau U (2016) Introductory Note to *Perinçek v. Switzerland* (2015): Judgement of the Grand Chamber (ECtHR). International Legal Materials 55:627–629

Belavusau U (2017) Hate Speech. In: Grote R, Wolfrum R, Lachenmann F (eds) The Max Planck Encyclopedia of Comparative Constitutional Law. Oxford University Press, Oxford, pp 1–12

Belavusau U, Gliszczyńska-Grabias A (2017) (eds) Law and Memory: Towards Legal Governance of History. Cambridge University Press, Cambridge

Belavusau U, Gliszczynska-Grabias A (2017) Memory Laws: Mapping a New Subject in Comparative Law and Transitional Justice. In: Belavusau U, Gliszczyńska-Grabias A (eds) Law and Memory: Towards Legal Governance of History. Cambridge University Press, Cambridge

Benjamin W (1997) Sul concetto di storia. Einaudi, Turin

Benz W (1992) Legenden Lügen Vorurteile. Ein Wörterbuch für Zeitgeschichte. Deutscher Taschenbuch, Monaco

Berger BL (2014) Constitutional Principles. In: Dubber MD, Hörnle T (eds) The Oxford Handbook of Criminal Law. Oxford University Press, Oxford, pp 422–444

Bernal del Castillo J (2016) La justificación y enaltecimiento del genocidio en la Reforma del Código Penal de 2015. Revista para el Análisis del Derecho 2:1–30

Bidasolo MC et al. (2015) Comentarios al código penal. Tirant, Madrid

Bifulco D (2012) Negare l'evidenza, Diritto e storia di fronte alla 'menzogna' di Auschwitz. Franco Angeli, Milan

Bifulco D (2015) Il disincanto costituzionale. Profili teorici della laicità. Franco Angeli, Milan

Bilbao Ubillos JM (2008) La negación del holocausto en la jurisprudencia del Tribunal Europeo de Derechos humanos: la endeble justificación de tipos penales contrarios a la libertad de expression. Revista de Derecho Político (UNED) 71–72:19–56

Bilbao Ubillos JM (2009) *La negación de un genocidio no es una conducta punible (comentario de la STC 235/2007).* Revista Española de Derecho Constitucional 85:314–328

Bin R (1992) Diritti e argomenti. Il bilanciamento degli interessi nella giurisprudenza costituzionale. Giuffrè, Milan

Bird P (2015) Virtual Child Pornography Laws and the Constraints Imposed by the First Amendment. Barry Law Review 16:161–177

Bisset A (2012) Truth Commissions and Criminal Courts. Cambridge University Press, Cambridge

Bizimana JD (2001) L'Eglise et le génocide au Ruanda: les Péres blancs et le négationnisme. L'Harmattan, Paris

Bloch P (2006) Response to Professor Fronza's The Punishment of Negationism. Vermont Law Review 30:627–643

Boas G, Bischoff JL, Reid NL (2009) Elements of Crimes Under International Law. International Criminal Law Practitioner Library Series. Cambridge University Press, New York

Boed R (2002) Individual Criminal Responsibility for Violations of Article 3 Common to the Geneva Convention of 1949 and of Additional Protocol II Thereto in the Case Law of the International Criminal Tribunal for Rwanda. Criminal Law Forum 13:293–322

Bonini S (2003) Quali spazi per una funzione simbolica del diritto penale? Indice penale 491–534

Booysen H (1976) Convention on the Crime of Apartheid. South African Yearbook of International Law 2:56–96

Borgwardt H (2009) Die Strafbarkeit der "Auschwitzlüge". In: Ostendorf H (ed) Rechtsextremismus. Eine Herausforderung für Strafrecht und Strafjustiz. Nomos, Baden-Baden, pp 233–266

Bricola F (1973) Teoria generale del reato. Novissimo Digesto italiano XIX 3–97

Bricola F (1981) Funzione promozionale, tecnica premiale e diritto penale. Questione Criminale 445–460

Bricola F (1984) Tecniche di tutela penale e tecniche alternative di tutela. Funzioni e limiti del diritto penale. Padua

Brunelli D (2016) Attorno alla punizione di negazionismo. Rivista italiana di diritto e procedura penale 2:978–998

Brugger W (2002) The Treatment of Hate Speech in German Constitutional Law (part 1). German Law Journal 3:1–44

Brugger W (2003) The Treatment of Hate Speech in German Constitutional Law (part 2). German Law Journal 4:1–44

Brugger W (2005) Ban on or Protection of Hate Speech? Some Observations Based on German and American Law. Tulane European and Civil Law Forum 17:1–21

Brunet F (2012) De la censure constitutionnelle de la loi "visant à réprimer la contestation de l'existence des génocides reconnus par la loi". Revue de science criminelle et de droit pénal comparé 2:343–354

Buratti A (2012) L'uso della storia nella giurisprudenza della Corte europea dei diritti dell'uomo. Rivista telematica giuridica dell'Associazione italiana dei Costituzionalisti 2:1–18

Burz A (2013) Redefining Apartheid in International Criminal Law. Criminal Law Forum 24:205–233

Buyse A (2014) Dangerous Expressions: The ECHR, Violence and Free Speech. International and Comparative Law Quarterly 63:491–503

Buzzelli S, De Paolis M, Speranzoni A (2012) La ricostruzione giudiziale dei crimini nazifascisti in Italia. Questioni preliminari. Giappichelli, Turin

Cadoppi A (2010) (ed) Laicità, valori e diritto penale. The Moral Limits of the Criminal Law. In ricordo di Joel Feinberg. Giuffrè, Milan

Cajani L (2008–2009) Historians between Memory Wars and Criminal Law: the Case of European Union. Annales International Society for Historic Didactis XXIX–XXX:39–55

Cajani L (2011) Criminal Laws on History. The case of the European Union. Historein, How to deal with tormented pasts 3:19–29

Calamandrei P (1939) Il giudice e lo storico. Rivista di diritto processuale civile XVII:105–128

Calamandrei P (1957) Verità e verosimiglianza nel processo civile. In: Studi sul processo civile IV. Cedam, Padua, pp 111–139

Camby JP (2012) La loi et le négationnisme: de l'exploitation de l'histoire au droit au débat sur l'histoire. Les Petites Affiches 70:11–22

Campisi MC (2014) From a Duty to Remember to an Obligation to Memory? Memory as Reparation in the Jurisprudence of the Inter-American Court of Human Rights. International Journal of Conflict and Violence 8:62–74

Cancio Meliá M (2005) "Feindstrafrecht"? Zeitschrift für die gesamte Strafrechtswissenschaft 117:267–289

Cancio Meliá M (2010) Los delitos de terrorismo estructura típica e injusto. Editorial Reus, Madrid

Cancio Meliá M, Jakobs G (2003) Derecho penal del enemigo. Madrid

Cancio Meliá M, Jara G (2006) (eds) Derecho penal del enemigo, el discurso penal de la exclusión. Edisofer, Madrid

Canestrari S (2006) Laicità e diritto penale nelle democrazie costituzionali. In: Dolcini E, Paliero CE (eds) Studi in onore di Giorgio Marinucci, I. Giuffrè, Milan, pp 139–166

Canestrari S, Cornacchia L, De Simone G (2007) Manuale di diritto penale. Parte generale. Il Mulino, Bologna

Caputo M (2014) La "menzogna di Auschwitz", le "verità" del diritto penale. La criminalizzazione del c.d. negazionismo tra ordine pubblico, dignità e senso di umanità. Diritto penale contemporaneo. Online: https://www.penalecontemporaneo.it/upload/1389084288CAPUTO%202014a.pdf. Accessed 1 October 2017

Caroli P (2015) La Corte europea in tema di offese pubbliche contro gli ebrei. Diritto penale contemporaneo online http://www.penalecontemporaneo.it/d/4368-la-corte-europea-in-tema-di-offese-pubbliche-contro-gli-ebrei. Accessed 16 July 2017

Caroli P (2017) La giustizia di transizione in Italia. L'esperienza dopo la seconda guerra mondiale. http://cprints-phd.biblio.unitn.it/1981/1/Paolo_Caroli_-_Tesi_dottorato_.pdf. Accessed 13 August 2017

Cartier E (2006) Histoire et droit: rivalité ou complémentarité? Revue francaise de droit constitutionnel 67:509–534

Caruso C (2008) Tra il negare e l'istigare c'è di mezzo il giustificare: su una decisione del tribunale Costituzionale spagnolo. Quaderni Costituzionali 3:635–639

Caruso C (2013) La libertà di espressione in azione. Contributo a una teoria costituzionale del discorso pubblico. Bononia University Press, Bologna

Caruso C (2016) Tolleranza per gli intolleranti? Una ragionevole apologia della libertà di espressione. DPCE online 1:99–114

Caruso C (2017) L'hate speech a Strasburgo. Il pluralismo militante del sistema convenzionale. Quaderni costituzionali 4:3–45

Cassano M (2013) Negazionismo e opportunità di una risposta penale. Criminalia 271–284

Cassese A (2002) Genocide. In: Cassese A, Gaeta P, Jones JRWD (eds) The Rome Statute of the International Criminal Court: A Commentary. Oxford University Press, Oxford, pp 335–351

Català A, Pérez Z (2007) La negación del holocausto. A propósito de la STC 235/2007, de 7 de noviembre de 2007. Revista Europea de Derechos Fundamentales 10:181–196

Cavaliere A (2016) La discussione intorno alla punibilità del negazionismo, i principi di offensività e libera manifestazione del pensiero e la funzione della pena. Rivista italiana di diritto e procedura penale 2:999–1015

Ceretti A (2004) Presentazione. In: Garland D, La cultura del controllo: crimine e ordine sociale nel mondo contemporaneo. Il Saggiatore, Milan

Clark RS (1990) Crimes Against Humanity at Nuremberg. In: Ginsburgs G, Kudriavtsev VN (eds) The Nuremberg Trial and International Law. Nijhoff, Boston, pp 177–212

Cohen-Almagor R (2009) Holocaust Denial is a Form of Hate Speech. Amsterdam Law Forum 2:33–42

Cohen Jonathan G (1999) L'apologie de Pétain devant la Cour européenne des droits de l'homme. Revue universelle des droits de l'homme 38:366–388

Cooper J, Williams AM (1999) Hate Speech, Holocaust Denial and International Human Rights Law. European Human Rights Law Review 6:593–613

Corboz B (2002) Les infractions en droit suisse. Volume II. Staempfli, Bern

Cortese F (2012) Memoria e diritto. Contributo per un approccio non necessariamente centripeto (tra storia, giustizia e letteratura). Rassegna Di Diritto Pubblico Europeo, 2:19–45

Cortese F (2016) What can the Perincek case teach? DPCE online http://www.dpceonline.it/index.php/dpceonline/article/view/93. Accessed 16 July 2017

Costa-Lascoux J (1976) La Loi du 1. juillet 1972 et la protection pénale des immigrés contre la discrimination raciale. Droit social 5:181–187

Couvrat P (1993) Les infractions contre les personnes dans le nouveau Code Pénal. Revue de Science Criminelle et de Droit Comparé 3:469–480

Cryer R (2009) The Definitions of International Crimes in the Al Bashir Arrest Warrant Decision. Journal of International Criminal Justice 7:283–296

Cryer R, Friman H, Robinson D, Wilmshurst E (2014) An Introduction to International Criminal Law and Procedure. Cambridge University Press, Cambridge

Cuerda Arnau ML (2008) Terrorismo y libertades políticas, Teoría & Derecho. Revista de Pensamiento Jurídico (El Estado de Derecho Frente a la amenaza del nuevo terrorismo) 3:88–103

Cueva Fernández R (2012) A propósito de la Sentencia del Tribunal Supremo 259/2011: Discurso del odio, incitación y derecho al honor colectivo. ¿Una nueva vuelta de tuerca contra la prohibición del hate speech? Eunomia 105–120

Cullen A (2008) Definition of Non-International Armed Conflict in the Rome Statute of the International Criminal Court: An Analysis of the Threshold of Application Contained in Article 8(2)(f). Journal of Conflict and Security Law 12:419–445

Cupido M (2011) The Policy Underlying Crimes Against Humanity: Practical Reflections on a Theoretical Debate. Criminal Law Forum 22:275–309

Damaska M (1991) The face of Justice and State Authority. A Comparative Approach to the Legal Process. Yale University Press, New Haven

Damaska M (2006) The Uncertain Self-Identity of International Criminal Courts. Criminalia: 9–55

Damaska M (2007) What is the Point of International Criminal Justice? Chicago Kent Law Review, 83:329–364

Danti-Juan M (2012) Contestation de l'existence d'un génocide. Revue pénitentiaire et de droit pénal 2:399–402

de la Rosa Cortina JM (2007) Negacionismo y revisionismo del genocidio: perspectiva penal y constitucional. Diario La Ley 6842

de Pablo Serrano A, Tapia Ballesteros P (2017) Discurso del odio: problemas en la delimitación del bien jurídico y en la nueva configuración del tipo penal. Diario La Ley 8911

Décima (2016) Terreur et métamorphose. À propos de la loi n° 2016- 731 du 3 juin 2016 sur la lutte contre le terrorisme. Dalloz, Paris

Decoeur H (2014) The Judgement of the European Court of Human Rights in Perinçek v. Switzerland: Reducing Genocide to Law. Cambridge Journal of International and Comparative Law 2:345–367

Delage C, Goodrich P (2012) (eds) The Scene of the Mass Crime: History, Film, and International Tribunals. Routledge, London

Della Morte G (2011) Le amnistie nel diritto internazionale. Cedam, Padua

Della Morte G (2014) L'introduzione del reato di negazionismo in Italia. Una prospettiva critica alla luce dell'ordinamento internazionale. Diritto pubblico comparato ed europeo 3:1181–1203

Della Morte G (2016) Sulla legge che introduce la punizione delle condotte negazionistiche nell'ordinamento italiano: tre argomenti per una critica severa. SIDI Blog, online: http://www.sidiblog.org/2016/06/22/sulla-legge-che-introduce-la-punizione-delle-condotte-negazionistiche-nellordinamento-italiano-tre-argomenti-per-una-critica-severa/. Accessed 17 November 2017

Della Morte G (2016) When is a criminal prohibition of genocide denial justified? The *Perinçek* Case and the risk of a double standard. Questions of International Law, online: http://www.qil-qdi.org/criminal-prohibition-genocide-denial-justified-perincek-case-risk-double-standard/. Accessed 17 November 2017

Della Morte G, Abdelgawad EL, Martin-Chenut K (2007) La clémence saisie par le droit: Amnistie, prescription et grâce en droit international et comparé. Collection de l'UMR de droit comparé de Paris 14, Paris

Delmas-Marty M (1980) Les chemins de la répression. Presses Universitaires de France, Paris

Delmas-Marty M (2004) Le flou du droit. Du code pénal aux droits de l'homme. Puf, Paris

Delmas-Marty M (2004) Le relatif et l'universel. Les forces imaginantes du droit. I. Seuil, Paris

Delmas-Marty M (2006) Le pluralisme ordonné. Les forces imaginantes du droit. II. Seuil, Paris

Delmas-Marty M (2010) Libertés et sûreté dans un monde dangereux. Seuil, Paris

Delmas-Marty M (2016) Aux quatre vents du monde. Petit guide de navigation sur l'océan de la mondialisation. Seuil, Paris

Delmas-Marty M, Fouchard I, Fronza E, Neyret L (2013) Le crime contre l'humanité. PUF, Paris

Delmas-Marty M, Mathieu-Izorche ML (2000) Marge nationale d'appréciation et internationalisation du droit: réflexions sur la validité formelle d'un droit commun pluraliste. Revue internationale de droit comparé 52:753–780

Derieux E (2012) Sanction de la contestation de génocides et garantie de la liberté d'expression. Revue Lamy Droit de l'Immatériel 80:6–8

Di Cesare SD (2012) Se Auschwitz è nulla: contro il negazionismo. Nuovo Melangolo, Genoa

Di Giovine A (2006) Il passato che non passa. «Eichmann di carta» e repressione penale. Diritto pubblico comparato e europeo 1:XIII–XXVIII

Di Martino A (2017) Assassini della memoria: strategie argomentative in tema di rilevanza (penale?) del negazionismo. In: Cocco G (ed) Trattato breve di diritto penale. Cedam, Padua, pp 193–216

Dietz S (1995) Die Lüge von der "Auschwitzlüge" - Wie weit reicht das Recht auf Meinungsäußerung? Kritische Justiz 28:210–222

Díez Ripollés JL (2003) El Derecho Penal Simbólico Y Los Efectos De La Pena. In: Arroyo Zapatero L, Neumann U, Nieto Martín A (eds) Crítica Y Justificación Del Derecho Penal En El Cambio De Siglo. Ediciones De La Universidad De Castilla, Cuenca, pp 147–172

Dolz Lago MJ (2016) Oído a los delitos de odio (algunas cuestiones claves sobre la reforma del art. 510 CP por LO 1/2015. Diario La Ley 8712

Domenico RP (1991) Italian fascists on trial 1943–1948. University of North Carolina Press. Chapel Hill

Donini M (2001) Alla ricerca di un disegno. Scritti sulle riforme penali in Italia. Cedam, Padua

Donini M (2001) Ragioni e limiti della fondazione del diritto penale sulla Carta costituzionale. Il significato dell'esperienza italiana. Foro italiano V:29–46

Donini M (2003) Alla ricerca di un disegno. Scritti sulle riforme penali in Italia. Cedam, Padua

Donini M (2004) Il volto attuale dell'illecito penale. La democrazia penale tra differenziazione e sussidiarietà. Giuffrè, Milan

Donini M (2007) Diritto penale del nemico. Scritti in onore di Federico Stella. Jovene, Naples

Donini M (2007) Diritto penale penale di lotta vs diritto penale del nemico. In: Gamberini A, Orlandi R (eds) Delitto politico e diritto penale del nemico. Monduzzi, Bologna, pp 73–98

Donini M (2008) «Danno» e «offesa» nella cd. tutela penale dei sentimenti. Note su morale e sicurezza come beni giuridici, a margine della categoría dell'«offense» di Joel Feinberg. Rivista italiana di diritto e procedura penale 4:546–1593

Donini M (2009) La gestione penale del passaggio dal Fascismo alla democrazia in Italia. Appunti sulla memoria storica e l'elaborazione del passato 'mediante il diritto penale'. Materiali per una storia della cultura giuridica 1:183–216

Donini M (2009) Principi costituzionali e sistema penale. Modello e programma. IUS17@unibo.it 421–453

Donini M (2012) L'eredità di Bricola e il costituzionalismo penale come metodo. Diritto penale contemporaneo 2:51–74

Donini M (2013) Il diritto giurisprudenziale penale. Collisioni vere e apparenti con la legalità e sanzioni dell'illecito interpretativo, in Diritto penale contemporaneo, online, 6-35.

Donini M, Papa M (2007) (eds) Diritto penale del nemico. Un dibattito internazionale. Giuffrè, Milan

Doward J (2017) New online generation takes up Holocaust denial https://www.theguardian.com/world/2017/jan/22/online-conspiracy-theories-feed-holocaust-denial. Accessed 13 August 2017

Droin N (2010) Les limitations à la liberté d'expression dans la loi sur la presse du 29 juillet 1881 - Disparition, permanence et résurgence du délit d'opinion. Fondation Varenne. Collection de Thèses n. 35, Paris

Droin N (2013) L'avenir del les lois mémorielles à la lumière de la décision du Conseil constitutionnel du 28 février 2012 relative à la loi visant à réprimer la contestation de l'existence des génocides reconnus par la loi. Revue française de droit constitutionnel 95:589–610

Droin N (2014) État des lieux de la répression du négationnisme en France et en droit comparé. Revue Trimestrielle des Droits de l'Homme 98:363–394

Drumbl MA (2007) Atrocity, Punishment, and International Law. Cambridge University Press, Cambridge

Du Bois-Pedain A (2007) Transitional Amnesty in South Africa. Cambridge University Press, New York

Dubber MD (2004) Toward a Constitutional Law of Crime and Punishment. Hastings Law Journal 55:1–77

Dubber M, Hörnle T (2014) Criminal Law: A Comparative Approach. Oxford University Press, Oxford

Dubuisson F (2007) L'incrimination générique du négationnisme est-elle conciliable avec le droit à la liberté d'expression. Revue de Droit Université Libre de Bruxelles 35:135–195

Eden P (2014) The Role of the Rome Statute in the Criminalization of Apartheid. Journal of International Criminal Justice 12:171–191

Eiroa PD, Otero JM (eds) (2007) Memoria y Derecho Penal. Fabián J. Di Plácido Editor, Buenos Aires

Elholm T, Colson R (2016) The Symbolic Purpose of EU Criminal Law. In: Colson R, Field S (eds) EU Criminal Justice and the Challenges of Diversity: Legal Cultures in the Area of Freedom, Security and Justice. Cambridge University Press, Cambridge, pp 48–64

Elster J (2004) Closing the Books: Transitional Justice in Historical perspective. Cambridge University Press, Cambridge

Feinberg J (1974) Doing and Deserving: Essays in the Theory of Responsibility. Princeton University Press, New Jersey

Feldman JP (1998) Peut-on dire impunément n'importe quoi sur la Shoah? Revue de droit international et de droit comparé 229–271

Feijoo Sánchez BJ (1998) Reflexiones sobre los delitos de genocidio (art. 607 del Código Penal). La Ley 6:2267–2285

Fernández Hernández A (2010) Delito de genocidio (art. 607). In: Álvarez Garcia FJ, Gonzáles Cussac JL (eds) Comentarios a la Reforma Penal de 2010. Tirant lo Blanc, Valencia, pp 533–536

Ferrajoli L (2009) Diritto e ragione. Teoria del garantismo penale. Laterza, Bari

Fiandaca G (2013) Populismo politico e populismo giudiziario. Criminalia 95–121

Findlay M, Henham R (2012) (eds) Transforming International Criminal Justice. Retributive and restorative justice in the trial process. Routledge, London

Finer SE, Bogdanor V, Rudden B (1995) Comparing Constitutions. Clarendon Press, Chicago

Finkelstein C (2000) Positivism and the Notion of an Offense. California Law Review 335–394

Finkielkraut A (1982) L'avenir d'une négation. Réflexion sur la question du genocide. Seuil, Paris

Fiore C (1972) I reati di opinione. Cedam, Padua

Fiore C (2002) I reati di opinione. In: Moccia S (ed) Diritti dell'uomo e sistema penale. Edizioni Scientifiche Italiane, Naples, pp 234–257

Fischer T (1986) Öffentlicher Friede und Gedankenäußerung. Dissertation. Würzburg University

Fischer T (2011) Störung des Öffentlichen Friedens (§ 130 Abs. 4 StGB): Strafwürdigkeit als Tatbestandsmerkmal. Zugleich eine Besprechung von BVerfG, Beschl. vom 4. November 2009 - 1 BvR 2150/08. In: Paeffgen HU (ed) Strafrechtswissenschaft als Analyse und Konstruktion. Festschrift für Ingeborg Puppe zum 70. Geburtstag. Duncker & Humblot, Berlin, pp 1119–1141

Fischer T (2017) Strafgesetzbuch und Nebengesetze, § 130 StGB. Beck, Munich

Fletcher GP (1998) Basic Concepts of Criminal Law. Oxford University Press, Oxford

Fletcher M, Lööf R, Gilmore B (2008) EU Criminal Law and Justice. Edward Elgar, Cheltenham

Flores M (2007) Il genocidio degli armeni. Il Mulino, Bologna

Flores M (2007) Revisionismo storiografico. In: http://www.treccani.it/enciclopedia/revisionismo-storiografico_%28Enciclopedia-Italiana%29/. Accessed 17 November 2017

Focardi F (2014) Il cattivo tedesco e il buon italiano. Laterza, Bari

Focardi F, Klinkhammer L (2004) The question of Fascist Italy's war crimes: the construction of a self-acquitting myth (1943–1948). Journal of Modern Italian Studies 3:330–348

Fornasari G (2013) Giustizia di transizione e diritto penale. Giappichelli, Turin

Fornasari G (2015) Giustizia di transizione. Enciclopedia del Diritto. Annali VIII:547–570

Fouchard I (2014) Crimes internationaux. Entre internationalisation du droit pénal et pénalisation du droit international. Bruylant, Brussels

Fourie P, Meyer M (2013) The Politics of AIDS Denialism: South Africa's Failure to Respond. Routledge, London

Fraisseix P (2006) Le droit mémoriel. Revue française de droit constitutionnel 3:483–508

Francillon J (2010) Questions prioritaires de constitutionnalité en matière d'infractions de presse (délits d'apologie de crimes de guerre, de contestation de l'existence de crimes l'humanité, et de diffamation), observations à propos de Crim. 2 et 19 mars 2010, n° 09-81.238 09-81.027, et 7 mai 2010, n° 09-80.774. Revue Sciences criminelles et Droit Comparé 3:640–655

Francillon J (2012) Pénalisation de la contestation de l'existence d'un génocide reconnu par la loi. Revue de science criminelle et de droit pénal comparé 1:179–182

Francillon J (2013a) Apologie de crimes contre l' humanité. Absence de portée normative de la "Loi Taubira" du 21 mai 2001 (Crim. 5 février 2013 n. 11-85.909). Revue de sciences criminelles et de droit comparé 1:1–24

Francillon J (2013b) Pénalisation des discours négationnistes et liberté d'expression. Mélanges offerts à Claude Bontems. L'Harmattan, Paris

Frangi M (2005) Les lois mémorielles: de l'expression de la volonté générale au législateur historien, Revue de droit public 1:241–266

Freeman M (2006) Truth Commission and Procedural fairness. Cambridge University Press, New York

Fronza E (2009) Italia. In: Ambos K, Malarino E, Elsner G (eds) Justicia de transicion. Konrad Adenauer Stiftung, Montevideo

Fronza E (2015) Negazionismo. Enciclopedia del Diritto Annali VIII:633–658

Fronza E (2016) Criminalizzazione del dissenso o tutela del consenso. Profili critici del negazionismo come reato. Rivista italiana di diritto e procedura penale 2:1016–1033

Fronza E (2016) Il crimine di genocidio. In: Amati E, Costi M, Fronza E, Lobba P, Maculan E, Vallini A (eds) Introduzione al diritto penale internazionale. Giappicheli, Turin, pp 323–350

Fronza E (2017) L'introduzione dell'aggravante di negazionismo. Diritto penale e processo 2:155–167

Fronza E, Cortese F (2017) Il *caso Perinçek* davanti alla Corte europea dei diritti dell'uomo. Quando il giudice fa la storia. In: Arslan A, Berti F, De Stefani P (eds) Il paese perduto. A cent'anni dal genocidio armeno. Edizioni Angelo Guerini, Milan, pp 213–234

Fronza E, Fornasari G (2009) (eds) Il superamento del passato e il superamento del presente. La punizione delle violazioni sistematiche dei diritti umani nell'esperienza argentina e colombiana. Università degli Studi di Trento, Trento

Fronza E, Gamberini A (2013) Le ragioni che contrastano l'introduzione del negazionismo come reato. Diritto penale contemporaneo, online: https://www.penalecontemporaneo.it/upload/1383000563FRONZA%20GAMBERINI%202013.pdf. Accessed 17 November 2017

Fronza E, Tricot J (2003) Fonction symbolique et droit pénal international. Une analyse du discours des Tribunaux pénaux internationaux. In: Fronza E, Manacorda S (eds) La justice pénale internationale dans les décisions des tribunaux ad hoc. Dalloz-Giuffré, Milan

Galazzo G (2016) Reato di negazionismo e libertà di manifestazione del pensiero: una riflessione. Giurisprudenza penale 9:1–10

Galli C (2007) Diritto e politica: profili teorici e politici del loro rapporto. In: Gamberini A, Orlandi R (eds) Delitto politico e diritto penale del nemico. Monduzzi, Bologna, pp 45–60

Gamberini A (1973) I "pensieri leciti" della Corte Costituzionale. Rivista italiana di diritto e procedura penale 1:161–184

Gamberini A (2005) Profili di diritto penale sostanziale dell'azione di contrasto al terrorismo. Relazione svolta presso la Corte di Cassazione nel 2005

Gamberini A (2013) Tutela della memoria e diritto penale: una riflessione sistematica e comparativa a partire dal reato di negazionismo. Diritto penale contemporaneo. Online: https://www.penalecontemporaneo.it/d/2716-tutela-della-memoria-e-diritto-penale-una-riflessione-sistematica-e-comparativa-a-partire-dal-reato. Accessed 17 November 2017

Gamberini A, Insolera G (2006) Legislazione penale compulsiva, buone ragioni e altro. A proposito della riforma dei reati di opinione. In: Insolera G (ed) La legislazione penale compulsive. Cedam, Padua, 2006, pp 135–143

Garapon A (1985) L'Ane portant des reliques: essai sur le rituel judiciaire. Le Centurion, Paris

Garapon A (1995) Bien juger: essai sur le rituel judiciaire. Odile Jacob, Paris

Garapon A (2002) Des crimes qu'on ne peut ni punir ni pardonner: pour une justice internationale. Odile Jacob, Paris

Garapon A (2008) Peut-on réparer l'histoire? Colonisation, esclavage, Shoah. Odile Jacob, Paris

García Arán M (2004) Artículo 607. In: Córdoba R, García Arán M (eds) Comentarios al Código penal, Parte especial, Tomo II. Marcial Pons, Madrid, pp 2688–2703

Garibian S (2006) Pour une lecture juridique des quatre lois «mémorielles». Esprit 322:1–18

Garibian S (2008) Taking Denial Seriously: Genocide Denial and Freedom of Speech in the French Law. Cardozo Journal of Conflict Resolution 9:479–488

Garibian S (2013) (Legally) binding memory? Uncertainties arising from decision no. 2012-647 DC of France's Constitutional Council'. Droit et Cultures 66:25–56

Garibian S (2014) Ghosts Also Die: Resisting Disappearance through the 'Right to the Truth' and the Juicios por la Verdad in Argentina. Journal of International Criminal Justice 12:515-538

Garibian S (2016) On the Breaking of Consensus: the Perincek case, the Armenian Genocide and International Criminal Law

Garland D (2002) Beyond the culture of control. Critical Review of International Social and Political Philosophy 7:160–189

Gasanabo JD, Simon DJ, Ensign MM (eds) (2015) Confronting Genocide in Rwanda: Dehumanization, Denial, and Strategies for Prevention. Apidama, Bogota

Gascón Cuenca A (2016) El discurso del odio en el ordenamiento jurídico español: su adecuación a los estándares internacionales de *protección*. Aranzadi, Pamplona

Geilen G (2008) Unvorsätzliche "Auschwitzlüge"? Bemerkungen zu § 130 Abs. 3 StGB. Festschrift für Rolf Dietrich. *Herzberg*

Gelber K (2016) Free Speech After 9/11. Oxford University Press, Oxford

Gil Gil A (2009) La Justicia de Transición en España: de la Amnistía a la Memoria Histórica. Atelier, Barcelona

Gil Gil A, Maculan E (2016) (eds) Derecho penal internacional. Dykinson, Madrid

Gil Gil A, Maculan E (2017) (eds) Colombia como nuevo modelo para la justicia de transición. Instituto Universitario General Gutiérrez Mellado, Madrid

Gil Gil A, Maculan E (2017) La influencia de las victimas en el tratamiento juridico de la violencia colectiva. Dykinson, Madrid

Ginzburg C (1991) Il giudice e lo storico. Considerazioni a margine del processo Sofri. Einaudi, Turin

Ginzburg C (2002) Beweis, Gedächtnis, Vergessen. Memory 30:50–60

Girard R (1987) Things hidden since the foundation of the world. Stanford University Press, California

Glet A (2011) Sozialkonstruktion und strafrechtliche Verfolgung von Hasskriminalität in Deutschland. Dissertation. Berlin

Gliszczyńska-Grabias A (2013) Penalizing Holocaust Denial: A View from Europe. In: Small CA (ed) Global Antisemitism: A Crisis of Modernity. Brill-Nijhoff, Leiden, pp 237–256

Gómez Tomillo M (ed) (2011) Comentarios al Código Penal. Lex Nova, Valladolid

Gordon RSC (2013) Scolpitelo nei cuori. L'Olocausto nella cultura italiana. Bollati Boringhieri, Turin

Gorton S (2015) The Uncertain Future of Genocide Denial Laws in the European Union. George Washington International Law 47:421–445

Grabenwarter C (2014) European Convention on Human Rights: Commentary. CH Beck/Hart/Nomos, Helbing Lichtenhahn

Graf JP (2013) BGH-Rechsprechung Strafrecht 2012–2013: die wichtigsten Entscheidungen mit Erläuterung und Praxishinweisen. De Gruyter, Berlin

Gramsci A (1994) Letters from Prison. Columbia University Press, New York

Grandjean G (2011) La répression du négationnisme en Belgique: de la réussite législative au blocage politique. Droit et Société 1:137–160

Grande E (2015) I mobili confini della libertà di espressione negli Stati Uniti e il metro della paura. Questione Giustizia 4:47–61

Greer S (2006) The European Convention on Human Rights. Achievements, Problems and Prospects. Cambridge University Press, Cambridge
Greppi E (2001) I crimini di guerra e contro l'umanità nel diritto internazionale. Utet, Turin
Grimm D (2011) The Holocaust Denial Decision of the Federal Constitutional Court of Germany. In: Hare I, Weinstein J (eds) Extreme Speech and Democracy, Oxford University Press, Oxford, pp 557–576
Guembe MJ (2005) Reopening of trials for crimes committed by the Argentine military dictatorship. http://www.scielo.br/scielo.php?pid=S1806-64452005000200008&script=sci_arttext&tlng=es. Accessed 13 August 2017
Gunter MM (2011) Armenian History and the Question of Genocide. Palgrave Macmillan, London
Gutiérrez Ramírez LM, Rodríguez JR (2016) Una comisión de la verdad en el modelo colombiano de justicia transicional: aproximación a través de la historia reciente y la experiencia comparada. Jurídicas 10:40–60
Guyaz A (1996) L'incrimination de la discrimination raciale. Verlag, Bern
Halbwachs M (1925) Les cadres sociaux de la mémoire. Presses Universitaires de France, Paris
Halbwachs M (1950) La mémoire collective. Presses Universitaires de France, Paris
Hamon F (2012) Le Conseil constitutionnel et les lois mémorielles. Revue française de droit administratif 2:7–11
Harcourt BE (1999) The Collapse of the Harm Principle. Journal of Criminal Law and Criminology 109–194
Harcourt BE (2002) Joel Feinberg on crime and punishment: exploring the relationship between "the moral limits of the criminal law" and "the expressive function of punishment". Buffalo Criminal Law Review 145–172
Hare I, Weinstein J (2011) (eds) Extreme Speech and Democracy. Oxford University Press, Oxford
Hartog F, Baruch MO, Thomas Y, Gaudard PY (1998) Vérité judiciaire, vérité historique. Le Débat 102:4–44
Hassemer W (1989) Symbolischer Strafrecht und Rechtsgüterschutz. Neue Zeitschrift für Strafrecht 170–188
Hassemer W (2008) Das Symbolische am symbolischen Strafrecht. In: Hassemer W (ed) Strafrecht. Sein Selbstverständnis, seine Welt, Berlin
Hassemer W (2009) Warum Strafe sein muss. Ein Plädoyer. Ullstein, Berlin
Haupt CE (2005) Regulating Hate Speech - Damned If You Do and Damned If You Don't: Lessons Learned from Comparing The German and U.S. Approaches. Boston University International Law Journal 23
Hayner P (1994) Fifteen Truth Commissions - 1974 to 1994: A Comparative Study. Human Rights Quarterly 16:597–665
Heinze E (2016) Hate speech and democratic citizenship. Oxford University Press, Oxford
Heinze E (2017) Beyond 'Memory Laws': Towards a General Theory of Law and Historical Discourse. In: Belavusau U, Gliszczyńska-Grabias A (eds) Law and Memory: Addressing Historical Injustice by Law. Cambridge University Press, Cambridge
Heller KJ (2011) The Nuremberg Military Tribunals and the Origins of International Criminal Law. Oxford University Press, Oxford
Hellmann M, Gartner J (2011) Neues beim Volksverhetzungstatbestand - Europäische Vorgaben und ihre Umsetzung. Neue Juristische Wochenschrift 961–966
Helz M (2012) The Content and Context of Hate Speech: Rethinking Regulation and Responses. Cambridge University Press, Cambridge
Hennebel L, Hochmann T (eds) (2011) Genocide Denials and the Law. Oxford University Press, Oxford
Herlin-Karnell E (2012) The constitutional Dimension of European Criminal Law. Hart, Portland
Higwedere P, Essex M (2010) AIDS Denialism and Public Health Practice. AIDS and Behavior 14:237–247

Hervieu N (2014) Le négationnisme, prisme révélateur du dilemme européen face à lutte contre l'extrémisme. Revue des droits de l'homme online https://revdh.revues.org/503. Accessed 16 July 2017

Hildebrandt M (2007) European Criminal Law and European Identity. Criminal Law and Philosophy 1:57–78

Hill LE (1989) The trial of Ernst Zundel. Revisionism and the Law in Canada. http://motlc.wiesenthal.com/site/pp.asp?c=gvKVLcMVIuG&b=395157. Accessed 13 August 2017

Hochmann T (2011) Faurisson, «falsificateur de la jurisprudence»? Droit et Cultures 61:235–256

Hochmann T (2012) Le négationnisme face aux limites de la liberté d'expression. étude de droit comparé. Pedone, Paris

Hochmann T (2013) Le problème des lois dites «mémorielles» sera-t-il résolu par les résolutions? La référence à l'article 34-1 de la Constitution dans le discours contemporain sur les relations entre le Parlement et l'histoire. Droit et cultures 66:57–69

Hochmann T (2016) Négationnisme: le Conseil Constitutionnel entre ange et démon. Revue des droits et libertés fondamentaux online http://www.revuedlf.com/droit-constitutionnel/negationnisme-le-conseil-constitutionnel-entre-ange-et-demon/. Accessed 16 July 2017

Hochmann T (2017) Pas de lunettes sous les oeillères: le conseil constitutionnel et le négationnisme. Revue des droits et libertés fondamentaux online http://www.revuedlf.com/droit-constitutionnel/pas-de-lunettes-sous-les-oeilleres-le-conseil-constitutionnel-et-le-negationnisme/. Accessed 16 July 2017

Hörnle T (2001) Anmerkung zu BGH. Neue Juristische Wochenschrift 624–633

Hörnle T (2005) Grob anstössiges Verhalten: strafrechtlicher Schutz von Moral, Gefühlen und Tabus. Verlag, Frankfurt am Main

Hörnle T (2010) Strafe als Reaktion auf grob anstößiges Verhalten am Beispiel von Bekenntnisbeschimpfungen und Holocaust-Leugnen (§§ 166, 130 Abs. 3 StGB). In: Rosenau H, Kim S (eds) Straftheorie und Strafgerechtigkeit. Deutsch-Japanischer Strafrechtsdialog. Peter Lang GmbH Internationaler Verlag der Wissenschaften, Frankfurt am Main/Berlin/Bern/Brussels/New York/Oxford/Vienna

Hörnle T (2015) Theories of Criminalization. In: Dubber MD, Hörnle T (eds) The Oxford Handbook of Criminal Law. Oxford University Press, Oxford, pp 679–701

Husak D (2008) Overcriminalization: The Limits of the Criminal Law. Oxford University Press, Oxford

Huster S (1996) Das Verbot der "Auschwitzlüge", die Meinungsfreiheit und das Bundesverfassungsgericht. Neue Juristische Wochenschrift 487–503

Ibáñez Majar JE (2014) Justicia transicional y las Comisiones de la Verdad. Aufklarung, Bogota

Igounet V (2000) Histoire du négationnisme en France. Seuil, Paris

Igounet V (2012) Robert Faurisson: Portrait d'un négationniste. Denoël, Paris

Imbleau M (2003) La négation du génocide nazi, liberté d'expression ou crime raciste? L'Harmattan, Paris

Insolera G (2006) (ed) La legislazione penale compulsiva. Cedam, Padua

Insolera G (2014) Negazionismo e controllo penale. Ius17@unibo.it Criminal law studies and materials 1:1–25

Jacobi K (2010) Das Ziel des Rechtsgüterschutzes bei der Volksverhetzung. Universität Köln, Cologne

Jahn J (1998) Strafrechtliche Mittel gegen Rechtsextremismus: die Änderungen der §§ 130 und 86a StGB als Reaktion auf fremdenfeindliche Gewalt im Licht der Geschichte des politischen Strafrechts in Deutschland. Frankfurt am Main/Berlin/Bern/New York/Paris/Vienna

Jakobs G (1985) Kriminalisierung im Vorfeld einer Rechstgutverletzung. Zeitschrift für die gesamte Strafrechtswissenschaft 97:751–785

Jakobs G (1995) Das Strafrecht zwischen Funktionalismus und alteuropäischem Prinzipendenken. Zeitschrift für die gesamte Strafrechtswissenschaft 107:843–906

Jakobs G (1997) Norm, Person, Gesellschaft. Vorüberlegungen zu einer Rechtsphilosophie, Berlin

Jakobs G (2000) Das Selbsverständnis der Strafrechtswissenschaft vor der Herausforderung der Gegenwart. In: Eser A, Hassemer W, Burhardt B (eds) Die deutsche Strafrechtswissenschaft vor der Jahrtausendwende, Munich, pp 47–71

Jakobs G (2003) Bürgerstrafrecht und Feindstrafrecht. In: Yu V, Hsu H (eds) Foundations and Limits of Criminal Law and Criminal Procedure. An anthology in memory of Professor Fu-Tseng Hun. Taipeh, pp 41–73

Jakobs G (2005a) Individuum und Person. Zeitschrift für die gesamte Strafrechtswissenschaft 117:247–265

Jakobs G (2005b) Terroristen als Personen im Recht? Zeitschrift für die gesamte Strafrechtswissenschaft 117:839–851

Jakobs G (2006) Enemy Criminal Law? An investigation of the conditions of legality. HRRS 289–312

Jakobs G (2014) On the Theory of Enemy Criminal Law. In: Dubber MD (ed) Foundational Texts in Modern Criminal Law. Oxford University Press, Oxford, pp 415–424

Jansen YO (2014) Denying Genocide or Denying Free Speech? A Case Study of the Application of Rwanda's Genocide Denial Laws. Northwestern Journal International Human Rights 12:191–207

Jean JP (2009) Le procès et l'écriture de l'histoire. Revue de sciences humaines 9:61–74

Jones JRWD (2003) Whose Intent Is it Anyway? – Genocide and the Intent to Destroy a Group. In: Vohrah LC et al. (eds) Man's Inhumanity to Man. Brill-Nijhoff, Boston

Jouanneau B (2008) La Justice et l'Histoire face au négationnisme. Au coeur d'un procès. Fayard, Paris

Kahn RA (1997) Who Takes the Blame? Scapegoating, Legal Responsibility and the Prosecution of Holocaust Revisionists in the Federal Republic of Germany and Canada. Glendale Law Review 16:17–64

Kahn RA (2004) Holocaust Denial and the Law. A Comparative Study. Palgrave, New York

Kahn RA (2006) Cross-Burning, Holocaust Denial and the Development of Hate Speech Law in the United States and Germany. University of Detroit Mercy Law Review 1:163–194

Kalichman SC (2009) Denying AIDS: Conspiracy Theories, Pseudoscience, and Human Tragedy. Springer, New York

Keane D (2007) Attacking Hate Speech under Article 17 of the European Convention on Human Rights. Netherlands Quarterly of Human Rights 25:641–663

Kindhäuser U, Neumann U, Paeffgen HU (eds) (2013) Strafgesetzbuch: Band 2. Nomos, Munich

Kiska R (2012) Hate Speech: a Comparison between the European Court of Human Rights and the United States Supreme Court Jurisprudence. Regent University Law Review 25:107–151

Knauer F (2014) Der Schutz der Menschenwürde im Strafrecht. ZStW 126:305–336

Knechtle JC (2006) When to Regulate Hate Speech. Pennsylvania State Law Review 110:539–578

Knechtle JC (2008) Holocaust Denial and the Concept of Human Dignity in the European Union. Florida State University Law Review 36:41–65

Kolb R, Scalia D (2012) Droit international pénal. Précis. Helbing & Lichtenhahn, Basel

Koltay A (2016) Comparative Perspectives on the Fundamental Freedom of Expression. Wolters-Kluwer, The Netherlands

Koposov N (2017) Memory Laws, Memory Wars. Cambridge University Press, Cambridge

Korman C (1989) Le délit de diffusion des idées racistes. La Semaine Juridique 50

Koskeniemmi M (1989) From Apology to Utopia. The Structure of International Legal Argument. Cambridge University Press, Cambridge

Krauß M (2009) Leipziger Kommentar Strafgesetzbuch: StGB Band 5: §§ 110-145d. De Gruyter, Berlin

Kress C (2001) War Crimes Committed in Non-International Armed Conflict and the Emerging System of International Criminal Justice. Israeli Yearbook on Human Rights 30:103–177

Kress C (2009) The Crime of Genocide and Contextual Elements. A Comment on the ICC Pre-Trial Chamber's Decision in the Al Bashir Case. Journal of International Criminal Justice 7:1–10

Kress C (2009) Vom Nutzen eines deutschen Völkerstrafgesetzbuchs. Nomos, Baden-Baden

Kučs A (2014) Denial of Genocide and Crimes against Humanity in the Jurisprudence of Human Rights Monitoring Bodies. Journal of Ethnic and Migration Studies 40:301–319

Kühl K (2003) Auschwitz-Leugnen als strafbare Volksverhetzung? In: Bernsmann K, Ulsenheimer (eds) Bochumer Beiträge zu aktuellen Strafrechtsthemen. Vorträge anläßlich des Symposions zum 70. Geburtstag von Gerd Geilen am 12./13.10.2001. Cologne, pp 103–120

Laitenberger A (2003) Die Strafbarkeit der Verbreitung rassistischer, rechtsextremistischer und neonazistischer Inhalte: Unter besonderer Berücksichtigung der Verbreitung über Netzwerke. Ein Rechtsvergleich. Peter Lang GmbH Internationaler Verlag der Wissenschaften, Frankfurt am Main

Lalieu O (2001) L'invention du "devoir de mémoire". Vingtième Siècle Revue histoire 69:83–94

Landa Gorostiza JM (1999) La llamada "mentira de Auschwitz" y el "delito de provocación" a la luz del "caso Varela": una oportunidad perdida para la cuestión de inconstitucionalidad. Actualidad Penal 36:691–692

Landa Gorostiza JM (2001) La política criminal contra la xenofobia y las tendencias expansionistas del derecho penal. Comares, Granada

Landa Gorostiza JM (2003) Nuevos crímenes contra la humanidad: el nuevo delito de lesa humanidad (artículo 607 Bis CP 1995) desde una perspectiva intrasistemàtica. In: Eguzkilore: Cuaderno del Instituto Vasco de Criminología 17:105–119

Landa Gorostiza JM (2012) *Incitación al odio: evolución jurisprudencial (1995–2011) del art. 510 CP y propuesta* de lege lata, (A la vez un comentario a la STS 259/2011 —librería Kalki— y a la STC 235/2007). Revista de Derecho Penal y Criminología 7

Lapage A (2013) Le Conseil Constitutionnel ne connaitra toujours pas du délit de contestation de crimes contre l'humanité. Communication Commerce Électronique 2

Lascuráin Sánchez JA (2010) La libertad de expresión tenía un precio. Revista Aranzadi Doctrinal 6:1–23

Lazerges C (2004) De la fonction déclarative de la loi pénale. Revue de science criminelle et de droit pénal comparé 59:194–202

Le Crom JP, Jean-Clément M (1998) (eds) Dossier vérité historique, vérité judiciaire. Droit et Société 38:9–67

Ledoux S (2012) Ecrire une histoire du "devoir de mémoire". *Le Débat* 170:175–185

Leotta CD (2015) Profili penali del negazionismo. Riflessioni alla luce della sentenza della Corte EDU sul genocidio armeno. Cedam, Padua

Lessa F, Payne LA (2012) (eds) Amnesty in the Age of Human Rights Accountability. Comparative and International Perspectives. Cambridge University Press, New York

Letsas G (2007) A Theory of Interpretation of the European Convention on Human Rights. Oxford University Press, Oxford

Levade A, Mathieu B (2012) Le législateur ne peut fixer des vérités et en sanctionner la contestation. La Semaine juridique. Édition générale 14:680–684

Levinet M (2004) La fermeté bienvenue de la Cour européenne des droits de l'homme face au négationnisme, obs. à la décision du 24 juin 2003, Garaudy c/ France. Revue Trimestrielle des Droits de l'Homme 653–662

Lippmann M (1997) Crimes Against Humanity. Boston College Third World Law Journal 17:171–278

Lipstadt DE (1994) Denying the Holocaust: The Growing Assault on Truth and Memory. Plume, New York

Lobba P (2011) La lotta al razzismo nel diritto penale europeo dopo Lisbona. Osservazioni sulla decisione quadro 2008/913/GAI e sul reato di negazionismo. Ius17@unibo.it 107–156

Lobba P (2014) A European Halt to Laws Against Genocide Denial? European Criminal Law Review 4:59–77

Lobba P (2014) Il negazionismo come abuso della libertà di espressione: la giurisprudenza della Corte di Strasburgo. Rivista italiana di diritto e procedura penale 57:1815–1853

Lobba P (2014) Punishing Denialism Beyond Holocaust Denial: EU Framework Decision 2008/913/JHA and Other Expansive Trends. New Journal of European Criminal Law 5:58–77
Lobba P (2015) Holocaust Denial Before the European Court of Human Rights: Evolution of an Exceptional Regime. European Journal of International Law 26:237–253
Lobba P (2016) Testing the “Uniqueness”: Denial of the Holocaust vs. Denial of Other Crimes Before the European Court of Human Rights. Diritto penale contemporaneo, http://www.penalecontemporaneo.it/upload/LOBBA_2016a.pdf. Accessed 13 August 2017
Lobba P (2017) From introduction to implementation: first steps of the EU Framework Decision 2008/913/JHA against racism and xenophobia. In: Behrens P, Terry N, Jensen O (eds) Holocaust and Genocide Denial: A Contextual Perspective. Routledge, London, pp 189–210
Lollini A (2003) Le rôle (pre)constituant de la Commission Verité et Reconciliation. Le renouvellement du constitutionnalisme en Afrique du Sud. Thesis
Lollini A (2011) Constitutionalism and Transitional Justice in South Africa. Berghahn Books, Oxford
Longman T (2011) Christianity and Genocide in Rwanda. Cambridge University Press, Cambridge
Longo S, Ubiali MC (2016) Articolo 10. In: Ubertis G, Viganò F (eds) Corte di Strasburgo e giustizia penale. Giappichelli, Turin, pp 290–305
Loraux N (1988) De l’amnistie et de son contraire. In: Yerushalmi YH, Loraux N, Mommsen H, Milner JR, Vattimo G (eds) Les usages de l’oubli. Seuil, Paris, pp 23–47
Loraux N (1997) La cité divisée. Payot. Paris
Lowenthal E (2014) Contro il giorno della memoria. Online: http://www.lastampa.it/2014/01/16/cultura/contro-il-giorno-della-memoria-GKkosn3Gh3Ddz5qNYBOQMJ/pagina.html. Accessed 28 September 2017
Loytomaki S (2014) Law and the Politics of Memory: Confronting the Past. Routledge, London
Luban D (2004) A Theory of Crimes Against Humanity. Yale Journal of International Law 29:85–167
Luther J (2008) L’antinegazionismo nell’esperienza giuridica tedesca e comparata. Diritto pubblico comparato ed europeo 1192–1221
Macaya A (2011) Lois mémorielles. In: Bernard G, Deschodt JP, Verpeaux M (eds) Dictionnaire de la politique et de l’administration. PUF, Paris
Maculan E (2012) Prosecuting international crimes at national level: lessons from the Argentine “truth-finding trials”. Human Rights Review 1:53–82
Maculan E, Pastor D (2013) El derecho a la verdad y su esercicio por medio del proceso penal. Hammurabi, Buenos Aires
Malarino E (2009) Il volto repressivo della recente giurisprudenza argentina sulle gravi violazioni dei diritti umani. Un’analisi della sentenza della Corte Suprema di Giustizia della Nazione del 14 giugno 2005 nel caso Simón. In: Fronza E, Fornasari G (eds) Il superamento del passato e il superamento del presente. La punizione delle violazioni sistematiche dei diritti umani nell’esperienza argentina e colombiana. Università degli Studi di Trento, Trento, pp 31–98
Mallet-Poujol N (2012) La loi de pénalisation du negationnisme: la censure constitutionnele ou le crépuscule des lois mémorielles. Légipresse 293:219–226
Manes V (2005) Il principio di offensività nel diritto penale. Giappichelli, Turin
Manes V (2007) Attualità e prospettive del giudizio di ragionevolezza in materia penale. Rivista italiana di diritto e procedura penale 2–3:739–789
Manes V (2012) I principi penalistici nel network multilivello: trapianto palingenesi, cross-fertilization? Rivista italiana diritto e procedura penale 1:839–874
Manetti M (2005) Libertà di pensiero e negazionismo. In: Ainis M (ed) Informazione, potere, libertà. Giappichelli, Turin, pp 41–51
Manetti M (2005) L’incitamento all’odio razziale tra realizzazione dell’eguaglianza e difesa dello Stato. In: Di Giovine A (ed) Democrazie protette e protezione della democrazia. Giappichelli, Turin, pp 103–128

Manzanares Samaniego J (2016) Código penal, 2 volúmenes. Comentarios y jurisprudencia. Dykinson, Madrid

Marcheri PL (2015) Legislação europeia de combate ao nazismo, doutrinas de ódio e discriminação racial. Cia Do Ebook, Timburi

Margalit A (2002) The Ethics of Memory. Harvard University Press, Cambridge/London

Martínez Sospedra M (1993) No todas las ideas son respetables. Racismo y nacionalsocialismo en el Estado constitucional democràtico. Acerca de la STC 214/1991, de 11 de noviembre. Revista General de Derecho 585:5785–5794

Martínez Sospedra M (2000) Aplastar la serpiente en el huevo. Acerca de la cuestión de inconstitucionalidad promovida contra el artículo 607.2 del CP. Revista general de Derecho 664:99–120

Mathieu-Izorche ML (2006) La marge nationale d'appréciation, enjeu de savoir et de pouvoir, ou jeu de construction? Revue de Sciences Criminelles 1:25–34

Matuschek M (2012) Erinnerungsstrafrecht. Eine Neubegründung des Verbots der Holocaustleugnung auf rechtsvergleichender und sozialphilosophischer Grundlage. Duncker & Humblot, Berlin

Matuschek M (2013) Thomas Hochmann, Le négationnisme face aux limites de la liberté d'expression, étude de droit comparé. Droit et cultures 66:231–234

Massias F (1993) La liberté d'expression et le discours raciste ou révisionniste. Revue Trimestrielle des Droits de l'Homme 183–213

Matuschek M (2012) Erinnerungsstrafrecht. Eine Neubegründung des Verbots der Holocaustleugnung auf rechtsvergleichender und sozialphilosophischer Grundlage. Verlag. Berlin

May L (2010) Genocide. A Normative Account. Cambridge University Press, Cambridge

Melloni A (2008) Per una storia della tribunalizzazione della storia. In: Marquard O, Melloni A (eds) La storia che giudica, la storia che assolve. Laterza, Rome-Bari, pp 5–68

Méndez J (1998) The Right to Truth. In: Joyner CC (ed) Reining in Impunity for International Crimes and Serious Violations of Fundamental Human Rights: Proceedings of the Siracusa Conference. Erès, Toulouse, pp 255–278

Méndez J (2009) An Emerging 'Right to Truth': Latin American Contributions. In: Karstedt S (ed) Legal Institutions and Collective Memories. Hart, Oxford

Méndez J, Bariffi F (2007) Right to Truth. In: Wolfrum R (ed) Max Planck Encyclopedia of Public International Law. Oxford University Press, Oxford

Mensching C (2014) Hassrede im Internet. Grundrechtsvergleich und regulatorische Konsequenzen. Duncker & Humblot, Berlin

Merkel R (2008) The Law of the Nuremberg Trial: Valid, Dubious, Outdated. In: Mettraux G (ed) Perspectives on the Nuremberg Trial. Oxford University Press, Oxford, pp 555–576

Merli A (2008) Democrazia e diritto penale. Note a margine del dibattito sul cosiddetto negazionismo. Edizioni Scientifiche Italiane, Naples

Meron T (1995) International Criminalization of Internal Atrocities. American Journal of International Law 89:554–577

Mettraux G (2008) (ed) Perspectives on the Nuremberg Trial. Oxford University Press, Oxford

Michel J (2010) Gouverner les mémoires – Les politiques mémorielles en France. PUF, Paris

Miebach K et al. (2012) Münchener Kommentar zum Strafgesetzbuch: StGB Band 3: §§ 80-184g StGB. Beck, Munich

Minow M (1998) Between Vengeance and Forgiveness: Facing History After Genocide and Mass Violence. Beacon, Boston

Moerland R (2016) The Killing of Death: Denying the Genocide Against the Tutsi. Intersentia, Cambridge

Moerland R, Nelen H, Willems J (2016) (eds.) Denialism and Human Rights. Intersentia, Cambridge

Montanari M (2013) Il disegno di legge in materia di negazionismo passa all'esame dell'aula del Senato. Diritto penale contemporaneo. Online: https://www.penalecontemporaneo.it/d/2597-il-disegno-di-legge-in-materia-di-negazionismo-passa-all-esame-dell-aula-del-senato. Accessed 28 September 2017

Morales Prats F, Quintero Olivares G (eds) (2016) Comentarios al código penal españo. 2 volúmenes. Aranzadi, Madrid

Morange J (2009) La liberté d'expression. Bruylant, Brussels

Morguet G (2009) Feindstrafrecht – Eine kritische Analyse. Dunker & Humblot, Berlin

Morozinis I (2011) Die Strafbarkeit der "Auschwitzlüge" im Internet, insbesondere im Hinblick auf "Streaming-Videos". Goltdammer's Archiv für Strafrecht 8:475–492

Mouysset O (2012) Pas de nouveau délit de contestation (ou de minimisation) de l'existence de crimes contre l'humanité: suite et fin? Droit pénal 6:26–27

Muñoz Conde F (2005) De nuevo sobre el «derecho penal del enemigo». Revista Penal 16:123–137

Musco E (1993) Consenso e legisazione penale. Rivista italiana di diritto e procedura penale 80–92

Mutua M (2001) Savages-Victims-Saviors: The Metaphor of Human Rights. Harvard International Law Journal 42:201–245

Naqvi Y (2006) The right to truth in international law: fact or fiction? International Review of the Red Cross 88:245–273

Nersessian DL (2002) The Contours of Genocide Intent. Troubling Jurisprudence from the International Criminal Tribunals. Texas International Law Journal 37:231–276

Niggli MA, Wiprächtiger H (eds) (2013) Strafrecht II. Article 111-392 StGB. Basler Kommentar. Helbing, Basel

Noll P (1981) Symbolische Gesetzgebung, Zeitschrift für Schweizerisches Strafrecht 347–364

Nora P (2016) Come si manipola la memoria. Lo storico il potere, il passato. La Scuola, Brescia

Nora P, Chandernagor F (2008) Liberté pour l'histoire. CNRS éditions, Paris

O'Keefe R (2015) International Criminal Law. Oxford University Press, Oxford

Ochoa JC (2013) The Rights of Victims in Criminal Justice Proceedings for Serious Human Rights Violations. Brill-Nijhoff, The Hague

Ohana D (2014) Günther Jakobs's «Feindstrafrecht». A Dispassionate Account. In: Dubber MD (ed) Foundational Texts in Modern Criminal Law. Oxford University Press, Oxford, pp 353–372

Oliver WM, Marion NE (2010) Symbolic Politics, Criminal Justice Policy, and Third Political Party Platforms. Criminal Justice Policy Review 21:476–499

Osiel M (1999) Mass Atrocity, Collective Memory, and the Law. Transaction, London

Osiel M (2008) In Defence of Liberal Show Trials – Nuremberg and Beyond. In: Mettraux G (ed) Perspectives on the Nuremberg Trial. Oxford University Press, New York, pp 704–726

Ost F (1999) Le temps du droit. Odile Jacob, Paris

Oster J (2015) Media Freedom as Fundamental Rights. Cambridge University Press, Cambridge

Palazzo FC (1985) Valori costituzionali e diritto penale (un contributo comparatistico). In: Pizzorusso A, Varano V (eds) L'influenza dei valori costituzionali sui sistemi giuridici contemporanei. Giuffrè, Milan, pp 529–615

Palazzo FC (2016) Il principio di legalità tra Costituzione e suggestioni sovranazionali. Online: www.lalegislazionepenale.eu. Accessed 2 October 2017

Palermo PG (2014) Mecanismos políticos y jurídicos aplicados durante la transición uruguaya para la superación del pasado. In: Sabadell AL, Simon JM, Dimoulis D (eds) Justiça de Transição. Das Anistias às Comissões de Verdade. Revista dos Tribunais, Sao Paulo, pp 101–150

Paliero CE (1990) Il principio di effettività nel diritto penale. Rivista italiana di diritto e procedura penale 430–544

Paliero CE (1992) Consenso sociale e diritto penale. Rivista italiana di diritto e procedura penale 3:849–922

Paliero CE (1993) Diritto penale e consenso sociale. Verso un nuovo codice penale. Milan 184–202
Paliero CE (2016) La laicità penale alla sfida del "secolo delle paure". Rivista italiana di diritto e procedura penale 59:1154–1191
Parenti P (2009) La persecuzione penale di gravi violazioni dei diritti umani in Argentina. A 25 anni dal ritorno della democrazia. In: Fronza E, Fornasari G (eds) Il superamento del passato e il superamento del presente. La punizione delle violazioni sistematiche dei diritti umani nell'esperienza argentina e colombiana. Università degli Studi di Trento, Trento, pp 13–30
Parisi S (2013) Il negazionismo dell'Olocausto e la sconfitta del Diritto penale. Quaderni costituzionali 4:879–904
Pastor D (2006) La deriva neopunitivista de organismos y activistas como causa del desprestigio actual de los derechos humanos. Jura Gentium online: http://www.juragentium.org/topics/latina/es/pastor.htm. Accessed 30 September 2017
Pastor D (2009) Processi penali solo per conoscere la verità? L'esperienza argentina. In: Fronza E, Fornasari G (eds) Il superamento del passato e il superamento del presente. La punizione delle violazioni sistematiche di diritti umani nell'esperienza argentina e colombiana. Università degli Studi di Trento, Trento
Pastor D (2010) ¿Procesos penales sólo para conocer la verdad? La experiencia argentina. Revista General de Derecho Procesal 22, online: https://dialnet.unirioja.es/servlet/articulo?codigo=3305216. Accessed 17 November 2017
Pavarini M (2006) La neutralizzazione degli uomini inaffidabili. La nuova disciplina della recidiva e altro ancora sulla guerra alle Unpersonen. Studi sulla Questione Criminale 2:7–30
Pavarini M (2006) Sicurezza dalla criminalità e governo delle città. In: Dolcini E, Paliero CE (eds) Studi in onore di Giorgio Marinucci. Vol. I. Giuffrè, Milan, pp 1019–1050
Pavich G, Bonomi A (2014) Reati in tema di discriminazione: il punto sull'evoluzione normativa recente, sui principi e valori in gioco, sulle prospettive legislative e sulla possibilità di interpretare in senso conforme a Costituzione la normativa vigente. Diritto penale contemporaneo. Online: https://www.penalecontemporaneo.it/upload/1412690237PAVICH-BONOMI_2014.pdf. Accessed 28 September 2017
Pech L (2011) Ruling Denial Prohibition. In: Hennebel L, Hochmann T (eds) Genocide Denials and the Law. Oxford University Press, Oxford, pp 183–234
Pech L (2011) The Law of Holocaust Denial in Europe. In: Hennebel L, Hochmann T (eds) Genocide Denials and the Law. Oxford University Press, Oxford, pp 185–234
Pelissero M (2015) La parola pericolosa. Il confine incerto del controllo penale del dissenso. Quest. giust. 4:37–46
Perra E (2016) Negazionismo e web: il caso inglese. Shoah e negazionismo nel Web. Rome
Petrović V (2008) From Revisionism to "Revisionism". Legal Limits to Historical Interpretation. In: Kopeček M (ed) Past in the Making. Historical Revisionism in Central Europe after 1989. Central European University Press, Budapest, pp 19–3420
Piciocchi C (2013) La dignità come rappresentazione giuridica della condizione umana. Cedam, Padua
Pisanty V (2000) Sul negazionismo. In: Collotti E (ed) Fascismo e antifascismo. Rimozioni, revisioni, negazioni. Laterza, Rome-Bari, pp 43–68
Pisanty V (2005) I negazionismi. In: Cattaruzza M, Flores M, Levi Sullam S, Traverso E (eds) Storia della Shoah. Volume I. Utet, Turin, pp 422–465
Pisanty V (2012) Abusi di memoria. Negare, banalizzare, sacralizzare la Shoah. Mondadori, Milan
Plessner H (2006) Potere e natura umana. Feltrinelli, Milan
Pollicino O (2011) Il negazionismo nel diritto comparato: profili ricostruttivi. Diritti umani e diritto internazionale 1:85–105
Poncela P (2016) Les naufragés du droit pénal. Archives de politique criminelle 38:7–26
Portelli A (2003) The Order Has Been Carried Out: History, Memory, and Meaning of a Nazi Massacre in Rome. Palgrave, Basingstoke

Portinaro PP (1992) Materiali per una storicizzazione della coppia amico-nemico. In: Morani M, Portinaro PP, Vitale A (eds) Amicus (Inimicus) Hostis. Le radici concettuali della conflittualità 'privata' e della conflittualità 'politica'. Giuffrè, Milan, pp 219–274

Portinaro PP (1996) Premessa. In: Demandt A (ed) Processare il nemico. Da Socrate a Norimberga. Einaudi, Turin, pp XII–XV

Poscher R (2005) Neue Rechtgrundlagen gegen rechtsextremistische Versammlungen. Neue Juristische Wochenschrift 1317–1328

Prittwitz C (2004) Derecho penal del enemigo: ¿análisis crítico o programa del Derecho penal? In: Puig M, Bidasolo C, Martín G (eds) La política criminal en Europa, pp 107–120

Pugiotto A (2009) Quando (e perché) la memoria si fa legge. Quaderni costituzionali 1:7–36

Puglisi G (2016) A margine della c.d. "aggravante di negazionismo": tra occasioni sprecate e legislazione penale simbolica. Diritto penale contemporaneo, online: https://www.penalecontemporaneo.it/upload/1468507001PUGLISI_2016b.pdf. Accessed 17 November 2017

Puig P (2012) La loi peut-elle sanctuariser l'Histoire? Revue trimestrielle de droit civil 1:78–84

Puig M, Queralt Jiménez JJ (2010) (ed) Constitución y principios del derecho penal: algunas bases constitucionales. Tirant lo blanch, Valencia

Pulitanò D (2006) Laicità e diritto penale. Rivista italiana di diritto e procedura penale 1:55–94

Pulitanò D (2013) Populismi e penale, sulla attuale situazione spirituale della giustizia penale. Criminalia 123–146

Pulitanò D (2015) Di fronte al negazionismo e al discorso d'odio. Diritto penale contemporaneo. Online: https://www.penalecontemporaneo.it/upload/1426333841PULITANO_2015.pdf. Accessed 17 November 2017

Quaritsch H (1992) Über Bürgerkriegs- und Feind-Amnestien. Der Staat 4:389–418

Quintero Olivares G, Valle-Muniz JA (2008) Comentarios al nuevo Código Penal. Aranzadi, Pamplona

Ramos Vázquez AJ (2008a) Presente y futuro del delito de enaltecimiento y justificación del terrorismo. Anuario da Facultade de Dereito da Universidade da Coruña 12:771–795

Ramos Vázquez AJ (2008b) Sobre la peculiar lógica de los procesos por terrorismo (las paradojas de la absolución de Otegui). In: Puente A, Zapico Barbeito M, Rodríguez Moro L (eds) Criminalidad organizada, terrorismo e inmigración. Retos contemporáneos de la política criminal. Comares, Granada, pp 371–392

Ramón Vázquez JA (2009) La declaración de inconstitucionalidad del delito de «negacionismo». Revista Penal 23:120–137

Rémond R (2006) Quand l'État se mêle de l'histoire. Stock, Paris

Renauld B (2010) La decision-cadre 2008/913/JAI du Conseil de l'Union europeenne: du nouveau en matiere de lutte contre le racism? Revue trimestrielle des droits de l'homme 21/81:119–140

Resta G (2013) Il contrasto al negazionismo e i limiti del diritto. Diritto informatico 6.

Resta G, Zeno-Zencovich V (eds) (2012) Riparare, risarcire, ricordare. Un dialogo tra storici e giuristi. Editoriale Scientifica, Naples

Resta G, Zeno-Zencovich V (2013) "Judicial "Truth" and Historical "Truth": The Case of the Ardeatine Caves Massacre". Law and History Review 4:843–886

Revenga Sánchez M (ed) (2015) Libertad de expresión y discursos del odio. Universidad de Alcalá/Defensor del Pueblo, Madrid

Ribeyre C (2016) Loi n° 2016-731 du 3 juin 2016 renforçant la lutte contre le crime organisé, le terrorisme et leur financement, et améliorant l'efficacité et les garanties de la procédure pénale - Et maintenant? Droit pénal

Ricoeur P (2000) La mémoire, l'histoire, l'oubli. Seuil, Paris

Rieff D (2016) In praise of forgetting: Historical Memory and Its Ironies. Yale University Press, New Haven

Rioux JP (2008) Les avatars du 'devoir de mémoire'. Le Débat 170:186–192

Robinson D (2003) Serving the Interests of Justice: Amnesties, Truth Commissions and the International Criminal Court. European Journal of International Law 14:481–505

Robinson D (2008) The Identity Crisis of International Criminal Law. Leiden Journal of International Law 21:925–963
Robinson J (1946) The Nuremberg Judgement. Congress Weekly: A Review of Jewish Interests 13
Rodríguez Montañés T (2012) Libertad de expresión, discurso extremo y delito. Una aproximación desde la Constitución a las fronteras del Derecho penal. Tirant lo Blanch, Valencia
Roets D (2004) Epilogue européen dans l'affaire Garaudy: les droits de l'homme à l'epreuve du negationnisme. Recueil Dalloz, 240–244
Rohrßen B (2009) Von der "*Anreizung zum Klassenkampf*" zur "Volksverhetzung" (§ 130 StGB). Reformdiskussion und Gesetzgebung seit dem 19. Jahrhundert. Walter de Gruyter, Berlin
Romano M (2007) Principio di laicità dello Stato, religioni, norme penali. Rivista trimestrale di diritto e procedura penale 495–512
Rosoni I (1995) Quae singula non prosunt collecta iuvant: la teoria della prova indiziaria nell'età medievale e moderna. Giuffrè, Milan
Roumelian O (1996) Un délit d'opinion au service des droits de l'homme? Petites affiches 21
Rousso H (1987) Le syndrome de Vichy. Seuil, Paris (tr. The Vichy Syndrome. History and Memory in France since 1944. Harvard University Press, Massachusetts)
Rousso H (2016) Face au passé. Essais sur la mémoire contemporaine. Belin, Paris
Roux J (2012) *Le Conseil constitutionnel et le génocide arménien: De l'a-normativité à l'inconstitutionnalité de la loi.* Recueil Dalloz, 12 April 2012, no. 15, pp 987–993
Rovatti T (2009) Fra politiche di violenza e aspirazioni di giustizia. La popolazione civile vittima delle stragi di Monchio e Tavolicci (1943–45). Carocci, Roma
Roxin C (2006) Was darf der Staat unter Strafe stellen? Zur Legitimation von Strafdrohungen. In: Dolcini E, Paliero CE (eds) Studi in onore di Giorgio Marinucci, I. Giuffrè, Milan, pp 715–738
Safi F (2017) A la recherche d'un fondement à l'incrimination du négationnisme. Recueil Dalloz 686–691
Salas D (2002) La justice entre histoire et mémoire. In: Jean JP, Salas D (eds) Barbie, Touvier, Papon. Des procès pour la mémoire. Autrement, Paris, pp 20–33
Salas D (2013) La volonté de punir: essai sur le populisme pénal. Fayard, Paris
Salomon TR (2012) Meinungsfreiheit und die Strafbarkeit des Negationismus. Zeitschrift für Rechtspolitik 48–50
Salvador Coderch P, Rubi Puig A (2008) Genocide- Denial and Freedom of Speech. Comments on the Spanish Constitucional Court's Judgement 235/2007, November 7th. Revista para el análisis del Derecho 4:1–30
Sánchez Melgar J (2016) Código penal. Comentarios y jurisprudencia. Sepin, Madrid
Sarkin J (2004) Carrots and Sticks: The TRC and the South African Amnesty Process. Intersentia, Antwerp
Satzger H (2002) German Criminal Law and the Rome Statute – A Critical Analysis of the New German Code of Crimes against International Law. International Criminal Law Review 2:261–282
Saul M (2015) The European Court of Human Rights' Margin of Appreciation and the Process of National Parliaments. Human Rights Law Review 15:745–774
Schabas WA (2009) Genocide in International Law. The Crime of Crimes. Cambridge University Press, Cambridge
Schabas WA (2015) The European Convention on Human Rights. A Commentary. Oxford University Press, Oxford
Schabas WA (2016) Article 6. Genocide. In: Triffterer O, Ambos K (eds) Commentary on the Rome Statute of the International Criminal Court. Observer's Notes, Article by Article. C.H. Beck/Hart/Nomos, Munich/Oxford, pp 143–157
Shermer M, Grobman A (2009) Denying History: Who Says the Holocaust Never Happened and Why Do They Say It? University of California Press, Berkeley
Schmitt C (1972) Le categorie del 'politico'. Bologna
Schmitt C (1981) Teoria del partigiano. Note complementari al concetto di politico. Milan
Schmitt C (2005) Un giurista davanti a se stesso. Saggi e interviste, Vicenza

Schwarzenberger G (2008) The Judgement of Nuremberg. In: Mettraux G (ed) Perspectives on the Nuremberg Trial. Oxford University Press, Oxford, pp 167–189

Schwelb E (1946) Crimes Against Humanity. In: British Yearbook of International Law 23:178–226

Seibert-Fohr A (2009) Prosecuting Serious Human Rights Violations. Oxford University Press, Oxford

Semprun J (2005) Vivrò col suo nome, morirà con il mio. Einaudi, Turin

Shahnazarova I (2015) Criminalisation of genocide denial and freedom of expression. Inderscience online 1:322–340

Silva Sánchez JM (2001) La expansión del derecho penal. Civitas, Madrid

Silva Sánchez JM (2007) Nullum crimen sine poena? Sobre las docrinas penales de la "lucha contra la impunidad" y del "derecho de la víctima al castigo del autor". Derecho Penal del siglo XXI 327–362

Simester AP, Du Bois-Pedain A, Neuman U (2014) (eds) Liberal Criminal Theory. Essays for Andreas Von Hirsch. Hart, Portland

Sivakumaran S (2012) The Law of Non-International Armed Conflict. Oxford University Press, Oxford

Sluiter G (2011) "Chapeau Elements" of Crimes Against Humanity in the Jurisprudence of the UN ad hoc Tribunals. In: Sadat LN (ed) Forging a Convention for Crimes Against Humanity. Cambridge University Press, Cambridge, pp 102–141

Sotis C (2007) Il diritto senza codice. Uno studio sul diritto penale europeo vigente. Giuffrè, Milan

Sotis C, Meccarelli M, Palchetti P (2011) (eds.) Le regole dell'eccezione. Un dialogo interdisciplinare a partire dalla questione del terrorismo. EUM, Macerata

Sotis C, Meccarelli M, Palchetti P (2012) (eds.) Ius peregrinandi. Il fenomeno migratorio tra diritti fondamentali esercizio della sovranità e dinamiche di esclusione. EUM, Macerata

Sotis C (2012) Le «regole dell'incoerenza». Pluralismo normativo e crisi postmoderna del diritto penale. Aracne, Rome

Spena A (2007) Libertà di espressione e reati di opinione. Rivista italiana di diritto e procedura penale 689–738

Spigno I (2008) Un dibattito ancora attuale: l'Olocausto e la sua negazione. Diritto pubblico comparato ed europeo 1921–1931

Stahn C (2005) The Geometry of Transitional Justice: Choices of Institutional Design. Leiden Journal of International Law 3:425–466

Stein E (1986) History Against Free Speech: The New German Law *Against* the "Auschwitz" – And Other – "Lies". Michigan Law Review 85:277–324

Sternberg-Lieben D (2014) § 130 StGB. In: Schönke A, Schröder H (eds) Strafgesetzbuch. Kommentar 29. Auflage. Beck, Munich, pp 1533–1547

Stofleth DE (2012) Memory Laws as Mechanisms of "remembering to forget": The Spanish Law of Historical Memory as an Archetype. https://www.academia.edu/11087676/Memory_Laws_as_Mechanisms_of_Remembering_to_Forget_The_Spanish_Law_of_Historical_Memory_as_an_Archetype. Accessed 13 August 2017

Stolleis M (2000) Der Historiker als Richter - der Richter als Historiker'. In: Frei N, Van Laak D, Stolleis M (eds) Geschichte vor Gericht. Historiker, Richter und die Suche nach Gerechtigkeit. Beck, Munich, 173–179

Stora B (2007) La guerre des mémoires: la France face à son passé colonial (entretiens avec Thierry Leclere). Éditions de l'Aube, La Tour d'Aigues

Stortoni L (1994) Le nuove norme contro l'intolleranza: legge o proclama? Critica del Diritto 14–20

Stortoni L (2002) Diritti dell'uomo ed emergenza: (l'eredità de)gli anni di piombo. In: Moccia S (ed) Diritti dell'uomo e sistema penale. Edizioni Scientifiche Italiane, Naples, pp 29–42

Stramaccioni A (2016) Crimini di guerra: Storia e memoria del caso italiano. Laterza, Bari

Suárez Espino ML (2008) Comentario a la STC 235/2007, de 7 de noviembre, por la que se declara la inconstitucionalidad del delito de negación de genocidio. Revista para el análisis del Derecho 2:1–20

Swart M, van Marle K (2017) (eds) The Limits of Transition: The South African Truth and Reconciliation 20 years on. Brill Nijhoff, The Hague

Sweeney JA (2005) Margins of Appreciation: Cultural relativity and the European Court of Human Rights in the post-Cold War era. International and Comparative Law Quarterly 2:459–474

Taguieff PA (2001) The Force of Prejudice: On Racism and Its Doubles. University of Minnesota Press, Minnesota

Tamarit Sumalla JM (2014) Memoria histórica y justicia transicional en España: el tiempo como actor de la justicia penal. Anuario Iberoamericano de Derecho Internacional Penal, Bogota

Taruffo M (1967) Il giudice e lo storico: considerazioni metodologiche. Rivista di diritto processuale XXII:438–465

Taruffo M (1992) La prova dei fatti giuridici. Giuffré, Milan

Teachout PR (2006) Making "Holocaust Denial" a Crime: Reflections on European Anti-Negationist Laws from the Perspective of US Constitutional Experience. Vermont Law Review 30, pp 155–181

Teitel RG (2014) Globalizing Transitional Justice. Oxford University Press, Oxford

Temperman J (2014) Laws against the Denial of Historical Atrocities: A Human Rights Analysis. Religion and Human Rights 9:151–180

Ternon Y (1999) Du négationnisme: mémoire et tabou. Desclée de Brouwer, Paris

Ternon Y (1999) Freedom and Responsibility of the Historian. The "Lewis Affair". In: Hovannisian RG (ed) Remembrance and Denial: The Case of the Armenian Genocide. Wayne State University Press, Detroit, pp 237–248

Terry N (2017) Holocaust denial in the age of web 2.0. In: Behrens P, Jensen O, Terry N (eds) Holocaust and Genocide Denial: A Contextual Perspective. Routledge, London, pp 34–54

Teruel Lozano GM (2015) La libertad de expresión a los delitos de negacionismo y de provocación al odio y a la violencia: sombras sin luces en la reforma del código penal. Revista para el análisis del derecho 4:1–51

Tesauro A (2013) Riflessioni in tema di dignità umana, bilanciamento e propaganda razzista. Giappichelli, Turin

Thomas Y (1998) La vérité, le temps, le juge et l'historien. Le débat 102:17–36

Thornberry P (2016) The International Convention on the Elimination of All Forms of Racial Discrimination: A Commentary. Oxford University Press, Oxford

Tiedemann M (1996) In Auschwitz wurde niemand vergast. Verlag, Berlin

Todorov T (1995) Les abus de la mémoire. Arléa, Paris

Todorov T (2001) The uses and abuses of memory. In: Marchitello H (ed) What Happens to History: The Renewal of Ethics in Contemporary Thought. Routledge, London, pp 11–39

Toma J (2014) Zur Strafbarkeit und Strafwürdigkeit des Billigens, Leugnens und Verharmlosens von Völkermord und Menschlichkeitsverbrechen. Kovač, Hamburg

Tondini M (2007) Beyond the Law of the Enemy. Recovering from the Failures of the Global War on Terrorism through Law. Jura Gentium http://www.juragentium.org/topics/wlgo/cortona/en/tondini.htm. Accessed 20 August 2017

Tourkochoriti I (2014) Should Hate Speech Be Protected? Group Defamation, Party Bans, Holocaust Denial and the Divide between (France) Europe and the United States. Columbia Human Rights Law Review 45:552–622

Tracol X (1997) L'affaire Faurisson devant le Comité des droits de l'homme des Nations-Unies. Légipresse 141

Traverso E (2006) Il Passato. Istruzioni per l'uso. Storia, memoria, politica. Ombre Corte, Verona

Trechsel S, Pieth M (eds) (2012) Schweizerisches Strafgesetzbuch. Praxiskommentar. Dike, Zurich

Triffterer O (2001) Genocide, its Particular Intent to Destroy in Whole or in Part the Group as Such. Leiden Journal of International Law 14:399–408

Triffterer O, Ambos K (2016) (eds) Commentary on the Rome Statute of the International Criminal Court. Observer's Notes, Article by Article. C.H. Beck/Hart/Nomos, Munich/Oxford

Troper M (1999) La Loi Gayssot et la Constitution. Annales Histoire. Science sociales 6:1239–1255

Tulkens F, Donnay L (2006) L'usage de la marge d'apprèciation par la Cour européenne des droits de l'homme. Paravent juridique superflu ou mécanisme indispensabile par nature? Révue de Sciences Criminelles et de Droit Comparé XXII:3–24

Turner JI (2012) The Expressive Dimension of EU Criminal Law. American Journal of Comparative Law 60:555–583

van de Kerchove M (1987) Les lois pénales sont-elles faites pour être appliquées ? Réflexions sur les phénomènes de dissociation entre la validité formelle et l'effectivité des normes juridiques. In: Ost F, van de Kerchove M (eds) Jalons pour une théorie critique du droit. Publications des Faculté universitaires Saint-Louis, Brussels, pp 317–351

van Drooghenbroeck S (2001) L'article 17 de la Convention européenne des droits de l'homme est-il indispensable? Revue trimestrielle des droits de l'homme 46:541–553

Vassalli G (2001) Formula di Radbruch e diritto penale. Note sulla punizione dei "delitti di Stato" nella Germania postnazista e nella Germania postcomunista. Giuffrè, Milan

Vassalli G, Sabatini G (1947) Il collaborazionismo e l'amnistia politica nella giurisprudenza della Corte di Cassazione. La Giustizia penale. Rome

Vecchio F (2016) La libertà di espressione dopo la vicenda "Perincek c. Svizzera": il nuovo atteggiamento della Corte europea in materia di criminalizzazione del negazionismo e i rischi residui di una storia imposta per via legislativa. Rivista della cooperazione giuridica internazionale 52:58–67

Vercelli C (2013) Il negazionismo. Storia di una menzogna. Laterza, Rome-Bari

Véron M (1990) Le renforcement du dispositif répressif contre la discrimination et le racisme. Présentation des lois des 12 et 13 juillet 1990. Droit Pénal chron. 1

Verpeaux M (2007) Liberté d'expression et discours politique. Table ronde: Constitution et liberté d'expression

Veyrat-Masson I, Blanchard P (2008) (eds) Les guerres de mémoires. La France et son histoire. La Decouverte, Paris

Vidal-Naquet P (1995) Les Assassins de la Mémoire. «Un Eichmann de Papier» et autres essais sur le révisionnisme. Seuil, Paris

Viganò F (2011) L'arbitrio del non punire. Sugli obblighi di tutela penale dei diritti fondamentali. In: Studi in onore di Mario Romano. Vol. IV. Jovene, Naples, pp 2645–2704

Villa-Vicencio C, Doxtader E (eds) (2003) The provocations of amnesty. Africa World Press, Trenton-Asmara

Visconti C (2008) Aspetti penalistici del discorso pubblico. Giappichelli, Turin

Visconti C (2009) Il reato di propaganda razzista tra dignità umana e libertà di espressione. Ius17@unibo.it 1:191–213

Vives Antòn TS et al. (2008) Derecho Penal. Parte especial. Tirant lo Blanc, Valencia

Von Bubnoff E (2009) § 130 StGB. In: Laufhütte HW, Rissing-van SR, Tiedemann K (eds) Strafgesetzbuch. Leipziger Kommentar. De Gruyter Recht, Berlin, pp 445–465

Von Dewitz C (2006) NS-Gedankengut und Strafrecht - Die §§ 86, 86a StGB und § 130 StGB zwischen der Abwehr neonazistischer Gefahren und symbolischem Strafrecht, in Strafrechtliche Forschungsberichte aus dem Max-Planck-Institutes für ausländisches und internationales Strafrecht, Band S. Duncker & Humblot, Berlin

Von Ranke L (1885) Sämtliche Werke Bd. 33/34. Leipzig

Vormbaum T (1995) "Politisches" Strafrecht. Zeitschrift für die gesamte Strafrechtswissenschaft 107:734–760

Vormbaum T (2009) Einführung in die moderne Strafrechtsgeschichte. Springer, Berlin

Vormbaum T, Bohlander M (2014) (eds) A Modern History of German Criminal Law. Springer, Berlin

Waldron J (2012) The Harm in Hate Speech. Harvard University Press, Cambridge

Walzer M (1997) On toleration. Yale University Press, New Haven/London

Wandres T (2000) Die Strafbarkeit des Auschwitz-Leugnens. Duncker & Humblot, Berlin

Wandres T (2008) Expanding Holocaust Denial and Legislation Against It. Online: http://jcpa.org/article/expanding-holocaust-denial-and-legislation-against-it/. Accessed 17 November 2017

Wartanian R (2008) Memory Laws in France and their Implications: Institutionalizing Social Harmony. http://www.humanityinaction.org/knowledgebase/117-memory-laws-in-france-and-their-implications-institutionalizing-social-harmony. Accessed 13 August 2017

Weber M (1998) Switzerland's Anti-Racism Law. Online http://www.ihr.org/jhr/v17/v17n4p13_weber.html. Accessed 16 July 2017

Weiler B (2012) Der Tatbestand "Volksverhetzung" im europäischen Vergleich: zugleich ein Beitrag zur Frage der Verfassungsmäßigkeit des § 130 Abs. 3 und 4 StGB. Kovač, Hamburg

Weiler JHH (2009) Fundamental Rights and Fundamental Boundaries: Common Standards and Conflicting Values in the Protection of Human Rights in the European Legal Space. In: Kastoryano R (ed) Am Identity for Europe: the Relevance of Multiculturalism in EU Construction. Palgrave, London, pp 73–77

Werle G (1992) Der Holocaust als Gegenstand der bundesdeutschen Strafjustiz. Neue Juristische Wochenschrift 2530–2543

Werle G (2006) (ed) Justice in Transition - Prosecution and Amnesty in Germany and South Africa. Berliner Wissenschafts, Berlin

Werle G, Jessberger F (2002) International Criminal Justice is Coming Home: The New German Code of Crimes against International Law. Criminal Law Forum 13:191–223

Werle G, Jessberger F (2014) Principles of International Criminal Law. Oxford University Press, Oxford

Wilson RA (2011) Writing History in International Criminal Trials. Cambridge University Press, Cambridge

Wolf RP, Moore Jr B, Marcuse H (1965) Critica della tolleranza. Mimesis, Turin

Yakis YA (2011) European Union Framework Decision On the Offence of Denying a Crime. Review of Armenian Studies 23:63–92

Yerushalmi YH (1988) Réflexions sur l'oubli. In: Yerushalmi YH, Loraux N, Mommsen H, Milner JR, Vattimo G (eds) Les usages de l'oubli. Seuil, Paris, pp 7–21

Yerushalmy Y (1990) Usi dell'oblio. In: Yerushalmi Y, Loraux N, Mommsen H, Milner JC, Vattimo G (eds) Usi dell´oblio. Parma

Zabel B (2010) Soll das Strafrecht Erinnerungen schützen? Zeitschrift für die Gesamte Strafrechtswissenschaft 122:834–853

Zaffaroni R (2006) El enemigo en el derecho penal. Buenos Aires

Zemon Davis N (1984) Il ritorno di Martin Guerre. Feltrinelli, Milan

Zimmerman JC (2000) Holocaust Denial: Demographics, Testimonies, and Ideologies. University Press of America, Maryland

Index

E. Fronza, *Memory and Punishment*, International Criminal Justice Series 19,
https://doi.org/10.1007/978-94-6265-234-7

H

I

L

M

Printed by Printforce, the Netherlands